THEOLOGY IN GLOBAL PERSPECTIVE SERIES
Peter C. Phan, General Editor

CHRISTIANITY AND THE POLITICAL ORDER

Conflict, Cooptation, and Cooperation

KENNETH R. HIMES, O.F.M.

ORBIS BOOKS

Maryknoll, New York 10545

Founded in 1970, Orbis Books endeavors to publish works that enlighten the mind, nourish the spirit, and challenge the conscience. The publishing arm of the Maryknoll Fathers and Brothers, Orbis seeks to explore the global dimensions of the Christian faith and mission, to invite dialogue with diverse cultures and religious traditions, and to serve the cause of reconciliation and peace. The books published reflect the opinions of their authors and are not meant to represent the official position of the Maryknoll Society. To obtain more information about Maryknoll and Orbis Books, please visit our website at www.maryknoll society.org.

Library of Congress Cataloging-in-Publication Data

Himes, Kenneth R., 1950–
    Christianity and the political order : conflict, cooptation, and cooperation / Kenneth
    R. Himes.
        p. cm. — (Theology in global perspective series)
    Includes bibliographical references (p.   ) and index.
    ISBN 978-1-62698-028-0 (pbk.)
    1. Christianity and politics. 2. Christian ethics. 3. Political ethics. I. Title.
    BR115.P7H53 2013
    261.7—dc23
                                                                        2012036328

To the Franciscan Friars of
Holy Name Province

For more than forty years they have taught me
a great deal about Christianity . . .
and a fair amount about politics

Contents

Foreword   xiii

Acknowledgments   xv

1. **Introduction**   1
   Clarifying the Terms   2
   Politics Matters   4
      Two Distinct Realms but No Simple Division   5
      Secularization and Privatization   6
   Christianity Matters   7
      Christianity and Domestic Politics   8
      Christianity and International Affairs   10
   Plan of the Book   13
   Questions for Reflection/Discussion   14

Part I
Biblical Perspectives

2. **The Old Testament**   17
   Politics and the Hebrew Tribes   17
   "A King Like Those of Other Nations"   19
      Saul and David   20
      The Monarchy under Solomon   23
   Reflections on the Monarchy   24
   Politics from the Divine Perspective   28
      Politics and Prophets   29
      Prophecy and Wider Social Criticism   32
   Conclusion   34
   Questions for Reflection/Discussion   35

3. **The New Testament**   37
   Jesus and the Reign of God   37
      Jesus the Messiah   38
      The Reign of God Is Like . . .   40
   Jesus and the Politics of His Time   42
      Render to Caesar   44
      Interpreting Jesus   46

The Earliest Christians and the Empire   48
    The Letter to the Romans   48
    Revelation 13   52
Forming a Framework   55
Conclusion   57
Questions for Reflection/Discussion   58

PART II
HISTORICAL PERSPECTIVES

4. The Patristic Era   **61**
Christians and the Empire   61
    A New Order   63
    Eusebius of Caesarea (d. ca. 340)   64
    Ambrose of Milan (d. 397)   65
Augustine (d. 430)   68
    Augustine and the Theology of History   69
    Augustine and Political Life   71
    Two Forms of Social Criticism   75
    Political Augustinianism   77
The Patristic Legacy   78
Questions for Reflection/Discussion   81

5. The Medieval Era   **82**
"Two There Are"   83
    Sacerdotium: The Emergence of the Papacy   84
    Regnum and Imperium: The Power of Kings
        and Emperors   86
    Europe after Charlemagne   90
The Investiture Controversy   93
    A Narrative of the Conflict   94
    Understanding the Controversy   96
    Theories of Authority   98
    Outcomes of the Confrontation   100
The Political Ideas of Aquinas   101
    Zōon Politikon   102
    Questions of Governance   102
Universal Papacy and National Monarchy   104
    A Narrative of Conflict   105
    Theories and Arguments   108
    Outcomes from the Confrontation   110

The Avignon Papacy   111
   Marsilius of Padua (d. ca. 1343)   112
   The End of Medieval Political Theory   113
The Medieval Heritage   114
Questions for Reflection/Discussion   115

6. **The Age of Reform**   **116**
Religious and Political Change   117
Martin Luther (d. 1546)   119
   Theology and Politics   121
   The Peasant Wars   126
   Luther's Political Legacy   127
John Calvin (d. 1564)   128
   Theology and Politics   130
   Calvinism   134
Religious War and Its Consequence   135
   The Theory of Divine Right   136
   A Right of Rebellion   137
   Jesuit Opposition   138
   The Onset of an Idea   140
Other Traditions of Reform   140
   Anglicanism and a National Church   140
   The Radical Reformers   144
The Political Legacy of the Reformation   147
Questions for Reflection/Discussion   149

7. **An Age of Revolution**   **151**
The End of the Religious Wars   152
French Catholicism, the Revolution, and Aftermath   155
   The Impact of the Clergy Constitution   157
   Revolutionary Aftermath   160
   Church and State under Napoleon   162
   The Trend to Restoration   165
The American Revolution   166
   English Protestantism in the Sixteenth and
      Seventeenth Centuries   167
   Christianity in the New World   171
   The Great Awakening and the Virginia Statute   176
   A Constitutional Commitment   180
Church and State in the U.S. Context   182
   The Public Schools Controversy   183
   Making Sense of the First Amendment   185

An Ongoing Conversation   188
Questions for Reflection/Discussion   191

PART III
CONTEMPORARY PERSPECTIVES

8. **The Nature, Purpose, Role, and Form of the State**   **195**
The Catholic Social Imagination   195
The Nature of the State   196
    Society, Community, and the State   199
    Sovereignty and the State   201
The Purpose of the State   203
    The Common Good   204
    An Evolving Idea   205
The Role of the State   207
    Justice and State Intervention   208
    Subsidiarity and State Intervention   211
    A Balancing Act   213
Democracy as the Form of the State   216
    Democracy and Catholicism   217
    Missing the Difference   220
    A New Context for Democracy   221
    Democracy and Protestantism   223
Conclusion   228
Questions for Discussion/Reflection   229

9. **Why the Church Is Engaged in Politics**   **230**
Vatican II on the Church in the Temporal Realm   231
    Church as Sacrament   232
    Church as Servant   233
    Church as Communion   235
    Church as People of God   236
    Church as Ecumenical   238
The Council on Church and Politics   239
    A Religious Mission with Political Implications   239
    The Council on Church and State   242
Other Theological Themes for the Church's Political Activity   243
    Evangelization and Human Development   244
    Sin and Conversion   248
    Christian Love of Neighbor   250
Conclusion   252
Questions for Discussion/Reflection   253

10. The Church and Domestic U.S. Politics 254

The First of Political Institutions 254

Contributing to a Public Philosophy 256

Public Virtue, Public Skills, and Public Spirituality 259

Single-Issue Politics 262

Causes of Single-Issue Politics 262

Churches and Single-Issue Voting 265

Responsible Voting 267

Conscience and the Exercise of Prudence 269

Guidance from the Tradition 270

Considerations in Voting 273

Law and Morality 275

Different Approaches 276

A Modern Thomistic Approach 279

Catholic Politicians and Catholic Bishops 281

Catholics in the United States 282

One Source of the Tension 284

A Second Source of the Tension 285

Moving Forward 287

Conclusion 288

Questions for Discussion/Reflection 289

11. Christianity and International Politics 291

Globalization 292

Authentic Humanism 294

Solidarity 295

Common Good 297

Justice 299

Human Rights 301

Participation 301

Subsidiarity 302

Human Rights 306

The Evolution of Rights Language 306

Human Rights and Catholicism 308

Vatican II and Human Rights 310

Postconciliar Catholicism and Human Rights 311

Church Activity on Behalf of Human Rights 315

War 317

The Teaching of Jesus 317

What Does Love Require? 319

Just War and Pacifism as Ethical Traditions 321

Catholic Theology and the Just War Tradition 325

Pacifism and the Catholic Tradition   327
Peace and Peacebuilding   331
    Contemporary Catholic Teaching on Peace   333
    A New Emphasis   334
Questions for Discussion/Reflection   337

Conclusion   **338**

Select Bibliography   **340**

Index   **345**

Foreword

by Peter C. Phan

Religion and politics are verboten topics for conversation, especially during electoral seasons, if you want to keep your friends with opposing political persuasions. Yet, as Kenneth Himes has convincingly argued, politics and religion are matters too important to be left to politicians and religious leaders. Rather, they must be discussed by rank-and-file citizens and Christians, and indeed by the followers of all faiths, since the future of their religions and of the world itself depends on their ability to engage in a thoughtful and serious dialogue on these themes.

By the time Himes's book is in print, the American presidential elections will have been over, and perhaps the combustible mix of politics and religion will cool off, at least for a while. But in no way does this lessen its opportuneness and import. On the contrary, it will remain a must-read and indispensable guide for those concerned not only with the bread-and-butter issues of church-and-state relations but also with the broader but no less relevant and urgent questions of the possible impact of one's faith commitment and one's religious community on the common good.

Right at the start Himes reminds us that politics is much larger than electoral campaigns and government. Of course, it includes these, but also, and more importantly, it has to do, as he puts it, "with how we ought to live together, how we should organize and govern our common life." By the same token, Christian faith is more than church, even if it must necessarily take on an ecclesial, institutional form. In other words, Christianity and politics is much more than church and state, and the latter theme cannot be fully understood unless placed within the larger frame of reference of Christianity and politics.

Underlying Himes's work is his deep conviction that both politics and Christian faith matter greatly, and that although the state and the church are distinct from each other as independent and autonomous institutions of human activities, they cannot be separated but rather must collaborate with each other. The reason for the necessity of an intimate cooperation between these two institutions is that, as Himes elegantly puts it, "the spiritual and political meet in the human person." In other words, the raison d'être of both church and state is the full flourishing of the human person. The Jeffersonian "wall of separation" and the nonestablishment of religion clause must not be construed to mean the privatization of religion or the prohibition of efforts by believers to transform society according to their beliefs and values through democratic processes.

This does not, of course, mean that Christianity and politics, alternatively, church and state, have always existed in harmony. Readers interested in the ups and downs and the twists and turns of this complicated relationship as it played out in the West will relish perusing Himes's lively account of it in chapters 4 through 7. But as every Christian theologian knows, no fruitful reconstruction of Christian thought, on politics and otherwise, can be achieved without a deep *ressourcement* in the word of God as recorded in the Bible. Hence, Himes supplies us with two rich chapters on the teachings of the Old and New Testaments on what can be called "politics." On this solid biblical and historical basis Himes proceeds to present the Christian, especially Catholic, thought on the state, the social mission of the church, U.S. domestic politics, and international affairs.

Politics is the art of the possible. But it is not an unprincipled compromise, driven only by personal and corporate interests. Rather it must be guided by considerations of national and global justice and peace and, for Christians, by the teachings of Jesus, as these are interpreted and lived by the Tradition. Steeped in both Scripture and Tradition, and with his trademark clarity and judiciousness, Himes presents a set of ethical theories and guidelines for achieving full human flourishing in society. Thanks to his work, religion and politics becomes a welcome topic for conversation, for the sake of mutual understanding among friends, even those with opposite political sympathies.

Acknowledgments

Writing a book may seem a lonely task at times, but this book would not have been written without the help of many people.

First, I thank William Leahy, S.J., president of Boston College; Dr. Bert Garza, provost at BC; Dr. Patricia DeLeeuw, vice-provost for faculties; and Dr. David Quigley, dean of the college, for granting me the sabbatical time to complete this volume. Without that generous support I could not have completed the manuscript.

During the time of my writing I have tried to distribute broadly the burden of being my friend. I am grateful to friends and colleagues who read portions of the manuscript and offered advice and criticism that improved the final text. Lisa Sowle Cahill, Boyd Coolman, Charlie Curran, David Hollenbach, Tom Massaro, John Paris, Pheme Perkins, Steve Schloesser, Tom Shannon, and David Vanderhooft all were kind enough to assist me.

Peter Phan has been a patient editor. He is also a friend who asked me to write this book several years ago and, without ever losing his good humor, put up with my delays. Susan Perry used her editorial skills to get the text in finished form, and Jim Keane saw the manuscript through the production stages. I am grateful to them both and all the staff at Orbis Books for their good work.

Finally, I am thankful to those students I taught at the Washington Theological Union and Boston College in a course on Christianity and Politics. They were the patient people on whom I tried out many of the ideas that show up in this book.

1

Introduction

Should churches and other houses of worship keep out of political matters or should they express their views on day-to-day social and political
questions?" That question regularly appears in an annual survey of American
attitudes conducted by the Pew Research Center's Forum on Religion and
Public Life.[1] For more than a decade a clear majority of those who were polled
answered that the churches should express their views on social and political
questions. Recently, however, the balance of opinion has shifted, and in the
2012 survey 54 percent of respondents thought the churches should keep out
of political matters while 40 percent thought they should express their views.[2]

There is uncertainty as to why the shift occurred in public attitude about
the role of the churches in political affairs, although several factors may be
involved. The most recent survey took place during an election year when people are sensitive to any risk of religion being used for partisan causes. In the
past few electoral campaigns there has been a marked increase in political candidates talking about their personal faith convictions, and the survey reveals
that is off-putting to a substantial majority of Americans. Also there has been
a significant movement among voters self-described as "liberal" or partial to
the Democratic Party who now view organized religion, especially Christian
churches, as being more friendly to political conservatism. That has led rising
numbers of the "liberal" segment of the population to be skeptical about the
role of organized religion in politics. Finally, there are Christians who take
offense whenever their religious leaders appear too partisan and seemingly ally
the church with a specific party, issue, or politician.

There is fluidity behind the survey numbers reflecting public opinion. The
views of Americans are a moving picture in reaction to events and personalities, whereas the survey provides only a valuable "still" shot of the public. For
the present moment, nonetheless, there appears to be a rising tide of concern
among Americans about mixing religion and politics. Yet separating the two

---

1. The Forum's website is http://www.pewforum.org/.

2. Six percent of respondents were listed as "don't know" in response to the
question. A summary of the 2012 annual survey is found at http://www.pewforum
.org/Politics-and-Elections/more-see-too-much-religious-talk-by-politicians.aspx. A
complete copy of the survey is also available as a pdf document at the above site.

is nearly impossible, even if it were desirable. And there is no established and firm consensus that such a divide would be desirable.

Politics has to do with how we ought to live together, how we should organize and govern our common life. The words "ought" and "should" in the previous sentence imply there is no clear, straight dividing line between politics and morality. There is an inevitable moral dimension to politics because questions of justice, the nature of a good community, and the rights and duties of citizens (as well as noncitizens) are fundamental to politics.

If there can be no bright line separating morality and politics, it is equally true there is no simple way to separate morality and the Christian faith.[3] Indeed, Christianity has always understood itself as teaching and witnessing to a distinct way of life. For many people, including a great many Americans, there is a Christian dimension to the way they understand and live out their ethical beliefs. It would appear, therefore, that efforts to remove all linkages between politics and religion or, more specifically, politics and Christianity, will prove to be difficult and likely fruitless.

CLARIFYING THE TERMS

One common bit of advice for those hosting a dinner party is "don't talk about religion or politics." The assumption, of course, is that raising either topic leads to argument rather than conversation among the guests. Presumably, putting the two together would be positively combustible. When people suggest that religion and politics don't mix, or that religion should have nothing to do with politics, what do they mean by "politics"? By "religion"?

Is politics always partisan politics, rival candidates seeking election to public office? If not, then what is politics? The word comes from the Greek language's *polis*, meaning "city." The famous cities of Athens, Sparta, Corinth, and Thebes, for instance, were designated by the term *polis*, and the citizens of these city-states were called *politeis*. Originally, therefore, politics was about matters pertaining to the city, the conduct of public affairs as distinct from private matters about personal life.

So running for public office or contesting an election is part of politics but hardly all of it. Politics, more broadly understood, has to do with how a society conducts its business, how people organize and govern themselves as a group. Politics includes the entire range of "rules, practices and institutions under whose guidance we live together in societies." It has to do with knowing "who

---

3. I do not claim that morality is logically dependent on religious belief. A great many people do not believe in a religious foundation for their moral beliefs and activity. My point is that Christians have always understood their religious beliefs as entailing certain moral attitudes, values, traits of character, and principles.

can do what with whom, who owns which parts of the material world, [and] what happens if somebody breaks the rules."[4] In sum, politics is about how we shall establish the processes of human cooperation necessary for people to live together.

From the outset of political philosophy, in the work of Greek writers such as Plato and Aristotle, there was a belief that the primary matter at stake in politics was justice. There might be disagreement and argument as to what justice meant and what it required, but such public discourse concerning justice was precisely what politics was about for the Greeks, and for just about every major political thinker since.

A few distinctions ought to be kept in mind by the reader of this book. Politics, as I use the term, is a more expansive realm than the state or the government. The state is the institution concerned with the law, the realm of public order, and the administration of public life. It is the key institution of politics but does not make up all of public life for there are other organizations and groups active in public life: families, corporations, schools, churches, fraternal and sororal groups, labor unions, voluntary associations.

The state is distinct from government, the latter term meaning those people who happen to be in authority at a given time in a society and are charged with running the structures of the state, that more permanent institution through which political authority is exercised. Government is the ordinary, everyday activity of enacting the aims of the state. Governments change regularly, but the state remains as long as the society effectively endures.

Another important word for this book is religion, which means a great many different things to people. Anthropologists, sociologists, jurists, psychologists, philosophers, and theologians all have their particular vantage on the phenomenon called religion, and those disciplines do not exhaust the differing perspectives. Some uses of the term are broadly inclusive, defining religion as just about anything that is of ultimate concern to an individual or group. Seen that way, religion need not be theistic.

Others, including myself, opt for a more narrow reading of religion, suggesting that it has to do with the human experience of the sacred or transcendent. Religion without God is a misnomer in the narrow interpretation. Since the subject matter of this work is Christianity and politics, it is clear that I will be following a more narrow view of religion than those who take the inclusive approach to religion. While there are reasonable grounds for adopting an inclusive view of religion in some scholarship, a book about Christianity will be concerned with a particular expression of religion, one that is convinced a

---

4. David Miller, *Political Philosophy: A Very Short Introduction* (Oxford: Oxford University Press, 2003), 4.

personal God engaged with human history exists and has revealed something of the divine self to creatures.

Another important distinction is between Christianity as a set of beliefs, ideas, and practices and Christianity as a visible set of institutions peopled by historical individuals. Or to put it simply, the Christian faith and a Christian church are not identical and coextensive. Christianity and politics, therefore, entails a larger framework of reference than church and state. The first pair has to do with the interaction of an array of thoughts and actions influenced by Christian faith with the public affairs of a society. The second deals with the interaction of two social institutions. At various points in this volume we will be discussing matters of church and state. At other points in the book we will be examining how Christian faith has shaped and been shaped by its engagement with the realm of public life.

POLITICS MATTERS

The simple reason for Christianity's engagement with politics is that politics matters. For Christians, politics does not matter as much as religion matters, but to say something is not the most important hardly results in concluding that it is unimportant. Politics matters because people matter; each individual human being matters as a child of God for those of the Christian faith. According to Pope John Paul II (d. 2005), "the name for that deep amazement at the human person's worth and dignity is the Gospel, that is to say: the Good News. It is also called Christianity."[5] This papal perspective of Christian humanism helps to explain both the church's role in politics and why politics matters.

If one lives within the relative comfort and security of a nation such as the United States it is possible to imagine that politics is not that important since the changes in government do not dramatically affect the structures of the state. For many Americans, especially the nonpoor, everyday life may not seem to change dramatically as a result of a given political development. And so it is possible to convince oneself that politics is not really important.

Yet even a brief recall of events in the past century quickly dispels such a casual approach to the political realm. Consider the Nazi regime in Germany under which government agents systematically slaughtered millions of innocent people, especially Jews, gypsies, and others deemed inferior. Or think of Stalin's repression and murder of political dissidents, rivals, and "threats" to the state. Under Mao Tse Tung millions died from avoidable hunger due

---

5. John Paul II, *Redemptor hominis* (1979), no. 10. In keeping with the usual citation style for such documents all references to church documents throughout the book will be to the paragraph number, not page number, unless noted otherwise.

to policies that refused to acknowledge the human cost of the communist state's reforms of Chinese agriculture and rural society. The political genocide that the Pol Pot regime inflicted on the Cambodian people in the 1970s amounted to millions dead in that nation's "killing fields." These evils were not historically necessary but resulted from political decisions. They are horrible reminders that politics matters, that good or bad governments can make a huge difference in causing untold misery or fostering human well-being.

Even within the recent history of the United States there are painful reminders of the difference that politics makes. The treatment of African-Americans under segregation, the sorry record of government policy toward Native Americans, along with U.S. foreign policies in Latin America, Southeast Asia, and the Middle East stand as refutations of a glib dismissal of politics as "the same old, same old." What a government does and does not do has a major impact on the everyday lives of ordinary people.

For Christians who stand in "deep amazement at the human person's worth and dignity," the political realm matters. It is true the Christian church has a spiritual mission, but it is also a mission with political overtones because the spiritual and the political meet in the human person, and the church must defend the dignity of the person.[6] Likewise the essential criterion for any political regime, system, program, or policy is the welfare of the human person.[7] Precisely because the spiritual and the political converge at the intersection of the human person there can be no indifference to the political realm on the part of church members.

Two Distinct Realms but No Simple Division

Politics matters to Christians, therefore, because it concerns the temporal well-being of God's children. As with other Christians, Catholics have been encouraged to take an active role in building the earthly city. Indeed, the Catholic bishops who attended the worldwide conference popularly called Vatican II[8]

---

6. Ibid., no. 13.

7. Ibid., no. 17.

8. Throughout the history of the Catholic Church there have been a series of meetings of the bishops throughout the entire world, or representatives of the global body of bishops. These assemblies, which may occur in multiple sessions spanning several years, are known as ecumenical councils. They are usually identified by the location of the meeting, e.g., the Council of Nicea or the Council of Chalcedon. The Second Ecumenical Council to be held at the Vatican from 1962 to 1965 is often referred to in shorthand as Vatican II. A result of that Council was the formulation of several influential documents that guided major reforms in the life of the Catholic Church in subsequent decades. One such important document was the *Pastoral*

noted that the "split between the faith which many profess and their daily lives deserves to be counted among the more serious errors of our age."[9] The bishops underscored that the realms of religion and politics cannot be divorced since both "under different titles, are devoted to the personal and social vocation of the same people. The more that both foster sounder cooperation between themselves with due consideration for the circumstances of time and place, the more effective will their service be exercised for the good of all."[10]

The bishops go on to state that in carrying out this cooperative effort between religion and politics the Christian church serves as a leaven in the society. "By preaching the truths of the Gospel, and bringing to bear on all fields of human endeavor the light of her doctrine and of a Christian witness, she respects and fosters the political freedom and responsibility of citizens."[11]

This entails two central claims that have run through the history of Christianity's engagement with politics. On the one hand, "the Church should have true freedom to preach the faith, to teach her social doctrine, to exercise her role freely among humankind, and also to pass moral judgment in those matters which regard public order when the fundamental rights of a person or the salvation of souls require it."[12] There cannot be a divorce between Christianity and political life.

On the other hand, the bishops explicitly affirmed the legitimate autonomy of the state in secular affairs. "The Church and the political community in their own fields are autonomous and independent from each other."[13] This statement about the legitimate independence of two realms reflects the processes of secularization familiar to modern life, but so unimaginable to earlier generations of Christians.

Secularization and Privatization

Secularization as a theory involves a contested set of claims. As an empirical observation, however, secularization is the process whereby various realms and institutions of social life have been removed from the hegemony of religion.[14]

Constitution on the Church in the Modern World, also known by its Latin title, *Gaudium et spes*.

9. *Gaudium et spes*, no. 43.

10. Ibid., no. 76

11. Ibid., no. 79.

12. Ibid.

13. Ibid.

14. Secularization as used here should be understood as distinct from the terms secular and secularism. The secular denotes a realm of life differentiated from the realm of the religious. The secular need not be viewed as opposed to religion or the religious realm but rather as a term to distinguish between what is overtly or explicitly religious

The production of the fine arts, the practice of law, scientific research, the operations of a market economy—all these are examples, and more could be cited, of realms of societal life that are no longer controlled directly or indirectly by institutional religion. Politics, as one more secularized realm, enjoys a legitimate independence from religious authority.

Independence does not mean complete separation; it does mean that the Catholic Church or any other church cannot exercise controlling authority over political life. This lack of controlling authority is not to be equated with a total absence of influence, but a church must rely on persuasion not coercion in exercising its influence. The teaching of Vatican II on the question of religious liberty corroborates this conclusion. The Council's Decree on Religious Liberty made clear that within the modern setting, that is, a constitutionally limited state in a pluralistic society, the church-state issue "was resolved in favor of religious liberty."[15] This meant attention should be given to the primacy of conscience; all efforts at shaping the political culture of a people must accept that individuals can only come to truth on the basis of free consent. Churches should reject resorting to the coercive power of the state instead of persuading others through preaching and witness to the truthfulness of their claims.

A second and more contested element of the theory of secularization is the prediction that religion in modern societies would become "privatized." This neologism was coined as a description of an expectation that secularization as a social phenomenon would lead to religion withdrawing from the *polis* to become a private affair. Religion might continue to matter to an individual, but it would not matter to society. In effect, religion would be reduced to something akin to a personal hobby. It might bring enjoyment and comfort and absorb a fair amount of one's time or resources. Yet, just as society is unaffected by whether one builds airplane models or raises tulips so it is with whether one believes in God, goes to church, prays in solitude, or reads the Bible. Religion would become a nonfactor in the public life of a society according to the tenets of privatization, even if religion mattered to individuals in their private lives.

CHRISTIANITY MATTERS

That things have not worked out as predicted by secularization theory is readily apparent. The role of Christian churches in U.S. public life remains significant.

---

and another realm of human existence. Secularism is the term for a philosophical position, a conviction that there is no such realm as the transcendent, the eternal. It is the belief that historical existence is all there is, and though religion may be a social phenomenon, it is also a mistaken belief in something beyond earthly experience.

15. David Hollenbach, *Justice, Peace and Human Rights: American Catholic Social Ethics in a Pluralistic Context* (New York: Crossroad, 1988), 10.

There are numerous church-related social service agencies providing legal aid to immigrants, counseling to the troubled, shelter to the homeless, food to the hungry, safety to battered women, health care to the sick, job training to the unemployed, financial aid to the poor, transportation to shut-ins, visits to prisoners, and a variety of other public services.

There is, of course, the extensive network of church-sponsored schools at every level from prekindergarten to research universities; there are numerous hospitals founded and staffed by members of Christian churches; and there is a wide array of organizations devoted to development programs and disaster relief that are sponsored by American Christians. In areas of social charity and social justice the Christian community has a public presence that is undeniably important to the national and local communities of the United States.

Mainstream church leaders and members were a public presence during the civil rights campaigns of the 1950s and 1960s as well as during the anti–Vietnam War activities of the 1960s and 1970s. Beginning with the 1970s there was a major upturn in political activism by evangelical Protestant figures. The role of evangelical Christians in the political life of the nation is now widely recognized. Today it is difficult for a Republican candidate to win the party's nomination to state or federal office without the support of evangelicals and the endorsement of prominent Christian leaders of churches and other organizations. Of course, the African-American church communities have long been an essential base for raising up African-American politicians and supporting their candidacies.

As was reflected in the Pew survey cited at the beginning of this chapter, the political activity of the churches is a source of controversy and tension, both for non-Christians and fellow Christians. Of late, a good deal of the controversy has involved the Catholic Church and its political activity. Roman Catholic clergy in the United States have traditionally been more circumspect in their political activity, both for historical reasons (fear of Protestant backlash against a Catholic voting bloc) and theological reasons (the emphasis placed on the unity of the church). Nonetheless, in several elections in past decades Catholic bishops have made high-profile comments about candidates, usually fellow Catholics, concerning their positions on issues of social morality, particularly in the areas of abortion and same-sex relations.

Christianity and Domestic Politics

Ever since the Supreme Court decision *Roe v. Wade,* the politics of abortion has been polarized in this nation. It has been the rare presidential campaign since 1972 in which abortion has not surfaced as an issue. A particular aspect of the tension after *Roe v. Wade* was that Catholic politicians sought national office and failed to espouse a view of abortion policy that reflected the church's teaching. In 1984 when Representative Geraldine Ferraro, a Democrat from Queens, NY, ran as the vice-presidential nominee, Cardinal John O'Connor, who was not her bishop, was public in his complaints. Ferraro never was successful in articulating her understanding of the connection between morality and public policy, and that failure cost her support among Catholics.

During that same electoral season, New York's Democratic governor, Mario Cuomo, took up the challenge of O'Connor and other bishops to explain how he could reconcile his Catholic beliefs on abortion with his policy position. In a speech at the University of Notre Dame that garnered much attention, he laid out his case for how someone personally opposed to abortion could support a pro-choice policy regime. While subtler and more nuanced than Ferraro in his views, Cuomo also failed to convince church leaders that his position was coherent.

Episcopal displeasure with Catholic politicians continued to grow throughout the decades of the '80s and '90s. The pontificate of John Paul II regularly voiced strong opposition to abortion, and the U.S. bishops consistently followed the papal lead. In 2002 the Congregation for the Doctrine of the Faith (CDF) under the leadership of then Cardinal Joseph Ratzinger issued a doctrinal note, "The Participation of Catholics in Political Life."

With heavy reliance on the teaching of *Gaudium et spes*, the document laid out the position "that a well-formed Christian conscience does not permit one to vote for a political program or an individual law which contradicts the fundamental contents of faith and morals."[16] The CDF statement went on to make a distinction between "the rightful autonomy of the political or civil sphere from that of religion and the Church—but not from that of morality."[17]

The CDF document emboldened a small number of American bishops to raise the stakes in their ongoing dispute with various Catholic public officials. These bishops went public with their assessments of the worthiness of certain candidates to receive the Eucharist. The most prominent public official who was threatened with this sanction was John Kerry, the Democratic senator from Massachusetts and presidential candidate in 2004. Abortion has remained a hot-button issue, but others will emerge in the future.

As the ensuing chapters will show, history is replete with examples of Catholic hierarchs and other Christian leaders who have made overreaching claims about the church's role in a secular political order. At the same time, history also demonstrates that the temporal realm cannot be divorced from the concerns of morality or religion, and public officials are often tongue-tied when trying to articulate a coherent view of that relationship. Life is simply

---

16. Congregation for the Doctrine of the Faith, "The Participation of Catholics in Political Life" (November 24, 2002), no. 4.

17. Ibid., no. 6.

more complex and interconnected than past and present theories of church and state can comprehend. The truth is that both realms, spiritual and temporal, continue to endure, and the persistent problem is how they relate to each other.

For most Christians public service is a noble and worthy vocation. Precisely for that reason, the church cannot be indifferent to the moral dimension of politics. Vatican II remains a watershed for understanding the church's role in public life. The call to be a leaven within the dough of society means the church must not abandon politics to the expedient and popular. Moral values must be maintained in the life of a political community, and this entails public policies that will inevitably enshrine some goods in preference over others. The challenge, according to the church's own teaching, is that people must be persuaded not coerced to accept the morally good.

The tensions of past election campaigns are likely to simmer and be stirred anew the next time a Catholic runs for national office. The line between religion and politics is not easily drawn even though the distinction is real. Needed at this point in the life of the American Christian community is less prophetic denunciation and more space for searching moral reflection by church leaders and public officials on how one translates sincerely held moral convictions into public policy when society lacks moral consensus on a topic. Whether the near future is a time when Christianity is seen as a tradition and the church as an institution that enriches American politics or as a source of polarization and intolerance in the body politic cannot be determined in the present. What is highly likely, however, is that Christianity will remain as an important presence in the nation's political life.

Christianity and International Affairs

It is not only in domestic politics that religion in general, and Christianity in particular, is making a mark. Beyond the domestic context the arena of international affairs also illustrates the continued importance of religion as a factor in world affairs. And this fact is even more notable because many practitioners and scholars of international relations in the past had largely relegated religion to the status of an afterthought.

The legacy of the Peace of Westphalia that ended the European religious wars of the 1600s included the principles of state sovereignty and nonintervention in the domestic life of other states. The latter principle declared that a state's religious preference was not a basis for external interference by another state. As a consequence, "[t]he historical experience of Westphalia indelibly associated the removal of religion with the establishment of international order and planted an enduring suspicion of injecting religion into international affairs."[18] Yet despite this long-standing aversion to mixing religion and international politics recent occurrences have forced a reconsideration of the role of religion in world affairs.

Among those events that have heightened awareness and interest in the role of religion in global politics are the Islamic revolution in Iran that overthrew the shah and established the present Islamic regime, the emergence of liberation theology and church-related movements for social justice in Latin America, the involvement of many churches in the antinuclear campaigns of the Cold War, religious protests over U.S. policy in Central America, the influence of the Catholic Church in the "people power" revolution that overthrew the Marcos regime in the Philippines, the papacy of John Paul II and the role of the Catholic Church in Poland's break from communism, the Lutheran Church's part in ending the communist regime in East Germany, the impact of Protestant evangelicals on U.S. policy toward Israel, and the terrorist attack by Islamic radicals on the United States on September 11, 2001.

From the above roster it would appear that just as with domestic politics, so, too, with global politics, privatization is a fundamental misunderstanding of the role of religion. Religion, including the Christian religion, matters in international politics. There is a new architecture for international relations. The old building blocks of nation-states have not disappeared, but they now operate within a different context. For one thing sovereignty is no longer an all-or-nothing proposition. States retain power but have to wield it in collaboration with other nations and nonstate actors. Governance of the new international system will involve not only states but also agencies that are not part of any government at all.

We are witnessing the transformation of the old Cold War world. And like the Cold War system of international relations, the new world order has its own logic, rules, institutions, and characteristics. The Cold War international system was built around nation-states and led by two superpowers. The new international system is built around four overlapping and interpenetrating sets of relationships: states and states; states and nonstate actors; states and markets; states and powerful groups/individuals (e.g., terrorists, philanthropists, educators). Even the lone superpower, the United States, must attend to these various relationships and cannot sustain a unipolar world.

The rise of transnational religious conflict, transnational religious forces, and the impact of religiously generated identities, values, and norms in foreign affairs were all blind spots for those who thought too exclusively in terms of the state as the political unit.[19] For example, one major error of the past has

---

18. Eva Bellin, "Faith in Politics: New Trends in the Study of Religion and Politics," *World Politics* 60 (January 2008): 315-47 at 318.

19. Ibid.," 339.

been the expectation that people defined their identity in terms of the state. We know now many millions of people, particularly those living in multi-ethnic or multireligious states, take their identity from religion or a blend of religion and ethnicity. Furthermore, religion is a very powerful force in the shaping of societal values, morality, and the practices of communal life among a people.

Since the 1970s there has been increased attention given to transnationality as a theme in international relations, and this has led to a growing appreciation for the role of nongovernmental organizations (NGOs) and intergovernmental organizations (IGOs) in shaping world order. The emergence of transnationality prompted commentators to consider the similarities between organized religion and other nongovernmental actors having an impact on issues of trade, investment, human rights, population, ecology, migration, and communications. That development has opened up space for religion to re-enter the arena of international relations. "The conceptual and factual journey from interdependence to globalization offered topics that drew religious voices and analysis closer to mainline analysis of international relations."[20] Increasingly, there is an awareness that excluding religion from discussions of international politics leads to an inadequate understanding of the world in which we live.

The changes noted above have been accompanied by what observers characterized as a "new internationalism" on the part of religious groups. Interest in the International Religious Freedom Act of 1998, campaigns against human trafficking, efforts to stop the slaughter in Darfur, assisting in the battle against the AIDS epidemic, and addressing climate change have led to the formation of alliances by religious groups that otherwise have significant differences.[21]

Of the many religious bodies that have participated in the new internationalism it is the Catholic Church, because of its history and structure, that has been best able to insert itself into global politics. The Vatican has full diplomatic relations with 176 nations. It also has permanent observer status at the United Nations. That status means it does not vote in the General Assembly, but it has both voice and vote at U.N.-sponsored conferences.[22] Since such meetings tend to run by consensus, having voice and vote translates into having real impact. Partly because of its status at the United Nations the Vatican

20. J. Bryan Hehir, "Why Religion? Why Now?" in *Rethinking Religion and World Affairs*, ed. Timothy Shah, Alfred Stepan, and Monica Toft (New York: Oxford University Press, 2012), 15-24 at 20.

21. James Guth, John Green, Lyman Kellstedt, and Corwin Smidt, "Faith and Foreign Policy: A View from the Pews," *Review of Faith and International Affairs* 3, no. 2 (Fall 2005): 3-10 at 4.

22. By its own choice, not being a voting member of the U.N. permits the Holy See to claim neutrality and nonpartisanship in its activity.

is accorded a presence in a number of other IGOs, such as the Organization of American States and the African Union.

While acting in the arena of IGOs the Catholic Church and its related agencies also function as NGOs in other venues. Many national and regional episcopal conferences sponsor organizations, such as Catholic Relief Services here in the United States, that play important roles in development programs in many poor nations. There are agencies that are Catholic in nature, not under the auspices of the bishops, but sponsored by or affiliated with religious communities, such as the Jesuit Refugee Service. There are also groups not formally sponsored by the church, such as the Sant'Egidio community and Pax Christi, that engage in peacebuilding efforts. Many of these lay-run groups partner with other Christian NGOs as well as secular NGOs to promote social justice through a variety of strategies and in numerous locales worldwide.

The passage of time and the enduring presence of religion in human society have raised doubts about the cogency of secularization theory, particularly its privatization corollary. Christianity's public presence remains evident in the United States, a nation that has undergone all the social processes that were supposed to lead to religion's decline according to secularization theorists. In Latin America, Asia, and Africa the ongoing public significance of Christianity is abundantly evident.[23] One can ask if the European experience of the post-Westphalian order, rather than being the precedent that other regions of the world will follow, is instead the exception to the norm. It would seem that Christianity is once more acknowledged as a significant element of global politics.

PLAN OF THE BOOK

The late Henry Chadwick, a church historian of immense learning, who during his career taught at both Oxford and Cambridge universities, once remarked on the unfortunate situation when the Christian community forgets its past. "Nothing is sadder than someone who has lost his memory; and the church which has lost its memory is in the same state of senility."[24] In order to have an informed viewpoint on Christianity and politics in our own time,

---

23. One of the important works to challenge the inevitability of privatized religion was Jose Casanova, *Public Religions in the Modern World* (Chicago: University of Chicago Press, 1994). A recent restatement of his disagreement with those who equated secularization with privatization is "Public Religions Revisited," in *Religion: Beyond the Concept*, ed. Hent de Vries (New York: Fordham University Press, 2008), 101-19.

24. An oral remark spoken during a debate of the Anglican Church's General Synod in 1988; as reported in his obituary in the *New York Times* (June 22, 2008).

it is imperative that we have some grasp of the persons and events that have exercised influence on how the Christian community has thought about and actually engaged the political order.

Of course, it is impossible to summarize in a few pages the entire sweep of the church's history regarding the political order. Instead, in the next six chapters I will consider several key persons, proceedings, and ideas that are of special significance to the historical narrative of Christianity and politics. Following two chapters that examine biblical views of politics, both Old and New Testaments, there will be four chapters that provide "look-ins" on important moments during the patristic era, the medieval period, as well as the ages of reform and of revolution. The purpose of these chapters is to highlight representative types of individuals, themes, and events, offering historical vignettes that will illustrate significant aspects of the story of Christianity and politics.

The final four chapters of the book turn to contemporary perspectives, offering an interpretation of how a present-day Christian might think about the state, the social mission of the church, as well as issues of domestic and international politics. These final chapters, like the earlier ones, make no claim to being comprehensive but aim to provide the reader with a theologically informed overview of significant topics that illustrate the present state of interaction between the Christian religion and the political order.

One additional point to note is that within the Christian tradition the author has a preference for the Roman Catholic understanding of the tradition. This preference will be more apparent in some of the following chapters than others. For the most part the preference will be reflected in the way that certain documents of the Catholic Church—for example, texts of Vatican II and papal social teaching—are used in the presentation of contemporary perspectives. This does not mean the rich heritage of other interpretations of the Christian tradition simply will be ignored, but I want to acknowledge from the outset that the author is more familiar with the Roman Catholic rendering of the tradition than other approaches.

QUESTIONS FOR REFLECTION/DISCUSSION

1. How would you define politics? Do you agree that its first concern is justice?
2. What is the difference between the state and the government?
3. What is the difference between secularization and privatization? How is secularization distinct from secularism?
4. Can you describe the "new internationalism" of religious bodies?

Available at http://www.nytimes.com/2008/06/22/world/europe/22chadwick.html?_r=1&scp=1&sq=henry%20chadwick&st=cse.

Part I

BIBLICAL PERSPECTIVES

2

The Old Testament

It has been said that making a claim such as "the Bible teaches X" is similar to saying "the library teaches X." That is, the Bible is a diverse anthology that represents the viewpoints of many contributing authors, writing over a vast period of time, with many different audiences in mind. To assume there is going to be a uniform teaching throughout the Bible on any particular topic, therefore, is a very large assumption indeed. An example of the diversity of viewpoints within the Bible itself, actually within the same book of the Bible, can be found when one reads the opposing traditions concerning the establishment of the Israelite monarchy found in 1 Samuel 9:1-10:6 and then 10:17-27. These passages will be discussed below.

For now, one must first be clear about what is meant when statements are made concerning the Bible's teaching on politics. In this chapter I make no claim that the treatment of biblical materials is exhaustive or comprehensive. Rather, in this chapter we will examine certain key figures and passages in an effort to formulate a biblically informed view of the political order. We will start with the early Israelite community and examine the Hebrew Scriptures first, before moving on to look at texts from the Gospels, as well as the letters of Paul and other Christian writers in the next chapter.

POLITICS AND THE HEBREW TRIBES

The history of the Israelite people extends for centuries prior to the period of the monarchy and the development of a central government. During the premonarchical period, the social organization was tribal and was led by occasional charismatic figures who inspired loyalty and unity among the tribes. Moses, of course, was such a figure and the dominant personality of the Torah, or Pentateuch. While understood as the great religious prophet of Judaism, he also exercised political authority, sometimes alone and sometimes in coordination with a larger group (Numbers 11:16-17), within the enslaved and then nomadic tribes that came into Canaan. Stories of later individual leaders who exercised aspects of religious and political leadership can be found in the books of Judges and Joshua.

The central feature of Israelite religion was the belief that Yahweh had entered into a covenant, a personal bond of commitment, with the Israelite people. Fidelity to the covenant between Yahweh and the people was an expectation not only for individual behavior but also served as a social norm that required a certain way of communal life, with the hallmarks of justice, compassion, and integrity. If we view politics in the broad sense of how a community organizes itself to make decisions and implement agreed-upon practices, then the individual tribes and the tribal confederacy of this pre-monarchical era do reflect a view of politics.[1]

Not surprisingly, the tribal form of organization was less formal and institutionalized than later Israelite society. The subsistence economy of the tribes may have helped to reinforce the sense of social solidarity and concern for the poor that fidelity to Yahweh required as religious and moral norms. It is possible, as some commentators have argued, that Israel at this point in time had less emphasis on class distinctions than its neighbors and that it was a distinctive social system when compared to its neighbors of the period.[2]

However, other scholars warn against romanticizing early Israel by emphasizing its distinctive social organization. There were more similarities with neighbors than dissimilarities, and there were class distinctions, including the categories of slaves and resident aliens. Women suffered from the customs of a patriarchal society, and the model of tribal organization still could leave power in the hands of a small elite of elders and charismatic figures. So a community of people modeled on equal respect and care was not the everyday experience of the Jewish believer. As biblical scholar Bruce Birch summarizes the matter, "Israel does not represent the full and perfect embodiment of the covenant vision, but a people living toward that vision."[3]

It is in the books of 1 and 2 Samuel that we read the story of Israel's transition from a tribal confederacy to something approaching a more unified set of acknowledged authorities, including the institution of a monarchy. Just what is to be made of the historical nature of this story is a topic of debate. More skeptical scholars give little credence to the biblical narrative, even to the extent of challenging the reality of the Davidic monarchy. A more commonly held viewpoint is that the stories reflect "an historically rooted memory of a tribal chieftain of quite modest proportion whose memory has been greatly enhanced through artistic imagination."[4]

---

1. The belief that covenant theology was operative during the tribal era reflects the view of the biblical authors. Determining whether the historical reality matched the canonical view is beyond the aim of this chapter.

2. Norman Gottwald, *The Hebrew Bible: A Socio-Literary Introduction* (Philadelphia: Fortress Press, 1985), 284-86.

3. Bruce Birch, *Let Justice Roll Down: The Old Testament, Ethics, and Christian Life* (Louisville: Westminster/John Knox Press, 1991), 179.

4. Walter Brueggemann, *An Introduction to the Old Testament: The Canon and*

The exact achievements of King David and the accuracy of accounts concerning the size of his kingdom are also topics of debate. For our purposes, the important point is what the biblical texts reveal about how the Israelite people understood the political developments that are described in the Bible. The focus is on the meanings conveyed within the texts, not the historical accuracy of every detail found in the biblical narrative.

It is possible to classify ancient polities as innovative or imitative. Innovative polities create and develop distinctive organizational models based on their own cultures. China, Egypt, and Mexico would be examples of innovative entities. Imitative polities emerge through contact and communication with others and follow the patterns of organization within those polities. The story of the Israelite tribes' evolution into a political kingdom with a monarchy and centralized government is an obvious example of an imitative polity, drawing on the experiences of neighboring kingdoms in the ancient Near East.

Scholars suggest that the settlement and eventual "conquest" of Palestine began sometime around the early 1200s BCE. The period described in the book of Judges may preserve reflections of this era. The tribes were not so much biological but cultural and geographic, with shared interests in trade, grazing, and agriculture within the region. It is believed that the tale of the Exodus from Egypt became a unifying founding narrative even for those who never left Palestine or sojourned in Egypt. These tribes forged a confederacy to protect themselves from hostile neighbors and perhaps in recognition of their shared religious belief in Yahweh.

"A KING LIKE THOSE OF OTHER NATIONS"[5]

The books 1 and 2 Samuel and 1 and 2 Kings pick up from that starting point of a tribal confederacy. They then proceed to offer a dramatic portrayal of the rise and fall of the monarchy among the Israelite people, as well as a narrative of moments of success and failure in the political fortunes of the kingdom.

In one sense the movement from a tribal confederacy to a monarchy could be explained as a practical choice designed to counter a threat to the Israelites from their neighbors, particularly the Philistines and Ammonites in the last quarter of the eleventh century BCE, that is, about 1025. Apparently, as the power of these neighbors grew, the Israelite tribal confederacy was incapable of maintaining an adequate armed force to guard against an ongoing threat. As one scholar observed, "An Israelite king might require taxes, but

---

Christian Imagination (Louisville: Westminster/John Knox Press, 2003), 132.
   5. 1 Samuel 8:19-20.

the alternative was to pay an even more onerous tribute to the Philistines, the Ammonites, or some other invading enemy."[6]

Another practical concern involved the growing population among the Israelite tribes who had inhabited the highlands of Palestine. Though originally living in somewhat isolated small villages, the expanding number of people introduced disputes over natural resources, water and grazing land, and also a need to facilitate the increasing trade and interaction among the tribes. Some centralization of governance seemed necessary to regulate and adjudicate conflicting claims among the tribes.

At yet another level, the development of a monarchy required some kind of explanation beyond the practical. There was also the need for a theological rationale, because the decision to have a king like other nations appeared to be a challenge to the Hebrew claim that Yahweh was their king. There was a long-standing belief that Yahweh's special relationship with the Israelite people involved an acknowledgment that the true king of the nation was Yahweh and that the Israelite people did not need to follow the practice of their neighbors.

The arguments that arose about the practical and theological explanations of Israelite kingship are evident in the biblical texts. For example, the central figure in the early narratives is Samuel, a man who plays a role that combines elements of judge, priest, and prophet. In both the pro- and antimonarchical narratives, he sometimes appears as a strong supporter of the monarchy and other times as an opponent who only reluctantly acquiesces to the idea. Given his prominence as an authoritative leader, both sides in the debate wanted to claim him, and it is a testimony to the compiler of the biblical narrative that both viewpoints were included in the canonical text.

Saul and David

In 1 Samuel 9:1-10:6 we read that Saul (d. ca. 1020 BCE) is made king with the blessing of Samuel and is even secretly anointed by Samuel. Just a few verses later, in 1 Samuel 10:17-27, we read that the king was chosen by chance, and Samuel tells the people that they have rejected Yahweh by seeking to have a king. Support for the monarchy came from those who saw the tribal confederacy as no longer adequate to the changing situation while "opposition probably came from those who had the most to lose and the least to gain from

---

6. J. J. M. Roberts, "In Defense of the Monarchy: The Contribution of Israelite Kingship to Biblical Theology," in *The Bible and the Ancient Near East: Collected Essays* (Winona Lake, IN: Eisenbrauns, 2002), 358-75 at 374.

such a change, that is, from tribal leaders whose own territories were least threatened by the growing Philistine and Ammonite power."[7]

So Samuel of the antimonarchical tradition warns that a king will set up a standing army that will require heavy taxes, or he will create a court that will use forced labor to maintain his lifestyle, and abuse the freedom and prerogatives of the tribes (1 Sam 8:10-17). Yet the pro-monarchical viewpoint tells of Samuel's selection of Saul and recounts Saul's success in defeating the Philistines, Ammonites, and others (1 Sam 14:47-48). And when Saul's flaws eventually lead to his undoing, Samuel is portrayed not as rejecting the institution of the monarchy but as being directed by God to choose a new king, the young David (1 Sam 16:1-13).

The story of David's rise to power and of his troubles with Saul constitutes the remainder of 1 Samuel, and the narrative of his kingship continues in 2 Samuel. The early chapters relate David's exploits and successes in stabilizing and then expanding the kingdom, while the later chapters tell the story of the various plots and counterplots of the king's sons to succeed him. David (d. ca. 965 BCE) is portrayed as a clever, brave, and passionate man who sincerely desires to be faithful to Yahweh's will. But David is also described as weak, calculating, and capable of serious wrongdoing after he is installed on the throne. He flirted with religious idolatry, mishandled his succession in various scrapes with his sons, and abused his power to the point of fomenting rebellion. The famous tale of his adultery with Bathsheba, his successful plot to have her husband killed, his unmasking by the prophet Nathan, and his repentance reveal the complex character of David (2 Sam 11:1-12:25).

Biblical scholar Lawrence Boadt describes David, for all his flaws, as possessing "both a military and a political genius."[8] He was able to defeat the Philistines decisively, a job that Saul never quite managed, and he extended the kingdom's borders far beyond what the Israelite people had yet known. Insofar as he actually accomplished this, he was undoubtedly aided by the fact that he ruled during a period when the Egyptian state was in a weakened condition and the Assyrians had not yet emerged as a great power. In sum, he had the good fortune to live at a time when the Israelite people were not in the shadow of a major empire. David also was able to unite all the tribes, both of the north as well as of the south, in their acceptance of him as king. This was accomplished not by force but by consensus.

Another great stroke of genius was David's decision to create a new city for his capital and to merge the political center with the center of religious practice of Yahwistic faith. In doing this David began to create the mythology

---

7. Ibid.

8. Lawrence Boadt, *Reading the Old Testament* (New York: Paulist Press, 1984), 231.

that surrounded Zion in Israelite life, establishing Jerusalem as both the home of the king and the resting place for the Ark of the Covenant.

Even though the Israelite people had been in Palestine for approximately two centuries by David's time, they never controlled Jerusalem. Jerusalem was a city belonging to the Jebusite tribe, a people we know little about; but what is known suggests they had similar religious beliefs to the Canaanites.

When David lay siege and captured the city it had no particular significance to the Israelite people. Thus, making Jerusalem his capital rather than an existing Hebrew city allowed David to avoid complaints about favoring one tribe or region. One might see David's choice of Jerusalem as a compromise similar to the decision to make the District of Columbia the capital of the United States, rather than the rival cities of Boston, New York, or Philadelphia. Given the lingering doubts and reservations that some tribal leaders had about a central government, David could not be indifferent to resolving concerns about the monarchy, and the choice of Jerusalem was a wise selection of a neutral site.

The second important element to the creation of Jerusalem as a symbol of unity among the people was the movement of the Ark of the Covenant to Jerusalem. The Ark was the wooden chest that was the repository for the tablets of the law given at Sinai. The Ark played a major symbolic role from the time of Sinai and throughout the period of the settlement in Canaan. It was venerated as both the locus of God's presence in the world and as the shelter of God's law. Kept at various shrines—Gilgal, Bethel, and Shiloh—since the arrival in the Promised Land it had for a brief time been captured by the Philistines during a battle with Saul's army. When David brought it to Jerusalem, in effect, he united the political and religious centers of Israelite life. During David's reign, the Ark was kept in a tent, but under Solomon a temple was built and the Ark was installed in the sanctuary, the Holy of Holies. Jerusalem, the city of David, was the capital of the unified Israelite kingdom; Jerusalem, the resting place of the Ark, was the cultic heart of Yahwism.

David was successful at forging a political ideology that united the monarchy and the faith of the people; the king was viewed as the great servant of Yahweh, not a rival vying for the people's loyalty. Even later, after Solomon's excesses led to the fracturing of the unified kingdom, the belief in the king's role as a servant of Yahweh was never erased. During the era of the great prophets one does not usually find a fundamental repudiation of the idea of monarchy. Instead, many of the prophets, such as Isaiah or Ezekiel, yearned for the rise of a just and faithful king; they did not seek to abolish the monarchy as an institution within the Israelite nation.

Walter Brueggemann sums up the story that the books of Samuel tell by calling it a "transition of Israel from Judges to Kings, from tribal barbarism to monarchical bureaucracy, accomplished through divine love that is enacted through the force of David" as God's chosen one despite his manifold failings.[9]

The Monarchy under Solomon

After much conniving and tragic twists of plot, it was Solomon, David's son with Bathsheba, who ascended to the throne of Israel. The books of Kings tell the story of Solomon's reign, the political and military successes as well as the religious and moral corruption that eventuated in the collapse of national unity, the fall of the northern kingdom, and the later destruction of the southern kingdom and Jerusalem, followed by the Babylonian Captivity. The two books sweep across several centuries in telling this story.

Two different portraits of Solomon (d. ca. 922 BCE) are found within 1 Kings. He was successful in extending and solidifying the power of the Hebrew state. Like his father, Solomon benefited from ruling at a time when the great powers were undergoing transitions and there was something of a void in the politics of the ancient Near East. Solomon is portrayed in the Bible as skillfully seizing the opportunity to build a kingdom that was never rivaled in the history of the Jewish people. In that sense one can interpret Solomon's reign as a great success, and it is portrayed that way in chapters 3 through 10.

Chapter 3 offers two related incidents about what is probably the best-known characteristic of Solomon, his wisdom. The first incident tells of the request that the king made of Yahweh to grant him wisdom that he might rule God's people well. And the second incident illustrates that his prayer was granted when he resolves the question of who was the mother of an infant claimed by two women.

Chapters 5 through 8 tell the story of the building of the Jerusalem Temple, the act for which Solomon is remembered to this day. The great symbol of Israel's faith, the Temple became the home of the Ark of the Covenant and markedly shaped Israelite religious practice. The great success of Solomon and the wealth of his kingdom is celebrated in the story of the visit of the Queen of Sheba in chapter 10. Had the narrative been confined to these chapters the figure of Solomon would be a tale of greatness that rivaled or surpassed the narrative of David. Solomon would be seen as the king of Israel during the period when the nation knew its greatest political, economic, and military significance.

If Solomon's story had ended in such a manner it would leave the reader to conclude that the monarchy was a singular blessing for Israel. The example of Solomon would be a lesson that God had blessed the people by choosing an

---

9. Brueggemann, *An Introduction to the Old Testament*, 142.

exceptional individual to bring to fulfillment the promise that had been made to David. The promise spoken of by the prophet Nathan was that Israel would be a great nation and that rulers from the house of David would guide the people in a path that happily blended faith and politics.

But there is a chapter 11 in 1 Kings, and it is a catalogue of Solomon's sins. Here the great king is roundly condemned and revealed as a man of huge abuses in matters of power, money, and sex—Solomon might be said to have hit the trifecta in terms of excess. He is portrayed as a tyrant whose lust for power disrupted the balance that David sought between a central monarch and the prerogatives of local tribal leaders. The affluence of his lifestyle, which required forced labor and crushing taxation, is described in scandalous terms. And his household is reported to have included a thousand wives and concubines.[10]

The desire to please his wives and lovers led him to what the biblical author views most harshly, his religious indifferentism. In violation of the Mosaic Law, Solomon marries non-Israelites who practice other religions. His support for these other traditions goes so far as to build temples to gods other than Yahweh, and Solomon himself participated in the rituals of the different cults. The king of the Israelite people was an idolater, unfaithful to Yahweh, who was a jealous God.

Rebellion and civil war ensue after Solomon's death, and the kingdom is divided into northern Israel and southern Judah. Israel eventually comes under Assyrian rule and later so does Judah and with it, Jerusalem. The city of David—the site of the Temple and home of the Ark of the Covenant—is laid waste. The political independence of the Israelite people is no more, and the religious life of the people is imperiled. The story of the Israelite political state is a tale of survival and even triumph in a world of major military and political powers, only to be followed by crushing loss and division of the monarchy into southern (Judah) and northern kingdoms (Israel).

REFLECTIONS ON THE MONARCHY

Regarding the monarchy, Bruce Birch has nicely summarized the biblical viewpoint with his capsule descriptions of prominent Hebrew kings: the story of Saul is a tale of "the promise aborted"; David's story is "the promise glimpsed"; while Solomon and his successors illustrate "the promise broken." This failure of the monarchy will lead to "the promise postponed" as the Jew-

---

10. There is much hyperbole in the polemical treatment of Solomon. Part of the genius of the Old Testament writers is their ability to see both the best and the worst in the character of their leaders. No hero is without flaws, yet the existence of such flaws does not cancel out the good the hero accomplishes.

ish people look to the coming of a messiah, a hope that is developed in later biblical writings.[11]

In one sense, with Solomon and his successors Israel got what it wanted, a king like other nations. The Hebrew people were led by men of ambition, with varying degrees of leadership skills and often of questionable character. But, in another sense, there was no single mode of kingship that Israel's kings could fit. Lawrence Boadt points out that there were at least three patterns of kingship in the ancient Near East. The kings of great nations such as Assyria, Babylon, and Egypt might identify themselves with great forces of nature and so become "the sun god" or "the storm god." Kings of smaller nations, who were essentially vassals to the great kings, were understood to be servants of a local god who was in charge of a particular region. In some cases these local kings were military leaders who had taken control by force and the gods they worshiped were not necessarily the gods of the local people. Rather they were the personal gods of the ruler's family or original homeland. Finally, a third type was the king who emerged from within a tribe or clan and who, if not elected, was at least legitimated by the support of their people. Saul, David, and Solomon all fit this third model of kingship, as did their successors in the Davidic dynasty.

Ordinarily, a king had three broad responsibilities: (1) to control and direct the military, (2) to be the arbiter of justice in disputed cases among his people, and (3) to serve in a quasi-priestly role at key moments of religious ritual. This latter task underscores the fact that the role of monarch in the ancient world was never purely secular. Even if not viewed as divine himself, the king was a symbol of god's presence in the land and was seen as a deputy or chosen instrument of the deity. And so the monarch would play a role in the significant rituals that marked the calendar year, for example, planting and harvest times, or at special public celebrations such as a military conquest or the end of a drought.[12]

The kings of Israel played such a religious role, although it is clear that Israel's true king was Yahweh and no Israelite king was ever divinized.[13] The king did have a cultic role in Hebrew worship, and both prophets and priests were understood as officials of the monarch. One sees this, for example, in the legitimation of Jerusalem as the religious center of the nation. Given the lack of religious significance of Jerusalem prior to when David brought the Ark to rest there, his decision needed to be explained. A prophetic oracle announces that Mount Zion is Yahweh's chosen dwelling place. Despite the

---

11. Birch, *Let Justice Roll Down*, 11.

12. Boadt, *Reading the Old Testament*, 240-41.

13. That is not to deny there was a high theological view of the king, illustrated by texts like Psalm 72.

earlier tradition that all of Palestine was God's home, "the divine authority of the prophet, presumably Nathan, backed by the impressive royal power of an undoubtedly pleased king, quickly overcame any resistance to this radical localizing of Yahweh's mountain abode."[14]

Consistently, the Israelite king was seen as subject to Yahweh; it is Yahweh who is acknowledged as the actual king and ruler of the people. Any earthly king might be viewed as Yahweh's viceroy or deputy. Therefore, the qualities of an Israelite king must reflect the qualities that mark Yahweh. "Yahweh's kingship remains the source of a royal ideal even when the royal reality of Israelite and Judean kings sought to turn the religious tradition to self-serving ends."[15] Consequently, when various Hebrew kings failed in their rule it was understood that the root source of a monarch's failure was disobedience to Yahweh and neglect of the law of the covenant. The earthly king was judged by how well he upheld the standard of Yahweh, the true and heavenly king, who embodied an ideal that was expressed in the norms of the covenant relationship.

An example of standards that were established in order to limit a king's authority and exercise of power is found in the book of Deuteronomy.

> [The king] must not acquire many horses for himself, or return the people to Egypt in order to acquire more horses, since the Lord has said to you, "You must never return that way again." And he must not acquire many wives for himself, or else his heart will turn away; also silver and gold he must not acquire in great quantity for himself. When he has taken the throne of his kingdom, he shall have a copy of this law written for him in the presence of the levitical priests. It shall remain with him and he shall read in it all the days of his life, so that he may learn to fear the Lord his God, diligently observing all the words of this law and these statutes, neither exalting himself above other members of the community nor turning aside from the commandment.... (17:16-20a)

Because the king was a deputy of Yahweh, he was to be an advocate and defender of justice in the land. This suggests two consequences. First, the monarchy ought to serve as a check on the abuses of justice that occurred as a result of decisions by tribal chiefs and elders at the local level. Second, the understanding of justice established by the covenant law provided a standard by which a prophet could lodge criticism of the king or the king's agents.[16]

---

14. Roberts, "The Davidic Origin of the Zion Tradition," in *The Bible and the Ancient Near East*, 313-30 at 328.

15. Birch, *Let Justice Roll Down*, 205.

16. Roberts, "In Defense of Monarchy," 374.

Or another way of putting it is, "what chiefly distinguished the Israelite monarchy from the same institution in neighboring countries was the absence in principle of absolute despotic power." This was due to the king being bound to the norms of the covenant established by Yahweh. In effect, the Israelite king was a sort of constitutional monarch, as the text of Deuteronomy 17:14-20 exemplifies, with its listing of the limits of power and the duties incumbent on the king. Again, when the Israelite monarchy is compared to its counterparts in the region, a "second distinguishing mark was the special status of the prophets as bearers of the word of God to the king."[17] The confrontation between Nathan and David over the killing of Uriah is a notable example of the prophet's role to confront the king (2 Sam 12:1-15).

However, the possibility of the prophet challenging the king should in no way be interpreted as meaning that the classical prophets were antimonarchical. While individual kings may be rebuked for specific actions in the biblical text, there is no evidence of prophets promoting abolition of the monarchy as a political institution. Indeed, Isaiah is typical when he yearns not for the end of monarchy but for a good man to fill the kingly role.

We can conclude this reflection on monarchy in the Hebrew Bible by noting along with the scholar J. J. M. Roberts that the inclusion of both the pro- and antimonarchical voices is a valuable contribution to our understanding of politics. "If the critique of kingship preserved in the biblical record relativizes kingship and destroys any claim which that form of human government may make to being the divinely authorized form of government, the positive appreciation for kingship relativizes the claims of any competing form of human government."[18]

Here at the origins of their tradition, Christians already find an insight that can inform how they should think about politics today. All those who wield earthly power are subject to God's law and are bound by norms not of their own design but by standards that transcend any specific form of political

---

17. Benjamin Mazar, *Biblical Israel: State and People*, ed. Shmuel Ahituv (Jerusalem: Magnes Press of Hebrew University, 1992), 63.

18. Roberts, "In Defense of Monarchy," 366. A much different reading of the lessons to be drawn from the competing narratives about the monarchy is found in Wes Howard-Brook, *"Come Out My People"* (Maryknoll, NY: Orbis Books, 2010), 93-211, esp. 98-133. Howard-Brook provides a creative interpretation of the story of Solomon that reads it as a harsh portrayal of the utter corruption of Yahwistic religion by the Israelite monarchy's embrace of a religion of empire. The Solomon narrative, according to Howard-Brook, is a fundamental text revealing the contested vision found within the Bible itself of two competing forms of religion, with one version being truthful and the other being the polar opposite of true Yahwistic religion. Solomon represents the temptation to turn away from God's rule to pursue the political economy of human imperialism abetted by a religion of empire that undercuts true Yahwistic faith.

order. Furthermore, no specific political institution can claim to be *the* divinely inspired or approved order of governance.

POLITICS FROM THE DIVINE PERSPECTIVE

The story of the monarchy and the various events and persons that constitute that history is one important strand for understanding politics as portrayed in the Hebrew Scriptures. Another essential strand is that of the classical prophets. Classical is used here in the sense that the biblical books that bear the names of these individuals became the common norm for later generations of both Jews and Christians for interpreting the rule of faith of the Israelite people.

Popular imagery may suggest that a prophet is one who foretells the future. This, however, is not the best way to understand the figures that make up the tradition of classical prophecy. Another recent view of prophecy tends to equate the prophetic with the countercultural, but this, too, is not the most accurate interpretation of the message of the classical prophets.

We might begin our discussion of prophets and politics, then, by asking what a prophet is. There are many possible answers to that question, but one particularly insightful description is found in the study of the Jewish theologian Abraham Heschel.

For Heschel, the Bible reveals a God who is intensely involved with human beings, who are created by divine action. Yahweh is portrayed as rejoicing, lamenting, suffering, and consoled over the situation of humankind. Humankind makes God angry, creates divine frustration, and also brings about Yahweh's joy. Above all, human beings are the objects of God's love. This is crucial to Heschel's understanding of God; God *feels*. There is such a thing as divine pathos.

God is deeply engaged in human history, hardly indifferent to what occurs in human life. The God of the Bible is not distant and aloof, but truly moved by the human creatures made in the divine image. "The God of Israel is never impersonal."[19] Yahweh desires to have an intimate relationship with men and women, and the biblical narratives relate how the Israelite people regularly forget, repudiate, ignore, and only occasionally attend to the God so passionately committed to their well-being.

"This divine pathos is the key to inspired prophecy," according to Heschel.[20] The prophet stands within the community as the one person who understands what Yahweh is *feeling*. The prophet gives voice to God's viewpoint, the divine

---

19. Abraham Heschel, *The Prophets*, vol. 1 (New York: Harper & Row, 1962), 24.
20. Ibid.

way of seeing things. "[T]he fundamental experience of the prophet is a fellowship with the feelings of God, a *sympathy with the divine pathos*. . . ."[21] In effect, the prophet is the one who can assess the situation from the perspective of how Yahweh sees it.[22]

The classical prophets of the Old Testament came from both the southern and the northern kingdoms. They were from aristocratic families and from humble roots. Some were eloquent and others less polished in their use of language. The differing personalities and temperaments are evident in their writings. What they all shared, however, was a sense that, for whatever reason, Yahweh had called on them to remind the Jewish nation of its infidelities and its need to return to the way of the covenant.

While the prophets frequently spoke to the general community, at particular moments, a prophet might direct his words mainly to those in authority. When the prophet did so, it usually was to remind rulers to be mindful that they, too, are subject to God's law. Earthly rulers are not autonomous but are bound by a moral code not of their own making. The obligation of fidelity to the covenant leaves even kings open to judgment, and the prophets are the voice of that message.

Politics and Prophets

Bruce Birch has described the politics of the covenant as being a "politics of justice." The fundamental premise of such a politics is the "equal claim of all persons before God." Therefore, the use of power and the decisions of those invested with authority ought to reflect as much as possible the equal worth of persons.[23] Political institutions that grant preferences to some, that establish a political elite capable of imposing burdens on the wider community but excusing themselves, are incongruent with the prophetic vision of the political order.

A proper political order is governed by justice not self-serving power. There are moral standards that even the most powerful must abide by because the author of the standards is Yahweh. Not even kings are exempt from what is

---

21. Ibid., 26. Italics in original.

22. At the same time the prophet is portrayed as one who appeals to God on behalf of the people, defending them against God's anger. The prophet stands between God and the rest of humanity as oracle on behalf of God and intercessor on behalf of humankind. See Yochanan Muffs, "Who Will Stand in the Breach? A Study of Prophetic Intercession," in *Love and Joy* (New York: Jewish Theological Seminary of America, 1992), 9-48.

23. Bruce Birch, *What Does the Lord Require?* (Philadelphia: Westminster Press, 1985), 55-56.

understood by the prophets to be divinely sanctioned norms. From one perspective, prophecy as an institution exists alongside monarchy, and almost not
at all without it. Without the achievements of the monarchy and existence of
the state, there would be no prophets nor the codification of Torah legislation.
There are many narratives illustrating how royal power is abused but many
other narratives about judicial and cultic reform credited to various kings.
There is a dialectic between royal accomplishment and prophetic critique that
is part of the politics of justice.

From a second perspective, however, the monarchy under Solomon became
a centralizing force that established a court culture with a hierarchy of privileged officials. Indeed, the inequalities that developed within the Hebrew
nation and the abuses of power that flowed from Jerusalem led to the collapse
of the united nation and a return to the two kingdoms of Judah and Israel. Yet,
the dual monarchies went on to exhibit no greater devotion to a politics of
justice than had the single state united under the Davidic monarchy.

It is the second perspective on the political context, the corruption first of
the united monarchy in Jerusalem and then the continued failings of the dual
kingdoms, that explains the harsh judgments to be found in the writings of the
prophets. For example, there is the prophet Hosea, who lived in the northern
kingdom of Israel during a time of struggle with the far more powerful nation
of Assyria. Hosea is best known for the interpretation of his own failed marriage and his wife's adultery as an image of Israel's infidelity to Yahweh. But
he had a strong political message as well, even echoing the earlier antimonarchical themes found in 1 Samuel that attack the very institution of kingship.

Just how far Hosea takes his critique of monarchy is a debated issue among
biblical scholars. Is he critical of a series of individual kings in northern Israel
or is he making a broader, more extensive criticism of the idea of monarchy?[24]
Certainly Hosea is troubled by more than just the failings of one or two kings
because he foretells the destruction not only of individuals but of the entire
monarchy and the state of the northern kingdom. For Hosea the fault lay
deeper than an occasional bad king; the trouble began with the sin of the
people in not trusting Yahweh.

At one point Hosea portrays Yahweh complaining of the people, "They
made kings, but not through me. They set up princes, but without my knowledge" (Hos 8:4). Later Yahweh is unmoved by Israel's perilous situation before
the Assyrian threat. "Where now is your king, to save you; where are all your

---

24. An even-handed discussion of the prophet's attitude toward kingship may be
found in Peter Machinist, "Hosea and the Ambiguity of Kingship in Ancient Israel,"
in *Constituting the Community: Studies on the Polity of Ancient Israel in Honor of S. Dean
McBride, Jr.*, ed. John Strong and Steven Tuell (Winona Lake, IN: Eisenbrauns, 2005),
153-81.

princes, to defend you—those of whom you said, 'Give me a king and princes'? I have given you kings in my anger, and I have taken them away in my wrath" (Hos 13:10). The prophet has a dark view of the near future, even if he holds out hope for a restoration in a more distant future. The kingdom of Israel will collapse.

Unlike Hosea, the prophet Jeremiah, who lived in the southern kingdom of Judah, did not attack the very institution of the monarchy. Yet Jeremiah was deeply distressed by the abuses of King Jehoiakim and did not recoil from confronting his ruler. In chap. 22 the reader finds Jeremiah being told by Yahweh to "Go down to the house of the king of Judah, and speak there this word. . ." (Jer 22:1). The message is at first an exhortation. "Thus says the Lord: Do justice and righteousness, and deliver from the hand of the oppressor him who has been robbed. And do no wrong or violence to the alien, the fatherless, and the widow, nor shed innocent blood in this place" (Jer 22:3). If the king would listen, the prophet declares that the Davidic monarchy would continue and flourish. But if Jehoiakim does not listen, he is told that his house would "become a desolation" (Jer 22:6).

Jeremiah then delivers the warning of what shall befall Jehoiakim because of his intransigence in misrule.

> Woe to him who builds his house by unrighteousness, and his upper rooms by injustice; who makes his neighbor serve him for nothing, and does not give him his wages; who says "I will build myself a great house with spacious upper rooms," and cuts out windows for it, paneling it with cedar, and painting it with vermilion. Do you think you are a king because you compete in cedar? (Jer 22:13-15)

The forced labor and lavish displays of wealth are indicators of the king's failure to practice justice. The prophetic judgment continues, "you have eyes and heart only for your dishonest gain, for shedding innocent blood, and for practicing oppression and violence" (Jer 22:17).

The prophet Ezekiel also writes about the southern kingdom but at a time when Judah had been overrun by Babylon and many leaders had been taken into captivity back to Babylon. Ezekiel sees this crisis—the kingdom has been conquered and the Temple destroyed—as one that was brought on in large part by the failures of Judah's political leaders. At one point he quotes Yahweh equating the kings who brought on the crisis with shepherds who neglect their flock.

> You eat the fat, you clothe yourselves with the wool, you slaughter the fatlings; but you do not feed the sheep. The weak you have not strengthened, the sick you have not healed, the crippled you have not bound up, the strayed you have not brought back, the lost you have not sought, and with

force and harshness you have ruled them. So they were scattered because there was no shepherd; and they became food for all the wild beasts. (Ezek 34:3-5)

Ezekiel is close to the spirit of Hosea in his dark view of kingship as being at the center of reasons for Judah's ruin. Yet Ezekiel maintains that there is hope for the future, a hope that Yahweh himself will become the shepherd of the people and will reestablish a just social order. Part of that social order will be a prince who rules the people with fairness and does not use power for personal gain. The powerful symbol of the messiah as the son of David who will usher in a future age that will end Israel's tribulations remains. There were other symbols of the future age, "but the royal messiah, it is fair to say, was and remains principal among them."[25]

Thus, even amidst great disorder and following the bitter conquest by Babylon, the last of the major classical prophets is still able to console the people with a vision of a more just future. Part of that future is the emergence of a just prince. It is hard to understand how that hope could have endured if the judgment on kingship in ancient Israel was that it was a failed institution pure and simple. The disappointment of past and present political leadership does not eradicate a belief in what God will do for the political renewal of the Hebrew people.

Prophecy and Wider Social Criticism

When discussing the criticisms of the classical prophets it should be pointed out that while the prophets were not afraid to challenge even the monarchs who ruled them, it was not only, or even mainly, the king who came under the scrutiny of the prophetic eye. Many of the prophets had harsh judgments to make about the economic elite of their society.

One of the socio-economic changes that accompanied the rise of the monarchy was the development of a court society that benefited from proximity to the king. Advisors, administrators, military leaders, the priestly class charged with control of the Temple, and other individuals who were necessary for the functioning of a monarchy were all in a position to profit from various royal decisions, be it taxation, public works projects, trade, military campaigns and plunder, as well as other activities that may be found among political elites, for example, bribery.

The prophets took aim at the luxury enjoyed by some while others lacked necessities. They were particularly angered by corruption that fostered the gap

---

25. Machinist, "Hosea and the Ambiguity of Kingship," 154.

between the wealthy and the poor. Amos, a resident of the southern kingdom of Judah who heard the call to prophesy in northern Israel, is among the bluntest of critics. He had the unenviable task to denounce injustice at a time when many in the northern kingdom were prospering and thought the existing socio-political order to be more than acceptable. One of his prophecies was aimed at the judges entrusted with legal order. "For I know how many are your transgressions, and how great are your sins—you who afflict the righteous, who take a bribe, and turn aside the needy in the gate" (Amos 5:12).

Isaiah, perhaps the greatest of the classical prophets, was himself a member of the court in Jerusalem. He, however, did not use his position for his own advantage but was an eloquent voice for those who were disadvantaged by a corrupt leadership.

> Woe to those who call evil good
>   and good evil,
> Who put darkness for light
>   and light for darkness,
> Who put bitter for sweet
>   and sweet for bitter!
> Woe to those who are wise in their own eyes,
>   And shrewd in their own sight!
> Woe to those who are heroes at drinking wine,
>   And valiant men in mixing strong drink,
> Who acquit the guilty for a bribe,
>   And deprive the innocent of their rights! (Isa 5:20-23)

Isaiah reminds us it is not social location that determines the prophet but the moral and religious sensitivity of the person that enables one to enter into a sympathetic union with Yahweh's purposes. It is the ability to feel what Yahweh feels and give voice to Yahweh's disappointment and anger, as well as divine compassion and consolation. Perhaps Isaiah's status as a court insider helped him to understand the character and skills necessary to be a good king. Being a member of the royal court may have enabled him to appreciate the merits of good governance: justice and prosperity within the kingdom.

Earlier, the prophet Jeremiah was quoted as expressing God's warning to King Jehoiakim in the following way: "And do no wrong or violence to the alien, the fatherless, and the widow, nor shed innocent blood in this place" (Jer 22:3). In several texts throughout the Old Testament we read that Yahweh has a special concern for the alien, the orphan, and the widow. The significance of this triad may be missed if we do not remember that Israelite society, like so many other societies, was thoroughly patriarchal and tribal.

In such a society, a woman had public standing by virtue of being the daughter of her father. Once married her public standing was related to being the wife of her husband. A child, male or female, without a father had no real public existence for it was most often the father of a family who gave the child status. A woman who was widowed was a woman who lost her social position. Her best hope might be to be taken back into her father's house, or, if her son were mature and married, taken into his house. To be a resident in a land that did not belong to one's own tribe was also to be in a situation where one had precarious public standing. To be an outsider, unrelated to the local tribe, was to be effectively without appeal to an authority to protect one's rights.

In other words, to be a widow, orphan, or alien was to be marginal to the life of a society characterized by patriarchy and tribalism. For the prophets and many biblical writers, the triad of widow, orphan, and alien was a shorthand way of capturing that group of people that today we might call the marginalized. It was a way to refer to all those individuals who were the forgotten, the exploited, the powerless.

Material deprivation, physical violence, illness, and accidents, as well as exposure to the harshness of nature, are all hallmarks of life in the ancient Near East. With such conditions it is easy to imagine that a significant number of people experienced life as a hardship. The prophets may not always have been able to analyze the exact causes of people's suffering, but they were a consistent voice on behalf of those vulnerable to judicial exploitation and who were symbolized by the triad of widow, orphan, and alien. The prophetic criticism was lodged at a society that neglected these "little ones," and no one was viewed as being more at fault than those who made up the ruling elite that was deaf to the cries of the poor all about them.

CONCLUSION

While the political institutions of the ancient Hebrews may appear quite different from the way that we think of the political order today, there are important lessons to be found in the Old Testament treatment of politics. Foremost is that politics was for the good order of the entire Jewish community. The movement of a people out of slavery in Egypt and eventual transformation into a confederacy of tribes in Canaan; the establishment of a monarchy and eventually two kingdoms; and the activity of that remarkable group of individuals we know as the classical prophets—all these moments in the history of Israel were meant to promote the common well-being of the people.

Mistakes in judgment were made, and the Bible itself contains a record of the differing viewpoints about such decisions. There were individuals who exemplified great virtue in political life and others who displayed extensive vice. However, the basic theme that is evident both in the praises of political actors and institutions as well as in the condemnations of actors and institutions is that politics matters to Yahweh, and the purpose of politics is to oversee and promote the good of the community. Important to note is that it is the entire community that is meant to flourish, not just elites. Indeed, the most common measure used to allot praise and blame was whether or not all the people were treated fairly by the political rulers and policies of Israelite society.

In concluding this overview of Old Testament perspectives on the political order we might note the following points.

- The biblical view of kingship as an institution, as well as of the individuals who embodied it, is ambivalent. Clearly the institution is affirmed as central to Israelite history, yet there are deep reservations about its legitimacy and achievements as well as criticisms of specific kings.
- There is a sure conviction that there are standards to which kings are accountable (e.g., Deut. 17:14-20). All human authority has limits established by a deity who reveals the standards. This revelation is not restricted to an elite but is available to all the people.
- The existence of standards limiting the king's power is a conviction widely shared in the ancient Near East. A relatively novel aspect of the Israelite view, when compared to nonbiblical sources, is the belief of some biblical writers that human kingship is a usurpation of Yahweh's role.
- Although the sharp criticism of kingship by some authors may not have been shared by all in Israelite society, the critical texts were included as part of the Bible's canon. Thus, for Judaism and later Christianity authority was granted to a discourse of negative criticism directed at kings and kingship.
- Despite the ambivalence toward monarchy the most common source of hope in the Old Testament is that Yahweh would be faithful to the Davidic promise and raise up a royal messiah who would restore Israel as a united nation freed from past misfortune.
- The movement of classical prophecy in ancient Israel reflects a tradition of both challenge and consolation. Because of the message of the prophets, the people, in general, and rulers, in particular, were challenged to live in fidelity to the covenant, including the ideal of justice as the legitimate expectation of all. The prophets also provided consolation to those denied justice and pleaded for divine mercy in the face of Israel's failures to be faithful.

QUESTIONS FOR REFLECTION/DISCUSSION

1. What accounts for the movement of the Israelites from a tribal confederacy to a monarchy? What are the arguments, pro and con, that the Bible records about the institution of monarchy?

2. What was the importance of David's establishment of Jerusalem as the capital?
3. How did the authority and power of the Israelite monarchy relate to belief in Yahweh?
4. How does the Bible describe a prophet? How do Hosea and Jeremiah agree and differ in their criticism of monarchy?
5. What is the significance of "the alien, the orphan, and the widow"?

3

The New Testament

The books of the New Testament include four Gospels (Mark, Matthew, Luke, and John), an account of the early history of the Christian community (Acts of the Apostles), a collection of letters written by Paul and other early disciples (Epistles), and a book that echoes the style of what is called apocalyptic literature, a literature of visionary insight written in crisis (Revelation). Each of these genres contributes insights for constructing a perspective on politics. In this chapter we will consider several specific texts that have been cited throughout the church's history as especially significant for thinking about the political realm. First, however, we begin by placing Jesus and his disciples in their first-century social context.

JESUS AND THE REIGN OF GOD

Now after John was arrested, Jesus came into Galilee, preaching the gospel of God, and saying: "The time is fulfilled, and the kingdom of God is at hand; repent, and believe in the gospel." (Mark 1:14-15)

In the opening chapter of the earliest Gospel, Mark, we are told that Jesus went throughout the hill towns of Galilee—places like Capernaum, Nazareth, and Cana—preaching that the kingdom of God, or the reign of God, was at hand.[1] The historical Jesus did not preach about himself but about the reign of God. As the German biblical scholar Rudolf Bultmann famously said, "only after Easter did the proclaimer become the proclaimed." In other words, after

---

1. Throughout this chapter I will use the expression "reign of God" rather than "kingdom of God" for three reasons. First, the term "reign of God" is more gender inclusive than "kingdom of God" since it does not require a male imaging of God as king. Second, the phrase "kingdom of God" is not a common expression in the Hebrew Bible. The more common term is the Hebrew *YHWH malak*, which can be translated as "the Lord reigns" or "the Lord is king." Third, the expression "kingdom of God" can imply a spatial meaning, an area or place with boundaries like any other kingdom. However, the expression as used by Jesus in Mark's Gospel is not a place, rather it is the experience of God as once more being present and active in history.

the experience of the resurrection the followers of Jesus preached about Jesus. But during his public ministry the historical Jesus preached about the reign of God. It was that reality that was the central religious symbol throughout his ministry of preaching and healing.

For Mark, the preaching of Jesus about God's reign is the announcement that God is at work in the world. God reigns over creation as the creator, but not in a manner that is distant and aloof. A deist can imagine a creator who fashions the world and then exits from the stage, allowing history to move through time while this disengaged God observes from a far-off heaven. That is not the God that Jesus called "Father."

Rather Jesus is portrayed in Mark as proclaiming that the God who brought about creation is also the God who rules over history and brings salvation to Israel and all nations. Like any devout Jew of his time, Jesus believed that God is deeply engaged in human history, even if most observers of history do not comprehend that truth.

Like any public speaker, Jesus wanted to arouse a reaction from his audience. In response to his proclamation of God about to inaugurate salvation, Jesus called for people to reform their lives and believe in this good news. This message, contained in Mark 1:15, is what may be called a summary verse of Jesus' preaching, a concise statement of the fundamental message that Jesus of Nazareth announced: the reign of God is *at hand* and people ought to change their lives in response to this imminent salvation; God is drawing ever nearer.

If the reign of God was the main religious message of Jesus, then conversion or reform of one's life was his central moral message. Again and again, throughout his public ministry Jesus invited men and women to live differently because of the nearness of the reign of God, the conviction that God was at work in the lives of the people to whom he was preaching.

Jesus the Messiah

As their understanding of him deepened, the disciples, or followers, of Jesus began to proclaim that he was the messiah. This was a royal title drawn from the Hebrew Bible. The messiah was "the anointed" (*christos* in Greek), and the use of oil to anoint both the high priest and the king was a well-known practice among the Jewish people for centuries. Within Israel the vibrant hope for a messiah continued to develop during the period after the books of the Hebrew Bible were written and before Jesus' birth.

It is not easy to know specifically what the expectation of a messiah was that was harbored in the hearts of the people living in Jesus' time. There were several options regarding the future circulating at the time of Jesus' ministry. The first was the hope for a royal messiah, a political figure from the ancestral line of David who would restore Israel to the role of light to the nations. Second was the idea of a heavenly figure, akin to Michael at the end of the book of Daniel, who would usher in the end-time when God's people would no longer suffer. This vision emphasized a religious message, the need for personal holiness, rather than a political message, the aim of regime change. And a third hope entailed the rise of a prophet or priestly figure rather than a royal one who would be the agent of change.

It is clear that the hope for a messiah was not uniform in nature and the title could awaken a variety of expectations among the contemporaries of Jesus. The Gospels indicate that the historical Jesus did not see himself as one destined to be an earthly king who would rule over a restored Israel. Indeed, the temptation narrative in the Gospels of Matthew and Luke reject such temporal ambition as "demonic" in character. Instead, Jesus preached not his own reign but the reign of God. In this he was in accord with the traditional view that Israel's king was Yahweh. Jesus saw himself as an agent of his Father, announcing a message of what God was doing through his ministry, initiating the reign of God.

Jesus' concern that his role not be misunderstood is reflected in a particular feature of Mark's narrative, called the "messianic secret." On a number of occasions throughout that Gospel—after encounters with unclean spirits who knew him (3:11-12), having performed various miracles (5:35-43; 7:32-36), and with the disciples after the Transfiguration (9:2-7)—Jesus is portrayed as urging people not to draw attention to him or to what he had done. It is almost as if Jesus does not wish to be recognized, which is in tension with the crowds who press in on Jesus everywhere he goes in Mark's narrative.

Mark's use of the literary device of the "messianic secret" may be meant to convey a lesson that many who sought out Jesus, including his closest disciples, did not always understand his mission. Often the crowds are responding to his reputation as a healer. Their expectations of Jesus as Messiah may have been too quickly settled, not fully understanding the divine mission to which Jesus was called. In his Gospel, Mark proposes that no one could understand who Jesus the Messiah was until after his passion and death. Prior to that, his messianic role might be easily misconstrued.

This understanding of the "messianic secret" finds support in the climactic scene at Caesarea Philippi, where Jesus asks his disciples, "Who do people say that I am?" And then after hearing reports that he is John the Baptist, Elijah, or another prophet, Jesus puts the question directly to the disciples, "Who do you say that I am?" and Peter replies that he is the Messiah. The Gospel reader is then told that Jesus warned the disciples not to tell others about him (Mark 8:27-30).

Immediately following these verses Jesus speaks about his passion and how he will suffer, be killed, and then rise to new life. Peter, who has just professed his faith in Jesus as Messiah, now criticizes him for such words. Jesus, in turn, rebukes Peter by claiming he does not reflect how God sees things but as Satan does (Mark 8:31-33). Even Peter, the eventual leader of the Christian community, is portrayed as still not understanding Jesus and his mission. Although a literary device employed by Mark, the use of the "messianic secret" may well reflect a historical memory that Jesus was reluctant to accept titles or designations that were open to misunderstanding or that evoked reactions that were unsuited to his own self-understanding.

Within the context of Jewish Christianity when Jesus was proclaimed the Messiah, it was with the hindsight of a community that had experienced not only Jesus' passion and death but also his resurrection. Using messianic language allowed the first disciples to show how Jesus was the promised one. He was of the line of David, anointed by his baptism from John; he received God's spirit, witnessed to that spirit's power through his public ministry, and was given a royal welcoming ceremony upon his entrance into Jerusalem.[2] But the Gospels make very clear throughout that Jesus was not hoping to become an earthly king, and had something very different in mind when he associated himself with the coming reign of God.

The Reign of God Is Like . . .[3]

To understand the message of Jesus, therefore, about how his followers ought to live in the world, it is necessary to understand what God's reign meant for Jesus and how he expected his listeners would have heard his message. Jewish contemporaries of Jesus would be familiar with the psalms of the Hebrew Bible; hence they would recognize the theme of Yahweh being enthroned as the true God, the one God who reigns over all. Other gods are "no gods," mere idols who count for nothing. Yahweh alone is the one who rules, not just over Israel but over all creation and all creatures. Yahweh, the Lord God, is "a great king over all the earth" (Ps 47:2).

Yet, the expression "reign of God" pointed the listener to a future reality because one had only to look around to grasp that God's reign was not fully realized. Those who heard Jesus preach also paid taxes to an occupying Roman Empire; they saw Roman authorities in control of their ancestral land; there was division among the Jewish people themselves; and for the majority of the people life was always difficult with economic insecurity and harsh experiences of illness, physical labor, lack of sufficient food, bodily injury, and early death.

---

2. The terms messiah and Son of David were so deeply anchored in the Jewish context that they did not carry over effectively as Christianity moved into Hellenistic regions. There the terms Lord and Son of God better convey the identity of Jesus.

3. In this section I draw on insights of Frank Matera, *New Testament Ethics: The Legacies of Jesus and Paul* (Louisville: Westminster/John Knox Press, 1996), esp. 14-25.

Thus, the reign of God as an image of salvation meant being freed from this situation. It was an eschatological reality, that is, it pertained to the end of history; it was incompletely actualized in the here and now of Jesus' preaching.[4]

When Jesus announced the reign of God as being near, his audience would have understood that he was claiming God's future was breaking into the present time; the hope that God's rule to be established over all creation was now coming to be realized. The need for such an earth-shattering hope was not evident to everyone. Even most of Jesus' listeners were more focused on such immediate concerns as the need for healing demonstrated by the miracles. Hence the approach of God's reign calls for repentance and belief. For Mark, the disciple of Jesus has to be willing to make a break with the customary way of life, to leave behind family, work, possessions, or whatever hinders the following of Jesus (Mark 10:17-30). And the disciple must have faith, which for Mark entails the ability to see what nonbelievers cannot apprehend, the in-breaking of God's reign.

Jesus' miracles are the first signs of God's saving power. The various miracles of Jesus are understood as evidence that God is at work in Jesus through his healings, exorcisms, and other wonders, such as the feeding of the multitudes. The reign of God is at hand. However, those who will not accept the nearness of God's reign question the witness value of the miracles. Scribes in Jerusalem tried to discredit Jesus' authority in the eyes of the crowd by attributing Jesus' miracles not to God's power but to Satan (Mark 3:22). In their world, persons suspected of practicing magic could be punished with exile or death.

Another important aspect of the presence of the reign of God is suggested by the various parables Jesus used in teaching. In the parable of the sower (Mark 4:1-10) the farmer sows seed that falls on various types of soil, much as Jesus' preaching falls on the ears of various types of people.[5] The response to the preaching of Jesus is not uniform (4:13-20). This disparity provides no cause for alarm, however, for as Jesus later explains to his disciples, the seed does grow in a way that the sower cannot understand. Just as the seed is at work below ground long before the crop springs up from the earth, so the reign of God is at work although not all are aware of it (4:26-30). Those persons who

---

4. Traditionally, eschatology is that branch of theology that studies the "last things"—final judgment, God's justice, heaven and hell. In much contemporary theology it is also the study of how present realities are influenced by and related to the future of God. Eschatology is still about the "end of days," the culmination of God's plan of salvation and the destiny of humankind with God. Yet the topic of eschatology now also includes reflection on how Christian hope for the future inflects, or should inflect, historical experience.

5. Mary Ann Tolbert, *Sowing the Gospel: Mark's World in Literary-Historical Perspective* (Minneapolis: Fortress Press, 1989).

believe, who have faith in Jesus, are capable of understanding this, but those without faith will look but not see, listen but not really hear (4:11-12).

Yet another dimension of the mystery of God's reign is that its modest beginning is not in proportion to the wonder of its final manifestation. Like the mustard seed, the tiny seed that grows to a ten-foot bush, the reign of God may have humble origins, but that does not forecast what its final state will be (4:31-33). Easily overlooked in its early stage, the reign of God is truly present and at work. Yet one must have proper vision to see this happening. The reign of God is not simply a future hope; it is a present reality. That is the message Jesus announced as he walked throughout the towns of Galilee, the northern region of Israel, quite removed from the religious, cultural, and political center of Jerusalem to the south.

JESUS AND THE POLITICS OF HIS TIME

During Jesus' lifetime, Israel was a client kingdom under the control of the Roman emperor. The Jewish people were divided in their response to this reality as they were with regard to several other aspects of their political life. Jesus did not live within a unified Jewish political community, not even on the subject of Roman rule.

About one hundred and sixty years prior to Jesus' birth an independent Jewish state was established by the revolt of the Maccabees from the Seleucid rulers. Though based in Syria, the Seleucids were a Greek dynasty that was constantly engaged in skirmishes with the other Greek-speaking legacy of Alexander the Great, the Ptolemaic dynasty in Egypt, from whom they captured Palestine. During this period the Seleucids had to contend with Roman expansion to the east. The Maccabean revolt was a guerilla war against the Seleucids that led to the establishment of a Jewish family, called the Hasmoneans, as the kings of an independent Palestine. They sought assistance from the Romans in the power struggles that plagued the small kingdom.

While many Jews supported the overthrow of the Seleucids, there was no unanimity in support of the Hasmoneans. The more devout Jews saw these rulers as far too enthralled with worldly power and the attractions of Hellenistic culture. Consequently, reactionary movements emerged in the second century BCE such as that of the Qumran community, Jews who chose to withdraw from the everyday life they encountered under the Hasmonean rulers. Some members clustered in family groups. Others chose a monastic style of life centered on study of the Mosaic Torah. Such groups of pious Jews were equally disillusioned with the Herodian dynasty put in place by Mark Antony several decades after the Romans took control of Palestine in 63 BCE. The inhabitants of Qumran, who were called the Essenes, effectively dropped out of secular politics and awaited a divine vindication.

Another group of the pious was the Pharisees, religious reformers who sought to purify the religion and culture infected by the Hellenistic influence of the Hasmoneans. Devoted to detailed observance of the Mosaic Law, the Pharisees did not remove themselves from Jewish society but sought to reform it through various strategies, including political activity. As experts in the law, they accepted an oral tradition of interpretation that provided detailed guidance about how to observe such general commandments as keeping the Sabbath holy. Though never in control of the court or the Temple, the Pharisees did serve as leaders for those who wanted a reformed religious practice. Their application of the Law allowed for some accommodation to changing economic, social, and political circumstances. They acknowledged the realities of Roman rule. However, the Pharisees were not as tolerant of Rome as our next group.

A third group, the Sadducees, included the religious aristocracy of Jewish faith. They were descendants of the ancient priest Zadok, who was installed as high priest in Jerusalem by Solomon. Whether every priest of Jerusalem was, in fact, a descendant of Zadok may be debated, but all Temple priests claimed to be of his family. While not a sizable number of the population, the Sadducees were the "movers and shakers" of Jewish society. It was they who made up the majority of the Sanhedrin, the leadership council that governed Jewish life in lieu of the city council of pro-Roman notables found in non-Jewish cities. Their preoccupation was safeguarding the centrality of the Temple in Jewish life, and the perquisites they enjoyed as guardians and ministers of the Temple. As a consequence of these concerns, the Sadducees were far more politically "flexible" than other Jews. During Jesus' lifetime the Sadducees were supporters of the Herodians, the puppet regime put in place by the Romans to govern the Jewish people. The Sadducees would have been seen as "collaborators" by the forces of opposition to Rome.

Finally, a fourth group at the time of Jesus was the Zealots. These were the nonaccommodationists who advocated violent resistance to the Roman presence in Palestine. Having arisen about the time of Jesus' birth, when Jewish leaders dissatisfied with the harsher regime of Archelaus (Matt 2:22) petitioned Rome to take over rule of southern Palestine, the Zealots resisted the taxation Rome imposed on subject peoples. The Zealots were true theocrats; they sought a society governed by Mosaic Law and hated not only their Roman occupiers but Jews who collaborated with the Romans. The Zealots looked for the coming kingdom of God, but they believed this could be brought about through human activity, namely, religious rebellion. In place of the Roman Empire, which they saw as idolatrous, the Zealots wanted to establish a new Jewish state that could base its political order on Mosaic tenets.

One should not confuse these "parties" with our contemporary experience of political or religious organizations. The majority of the population did not belong to any of the four groups. Still, it is important to remember that a potent mix of religious and political viewpoints was the complex setting for Jesus' public ministry. In addition, of course, to the conflicting political outlooks within the Jewish community, there was the presence of the Roman Empire as the dominant political and military entity. For that reason, a particular scene in Mark's Gospel merits special attention.

Render to Caesar

And they sent to him some of the Pharisees and some of the Herodians to entrap him in his talk. And they came and said to him, "Teacher, we know that you are true, and care for no man; for you do not regard the position of men, but truly teach the way of God. Is it lawful to pay taxes to Caesar, or not? Should we pay them, or should we not?" But knowing their hypocrisy, he said to them, "Why put me to the test? Bring me a coin, and let me look at it." And they brought one. And he said to them, "Whose likeness and inscription is this?" They said to him, "Caesar's." Jesus said to them, "Render to Caesar the things that are Caesar's, and to God the things that are God's." And they were amazed at him. (Mark 12:13-17)

In chapter 12 of Mark, we find Jesus in Jerusalem, moving toward the great climax of his public life, his passion and death. Jesus is now in his third day within the city, and he is engaged in a series of controversies through which Mark reveals both the opposition to Jesus and the issues that brought him into conflict with the authorities of Jerusalem.

One of the exchanges is with the Pharisees and Herodians on the topic of paying taxes to Caesar. It is a story that appears in all three of the Synoptic Gospels (Mark, Matthew, and Luke). Paying the tax to Rome was a "hot button" issue within the Jewish community. It represented "tribute" paid to the Roman emperor, and as such was a direct reminder of Israel's subjection to a foreign power. For Jewish nationalists the experience of paying the tax would be deeply offensive, quite apart from any financial burdens it entailed.

The question posed to Jesus was whether, according to the Mosaic Law, it was proper to pay the tax that Rome required. By asking the question, his interlocutors hoped to put Jesus in an unwinnable position. The Zealots, of course, advocated outright resistance to the tax. (In this resistance they adopted a stronger stance than Old Testament prophets such as Ezekiel and Jeremiah, who did not present any religious objection to taxes exacted by foreign rulers like Nebuchadnezzar.) The Sadducees, supporters of the puppet government of Herod Antipas installed in Galilee by Rome, certainly would have supported paying the tax. Pharisees, though occasionally accommodationist, may have been opposed to the tax as individuals, though we have no evidence that they would have told people not to pay what was due. Hence, Jesus would be sure to alienate some group in the audience no matter how he answered. Furthermore, if he challenged payment of the tax he might well have gotten the attention of Roman authorities always wary of any leaders who might spark civic unrest in cities under their rule.

Jesus' initial reaction to the tax question is to ask his interrogators to show him the Roman silver coin required to pay the tax. When they produce the coin and are able to answer his next question about it, Jesus has demonstrated the insincerity of those individuals: the image on the coin would have been that of Tiberius Caesar, wearing a laurel wreath symbolizing his divinity.[6] He then states, "Render to Caesar the things that are Caesar's, and to God the things that are God's" (Mark 12:17). This statement of Jesus continues to circulate as a maxim independently of the situation that provoked it. Therefore it requires additional comment.

It is a mistake to read into Jesus' statement the separation of religion and politics or anything like our modern notion of separation of church and state. Throughout the ancient world, whether in Rome or in ancient Israel, religion and nation are understood to be a necessary unity. For Jesus, or any pious Jew, God is the creator and Lord of all of life. Those who rule the state have certain rights, but these rights are circumscribed by the all-encompassing claims of God.[7]

All that Jesus preached about the sovereignty of the reign of God would make it impossible for him to treat the realm of politics as sealed off from a person's higher loyalty to God. Nor is this saying a biblical warrant for separation of the institutions of church and state; that reading places contemporary ideas into a very different culture that closely allied religious and political institutions.

What then is going on in this passage? First of all, Jesus' reply is a positive answer to the question; the tax can be paid. This would surely have disappointed, even angered, the Zealots; Jesus does not reject the emperor's authority in principle. But the reason offered for paying the tax is not that Rome is the legitimate ruler of Palestine or that there is a moral duty to pay such a tax. Rather, Jesus offers a simple observation: the money is Roman money; give it back to the person who issued it. In effect, the money is Caesar's so let Caesar have it.

Notice that those questioning Jesus were able to produce a Roman coin when he asked for it even though they were in Jerusalem to celebrate Passover, not to pay taxes. The Pharisees and others used Roman money, which suggests

6. Wolfgang Schrage, *The Ethics of the New Testament* (Philadelphia: Fortress Press, 1988), 113.

7. Karl Hermann Schelkle, *Theology of the New Testament*, vol. 3 (Collegeville, MN: Liturgical Press, 1973), 337.

that they were willing to participate in the everyday affairs that Rome administered. Jesus' answer points out that since his questioners already are participating in the economic relationships enabled by Caesar's rule, they should acknowledge Caesar's claim.

It is the second part of Jesus' answer—one should pay to God what is God's—that moves the exchange to another level. Jesus' reply does not divide the world into political and religious realms that do not interact. That was the approach of the Herodians and other willing collaborators with Rome. They claimed Jewish identity, but they did not permit their faith to interfere with obeying Rome. They thought that their everyday politics did not shape their religious life.

As discussed above, Jesus, on the other hand, had been proclaiming the onset of the reign of God. It would have been obvious to his listeners that Jesus believed God's sovereignty over creation and history was higher than that of Caesar's. His second statement, therefore, reminds those gathered around him that they ought to be as concerned about obeying God as they are Rome. And this is what limits the claims of Caesar; the human person is claimed by God. Caesar may have a right to the coin, but he does not have the right to the ultimate loyalty of the person. That belongs to God alone, so "the demands of the state can have only limited authority and relative importance"[8] at best.

Interpreting Jesus

The Gospel passage about payment of the Roman tax recounts a scene in which opponents of Jesus were trying to put him in an awkward situation from which he could not escape without angering one or another group in society. Yet, as F. F. Bruce writes, the story "was not remembered and recorded simply as an interesting incident in the life of Jesus: it was recorded as precedent for the guidance of his followers."[9]

But what exactly is the guidance to be taken from the precedent? The saying about rendering to Caesar the things that are Caesar's, and to God the things that are God's, has generated no consensus among biblical experts. One scholar, Walter Pilgrim, has suggested three main schools of thought, and adds a fourth representing his own viewpoint.[10]

The first interpretation, the most traditional, reads Jesus as recognizing two realms, each of them legitimate. Respect and obedience are to be given to each,

---

8. Schrage, *Ethics of the New Testament*, 114.

9. F. F. Bruce, "Render to Caesar," in *Jesus and the Politics of His Day*, ed. Ernst Bammel and C. F. D. Moule (Cambridge: Cambridge University Press, 1984), 249-63 at 263.

10. Walter Pilgrim, *Uneasy Neighbors* (Minneapolis: Fortress Press, 1999), 64-72.

and there is no need to posit any inherent contradiction or tension between the claims placed on the believer who is also a citizen. The ideal is "a divinely intended partnership" between the earthly kingdom and the heavenly one.[11]

The second interpretation directly challenges the first, insisting that Jesus preached radical obedience only to God, ignoring Caesar. Render to Caesar what belongs to Caesar actually meant render nothing to Caesar for everything belongs to God. Some adherents of this position argue that Jesus believed in an imminent end to human history and thereby had little regard for the empire or any institution that was soon to pass away.

A third school of thought maintains that Jesus, indeed, acknowledges two legitimate kingdoms, political and religious, but that the kingdom of God must always be given clear priority. In principle, there is nothing wrong with paying taxes nor is there any moral obligation to oppose or rebel against all political authority. But no political ruler can be treated as divine or given unconditional loyalty or obedience.

Pilgrim accepts the basic contours of the third interpretation but offers a nuanced version of that approach. Without question God alone can claim our highest loyalty, but that does not deny "the necessity and significance of the political realm for daily existence."[12] Still, when the "render to Caesar" statement is placed within the wider context of Jesus' teaching and ministry, one sees that there is no easy peaceful coexistence between God's reign and any earthly kingdom. There is an inbuilt tension between the two realms as the passion and death of Jesus at the hands of the earthly rulers demonstrated. Many of the values and practices that Jesus endorsed and lived out himself will regularly put the followers of Jesus at odds with the claims of political rulers. Thus, what specifically ought to be rendered to Caesar in a particular situation is not always easy to discern for one can render only secondary, never primary, loyalty to political authority.

Summing Up

In the brief exchange between Jesus and his interlocutors, one sees a tension that will continue throughout the history of Christianity. Jesus, unlike the Zealots, acknowledges Caesar and obligations owed to government; yet Jesus insists that God makes claims as well and that people ought not to shirk their obligations to God. The Roman emperors had the most prominent offices within the religious cults that upheld their state. They permitted conquered peoples, including Jews, to follow their own religious rites as long as they did not stir up social conflicts within the cities. Yet, Jesus, even as he acknowledged

---

11. Ibid., 66.
12. Ibid., 71.

that Caesar might have some authority, made it clear that neither Caesar nor any other leader could assume to govern all realms.

The difficulty that will persist through the ensuing centuries, however, is that nowhere does Jesus provide a clear delineation of exactly *what* belongs to Caesar and *what* belongs to God. As a result there have been competing interpretations of what his statement means practically. In his reply Jesus does not indicate opposition to the state per se, but it is evident from all his teaching that he must oppose any state that makes absolute claims of sovereignty over a person's life. The latter claim would demand from Christians a loyalty and obedience to an earthly kingdom that is owed to the reign of God alone.

THE EARLIEST CHRISTIANS AND THE EMPIRE

Two passages from non-Gospel texts reveal how different the assessments might be concerning what it is that the disciples of Jesus owe to Caesar. These two passages from Romans and Revelation must be considered when seeking a biblically informed perspective on the political realm. The first is found in St. Paul's letter to the Romans. In Romans 13:1-7, Paul considers the issue of obedience to the political rulers and their decrees, including tax levies, even as he has taught that non-Jewish followers of Jesus are free from the religious obligations of Judaism. They are expected to observe the Ten Commandments given to Moses on Sinai (Rom 13:8-10).

In chapter 13 of the book of Revelation we find a very different sort of reflection written by an author named John who was a Christian prophet exiled to the island of Patmos. Here the conflict between church and empire is starkly drawn. It reaches its most direct form in the prophecies of Rome's collapse. By examining each of these texts we will see the range of reactions that early Christians had toward Roman imperial rule.

The Letter to the Romans

Let every person be subject to the governing authorities. For there is no authority except from God, and those that exist have been instituted by God. Therefore, he who resists the authorities resists what God has appointed, and those who resist will incur judgment. For the rulers are not a terror to good conduct, but to bad. Would you have no fear of him who is in authority? Then do what is good, and you will receive his approval, for he is God's servant for your good. But if you do wrong, be afraid, for he does not bear the sword in vain; he is the servant of God to execute his wrath on the wrongdoer. Therefore one must be subject, not only to avoid God's wrath but also for the sake of conscience. For the same reason you also pay taxes, for the authorities are ministers of God, attending to this very thing. Pay all of them their dues, taxes to whom taxes are due, revenue to whom revenue is due, respect to whom respect is due, honor to whom honor is due. (Rom 13:1-7)

Romans 13:1-7 is a key passage in the letter to the Romans, but these verses must not be read as if they were unrelated to what is before and after them. The verses are part of the closing section of the letter in which the apostle usually provides advice about how Christians should conduct themselves. Paul urges his readers to live as a people transformed by God and who will be devoted to what is right and good. He reminds them to live with an awareness that they are all members of the same body and that "all the members do not have the same function" (Rom 12:4).

Despite "having gifts that differ according to the grace given" by God (12:6), each Christian is called to "love one another" and "outdo one another in showing honor" (12:10). Such an approach to living is not restricted to behavior toward fellow Christians, but is extended even to those who persecute the believing community. Christians are not to repay evil with evil, nor take vengeance against one's enemies. Instead, Paul exhorts his fellow believers to "live peaceably with all" (12:18) and "do not be overcome by evil, but overcome evil with good" (12:21). That is the final verse of Romans 12, written directly before Paul states, "Let every person be subject to the governing authorities" (13:1).

After Paul offers his remarks about how Christians should live within the state in 13:1-7, he then writes in 13:8: "Owe no one anything, except to love one another; for he who loves his neighbor has fulfilled the law." He continues to urge his readers that to love others fulfills all the commandments. In other words, Paul's comments about obedience to public authority, payment of taxes, and the proper attitude toward the state and its leaders is of a piece with his general exhortation to Christians to enact a life marked by love and honor toward others, living peaceably with all. Romans 13:1-7 spells out what the ethic of love looks like in the political realm: an ethic of respect and obedience shown to authority.[13]

---

13. Schrage, *Ethics of the New Testament*, 236. I agree with Schrage's suggestion that seeing Paul's teaching in Romans 13 as part of the general love ethics enjoined on Christians helps to make sense of another text of Paul where he discourages Christians from using civil courts to adjudicate disputes (239). In 1 Corinthians 6:1-7, Paul is not attacking the legitimacy of the civil courts, he is opposing their use by Christians because that way of resolving disputes does not serve the public ethic of love of neighbor and service. In Romans 13, as we shall see, Paul encourages Christians to do certain things such as paying taxes and respecting civil authority because those behaviors do serve the ethic of love.

Paul did not develop this approach to the political authorities on his own. He adopted a position held by diaspora Jewish communities living as a noncitizen minority group in cities throughout the empire and beyond. These were communities of Jewish émigrés, who over the centuries had left Palestine either voluntarily or as slaves taken in war. Rome's Jewish community included many descendants of such captives, for example. As a minority community with distinctive traditions that often aroused suspicion or unfair treatment, "Jews in the provincial cities habitually depended upon good relations with the imperial court and its delegates, especially when local oppositions arose."[14] Paul, who grew up in the diaspora community of Tarsus, treated the civil authorities as part of God's plan for a just order and as defenders of the good. This evaluation was not due to naïveté; Paul had already been ill treated, beaten, thrown out of cities, and imprisoned by local authorities when his preaching caused controversy, so he knew individual governors could act unjustly. However, the experience of diaspora Judaism had proven that adopting a generous view of the state was expedient, and Paul simply urged the Christian community to do likewise.[15]

The positive view of rulers found in Romans 13 may also reflect Paul's experience in his work as the apostle to the Gentiles. Rome preserved a measure of order and peace throughout the Mediterranean region. The system of roads that Rome created, the relative safety of sea travel because the empire fought piracy, the establishment of order across the region, and a measure of religious toleration—all this facilitated Paul's travels to spread the gospel, which he soon hopes to take as far west as Roman Spain (Rom 15:22–29). And that is what was paramount for Paul, that he be allowed to proclaim the good news of Christ. So the state deserved a measure of respect because it helped, however unwittingly, Paul's apostolic ministry.

Finally, there is an additional rationale for Paul's teaching in Romans 13:1–7. Christians are bound to obey civil authorities because such authority ultimately comes from God. For Paul this is a matter of conscience (13:5) because he accepts the customary position of Jewish teaching, found in the Wisdom literature, that secular rulers hold their positions because God consents to it (Prov 8:15–16; Wis 6:1–3). This obligation applies not only to the leaders of Israel but to other nations as well. So, Paul reflects the traditional respect for the offices of the state that he has found in the Hebrew Scriptures.[16] If Paul

---

14. Wayne Meeks, *The First Urban Christians* (New Haven: Yale University Press, 1983), 106.

15. Ibid.

16. Yet, note that Wes Howard-Brook sees the Wisdom literature as representative of the biblical religion of empire to be opposed. See *"Come Out, My People!"* (Maryknoll, NY: Orbis Books, 2010), esp. 290–93.

was aware of the saying of Jesus concerning taxation, he does not invoke its authority. But he does concur with its sentiments.

The statement that God stands behind civil authority should not be understood as "divinizing" the state or its rulers. What Paul is stating is that civil government's power does not exist simply as an accident of history or by virtue of a social contract, but that it serves a divine purpose: the maintenance of good order and restraint of evildoers. Therefore, civil authority should be respected and obeyed, taxes ought to be paid, and civil law ought to be observed (Rom 13:7). Christians do these things not merely "for opportunistic reasons" but "out of responsible and conscientious obedience to God's will."[17]

Paul writes that there is no reason to fear civil rulers as long as one lives rightly, for civil rulers only use their violent force against wrongdoers (Rom 13:3-4). He does not take up the question about the possibility that the state is the one engaged in wrongdoing and what that might mean for the Christian community. Is this because he did not believe the state could be unjust? Hardly, given his reminders that Jesus was executed as though he were a disgraced criminal, by crucifixion. Paul prided himself on sharing similar punishments as an authentic apostle of Christ. He had to flee unjust imprisonment in Damascus and was beaten by authorities in Philippi, to cite just two instances.

What cannot be forgotten is that Paul was writing an exhortation to encourage people to live out the Christian ethic even in public life; he was not trying to present an exhaustive treatment of every question that might arise in the realm of politics. For example, Paul also did not treat the duties of government officials beyond the observation that they are to punish wrongdoers and reward the good.

Yet if Paul is aware that Roman authorities could and did condemn the innocent and enslave those they conquered, why then does he not preach social reform? Remember the first Christians were a mixture of social classes, but there were few who exercised any significant power. The cities and states that made up the empire were not democratic; there were no realistic opportunities for common people to exercise political power, to hold public officials accountable, or to reform political and social institutions. Such changes as did occur were initiated at the top by the governing elite. Furthermore, Paul does not think the existing world order is destined for a long life, as he observes in Romans 13:11-12, just a few verses after his comments on the state. The end-time is not far off, so what really matters is not a political program of reform but preaching the good news of salvation to those who have not yet heard it.

---

17. Schrage, *Ethics of the New Testament*, 238.

Summing Up

It would be a mistake to read Romans 13:1-7 as the Christian doctrine of the state. What is presented in this brief passage is not an abstract theory of government or an attempt to describe the ideal political order like Plato's *Republic*. Paul is writing as a pastor, describing how Christians ought to act toward civil authority in the concrete situation of first-century Rome.

It is a political order that is not going to last long; yet while it exists it represents part of God's plan for maintaining some measure of justice and peace in social life. As a result, Christians ought to be respectful to rulers, obedient to civil laws, and dutiful in paying taxes.

What we do not get from Paul, any more than from Jesus, is a theory of government that is meant to transcend the historical context for which he writes. Paul does not take up the question of what Christians ought to do in the face of gravely unjust rulers, or a state that acts deliberately to repress the Christian faith. Paul assumes that the existing social order reasonably reflects the purposes for which God has instituted political authority, and he then offers his counsel on how Christians should practice their ethic of love in public life. On what should be done by Christians when Paul's assumption is not the case, Romans 13 does not provide an answer.

Still we may recall an important corollary to Paul's assertion that civil government is instituted by God. It is a lesson we have already seen in the Old Testament. Civil rulers, be it Jewish monarch or Roman emperor, have legitimate authority granted them by God; but it is authority that is linked to God's purposes and therefore can be measured and held accountable when it fails to act in accord with those purposes. Prophets arose in ancient Israel to fulfill that role of challenging unjust kings, and the spirit of prophecy gave rise to men and women in early Christianity who opposed the injustices of Rome.

Revelation 13

To see just how context dependent the Pauline teaching was, consider another chapter 13, this time from the book of Revelation. Revelation was written ca. 90 CE, about thirty-three years after Paul wrote Romans and twenty years after Mark's Gospel, and the situation for Christians in the cities of Asia Minor had changed. Those earlier texts suggested, somewhat indirectly, there was "conflict between the will of God and that of the state." With the book of Revelation, however, there is a clear and direct statement of "the collision between the Christian faith on the one hand and the Roman Empire and emperor worship on the other."[18]

---

18. Ibid., 342.

A key factor that helped bring on the collision was the change in how Rome saw the Christian community. At first, Christian believers were not readily distinguished from the larger Jewish community by Roman authorities. Therefore, the first Christians "shared the privileges of the Jews and Roman toleration of Judaism" within the empire.[19] As the Christian church became largely non-Jewish and so divided from its Jewish roots, however, the Roman authorities saw Christianity as a disruptive, new religious movement. Christians refused to participate in the official state cult or acknowledge the divinized emperor, activities not expected of Jews. For non-Jews to exempt themselves, however, looked like rebellion. Moreover, cities in the imperial province of Asia were beginning to compete with one another to become centers of emperor worship, among them Ephesus and Pergamum, which are mentioned in Revelation.

Scholars disagree about the immediate context for John's ferocious hostility toward Roman imperial rule in the east. Some posit that the church was experiencing extensive persecution during the reign of the emperor Domitian; other experts argue there is no evidence for a situation worse than the customary hardships faced by Paul, Peter, or other early martyrs. Perhaps the exile suffered by the prophet John sharpened his critique. For our purposes what matters is not the actual historical situation but how the author of Revelation viewed it. For whatever reason, the writer had come to see the empire as idolatrous and considered it a grave threat to the life of the Christian church.

The prophet saw his time as one of crisis. The empire was not seen as tolerably just or as an unwitting ally of the missionary expansion of Christianity. Rather, the emperor and his allies had become an avowed enemy of the Christian community. In Revelation 13 we find a far different tone and set of recommendations to follow than in Paul's letter to the Romans.

> And I saw a beast rising out of the sea, with ten horns and seven heads, with ten diadems upon its horns and a blasphemous name upon its heads. . . . And to it the dragon gave its power and his throne and great authority. . . . Men worshipped the dragon, for he had given his authority to the beast, and they worshipped the beast, saying, "Who is like the beast, and who can fight against it?" And the beast was given a mouth uttering haughty and blasphemous words. . . . And it was allowed to make war upon the saints and to conquer them. (Rev 13:1, 2b, 4-5a, 7a)

This symbolism depicts an oppressive and idolatrous political system in which Rome had drawn all the kings of the earth into its orbit. Christians

---

19. Ibid., 343.

are facing the mythic power of the ancient Satan instantiated in the empire. So what to do? First, deny the state's legitimacy. Now there is no discussion of authority coming from God. On the contrary, using the imagery of earlier Jewish visionaries such as Ezekiel, Daniel, and noncanonical apocalypses, the state is likened to a mythic beast that commits blasphemy: its power comes from a dragon, Satan; its emperors force the populace to practice idolatry; and it wages war against God's holy ones.

"If you are to be taken captive, into captivity you go; if you kill with the sword, with the sword you must be killed. Here is a call for the endurance and faith of the saints" (Rev 13:10). The audience of the prophet is not urged to attack the empire but is warned that if one is destined for captivity or to be slain, then that is what will happen. What is called for is not violent rebellion but faithful endurance under trial. Despite the author's confrontational stance, denying any legitimacy to the state, there is no denial of the state's power. There is no call to reform the empire or even to fight against it. Instead, the only realistic option open for a small, powerless minority is to endure the empire's force, yet hold firmly onto the true faith. Christians can ridicule the pretensions of an idolatrous empire, but they must also acknowledge what the empire will do to its victims. And so the author exhorts his readers to fidelity when the inevitable suffering comes.

Romans 13 and Revelation 13 each paint a very different picture of Christians and the political realm. Paul, presuming a relatively just political order, urges Christians to meet their political obligations because of religious, ethical, and pragmatic reasons. The author of Revelation experiences the horror of state power put to the purposes of religious persecution and violence. The response is to challenge the legitimacy of such a state, while recognizing that the end result will be suffering and possibly martyrdom, not political reform.

Yet, it is important, as Christopher Bryan suggests, to see that the differences between Paul and John are differences of attitude to the experience of Roman rule, not differences of theological principle. That becomes clear if we "perceive correctly the object of John's attack."[20] It is not an attack on the idea of the Roman Empire; rather, it is an assault upon the idolatrous nature of the empire, as perceived by the author. As with the Jewish tradition, John sees idolatry as the root sin that leads to other sins, such as injustice and oppression. In that sense one might suggest, as Bryan does, that if Paul had viewed the empire in the same way that John did he would have come to the same conclusion about the right response. Paul would have agreed in full with John that any state that is idolatrous in its claims must be opposed.

---

20. Christopher Bryan, *Render to Caesar* (Oxford: Oxford University Press, 2005), 107.

Summing Up

The difference between Romans 13 and Revelation 13, therefore, lies in the differing assessments made about the actual state that Paul and John encountered in their different times and places. It is not a difference about Paul's reluctance to criticize political authorities, nor is it a difference due to John's opposition to all political institutions in principle. These writers were not developing political philosophies, but each was acting as a pastor addressing a particular community living in a specific social and historical setting.

FORMING A FRAMEWORK

Following the insights of Walter Pilgrim, I will describe a framework for church and state relations that takes the three New Testament perspectives seriously.[21] In accord with the Pauline approach there is a "critical constructive stance" that is appropriate when it is clear that political authorities are seriously engaged in the pursuit and establishment of justice. This stance affirms that God has supported the institution of the state for the purpose of promoting the common good, restraining evil, and maintaining public order marked by peace and justice for all.

Such an affirmation does not require a perfect public order, but the presence of the clear intent of political authorities to pursue the purposes behind God's institution of the state. In such a situation the Christian community can point out failings (critical) and pledge support for efforts to bring about necessary corrective changes (constructive).[22]

When citing failings and recommending changes, there is no assurance that those who adopt such a stance will agree with each other. The stance is broad enough that a spectrum of political choices and loyalties can fall within the confines of the critical-constructive outlook.

The second perspective is that of a "critical-transformative stance" that may be adopted when the government is seen to be seriously deficient in some important respect regarding a sound public order, but the judgment is also made that the authorities and institutions of government are capable of significant change. This approach attempts to express Jesus' teaching in Mark 12 that political authority rightly exists but that it cannot simply be blessed and

---

21. Pilgrim, *Uneasy Neighbors*, 192. In developing his framework Pilgrim acknowledges his indebtedness to an essay by Thomas Strieter, "Two Kingdoms and Governances Thinking for Today's World," *Currents in Theology and Mission* 16, no. 1 (1989): 29-35. Throughout this concluding subsection I will utilize material found in chapter 5 of Pilgrim's book.

22. Pilgrim, *Uneasy Neighbors*, 192-94.

accepted in light of the large gap between the existing situation and the claims of the reign of God.

Like the first perspective, this stance continues to view the state as a necessary institution that can embody God's purposes in history. The difference between the critical-transformative stance and the first perspective is that there is a sharper critique of the existent political order and its failings. The Christian community may continue to work within existing institutions but as much by way of challenge to, as cooperation with, authorities.

Within the proposed framework it is entirely possible that members of the Christian community may differ (1) on the degree of deficiency existing on a matter deemed important, and (2) on the proper remedy to pursue in order to correct the failing. Thus, some Christians may hold for a critical-constructive stance while others embrace a critical-transformative stance due to differences over point one. And Christians who agree on the need for a critical-transformative stance may differ widely over the method and substance of the change that is sought.

The third, biblically informed, perspective on politics is the critical-resistance stance. Shaped by the teaching of Revelation, this approach is deemed appropriate in the face of political rulers who are complicit in profound injustice and wrongdoing and who demonstrate little commitment to changing the policies and institutions that are wrong.

An ethic of resistance is necessary when the state embodies a politics that is fundamentally evil, making claims or propagating ideologies that are idolatrous. Faced with such a political order the Christian community must disassociate itself from the state and stand in direct opposition to the politics of evil.

There will be diversity in the strategies of resistance that are recommended to the church. For some, resistance may include violence in the form of rebellion; for others, resistance may be firm and public but nonviolent. In other situations it may be clear that resistance will simply entail noncooperation that leads to suffering and persecution. It is evident that the stance of critical resistance arises in periods of crisis and puts the church in a situation where collaboration with the state would be equated with a loss of integrity and false witness to the Christian message.

These three broad stances have been briefly sketched to indicate that the message of the New Testament may fairly be interpreted to include differing perspectives toward the political order, depending on one's prudential judgment concerning a range of contingent matters. At the same time, the witness of the New Testament should necessarily inform the Christian tradition in regard to politics.

CONCLUSION

As the biblical scholar Karl Schelkle states, "Political theory and abstract teaching on law and government, such as was produced by ancient learning, is utterly foreign to the (Old and) New Testament."[23] Biblical texts must be examined with respect for their particularity. Thus, I have presented the historical context of the material in order to understand it properly.

It is evident that one can find biblical texts that take contradictory viewpoints, even though all the texts under review were concerned with the same political reality—Roman imperial rule. "Any utterances of the New Testament about the State are never to be taken as purely theoretical and about government in general, but always in relation to this particular governmental organization."[24] The differences among the New Testament materials are due to the fact that the Roman Empire was experienced in a variety of ways by Jesus, the Gospel writers, Paul, and the author of Revelation. What then are we to make of these differences? First, the existence of differences suggests there are perspectives on politics in the New Testament, a variety of views, not one singular perspective.

Second, relying on the work of Walter Pilgrim, three basic perspectives within the New Testament materials were delineated and examined. These three perspectives should continue to inform Christian ideas about political life.

Pilgrim labels the three perspectives as an "ethic of subordination," exemplified by Paul in Romans; an "ethic of critical distancing," as found in Jesus' teaching in the Synoptic Gospels; and an "ethic of resistance," embodied in Revelation.[25] It would be a mistake to ignore this diversity in the pursuit of some unitary biblical treatment of politics. As subsequent chapters will show, the Christian community has fallen prey to this error at various times and reduced the biblical witness to one perspective in different eras. Far better to hold onto the diversity in order to avoid a reductionist treatment of politics according to the Bible.

At the same time, the plurality of biblical perspectives adds to the difficulty of relating politics and the Christian tradition because the tradition is rich and multilayered. Thus, differing assessments of the degree to which the political order reflects God's purposes are to be expected. Those differences in assessment will generate a variety of perspectives on politics, and it is possible that each of these perspectives will be able to claim biblical support.

Without denying the diversity of perspectives it does seem possible to pull together a few axioms that the New Testament provides which inform the Christian tradition in regard to the political order.

---

23. Schelkle, *Theology of the New Testament*, 333.
24. Ibid., 334.
25. Pilgrim, *Uneasy Neighbors*, 181.

- The political order is understood to be part of God's plan for human history. As such it is subject to God's reign in the present moment, and is destined to be incorporated into God's future reign.
- While the political order is related to the realm of religion in the present it is also distinct from it. It is clear that there is no confusion of the two realms by the New Testament authors.
- The claim that God's reign makes on the political order is that it is to be a vehicle for establishing justice, peace, and the common good in community life.
- Because of their role in God's plan, the authorities and institutions of the political order deserve respect and obedience as they embody the values of the reign of God. Obedience to political authority, under proper circumstances, is a form of obedience to God, for God's reign is not limited solely to the sphere of religion.
- Unlike politics in the Old Testament there is no expectation in the New Testament of a theocratic government to be established by Christians. At various points in their ancient history, the Israelite people were ruled by non-Israelites, but they always regarded such rulers as outsiders and yearned for a time of restoration to the rule of a just Israelite king. The New Testament writers also perceive the Roman Empire as an outside power, but the New Testament expresses no hope that God will establish a Christian leader to assume political rule.

Finally, fairly quickly after Jesus' death and resurrection, the new community began to break out of the ties that identified Christian faith with a particular ethnicity or nation. So the early church did not envision a future involving a Christian ruler governing all Christians. The next chapter will look at what happened when that unexpected future came to be.

QUESTIONS FOR REFLECTION/DISCUSSION

1. What were the expectations surrounding the messiah at the time of Jesus? How did Jesus understand messiahship? What is meant by the "messianic secret"?
2. How would you describe the political atmosphere that was the context of Jesus' public ministry?
3. What are the main political implications of Jesus' teaching about the reign of God?
4. What is meant by saying that neither Romans 13 nor Revelation 13 presents a *theory* of government?
5. Which of the three New Testament perspectives—critical constructive, critical transformative, critical resistance—do you think is most applicable in our political situation today?

Part II

HISTORICAL PERSPECTIVES

4

The Patristic Era

The patristic age takes its name from the several generations of learned and venerated figures called "Fathers (Latin: *patres*) of the Church." These figures represent the teaching and practice of Christians in the centuries following upon the death of the persons and authors of the New Testament period. While there is no specific date that can be cited as the beginning of the era, or for that matter the exact close of the era, it is generally understood that the patristic age encompasses the second century into the seventh in the West, and on into the eighth century in the Eastern empire. The exact dating of the period, however, is not a concern for our purposes; more important is to examine decisive developments that affected the relationship of Christianity and the political realm during this formative period in the life of the church.

CHRISTIANS AND THE EMPIRE

A commonly accepted division of the patristic era is that of pre- and post-Constantine (d. 337), the Roman emperor who converted to Christianity. There is good reason for seeing this as an important divide in church history, and it is especially so for the topic of Christianity and politics. The church of the second and third centuries, the years between the New Testament age and before the conversion of Constantine, are marked by concerns that had to be addressed if the young religious community was to survive and expand. The church after Constantine's baptism was confronted with a new set of issues that demanded a different pastoral agenda when survival was no longer an issue.

Certainly, one of the striking aspects of the entire patristic period is the extensive spread of the Christian faith throughout the Mediterranean world. The apostle Paul, of course, is recognized as the great figure in the early missionary life of the church, but he was hardly a lone agent of evangelization. There were many missionaries who helped to bring the message of the Christian faith to regions far beyond Palestine. In doing so, these early missionaries were frequently assisted by the presence of Greek-speaking Jewish communities throughout the major cities of the Roman Empire. As the Christian faith drew many adherents from these communities, it also reached out to the

Gentile population, which had little or no awareness of the Hebrew tradition. Gradually, the newly forming Christian communities developed a sense of their differences from those Jews who did not accept the message about Jesus. At the same time the early church recognized its distinctiveness from the dominant culture of classical Roman society.

A particular focus of the early church was to create a community of sharing among its membership and also to develop a practice of social charity to others within the society. The latter task included not only almsgiving, but hospitality to migrants, care for the sick, burying the dead, and aid to the imprisoned. It is likely that the effectiveness of this social witness was such that it became a compelling reason for many to join the church, some because they were beneficiaries of Christian charity but others because they wished to participate in a community that practiced such a virtue.

In the early decades of Christianity most converts were drawn from what was considered the lower class. However, given the nature of ancient Greek and Roman societies, it should be understood that the lower class included not only slaves and unskilled laborers but also craftspeople and small-business owners. These were people who could not easily take up the pursuits of philosophy, politics, and enjoyment of the arts that occupied the elites; rather, the lower class were people who had to work for a living. Such people possessed many practical skills and talents that could be put to good effect in organizing and maintaining a growing community of believers.[1]

There is clear evidence, however, that by the end of the second century, people of higher social rank also were seeking entrance into the church through Baptism. While it is not easy to ascertain the motivations of people from another time, it does appear that part of the attraction of Christianity was its commitment to caring for the individual. This was at a time when much of the dominant culture reflected a lack of respect for the dignity of the individual person.[2]

The political philosopher Kenneth Minogue has pointed out that Christianity's appeal in the ancient world was that it was "a religion of moral challenge." Greek and Roman religion were "highly elitist" with only military heroes and philosophers seen as fully human while large numbers of people were relegated to inferior status. "Christianity often reversed this judgment: it was the humble people who were closest to the spirit of love" the Christian gospel proclaimed. According to Minogue, "the real significance Christianity had for political life lay in its transformation of human values." Chief among

---

1. Wayne Meeks, *The First Urban Christians* (New Haven: Yale University Press, 1984), 73.

2. Rodney Stark, *The Rise of Christianity* (Princeton, NJ: Princeton University Press, 1996), esp. chaps. 7 and 10.

those transformations was that "Christianity affirmed the equal value in the sight of God of each human soul."[3] In cultures shaped by social hierarchies the commitment of the Christian community to the fundamental equality of each person before God was a distinctive and compelling claim.

So the early church, despite occasional persecutions, was making significant strides in spreading its message and attracting new adherents. By the latter half of the third century, from 250 CE onward, there was a network of churches firmly established throughout the major population centers of the empire. In both its intellectual apologetic against criticisms and by virtue of its social witness as an inclusive and loving community, the Christian church was succeeding. But a dramatic event at the beginning of the fourth century was to promote even further the rise of the church's presence within the empire. In 312 CE the emperor Constantine acknowledged his Christian faith, and in the next year he issued a decree establishing official toleration of the Christian faith.

A New Order

For almost three centuries the Christian community had existed within a political order that was at varying points indifferent, hostile, or unwittingly helpful to the new faith. Now in 313 a different situation prevailed. The relationship between Christianity and the political order was entering a novel phase because the emperor was a baptized believer. Constantine had proclaimed that the Christian faith was to enjoy full freedom of public practice and was to be given legal protection that permitted the expansion of church-owned property and wealth. As the empire underwent strains that were political, economic, demographic, and military, the new religion came to be viewed positively for at least three reasons: as a force for social unity, as a means of combating various social ills, and as a resource for talented and loyal personnel.

However, as the political theorist Robert Dyson reminds us, the new relationship between church and empire came with a cost. "That price was a pronounced ambiguity as to the standing of the Church in relation to the pre-existing institutions of power."[4] Constantine assumed, as his predecessors all did, that the emperor had sovereignty over not only government and secular law, but also over the laws relating to religion. The emperor's ancient title as *pontifex maximus*[5] reflected the presumption that he was head of the

---

3. Kenneth Minogue, *Politics: A Very Short Introduction* (Oxford: Oxford University Press, 1995), 31.

4. Robert Dyson, *St. Augustine of Hippo: The Christian Transformation of Political Philosophy* (New York: Continuum, 2005), 146.

5. Literally the term means "greatest bridge builder," but it was used to designate the emperor's role as high priest of Roman religion. The metaphor of bridge builder

church as well as the state. And, indeed, many Christian leaders appealed to Constantine to adjudicate ecclesiastical disputes, including his presiding role at the Council of Nicea where the basic creedal statement of the Christian dogma of the Trinity was decided.

It was only to be expected that in time the relationship between the imperial state and the church should undergo rethinking and experimentation. At first consideration, little in the New Testament materials on the political order would have prepared fourth-century Christians to encounter an emperor who was Christian. Yet, as the historian Francis Oakley suggests, there were strands of Christian thought that made possible a positive approach to the developments that followed Constantine's embrace of Christianity. This positive approach he calls the "Eusebian accommodation."[6]

Eusebius of Caesarea (d. ca. 340)

Broadly speaking, two strands of thought became characteristic of the Christian approach. Examining the thought of two important figures, Eusebius of Caesarea and Ambrose of Milan, can serve to summarize the diverging approaches. Eusebius is often called the first church historian; a man of learning who served as a bishop, he was an important participant in the deliberations of the Council of Nicea in 325. Several of his important works provide information about the early life of the church that otherwise would not be known to us. Eusebius was also a person held in esteem within the Constantinian court, and he returned the respect by writing a laudatory biography of the emperor.

Eusebius's portrayal of Constantine must be understood within his larger reading of history. Although having lived through persecution himself, Eusebius adopted a view of the Roman Empire as an instrument in God's plan—not unlike Paul's outlook in Romans whereby the empire, unintentionally, facilitated the spread of the faith. Also St. Luke, in both his Gospel and the Acts of the Apostles, correlated events in the history of the Roman Empire with the Christian narrative, for example his pairing of Christ's birth with the onset of the reign of Augustus and a time of peace and unity within the empire.[7] Thus, it was not unprecedented to interpret key moments in the political story of the empire as moving in sync with the salvation history of Christian revelation.

With the conversion of Constantine, Eusebius believed history had come to a decisive new era because God had led the Christian faith to become the

---

indicated the role of the priest as a point of connection between the spiritual and the temporal realms.

6. Francis Oakley, *Kingship* (Malden, MA: Blackwell Publishing, 2006), 69-76.

7. Ibid., 63.

recognized foundation not only of the spiritual realm but of the worldly one as well. The emperor was seen as an agent bringing about the victory of the true faith over all the false religious cults previously practiced within the empire. As the emperor embraced Christianity, "Eusebius saw those two social structures [empire and Church] move towards unity," and so the Christian society that emerged from this union was viewed as being in close relation to the reign of God.[8]

This benign and sweeping view of the course of historical events allowed Eusebius to be untroubled by the idea that the emperor should play an active role in the life of the church. For Eusebius, the role of Constantine as Christian emperor was to be God's chosen minister over worldly affairs, and also to serve as God's vicar or regent mediating the divine presence within history. Consequently, it seemed only right that the emperor would be deeply involved in the affairs of church life. Thus the "Eusebian accommodation" established a trajectory in church and politics, one that became dominant in the East when the empire later divided after Constantine. It saw church and state cooperation as natural and viewed imperial intervention in ecclesiastical affairs positively.

Indeed, later Byzantine treatments of the relationship between church and empire never gave up on the idea of a basic *symphonia*, or harmony, between the two institutions. As historian of the early church Henry Chadwick put it, "the Byzantine world did not think of itself as two 'societies,' sacred and secular, but as a single society in harmony with the emperor as the earthly counterpart of the divine Monarch."[9] By contrast, the West took a different path, one that adopted a more dualistic view of empire and church.

Ambrose of Milan (d. 397)

A clear representative of another trajectory regarding church and politics was Ambrose, bishop of Milan. His viewpoint became the one that prevailed in the Western empire after Constantine. The child of an imperial official, Ambrose pursued an administrative career and eventually served as governor of the province of Milan. As such, Ambrose was familiar with the realm of politics and power before he was baptized and elected bishop. Milan was home to the imperial court for part of the year. Thus, Ambrose was pastor to the imperial leadership and exercised influence upon a number of emperors, including the decision of Theodosius to make Christianity the official religion of the empire in 380. Similar to Eusebius, Ambrose believed that the church and empire had

---

8. Ibid., 76.
9. Henry Chadwick, *The Early Church* (New York: Penguin Books, 1967), 166.

a positive relationship. He accepted the idea that church and state should collaborate in advancing the causes of justice, peace, and good social order.

However, unlike Eusebius, Ambrose was determined to defend a realm of church freedom from the emperor. For Ambrose, the internal life of the church—meaning the formulation of religious doctrine, its teaching on morality, and the establishment of ecclesiastical discipline—was subject not to the emperor but to the ordained leaders of the church. This division of power, as an alternative to Eusebius's approach, took hold in the West. It was a position that recognized the legitimacy of the empire and its rule, while defending the freedom of the church from imperial interference in certain areas of church life.

The dualism of Ambrose did not imply a negative view of the state. One of his writings was *De officiis*, a title taken from Cicero's earlier work on the duties of public office. Essentially, what Ambrose provided in his essay was teaching on the appropriate behavior for clergy who had not only personal but also public responsibilities. The work is an extended reflection on what should be the appropriate lifestyle and behavior for an educated Christian in Roman society. Part of that appropriate behavior was practicing those virtues necessary for what we might call good citizenship. Whereas patristic authors who were pre-Constantinian also defended Christians as good citizens who paid their taxes and prayed for the emperor, one now finds in Ambrose the new theme of the proper exercise of public office as an important form of Christian service to the society.

Nonetheless, there was a limit to the loyalty the Christian believer owed to the state. Ambrose was once reported to have refused to celebrate the Eucharist in the presence of the emperor Theodosius, who had been excommunicated because he ordered a massacre of civilians in 390 at Thessalonika. This public opposition to the emperor happened despite the fact that Theodosius was an admirer of Ambrose and had supported him in several controversies with nonorthodox Christians.

On an earlier occasion in 386, Ambrose engaged in an even more high-stakes confrontation with the emperor Valentinian II. The emperor was a young boy, and his mother supported the cause of the Arian heresy, a belief that Jesus was not of the same nature as God the Father. She persuaded her son to give one of the churches in Milan to the Arian bishop, Auxentius, who challenged Ambrose's authority as the rightful leader of the local church.

In a sermon against Auxentius, Ambrose took up the biblical passage concerning taxation to Caesar, declaring, "So, I, too, say to those who oppose me, 'Show me the denarius!' Jesus saw the imperial denarius and said: 'Pay to Caesar what belongs to Caesar, and to God what belongs to God.' But when it comes to seizing churches, have they an imperial denarius to produce?"[10]

---

10. Ambrose of Milan, "From the *Sermon Against Auxentius*," in *From Irenaeus to*

Ambrose later exclaimed, "the Church is God's, and so it ought not to be given over to Caesar, because Caesar's sway cannot extend over the temple of God."[11]

Ambrose and his congregation staged what we would think of today as a sit-in at the church, refusing to surrender it to the heterodox bishop Auxentius. After several days of tense standoff, the emperor backed off and eventually acknowledged Ambrose's claim to be in charge of the church's property.

With a keen sense of the history of martyrdom, Ambrose recognized that challenging imperial authority might result in the emperor using force to achieve his aims. The response even to violent force, however, was not to deny outright the authority of the state but simply to hold fast to the claims of a higher authority. During the dispute with Valentinian, Ambrose made clear that his loyalty was to the Lord of all history, not the emperor of the moment, even though this might lead to a martyr's fate: "I am ready to bear the usual fate of a bishop, if he follows the usual practice of kings."[12]

Notable in the controversy is that although Ambrose strongly asserted the authority of the church over its own affairs, he did not deny the basic authority of the emperor. Indeed, he granted the right of the state to tax church property and pass laws that could oblige Christians in conscience. His resistance to some of the state's claims never crossed over into rebellion against the state as an institution. The divide between Ambrose and the emperor was over the boundaries between the spiritual freedom of the church and legitimate temporal authority.

By acknowledging that the emperor had rightful authority to govern in temporal matters, Ambrose was following the prevailing view of Christians. Writers of the patristic era accepted the Pauline teaching that civil authority stemmed from God and that even non-Christian rulers, if they ruled properly, provided a valuable service to society. Most of these writers also held that the state existed because of the social nature of human beings. This belief might be expressed by the answer to a question that today we would find quaint: "Would there have been a state in the Garden of Eden?" To that query the majority of church fathers answered "yes."

Remember that Christian authors writing in this period accepted the general historicity of the Hebrew Scriptures, including the creation accounts found in the book of Genesis. To ask if the state would be found in the Garden of Eden, prior to the sin of Adam and Eve, was simply another way to inquire whether the state is an institution willed by God. Or is it an institution that only came to exist because of human sinfulness? The majority of early

---

Grotius: A Sourcebook in Christian Political Thought, ed. Oliver O'Donovan and Joan Lockwood O'Donovan (Grand Rapids, MI: Eerdmans, 1999), 70-75 at 74.

11. Ibid., 75

12. Ibid., 70.

Christian authors saw the emergence of the state as due to humankind's natural orientation to social life and not mainly because of human evil.

Certain tasks of the state, such as the use of coercion to restrain wrongdoers, might be a consequence of sin, but life in the paradise of Eden would have required some measure of organization and governance if the human community were to flourish. In other words, the state is an institution meant positively to serve human well-being and is not primarily negative, aimed at merely restraining human sinfulness.

Ambrose was somewhat more jaded than his fellow Christian authors of the period. He, too, thought that the state, as an institution of social organization, was a necessary and natural component of human community. Had humanity continued to live in paradise the state's rule would have been broadly participatory, with each person having a say in governance. As a result of human sinfulness, however, the state was now dominated by a few—its power used for the aggrandizement of elites, its activity linked to coercion and violence. For Ambrose, therefore, the state was not only a necessary institution to check injustice in a fallen world; it embodied that same injustice through its manner of exercising power.

AUGUSTINE (D. 430)

Among those believers attending the "sit-in" at the church in Milan during Ambrose's dispute with the emperor Valentinian was a widowed mother named Monica. Her son, who eventually came under Ambrose's tutelage and accepted baptism, was Augustine, perhaps the most influential figure in Western Christianity after Jesus and St. Paul. He was a prolific writer on a variety of theological and moral topics, ranging from the Trinity to war, from Baptism to marriage. Regarding politics, his famous work the *City of God* was the most extensive treatment of the Christian understanding of political life for centuries. It still remains one of the most influential works of political theology ever written.

Yet, as with other Christian authors of this era, Augustine was not a political philosopher intending to develop a systematic theory. His political insights were by-products of various doctrinal and pastoral controversies in which he engaged as bishop. Even the *City of God*, as lengthy as that book is, cannot be considered a book intended primarily to treat political questions. Rather, Augustine is interested in defending Christianity against the charge that the new faith of the empire was the cause of the empire's undoing.

To understand Augustine's views on politics it is helpful to know something of his viewpoint on the dilemma of the human situation.[13] Reading

---

13. Many commentators have proposed understanding Augustine's theological

Genesis in a matter-of-fact manner, Augustine believed Adam and Eve were created sinless and with free will. By their disobedience in eating the forbidden fruit they freely chose their own self-love before love of God and, thereby, distorted the natural order of creation.

This original sin has had consequences for all descendants of Adam and Eve. Since this original sin each descendant of Adam and Eve has been born with a corrupted will that is not properly moved by love of God; instead people are governed by an inordinate love of self or love of the world. In effect, the human will is no longer free to choose the good, but only which evil it will pursue, with pride, greed, and self-love being chief among the evil options. As such, human beings deserve to be judged harshly by a just God.

Although God foresaw that humans would sin, that is not the same as God willing that humans sin. Mercifully, God decided to save at least some human beings from themselves. This was done by the divine decision to bestow grace upon a few chosen ones, a grace that would allow the redeemed elect to respond to the love of God. This gift of grace is freely given and cannot be earned.

Augustine adopted a scheme of predestination. God alone determines who receives the gift of grace and the possibility of salvation, and God alone determines the number of those chosen. That the vast majority of humankind is damned due to lack of grace only demonstrates God's justice; the fact that a select minority is granted the grace of redemption is proof of God's mercy. This pessimistic and deterministic view of the human situation sets the stage for Augustine's reading of history and his defense of Christianity against pagan critics.

Augustine and the Theology of History

Written by Augustine after Alaric and the Visigoths had sacked Rome in 410, the *City of God* is a defense of the Christian faith. Augustine responds to criticism that the spread and influence of the Christian religion contributed to the decline of the empire in general, and particularly the fall of Rome. For centuries Rome had stood as the center of civilization, and in the brief span of a few Christian emperors the empire had collapsed. For critics of Christianity, what good was this new faith if it led to such ruin? Augustine did not respond to critics on a specific point-by-point basis but took on the larger task of providing a critique of classical paganism and an interpretation of history that explained the place of Rome, or any empire, in the grand scheme of human events.

---

anthropology as the entryway into his politics. See, for example, Herbert Deane, *The Political and Social Ideas of St. Augustine* (New York: Columbia University Press, 1963), chaps. 1-2; and Dyson, *St. Augustine of Hippo*, chap. 1.

At the same time, he did not want his defense of Christianity to rest on overreaching or false claims about the gospel message and its relationship to political life. Augustine wanted to disabuse pagan critics about the glory that was Rome, but he also wanted to undercut those defenders of the faith who too closely identified the gospel message with the establishment of a Christian empire here on earth.

For Augustine, the story of humanity is a narrative about the inhabitants of two cities, the city of God and the earthly city. Everyone belongs to one of the two cities, depending on how God has predestined them by the bestowal or withholding of grace. History reveals to those with insight born of faith the underlying meaning to be found in the interaction of these two cities. Only believers accurately see what is really going on all about them.

Crucial for reading Augustine correctly is to know that the city of God is not identical to the Christian church, nor is the earthly city identical to the Roman Empire. Relying on such a misidentification became the error of a number of medieval interpreters of Augustine who thought he used the two cities as a metaphorical way to refer to the church and temporal government.

The church, as a historical institution, cannot be equated with the city of God although, admittedly, Augustine occasionally writes as if the church is truly representative of it. More accurately, however, for Augustine the church is the crucial historical institution that mediates God's reign in history. Thus, the church's vital importance for its emergence is a signal moment within human history. Yet, the historical institution of the church is composed of baptized members who are sinful and fail dramatically to live as faithful residents of the city of God.

The city of God, rightly understood, is what theologians call the communion of saints, the body of believers who extend through time and space. There is no single place or era in which they are to be found. The residents of the city of God move through life as *peregrini*, pilgrims or sojourners who know that their true home is not to be found in history. They are the ones who love God properly, putting nothing else before God. It is the common love of God that unites the residents of the city of God.

The earthly city is composed of the great majority of humanity who live by inordinate love of self or of the world. The inhabitants of this city also cannot be confined to a specific time, place, or institution, although various empires, especially Rome, are used by Augustine to illustrate the human city. Nonetheless, it is important to temper the tendency for human beings to think they can build institutions, enact policies, and choose persons on the basis of knowing the difference between the earthly city and the city of God. The inhabitants of the two cities dwell together throughout history and are not easily sorted out because both are subject to the same historical trials.

For Augustine, the appropriate passage from the Gospels for understanding the interplay of the two cities is the parable of the wheat and the weeds found in Matthew 13:24-30. Recall that the master in the story forbids the servants from precipitously pulling out the weeds in the field lest the wheat be uprooted as well. Better, the master says, to let both wheat and weeds grow together and save the time for separation till the harvest at the end. So, too, no one should be quick to divide humankind into the residents of the earthly city and of the city of God. Let them dwell together, interacting with one another, and allow God to separate them at the time of final judgment.

The inhabitants of the city of God, even if they were to be known, cannot simply withdraw from life in the earthly city. People are composed of both a spirit and a body, and all people experience both dimensions by the fact that every person has multiple interests. On the one hand, any human being, even the saintly, is concerned with satisfying this-worldly needs; on the other hand, any individual, even the sinner, is aware of another set of interests arising from the spiritual dimension of personhood.

That humans have this double dimension to their makeup was not a new claim by Augustine; many ancient writers, Christian and non-Christian, had noted it. What Augustine does is use this insight into the human situation as the interpretive key to all of history. The inhabitants of the earthly city are those who are preoccupied with temporal desires and needs to the detriment and disorder of their spiritual good; they love finite things more than God. The residents of the earthly city cannot be at peace for they are ever restless, for no earthly good can satisfy their longing. This is the penalty of loving one-self and the world out of proportion to one's love of God. The history of the ancient world and its great empires is the story of the earthly city. Rome is but one more chapter, albeit an impressive one, in the narrative.

Simultaneously, there is the story of the city of God, and it can be seen not in the armies and wealth of the earthly city, but in the story of those who live a life of *caritas*, the genuine love of God and humanity. In the end any achievement of the earthly city must fail for it is built not upon a solid foundation but upon the lesser aims of ambition, power, wealth, lust, and fame. The city of God will endure for it is built on wisdom, goodness, and, ultimately, love properly directed to God above all else.

Augustine and Political Life

How does Augustine understand the realm of politics, given his view of humans and history? For writers of classical culture who addressed politics—Plato, Aristotle, Cicero, Seneca—the human person was naturally a political animal because humans were perceived as rational and social. For Augustine, the flaw that sin introduced into human nature made the classical pagan writers appear fundamentally misguided. For him people do not enter into politics to cooperate but to dominate; the leaders of the earthly city are driven by what Augustine called the *libido dominandi*, which stands in direct contradiction to the desire to serve that marks the residents of the city of God. Consequently, Augustine had a low opinion of the Roman Empire, or any state for that matter, since it represents the institutional expression of the will to dominate.

The Augustinian critique of the empire extended to the point where he denied that Rome ever was able to embody justice, the essential virtue of social life in classical political philosophy. Justice is what makes a state, and Augustine charged that no state had ever embodied true justice. After all, justice requires rendering to each their due, and a state that ignores what God is due cannot be just. Rome, like every other earthly city, never rendered the true worship that was properly due to God. Therefore, prior to Christianity no state was capable of true justice. Yet, even an empire that embraces Christianity will be made up of a majority of people who do not really worship God in love and truth. And so the empire, even a Christian empire, could never claim to be a genuine state because it had no claim to represent true justice within a community of citizens.[14]

In the *City of God* there is a story that Augustine took from Cicero to express his attitude toward the state. He related with approval an anecdote that Alexander the Great once interrogated a captured pirate, asking, "What is your idea, in infesting the sea?" To which the pirate replied, "The same as yours, in infesting the earth! But because I do it with a tiny craft, I'm called a pirate: because you have a mighty navy, you're called an emperor."[15] For Augustine, the lesson was that a state without justice is no different than a criminal gang.

Yet, as so often with Augustine's writing, his viewpoint is more complicated than one side of an argument can capture. For, despite his bleak assessment concerning its nature, Augustine maintained the state can play a helpful role. Perhaps it cannot represent true justice, but it can enforce a lesser or earthly justice that still is of value.

Due to sin, human beings if left on their own would engage in constant strife, each driven by some form of evil desire. Inhabitants of the earthly city, despite their flawed motives, are not bereft of human intelligence. They can understand their plight and conclude that imposing a measure of restraint upon themselves and others may allow for creation of common goods that otherwise would be lost. And when people agree "to accept a share of the common good, and to punish those who exceed their shares, we call the result

---

14. Augustine, *City of God*, ed. David Knowles; trans. Henry Bettenson (New York: Pelican Classics, 1972), book XIX, chap. 21.

15. Ibid., IV, 4.

a state."[16] The state cannot do away with all strife; indeed, it uses violence and coercion to suppress disorder. But it does so in a way that establishes a measure of civic peace and protection of a society's way of life. In effect, the state uses certain means that ultimately stem from human sinfulness to minimize greater evils that otherwise would overwhelm any possibility of human society.

The state may owe its origin to the original sin of Adam and Eve, but the state at least can serve to limit the social effects of human sinfulness by establishing a semblance of order, as well as correcting and punishing those wrongdoers who violate that order. This way of thinking about the role of the state is still largely negative; it is a role that essentially amounts to damage control.

Because political authority is exercised in a manner that reflects the human drive to dominate there must be limits to what the state can do. For Augustine that means describing political authority not in a positive way, as Greek and Roman philosophers did with their talk of justice and the common good as the aim of the state. Rather, the negative cast given to political authority by Augustine sees its role as restraining sin. Political authority is coercive, but that is a tragic necessity of life in the earthly city.

What of the Christian empire? Is there a more positive role for the state that is led by a Christian ruler? The answer, basically, is no. So-called Christian states are not to be equated with the city of God, anymore than the church is to be identified with it. Augustine was certainly less enthusiastic about the idea of a Christian empire than Eusebius; in truth, he was less hopeful about such a political option than just about all of the other writers, East or West, of the later patristic era. There is, in Augustine, a profound skepticism about what any human undertaking can really accomplish, and politics is not exempt from that sober perspective.

There are two possible benefits to a Christian empire, however. First, the emperor and other rulers, if they truly are Christian, can provide good example to subjects by living in such a way that they encourage and educate others in virtue. Second, and this is a point that underwent evolution in Augustine's thinking, Christian rulers can put themselves in service to the church; they can facilitate its work.

When Augustine became a bishop he inherited a dispute among Christians that was almost a century old. The Donatist controversy involved a group of churches in the region of North Africa, the locale of Augustine's diocese, which held to a rigid code of holiness for church membership. Among the Donatist axioms was that the sacraments were valid only if performed by ministers who were free of serious sin. In brief, the holiness of the minister

---

16. Dino Bigongiari, "Appendix: The Political Ideas of St. Augustine," in Henry Paolucci, ed., *The Political Writings of St. Augustine* (South Bend, IN: Gateway Editions, 1962), 343-58 at 349.

was determinative of true sacraments. Augustine and the majority of bishops opposed this viewpoint by arguing that sacraments are valid based on God's action and grace, not human worthiness and effort.

For our purposes here, the important point is not the disputed theological claim by the Donatists but that at a certain point the imperial government ceased to grant religious toleration to the Donatists. The government enacted a series of measures that sought to pressure the Donatist believers to change their views and accept the orthodox viewpoint represented by Augustine. Initially hesitant to accept this role for the state, Augustine eventually endorsed and encouraged the use of the coercive power of the state in a religious dispute.

Henry Chadwick summarizes Augustine's view: "Augustine knew that the motives which bring men to the truth are often complex, and may include elements of fear or self-interest that have to be regarded as a temporary stage towards a full, glad, and willing assent."[17] In Augustine's thinking, the state in this case was doing something quite similar to its accepted function of inflicting punishment for the sake of correction. It was, to his mind, playing a legitimate paternalistic role in the use of penalties as remedial education for the Donatists to come to the truth.

The position that Augustine took is not exactly the same as advocating state coercion to make nonbelievers accept Christianity. Augustine never supported persecution of Jews or pagans. The Donatist case was about Christians who had gone astray from the accepted orthodoxy. For Augustine, the emperor's role in the dispute with the Donatists was akin to a family fight when a parent uses his authority to resolve the disunity. In the situation with the Donatists, a Christian ruler was simply using state power to correct those in error and induce them to reconcile with the authentic church.

While Augustine thought that Christian rulers could be called upon to use their temporal power against heretics and schismatics, it would be a mistake to think Augustine believed that a Christian state was subordinate to the church and should simply do its bidding. Rather, he believed that Christian rulers, like Christian parents, sailors, soldiers, or teachers, should serve their Lord in the roles that they inhabit. Christian rulers should ask how to follow God's will by being good at their calling or vocation. The means of service to God may change with different vocations, but there is nothing unique in the claim that the ruler has a duty to serve God.

So if Christians in their role as rulers have duties to fulfill, what of Christians as citizens? Even though the state is the result of sin, Augustine upheld the duty of obedience to it. Like St. Paul and the majority of patristic writers, Augustine believed that Christians should respect civil authority because all earthly authority comes from God. As long as temporal rulers did not com-

17. Chadwick, *The Early Church*, 223.

mand direct disobedience to God they were to be obeyed. Even when an unjust ruler enjoined obedience in doing evil the obligation of the believer not to comply did not extend to open rebellion or violent resistance. From Augustine's standpoint, an unjust ruler was God's just punishment on sinners and an ascetical discipline for saints.

The state was a flawed institution, to be sure, but Augustine maintained that God employed such an entity for the attainment of an earthly order of civic peace. Therefore, Christians ought to pay taxes, obey the law, and defend the state from external enemies. This last point reminds us that Augustine was an important figure in the development of the just war tradition within Christian theology.[18]

Two Forms of Social Criticism

One approach to Augustine's way of thinking about the earthly city is to see him as employing two methods of social criticism. Seen from the spiritual perspective, all human activity, including our grandest political achievements, falls short of the city of God. Reciting the many accomplishments of the Roman Empire, Augustine could acknowledge the system of law, the beauty of the art, the bravery of the army, the practical feats of engineering, and other impressive deeds. Behind all of it, however, was the driving force of pride; so, impressive as the empire might be, it was all an example of "splendid vice."[19] The Augustinian assessment of Rome reflects what might be called principles of transcendent and historical criticism.

Seen from the perspective of the city of God, even the highest attainments of the earthly city fall short and are subject to critique. From this transcendent perspective Rome is no more immune from criticism than the invaders who sacked it. Augustine denied that Rome was ever worthy of the praise that was showered on it by pagan writers. For Rome never embodied justice, the alleged aim of the state according to classical political thought. How could a state that denied what was due God pretend to be just? Rome may have had its accomplishments but they were built on the false foundation of human pride. The earthly city and its residents deserved their fate.

Because human beings lived in both cities, however, Augustine was not simply dismissive of the earthly city and human achievement. There was another side to the story. Augustine did not ignore the temporal dimension of existence, even if he thought it secondary to the spiritual. The accomplishments

---

18. The topic of Christianity and warfare will be treated in chap. 11.

19. This expression, though commonly attributed to Augustine, nowhere appears in the *City of God*. The expression, however, does capture in a succinct formula an important aspect of Augustine's assessment of the Roman Empire.

of Rome may have been built upon "splendid *vices*," but they were, indeed, *splendid*. Though built upon pride and the desire to dominate, the achievement of Rome is, undoubtedly, impressive. Though not virtuous, they are seemingly less evil than vices that could not be called "splendid."

In other words, while being comprehensive and harsh in his dismissal of Rome when it is compared to the city of God, Augustine was willing to consider that various incarnations of the earthly city might be more or less evil, closer or more distant as an approximation of justice in social life. Viewed from the vantage point of historical experience, from within the earthly city, there are important differences of degree between one government and another, one system of law and another, one ruler and another.

Consider a modern example to understand what Augustine was doing in his dual method of criticism. If we look directly down on a town from an airplane flying several thousand feet high, it is difficult to see much distinction between a one-story and a three-story building. From an airborne perspective the height of the buildings appear much the same. This is akin to the principle of transcendent criticism; the differences of degree seem minor or insignificant. To see those same buildings as a pedestrian, however, is to gain an entirely different perspective. At ground level the height difference between the buildings is significant and can make a huge difference in how we assess the beauty, utility, and value of the properties. This is similar to the principle of historical criticism; the differences between historical realities matter to people.

Augustine's approach to politics in the *City of God* embraced both methods of criticism. The transcendent method allowed Augustine to dismiss all claims of the empire's achievements as but passing moments in the ongoing story of the flawed earthly city. For him these achievements carried within themselves the seed of their own corruption and, ultimately, did not mean much more than what other empires had attained—empires that had come and gone. The city of God relativized the importance of all human achievement.

The method of historical criticism, on the other hand, provided Augustine with the means whereby he could make judgments that one set of institutions or practices within the earthly city was to be preferred to an alternative, even if the preferred set still was subject to challenge because it was part of the earthly city. And so Augustine could judge the empire harshly; yet, at the same time, he could mourn its passing. Granted, all earthly states are to be judged wanting, but some achieve a far greater measure of justice, peace, and social order than others. This explains why the same author who criticized the empire for its fundamental failings could still in a letter to one Count Boniface encourage Christian military leaders to fight on behalf of the empire.[20] The politics of the

---

20. "Letter 189," in O'Donovan and O'Donovan, *Irenaeus to Grotius*, 133-36.

earthly city, even at its best, might be but a weak approximation of true justice and community; yet, for all that, it still mattered.

Political Augustinianism

The vast influence of Augustine left a lasting impression on Western Christianity. Whether the impression held of Augustine was always an accurate one, however, may be questioned. Later writers used Augustine's view concerning the state's role in the Donatist controversy to portray an Augustine who was far more favorable to the idea of a Christian empire than was the case in the *City of God*. For this reason scholars of Augustine have adopted the term "political Augustinianism" to describe a theocratic view of societal governance that was ascribed to Augustine, though not accurately so.[21]

Medieval writers who disagreed with Augustine's theory of predestination and his belief that grace was given to only a minority preferred a more generous understanding of the availability of grace, as if every baptized member of the visible church was also a citizen of the city of God. By so doing these writers broached the gap Augustine had maintained between the city of God and any earthly institution, including the church. And so it became possible, while citing Augustine as an intellectual authority, for medieval scholars to discuss a society, populated and ruled by church members, that would be a Christian society: that is, a set of temporal institutions (church and state) that would promote the reign of God.

One reason for this revision of Augustine's view was that later church writers wished to use his authority to argue that a state subject to the supervision of the church could be just. This is quite a different position than that held by Augustine, who not only denied that the empire, even one ruled by a Christian, could embody true justice, but also denied that the church in history could be identified with the city of God.

Medieval authors mistakenly interpreted Augustine's suggestion that a Christian ruler should serve God in that capacity, just as a Christian farmer should serve God as a farmer, to mean that a secular ruler should be incorporated into a ministerial role at the service of the church. An emperor or king might be treated as the temporal arm of the church. As noted, such a theory could be used by clerics to justify their authority over a secular ruler, but the theory could also be used to legitimate the secular ruler as divinely chosen to bring about God's rule.[22]

---

21. The term was coined by H. X. Arquilliere, *L'augustinisme politique* (Paris: Librairie Philosophique J. Vrin, 1955).

22. "In effect, and by one of those superb ironies in which the history of ideas abounds, the name and prestige of Augustine became one of the instrumentalities

In this way, as we shall see in the next chapter, the Frankish king Char-lemagne could envision himself another Constantine, and would have his Eusebius in the person of Alcuin of York. All of this is a far cry from the *City of God* and the Augustine who believed that even the best empire is but a modestly successful device for establishing some social order in a fallen world.

THE PATRISTIC LEGACY

It is difficult to synthesize the outcome of the patristic era for several rea-sons. First, the number of authors to consider constitutes a much wider group than the three figures we have noted above. Important as they are, Eusebius, Ambrose, and Augustine are simply representative of this period of church history. A more comprehensive account of the political ideas of the church fathers would surely include Tertullian, Lactantius, Clement of Alexandria, John Chrysostom, and Gregory I.[23] Each of these writers offers a different perspective and has contributed to the legacy of the era.

Another difficulty with any neat synthesis of patristic teaching is that few of the church fathers had an interest in political theory per se. All of these individuals were primarily pastors and theologians; they addressed political issues to the extent to which they thought they must in order to advance their primary religious concerns. As a result there is no effort at providing a complete theory of the political order; rather, politics is examined as it relates to the faith and practice of the Christian community. This latter point under-scores another important factor, namely, most of the writing of this age may be described as occasional. Even a work as extensive as *The City of God* was written to address a specific situation and challenge. It is relatively easy to find patristic authors devising different responses in one text than what is found in another work by the same author.

Nonetheless, there are some topics where one can find a broad measure of consensus if not detailed agreement.

- First, political authority is widely viewed as being derived from God, at least in the sense of God being the author of authority. This remains the case even when a specific leader abuses his authority.
- Second, the state is considered a necessary and useful institution given the human condition. Many authors emphasize that the state is a devel-

---

whereby archaic notions of sacral kingship . . . were able to survive in Latin Christen-dom" (Oakley, *Kingship*, 91).

23. A useful anthology of many patristic texts regarding political life is Peter Phan, ed., *Social Thought* (Message of the Fathers of the Church 20; Wilmington, DE: Michael Glazier, 1984).

opment of humanity's social nature, while others, like Augustine, place greater stress on the state as an outgrowth of sin. Clearly, the state wields power, and the way it wields power, coercively, reflects the reality of humanity's sinfulness. But for most patristic writers, the state also has the duty to promote the cause of justice within the community and between societies.

- Thus, a third area of general agreement, the value of the state to social order generates moral duties for the Christian, including payment of taxes, obedience to law, respect for the office of ruler, and, as time passes, the use of violence in defense of the state.

In working out the details that follow from acceptance of the above convictions there is a good deal of room for disagreement. One of the fundamental divergences that went forward from this time onward is the differing emphases that Eusebius and Ambrose exemplify in their positions regarding the relationship between church and empire. The Eusebian approach set the trajectory for the church-state relationship in the East after the empire divided. Ambrose's position established the trajectory that Augustine confirmed for church-state relations in the West.

Whereas the church in the eastern portion of the empire gave greater sway to the emperor's role in ecclesiastical affairs, the church in the West held to a far sharper distinction between secular and ecclesial matters. The emperor and his ministers, it was argued, must respect the line between temporal and spiritual power and not seek to intervene in a realm that operates under a different authority. Furthermore, in the spiritual realm the emperor in the West, like any of the baptized, must submit to the authority of the church and its ministers, even as clergy must obey the legitimate temporal laws of the empire.

These claims of Western theologians and church officials established a different path than what the ancient world knew. It was also a new path that would have momentous consequences for how politics developed because it separated the realms of religion and politics at the institutional level. George Sabine, the author of a commonly used text, *A History of Political Theory*, wrote that the emergence of the Christian church as "a distinct institution entitled to govern the spiritual concerns of humankind in independence of the state, may not unreasonably be described as the most revolutionary event in the history of western Europe."[24] Prior to this development the common assumption of the ancient and classical worlds had been that the state was the supreme institution in society. The political leader was also understood as a religious figure, and there was no institution that might generate a competing sense of

---

24. George Sabine, *A History of Political Theory*, 4th edition revised by Thomas Thorson (Hinsdale, IL: Dryden Publishing, 1973), 176.

allegiance to what was owed to the state. Now that assumption was altered by the emergence of the Christian church.

Yet there was another commonly held assumption that was not challenged by the authors of this era. This was the conviction that in order to have a unified political society there must be unity at the level of religious belief. The necessary union of politics and religion was a widely held view throughout the ancient world. There might be empires that permitted the local religions of the conquered to continue, but there was an expectation of unity in religion and politics among the ruling group of the empire.

Further adding to the desire for unity was the Christian church's claim that it was not a tribal faith or the religion of a region; rather, the strongly held conviction was that the church was a universal society, meant to include all peoples and nations. Thus, no distinction could be easily drawn between membership in society and in the church. There might be distinct institutions, church and state, both exercising power, but it was power over one, unified society.

Patristic authors writing after Constantine shared that inherited belief. The empire should be animated by Christian belief; the state should be a Christian state in a society where the Christian faith is the "social glue." The patristic authors helped to solidify this viewpoint, which prevailed for over a thousand years more of European history. In subsequent centuries there might be differences on religious matters, yet all sides in disputes maintained that their religious belief was necessary for social and political unity to survive. No thinker was more influential in embedding that idea in the European mind than Augustine. Political unity required religious unity. Sabine has observed that this view of society was so dominant that when the eventual fracturing of Western Christianity made religious unity unattainable, "no idea was harder for a seventeenth-century thinker to grasp than the notion that the state might stand entirely aside from all questions of religious belief."[25]

Emphasis on the need for unity in religion so that there be political unity should not, however, be confused with theocracy. Here was the importance of the shattering of the first assumption regarding state supremacy in all matters. For if there are two distinct realms, and the church must be autonomous in order to govern and minister in the realm of the spiritual, there is the further implication that the state is autonomous and rightly governs and ministers in the realm of the secular.

No patristic author doubted the spiritual realm was the more important, and therefore gave precedence to the church over the state in terms of loyalty. Still, the same authors did not deny that the state deserved loyalty and obedience as long as it acted within its realm of competence. Local bishops and,

---

25. Ibid., 186.

particularly, the bishop of Rome would insist on the right of the church to rule over the spiritual realm, but they also were clear that the state and its leaders had legitimate authority and power to rule in secular affairs.

Thus, the patristic age gave us the famous dictum of Pope Gelasius I (d. 496) in his letter to Emperor Anastasius: "Two there are, august Emperor, by which this world is ruled."[26] The ongoing tensions of working out the meaning of the hard-won distinction between sacred and secular authority is the focal point of the next chapter.

QUESTIONS FOR REFLECTION/DISCUSSION

1. What do you think was the most important consequence of the conversion of Constantine for the church?
2. How would you describe the differences in the "trajectories" represented by Eusebius (*symphonia*) and Ambrose (dualism)?
3. How does Augustine's view of human nature and history influence his politics?
4. According to Augustine, can the empire, if it is led by a Christian, ever be described as a positive force?
5. What is meant by Augustine's employment of two forms of socio-political criticism?
6. What is political Augustinianism?

---

26. Gelasius I, "Letter to Emperor Anastasius," in O'Donovan and O'Donovan, *Irenaeus to Grotius*, 179.

5

The Medieval Era

As was discussed in the previous chapter, Eusebius of Caesarea illustrated the Eastern style of deference to imperial claims, but by 390 the situation in the West was so different that Ambrose could dare to excommunicate the emperor Theodosius. The diverse trajectories exemplified by Eusebius and Ambrose continued in subsequent centuries, with Augustine becoming the dominant figure in Western Christianity's understanding of political life, even if he was sometimes misinterpreted.

Patristic thinkers introduced a different understanding of society than that held by ancient Greek and Roman writers. The writings of Ambrose, Augustine and others in the West had established there was both sacred and secular power within the empire and that the two powers were not to be exercised by the same authority. Remaining unsettled, however, was just where to draw the boundaries between the realms of sacred and secular and how to understand the relationship of emperor and bishop.

Throughout the post-Constantine period there was an effort to reconcile Christianity with the social institutions of the Roman Empire. According to British political scientist Kenneth Minogue, the next great social experiment that followed that effort was the encounter of Christianity with the barbarian kingdoms. This merger morphed into the medieval order, and it was the medieval order that gave rise to modern politics.[1]

The time period covered in this chapter reveals a story of how the power and authority of popes and kings waxed and waned.[2] There were numerous incidents where spiritual and temporal powers jousted with each other. And always remaining at the heart of the medieval era was the ongoing effort to strike a balance of power among these competitors within the social order. In this chapter, organized under five major headings, we will consider the story

---

1. Kenneth Minogue, *Politics: A Very Short Introduction* (Oxford: Oxford University Press), 4.

2. I use the word "king" in this chapter to refer to the chief or sovereign ruler of an independent state or territory. I use "emperor" to refer to one who rules over a larger territory that may be composed of subordinate kingdoms recognizing the superior authority of the greater entity. In my usage, an emperor is a king, but not all kings are emperors.

of two great confrontations between papal and secular rulers, the ideas of an influential scholar, and a period of papal exile, all during the period spanning the eleventh to the fifteenth century. Before treating those parts of the story it will be helpful in our first major section to survey developments from the end of the patristic age and prior to the eleventh century.

"TWO THERE ARE"

The formula of Gelasius—"two there are"—was concise but not precise. The Gelasian position that two powers govern the world stated a crucial principle but allowed plenty of specifics open to argument. Like the formula of Jesus, "render to Caesar the things that are Caesar's and to God the things that are God's," there was a lot of room left to debate what was whose.

As pope at the end of the fifth century, Gelasius argued that the clergy had the duty to teach and correct political rulers in matters of faith and morals, and that the church should have the prerogative to discipline its members when the offense was spiritual. At the same time he maintained that the emperor was subject to the papacy only on religious matters and that the bishop of Rome had no direct exercise of power in temporal affairs.

In the letter to Emperor Anastasius, where he stated his formula of two swords, Gelasius also claimed that the responsibility of priests was more weighty than that of kings, for the priests will have to answer to God at the final judgment for the people entrusted to their care, including those who are secular rulers.[3] This statement would in later centuries become one of the texts cited to support papal claims of supremacy over secular rulers. Whether Gelasius intended that by his statement remains a matter of dispute among scholars, although he did not assert such authority during his papacy.

For centuries after Gelasius most of the leading actors would nod toward the theory his formula summarized. There are two authorities ordained by God to rule, one has power to govern in matters temporal and the other in matters spiritual. Both are necessary and both are to be obeyed. Neither authority is autonomous; ordained by God they are subject to God's divine revelation and to the moral law known through reason, which reflects God's purposes and plan for creation. Both the spiritual (*sacerdotium*) and temporal (*regnum* or *imperium*) powers have their distinctive areas of competence and ought to cooperate with each other in guiding the society of Christian Europe.

Theories, however, may be more descriptive of what reality *ought* to be

---

3. Gelasius I, "Letter to Emperor Anastasius," in *From Irenaeus to Grotius: A Sourcebook in Christian Political Thought*, ed. Oliver O'Donovan and Joan Lockwood O'Donovan (Grand Rapids, MI: Eerdmans, 1999), 179.

rather than what it *is*. For over five hundred years there was not much theoretical elaboration of how the two authorities should collaborate yet remain distinct. There were, however, numerous instances of matters being decided at the level of practical activity that did not easily coincide with the simple formula of Gelasius.

Sacerdotium: The Emergence of the Papacy

When in the year 330 Constantine moved the imperial capital from Rome to Constantinople he set in motion a development that was not foreseen but which in hindsight seems almost inevitable.[4] Constantine's and his successors' influence and watchfulness over the church in the eastern half of the empire grew, and clerics within the region largely accepted an imperial role in ecclesial matters. At the same time the emperor's physical absence in the West tended to mean a diminution of his influence over the church in the region.

Papal involvement in temporal matters was immensely impacted by the dissolution of the Roman Empire in the West. As medieval historian Brian Tierney suggests, the end of the emperor's power in the region led to two consequences of great significance: first, the papacy (an office held by virtue of being the bishop of Rome) became by default the temporal as well as spiritual ruler of central Italy; second, the papacy would, in time, look elsewhere than to the Byzantine emperor for a political alliance to assure order and security. That alliance would be with the Frankish king, and it would eventuate in a new emperor in the West supported by the papacy.[5]

The migration of peoples throughout western Europe during the period from 300 to 700 CE brought forward secular rulers from the tribal leadership of Visigoths, Lombards, Franks, Angles, and Saxons. As early as 452 it was Pope Leo I (d. 461) who had to fill the power vacuum left by the emperor. Attila, the king of the Huns, had invaded northern Italy, and it was Leo who obtained the agreement that avoided further violence. Just a few years later, to protect the residents of Rome, Leo again negotiated a settlement with Genseric, leader of the Vandals, who had invaded the city.

Before the end of the sixth century the Byzantine emperor's holdings in the West were reduced to Sicily and southern Italy, along with some areas of the eastern coast of the peninsula. By the time of the papacy of Gregory I (d. 604) it was evident that the pope was the true ruler of Rome and its environs. The

---

4. Because Constantine built the eastern capital of Constantinople on the site of the ancient Greek city of Byzantium, the empire and emperor in the East were often described by the adjective Byzantine. Istanbul is the present name of the Turkish city.

5. Brian Tierney, *The Crisis of Church and State, 1050–1300* (Englewood Cliffs, NJ: Prentice-Hall, 1964), 16.

papal break with Constantinople did not come at once, however. Although he was in practice a temporal and spiritual leader, Gregory never made any such claim for himself or his office. The split between the Byzantine emperor and the papacy came later and involved both a theological divide, when the emperor announced a policy of iconoclasm[6] in 726, and the papal need for material assistance in maintaining political order.

While the temporal power of the papacy grew in the fifth, sixth, and seventh centuries, there was also growth in the spiritual authority of the bishops of Rome. Already in the New Testament era there are signs that the Jerusalem community was honored but that Gentile Christians did not look to Jerusalem as the authoritative community. During the second century, the Roman church played a role in settling disputes among other churches over orthodox belief. Rome was also respected as the site of Peter's and Paul's martyrdoms. Of course, there was also the fact that Rome was the center of the Gentile world and capital of the empire.

For most of the first three centuries of the church's life there was an unarticulated recognition of the church in Rome as being of special importance. In a dispute between the bishop of Rome and the bishop of Carthage in the mid-third century there was a more formal assertion of Rome's primacy among the churches, and by the end of the century there are increased incidents of the bishop of Rome claiming an authoritative role in the wider church and not just within his local church.

In the East there were a number of important local churches that might claim an authoritative role—Jerusalem, Antioch, Constantinople, and Alexandria.[7] But in the West, Rome was the lone candidate; and as the empire divided into eastern and western sectors, one sees Rome growing in significance for the other churches in the West.

Pope Damasus I in the latter part of the third century adopted the argument that Peter was the leader of the apostles and that the bishop of Rome was the direct successor to Peter. Over time, as various bishops sought guidance or advice from their counterpart in Rome, the bishop there imitated the format of imperial responses to requests from provincial governors. And so the idea developed that the bishop of Rome's decisions carried a special weight within the church.

A number of those who served as bishop of Rome—especially Damasus,

---

6. Iconoclasm (Greek for "image breaking") refers to a theological position that opposes the use of imagery in religious practice. It was a viewpoint adopted by several of the Byzantine emperors and opposed by the papacy.

7. These four churches along with Rome are known as the ancient patriarchates. Due to their historical significance, the bishops of these five churches were viewed as having a patriarchal, or fatherly, relationship with other churches and enjoyed a religious and moral authority in doctrinal teaching and ecclesial governance.

Leo, and Gelasius—brought a variety of administrative skills, personal charisma, and theological argument to advance the cause of Rome's primacy, at least in Western Christianity. The papal office under these leaders developed as an institution in ways that would be crucial for the medieval era.

By the seventh century the papacy had a spiritual authority to be sure; its preaching and teaching were important, but it was also clearly exercising a jurisdictional authority. After all, the body of baptized Christians was not simply a spiritual movement; it was a corporate entity, and so required an institutional organization and method of governance. The office of the papacy developed along the lines of Roman governance with popes issuing and overseeing laws that helped the church function as an effective institution. This jurisdictional role of the papacy was not viewed as being at odds with the church's spiritual mission, but as a necessary task that enabled the spiritual mission to survive and prosper over time.

By way of summing up, after Gelasius, the virtual disappearance of the Byzantine emperor's presence in Italy combined with the invasion of the Lombards created a new situation. The absence of the emperor and irregular communication with the Eastern patriarchs created an opportunity for the bishop of Rome to step forward as a spiritual and temporal authority. Following upon several less gifted popes, it was Gregory I who rose to the occasion and restored the credibility of papal claims to possessing a unique authority in the Western church. From Gregory onward, the papacy would become increasingly independent of the emperor in Constantinople, while exercising its own authority over temporal matters in central Italy.

Regnum and Imperium: The Power of Kings and Emperors

It was not only the papacy that was undergoing change in the West. The other great social institution of the medieval era was also experiencing important development. There is much scholarly debate over the emergence of the idea of kingship in the West. What can be stated without question is that barbarian kings in the sixth century already understood that the source of their authority was God. The formula *rex dei gratia*, "king by the grace of God," "became fundamental to medieval conceptions of kingship and was the distant ancestor of early modern divine right monarchy."[8] By the time of Charlemagne in the eighth century the phrase was used as part of his royal title.

The source for this idea of kingship was to be found in the Bible. The Old

---

8. Joseph Canning, *A History of Medieval Political Thought 300-1450* (London: Routledge, 1996), 17. For the first part of this presentation on early Christian kingship I am indebted to Canning and to Francis Oakley, *Kingship* (Malden, MA: Blackwell Publishing, 2006).

Testament, as we have seen, was ambivalent about monarchy, including negative as well as positive treatments of the institution. However, during the period surveyed in this chapter, it was those texts indicating a positive view that received the most attention. New Testament texts were also cited to provide support for the idea that the king was God's chosen one. Although a text such as Christ's response to Pilate, "You would have no power over me unless it had been given you from above" (John 19:11), was not exactly a comment on kingship, nonetheless in a context where the centrality of the king was a political reality, the text was read as rendering divine approval of the ruler.

One implication of this understanding of kingship was that the king derived authority directly from God and was not beholden to those ruled for his authority. The people were entrusted by God to the king's care and had no real recourse if their king ruled harshly or unfairly. Gregory I, for example, held that a good king was God's gift to a people, and a bad king was God's punishment upon a people. In both cases the king was to be obeyed.

There were, however, other implications of the Christian understanding of kingship that modified the seeming uncontestable authority of the king. Since the role of king was instituted by God it could be argued that the king ruled in order to play a part in God's plan. The king's power, therefore, was not to be exercised arbitrarily but in accord with the Christian understanding of creation and providence. In sum, there were moral norms that ought to guide the use of the king's authority. This would eventually lead to a positive understanding of the role of government, eclipsing the rather negative and limited view that we saw in Augustine.

Gregory went so far as to assert that the role of king should be described in terms of service or ministry. And Isidore of Seville (d. 636), perhaps the second most influential Christian writer after Augustine on medieval political thought, maintained that the king ought to aim at justice as the goal of his rule. Thus, there was a retrieval of the Greco-Roman notion that the purpose of political authority was the promotion of the common good. The common-good theme suggests that the people are not simply an extension of the king; rather, they have their own ends and purposes that the king should serve well. Such an approach helps to explain the practice of the people—at least their representatives in the persons of the nobility, tribal chiefs, and elders—in giving consent or acclamation to a new king's appointment.

How did a king, ruling by the grace of God, relate to the church and its ministers? There is no evidence that these Christian kings performed a priestly role if is meant by that a sacramental role. The cleric-lay distinction was maintained. However, as with Constantine and later Roman emperors, there are abundant examples of kings exercising authority over matters that today we would think of as internal church affairs. Kings nominated bishops, presided at church councils and meetings, and enforced both doctrinal and moral teachings of the Christian church.

King of the Franks

About the middle of the eighth century, following the tensions occasioned by the iconoclast controversy and the break with the Byzantine emperor, the papacy sent a legate, or representative, to establish regular communication with the Frankish kingdom. The Frankish kings from the time of Clovis (d. 511) had been expanding their territory through conquest, to the point that by the time of the papal diplomatic mission, much of western Europe was under Frankish rule. By the mid-eighth century, however, a series of uninspired monarchs had led to dissatisfaction with the prevailing dynasty. The most powerful court official in the kingdom, Pepin (d. 768), wished to claim the monarchy for himself and sought the advice of the pope regarding the moral issues involved in such a plan.

Pepin was the son of Charles Martel (d. 741), the Frankish military leader who defeated the Saracen army at Tours and who stopped the spread of Islamic expansion in western Europe. Prior to his battles with the Saracens, it was Martel who over the course of several decades unified the Frankish nobility through a series of military campaigns reasserting Frankish dominance over territories that the prior dissolute dynasty had governed ineptly. Although Martel never claimed the title of king, it was clear that the official monarch had little power or interest in ruling and that Charles Martel was the true military and political leader of the Franks.

Pepin, too, held much of the power of the Frankish kingdom, but unlike his father he desired the actual title of king. When Pope Zachary I indicated in his response to Pepin's inquiry, that it seemed only proper that the person who actually wielded power should have the formal title of king, Pepin deposed the sitting monarch and declared himself King of the Franks. He received the approval of the Frankish nobility and in 752 was crowned king by St. Boniface, the famed missionary bishop, who was the original papal legate sent to the Frankish court in 742.

The year after his coronation Pepin had an opportunity to repay the papacy for its support. The Lombards in northern Italy moved to invade Rome, and a new pope, Stephen III, called on the Frankish king for assistance in repelling the Lombard aggression. Pepin not only agreed to defend the pope but offered to hand over to the papacy any of the land he took from the Lombard kingdom. The land secured for the papacy by Pepin in 756 was the beginning of the territory known as the Papal States, and established the pope as temporal ruler of a region as well as spiritual ruler of the universal church.

An Emperor in the West

Pope Stephen III and his successors realized that both the territories they held and the temporal authority they now claimed were not seen as fully legitimate in the eyes of all. Certainly, the Byzantine emperor would look askance at the papacy's formal claims to temporal authority. It was apparent there needed to be a source of legitimation for the papal holdings, to secure them against the opposition of the emperor in Constantinople. And so on Christmas Day in the year 800, while attending Mass in Rome, Pepin's son Charlemagne (d. 814), the second king of the Carolingian dynasty, found to his surprise that Leo III had arranged to coronate him and pronounce him Emperor of the West. Thus, the papacy's alliance with the Frankish kings led to the creation of the Holy Roman Empire.[9]

Historians debate whether Charlemagne was entirely surprised by the decision to be made emperor or just that he was troubled by the part of the pope in the coronation. Traditionally, a new emperor participated in a ceremonial rite of acclamation by nobles and others. There was no history of a papal role bestowing a crown on the emperor's head. Yet, as Tierney writes, "By one brilliant gesture Pope Leo established a precedent, adhered to throughout the Middle Ages, that papal coronation was essential to the making of an emperor, and thereby implanted the germ of the later idea that the empire itself was a gift to be bestowed by the papacy."[10]

Whatever later theorists were to make of Charlemagne's coronation, it is clear that he was not overly deferential to papal prerogatives. Throughout his reign Charlemagne expanded and solidified the Frankish kingdom. Possessing a genius for organization, he established an effective, centralized system of governance. By his rule he appointed bishops for major cities and regions, and established monasteries that became important centers for education and the training of a new generation of men who might take up leadership roles, either within the church or kingdom. Because of their education he relied upon numerous clerics to fill positions that entailed political as well as ecclesiastical power. For many of the clergy within his extensive kingdom, there was no question that it was Charlemagne, not the bishop of Rome, who was the object of loyalty and who commanded obedience. Although broadly supportive of the church, Charlemagne saw his role in a manner more akin to the Israelite monarchy with its sacral elements, than as a ruler of Augustine's earthly city.

---

9. An old joke of historians is that the Holy Roman Empire was neither holy (violence was endemic) nor Roman (it was Frankish) nor much of an empire (soon after Charlemagne it devolved into a network of tribal and ethnic kingdoms).

10. Tierney, *The Crisis of Church and State*, 18.

Charlemagne's descendants could not maintain the unity of his legacy, and the imperial organization he had built by the end of his life was short lived. Pressured by invasions from north and south, along with continued immigration from the east, the political unity of the Carolingian territories dissolved. The results were the political and economic arrangements called feudalism, although this label falsely suggests there was a single and uniform system that emerged throughout Europe.

Europe after Charlemagne

Throughout the ninth and tenth centuries a diffuse set of social arrangements developed, reflecting new allegiances and emergent political identities, though they were largely local or regional. The authority and power of the Holy Roman Emperor had reached its high-water mark under Charlemagne. It was never to be equaled by his successors.

The eventual breakdown of Charlemagne's empire and the persistent danger of invasion from peoples outside the empire's boundaries left individuals at the local level to seek security and order where they could find it. Oftentimes regional nobility and military leaders found they could provide the hope of protection in exchange for an individual's loyalty and obedience. The authority of the local lord extended to the power to collect rents for property, levy taxes, and act as the officer of public justice. The absence of strong government and central authority permitted local rulers to provide what services they wished and to exact profit from those on their land. In a real sense, the activity of such local lords was less like public governance and more like a private, for-profit protection agency.

The church in the ninth century remained an omnipresent social reality throughout western Europe, but its form, too, varied from region to region. In some settings it was large monasteries that dominated social life; in other areas it was a strong bishop-prince exercising control over spiritual and material matters; in the region of central Italy the bishop of Rome ruled, though often dependent on a military protector. Popes did make claims to universal jurisdiction, but these were largely ineffective given the fragmentation of Europe. The resources of the church—its land holdings, educational and cultural institutions, personnel, and spiritual power that might serve as a source of social legitimation—made it attractive for ambitious secular rulers to seek influence over ecclesiastical affairs. This was a period where much of the church's religious witness was compromised by internal corruption and external manipulation.

The property and offices of the church came under the control of regional rulers, and individual clergy discovered that the distant, central authority of the papacy was no match for the security and power offered by a local noble.

Even great monasteries were put under the "protection" of a member of the nobility, while the resources of important bishoprics would be "overseen" by the local ruler. The lands, endowments, and other benefits of the church's holdings were then treated as the nobility's private property to be passed on to children, favored military leaders, or some other chosen beneficiary.

Church leaders anxious about such consequences looked to kings for leadership, as the lone realistic alternative to the rapaciousness of the petty nobility. Strong monarchs were seen as the means to rein in the worst excesses of the age. In addition, churchmen found many biblical texts, particularly in the Old Testament, that gave a religious overlay to the authority of kings. During the tenth century there developed church ceremonies to anoint and confirm monarchs that were akin to those used to consecrate bishops. Kings were praised by preachers as ministers of God's justice to rule over the people, including the clergy.

Of course, kings welcomed these developments. Not only did the church's actions add luster to the dignity of royal office, it also provided a very practical benefit to a monarch's power. Although lesser nobles, often little more than ruthlessly violent military leaders, owed fealty to a king, there was a good deal of autonomy exercised by the nobility in this period. In particular, many of the temporal goods that, in theory, were bestowed by the monarch were, in practice, treated as if they were a noble's by right. Kings frequently had little say in who would inherit the fiefdom when a local lord died. Therefore, the true loyalty of some nobles toward the king was suspect.

However, if the king granted territory and jurisdiction over it to a bishop, then when the bishop died the fiefdom returned to the monarch. The king could then seek out an acceptable successor from the ranks of clergy in the region to be made the new bishop and recipient of the fiefdom. In brief, the use of clergy as bishop-nobles, possessing spiritual and temporal authority in a region, was an effective stratagem for increasing royal power. Understandably, the practice, though useful to kings, often resulted in bishops more interested in temporal than spiritual concerns.

The Need for Reform

As is often the case when institutions slip into a state of disrepair, there is a reaction that gives birth to calls for reform. In the tenth century one particular movement for change arose at the monastery of Cluny in the region of Burgundy. This Benedictine monastery was granted certain rights by royal decree that prevented external forces meddling in its internal life. As a consequence, the residents of Cluny were able to develop a rigorous monastic lifestyle that became an example of authentic Christian virtue. Along with other reform-minded monasteries, the monks of Cluny established a network of institutions that spurred spiritual renewal.

The influence of this monastic reform spread broadly over time; and, although not the only force for change, what historians have called the "Cluniac reform" was a moment in church history when strategies and actions for internal church renewal prospered. Yet, as we shall see below, the reform also occasioned an important historical marker in the story of Christianity and temporal politics.

By the end of the first millennium of the church's life there was clear evidence that change was needed. Not only clerics and monks participated in the movement for church renewal. Henry III, king of Germany, was instrumental in pushing forward the cause of church reform. Like several of his predecessors, Henry traveled to Rome to be crowned emperor of the Holy Roman Empire in the year 1046. Once there he was scandalized to find that there were three rival claimants for the papacy, an illustration of how even the bishopric of Rome had turned into an office that various bidders sought for temporal not spiritual reasons.

Henry simply decided to dismiss all three claimants and appoint his own choice to be pope. To his mind, he had the same authority to appoint the bishop of Rome as he did to appoint other bishops within his realm. His first two appointees to the position died shortly after assuming the office, but his third choice was a family relative who had served as bishop in Germany and was familiar with church reform movements there. Leo IX served as bishop of Rome for five years and during that relatively brief time initiated a wide range of reforms that were to be of lasting importance.

For example, Leo appointed a group of ecclesiastical reformers to be cardinals and then began the practice of keeping cardinals in Rome as his closest advisors and administrators. He decreed various norms for reforming the lifestyle of clerics and took the extraordinary measure of traveling throughout Europe to hold bishops and clergy publicly accountable for following the new norms. In many ways he restored the prestige and authority of the papacy in the eyes of fellow bishops and lower clergy who had never seen or heeded the bishop of Rome.

Leo as pope and Henry as emperor worked cooperatively in bringing about needed reforms. As long as they did so the movement for change proceeded, backed as it was by the two great forces that dominated the eleventh century, the pope of Rome and the German king, who was Holy Roman Emperor. However, when both Leo and then Henry died in the 1050s the agents of renewal did not find cooperation so easy to achieve. What became apparent was that calls for change do not always ensure agreement among all actors about the direction or pace of change.

Conclusion to Historical Survey

Many figures, movements, and events are overlooked in the above brief overview of more than five centuries. The aim of the previous pages was not to present a fully adequate history of the period but to indicate how events can overwhelm ideas, thereby making it difficult to maintain any neat theoretical distinction between temporal and spiritual power. Sometimes because of the designs of secular and religious leaders the lines of authority were deliberately blurred; at other times, the mixing of authority was necessary because of social emergency and historical chance.

In what follows, two disputes, each involving a pair of figures, will illustrate the changing fortunes of religious and secular authority in the medieval period. In both cases there was a conscious and sustained effort not only to press for change but also to present arguments that would justify the change. Disputants employed principles and precedents as the two-powers formula of Gelasius was applied to particular circumstances. The first confrontation, between Pope Gregory VII and the Emperor Henry IV, is known as the Investiture Controversy; the second was the struggle between Pope Boniface VIII and King Philip IV of France.

THE INVESTITURE CONTROVERSY

In the mid-eleventh century when a bishop died it was the usual practice that the king chose a person to fill the vacancy. As a consequence stemming from the confusion of roles in the prior centuries, there had developed the practice of secular leaders "investing" a local bishop with the symbols of his authority, the crozier, or staff, that spoke of his role as shepherd of the people, and the episcopal ring signifying his "marriage" to the local church. Part of the ritual also entailed the episcopal nominee doing homage to the lay ruler and receiving the grant of land and jurisdiction that was attached to the bishopric.

Leo IX, as part of his reform agenda, had condemned the practice of simony, the selling of church offices to the highest bidder. But as his own appointment to the papacy attested, the practice of lay rulers selecting bishops for dioceses or bishoprics in their domain was common. As reform movements developed, however, the practice of laymen bestowing the symbols of religious authority on a bishop was deemed unacceptable. The proposed reform was not due to an offense taken at a ritual impropriety; rather it expressed a desire to clarify whose power was greater concerning church life and which authority had stronger claims on a bishop's loyalty. It was, in other words, a dispute about the appropriate boundaries between secular and ecclesiastical authority, boundaries that had been thoroughly blurred over the prior centuries.

On the level of ideas it is easy to distinguish two roles—bishop and prince-vassal—that are joined in one person. On the level of practice in the mid-1000s neither side in the dispute was able to separate the elements of one role from the other.[11] For advocates of church reform the practice of lay investiture was an intolerable intrusion by secular authority into ecclesiastical affairs. For defenders of the practice, the ability of the monarch to control appointments that brought with them significant temporal authority was vital to good social order.

A Narrative of the Conflict

In the year 1059, Pope Nicholas II issued a decree that changed the entire process of papal elections. Nicholas determined that future elections of a pope were to be in the hands of the cardinals of the church, establishing a new function for the reform-minded body promoted by Leo IX. The pope's decree ignored the role of the emperor, dating from the days of Charlemagne, in nominating the candidate. The papal decision also effectively marginalized the influence of the Roman nobility, who vied for influence in the selection of the bishop of Rome. Aware that acting on such a decree would incite hostility from the emperor, the papacy formed an alliance with the leader of the Norman invaders who had taken over much of southern Italy.

Then in 1073 one of the original reformist cardinals brought to Rome by Leo was elected pope. Hildebrand, a former abbot of Cluny, and at the time of his election a powerful figure among the college of cardinals, became Gregory VII. The emperor, Henry IV, was preoccupied at the time with quashing a rebellion in the region of Saxony and did not contest the new pope's election, even though he had played no part in it.

Henry IV, unlike his father, had no particular interest in assisting with ecclesiastical reform and had been uncooperative in his dealings with Gregory's predecessor. Had the focus of papal efforts been restricted to the moral reform of the clergy, the emperor may not have objected. But when Gregory sought to alter the manner of episcopal appointments it was clear there would be conflict with the emperor.

---

11. Kings did not want to see the temporal and spiritual elements separated because the prince-bishop had become a vital office for public administration and organization of a realm. Reformers did not want to see the elements separated because of their opposition to simony. If the spiritual and temporal elements were separate, a candidate for office might argue that he was only paying a tithe to the king for the temporal benefits of the office and not for the spiritual office of the episcopacy. Separation of the two elements of the office would permit an easy defense against the charge of simony. The reformers' concern about simony would not allow such a possibility.

Much was at stake, for Henry viewed his control of episcopal appointments as essential to his ambition to unify the monarchy and empire. Gregory, in turn, did not see how the movement for church reform could continue if the papacy surrendered to the imperial claims about its authority to determine the makeup of the church's hierarchy, including the bishop of Rome.

The immediate context for the crisis was 1075, when both pope and emperor each nominated a candidate to fill the vacant bishopric of Milan. Gregory wrote a letter, essentially upbraiding the emperor and reminding him that the bishop of Rome was the successor to St. Peter and that all Christians were subject to the pope, including the emperor. In response Henry convoked a council of German bishops and denounced Gregory as a false pope and guilty of various abuses of authority. In early 1076 the pope excommunicated Henry and, most significantly, took the bold move of declaring that since the emperor was no longer a member of the church all his vassals were released from their oaths of obedience. Henry replied in his defense that he was king by divine election and that Gregory had no power to deny his authority.

During the course of the ensuing months it became clear that the tide was turning against Henry. Many of the German nobility were uneasy with Henry's efforts at centralization and claims of authority over them; the German bishops were troubled at the idea of breaking with Gregory and backed away from their initial support of the emperor. Eventually, it became clear that Henry was in a weak position, and he underwent a humiliating about-face, calling for a meeting in Augsburg, to be presided over by the pope, that would determine his suitability to remain as king as well as the continuation of the ban of excommunication.

Early in 1077 Gregory started his journey north for the Augsburg gathering, stopping on his journey at a castle in Canossa, Italy, before crossing the Alps into Germany. This became the site of a dramatic encounter when Henry crossed into Italy with a small escort and called upon the pope in Canossa. Accounts of the event describe Henry dressed as a public penitent standing at the castle gates in winter seeking forgiveness and reconciliation.

The conflict inherent in Gregory's role was clear. As a minister of the church, the pope could not turn away a sinner seeking absolution; as a key political figure in the crisis, Gregory should have told Henry to return to Germany to await the hearing on his case before the assembly of German nobles. In the end Gregory met with Henry and lifted the excommunication but did not pronounce him restored to royal rule.

The reaction was not what the pope would have hoped. Now reconciled with the church, Henry's supporters once again rallied to his side. His opponents felt betrayed by Gregory's unilateral action, and they proceeded to elect a new king. This decision put the pope in the uncomfortable position of having to choose whom to support, and he delayed a decision for so long that civil war broke out in Germany. When Gregory finally did choose to favor the rival claimant to the throne, he once again excommunicated Henry.

By now many were angry with the pope, blaming his indecisiveness for bringing about the suffering of war. The papal choice was also unwise in that Henry's side had recently gained the momentum in the struggle. Once he defeated his rival, Henry sought his revenge, nominating his own choice for pope and setting siege to Rome. In time, the imperial army retreated from Rome when the Norman forces in the south very belatedly acted on their promise to be papal protectors. The Normans, however, treated Rome as theirs to loot, and after having done so they returned to the south, taking Gregory with them, allegedly as his defenders. Gregory died shortly thereafter, in 1085, without ever returning to Rome.

The dispute over lay investiture outlived the two major figures. In 1122 a treaty signed at the city of Worms in Germany settled the matter. By the terms of the treaty, the emperor was granted the right to oversee any election of bishops and abbots within Germany to guarantee that the process be fair. But the emperor was not to bestow the symbols of their authority on the bishops, nor was he to have any role in the appointment of bishops outside of German territory. Basically, it was a victory for the papal view of investiture.

Understanding the Controversy

The papal argument against lay investiture was fueled by two factors. First, there was a movement toward increased centralization of church authority in the office of the papacy and a developing organizational apparatus that permitted that development. Second, there was energy for renewal prompting a desire for the church to have autonomy and authority in matters spiritual that had been granted in theory but eroded in practice over the centuries.

The supporters of Henry's position on investiture were, practically speaking, defending the status quo as things had evolved over time since Charlemagne. Their argument was based more on precedent than principle. There was little doubt that Charlemagne and his successors stood in judgment of clerics and had even deposed popes, had exercised leadership in church councils, and promoted occasional church reforms. Furthermore, with the breakdown of central authority during the ninth and tenth centuries, local rulers, not papal leadership, often provided for church governance, at least in the sense of selecting bishops.

There is no question that the papacy had the better side of the theoretical argument concerning lay investiture. Where the papal argument went too far was Gregory's declaration that all oaths of obedience by vassals to the emperor were illegitimate. That was, for all intent and purpose, to equate the power to excommunicate, a legitimate papal prerogative, with the right to depose.

Given the facts in this case, and as would be the situation in many cases, that a substantial portion of a king's vassals were clerics, there was a genuine risk to Henry's ability to rule. In short, by his decree Gregory was setting himself up to be the determiner of political legitimacy.

There were no precedents for Gregory's claim that a pope had the right to depose a monarch. Even at the time papal opponents made that point. Gregory argued that spiritual power was inherently superior to temporal power. Others had believed that as well, including Gelasius. The error in Gregory's argument, however, was to move from claims of higher responsibility as spiritual leaders to a claim of authority over temporal rulers. Ambrose, Augustine, Gelasius, Gregory I, and other church figures we have previously discussed may have thought the temporal realm inferior to the spiritual realm, but the key point is that they thought there were two realms, and authority in one realm ought not be mixed with authority in the other. Gregory VII acted as if there was one realm with temporal power subordinate to spiritual power.[12]

Gelasius had argued in his two-powers formula that all power is from God, the emperor's no less than the pope's. Thus, when the issue moved from lay investiture to the question of deposition of a temporal ruler, the imperial position had a sound principle to rest upon. What Gregory VII tried to do was exercise supremacy in both temporal and spiritual rule. This, the emperor's supporters argued, no one should be permitted to do. In effect, the argument that the papal side used against the imperial in the investiture matter, about meddling in an area that should be off limits, was turned around by the imperialists to good effect against the papal position on deposition of a ruler. The nub of the problem was that both sides had violated the Gelasian formula by making overreaching claims of power.

Neither Gregory nor Henry worked out with any coherence the full implications of their stands over lay investiture, for each the focus was on winning that single point; in order to do so they took positions that they might have reconsidered had they broadened their focus. Brian Tierney reminds us that although Gregory "asserted a right to depose Henry he never suggested that the king's authority was in principle delegated to him by the pope; nor did he claim in practice the right to choose anyone he wished as king, but rather acknowledged the right of election belonged primarily to the princes. Least of all did he ever suggest that he could himself assume the role of a king of Germany and so combine in his own person supreme spiritual and temporal power."[13]

Regarding Henry, his insistence "that his authority came from God alone

---

12. In the *Dictatus Papae*, Gregory famously declared that "the Pope is the only one whose feet are to be kissed by all princes" (*From Irenaeus to Grotius*, 242).

13. Tierney, *The Crisis of Church and State*, 57.

and that only God could depose him" did not lead him to deny "that the two swords of spiritual and temporal government should remain separate," nor did he claim both swords for himself. While his claim that he should nominate bishops, including the bishop of Rome, would seem to transgress the boundary between the two realms in practice, Henry never declared as a theoretical principle "that all spiritual and temporal authority belonged to him as vicar of God. The assertions of both rulers thus fell far short of claims to absolute theocratic power."[14]

Theories of Authority

The dispute between Gregory and Henry did not resolve the theoretical issues so much as confuse them. It fell to others to develop the arguments that were needed for clarification in order to attain a settlement. Whether a pope could depose a king and determining the proper role of bishops were two significant elements of the controversy.

Deposing a King

There were any number of authors who leaped into the fray as partisans for either Gregory or Henry. However, there were also others willing to make more principled and extended arguments that explored both the imperial and papal positions.

Perhaps a text written by an unknown author—thought to be from York in England or Rouen in Normandy—was the clearest example of a pro-royalist position. The tract, circa 1100, developed a theological argument that there was a sacral nature to kingship, a view that was even at this time beginning to wane.[15] The anonymous writer argued that kings no less than priests receive the sacramental image of Christ at their consecration.

Priests receive the image of Christ as high priest who redeems humanity through his sacerdotal function of offering himself as the sacrifice pleasing to God. Kings, on the other hand, receive the image of Christ as king and are to provide the functions of governance and rule. Earthly kings, much like the Old Testament kings, rule over the entire body of society, both clergy and laity. Kings govern the institution of the church just as they do any other area of social life. Thus, the argument of the anonymous author helped to continue the belief in the divine nature of kingship, a motif to which later royalist thinkers would return.[16]

---

14. Ibid., 57.

15. See Norman Anonymous, "The Consecration of Bishops and Kings," in *From Irenaeus to Grotius*, 251-59.

16. Oakley, however, maintains that despite such pro-royalist argumentation

On the papal side, one of the more intriguing arguments put forth was by Manegold of Lautenbach. A strong supporter of the papal action to depose the emperor, Manegold did not argue from the premise that the pope had temporal jurisdiction greater than the king. Rather he argued from the claim that government and law ought to contribute to justice. Consequently, one can draw a clear line of demarcation between a just king and a tyrant, with the implication that under the right conditions a tyrant can be deposed.

It is the office of kingship that must be honored, not any particular holder of it. When the actual king fails to promote justice his claim to the office cannot be treated as absolute. Manegold concluded that a king might be deposed when the king has undermined the very goods that royal office is supposed to secure. A people and a king forge a pact to endow the ruler with power for the purpose of establishing just rule. Should the ruler break faith with the people, "reason dictates that he absolves the people from their obedience."[17] According to Manegold, what Gregory did was simply to declare publicly that the pact had been voided by Henry's own actions invalidating his rule.[18]

The Role of Bishops

A second issue that required further exploration was the function of a bishop. Here the way forward was indicated when arguments were made that the spiritual office of the episcopacy was distinct from any temporal jurisdiction that might have accrued to a particular bishopric.

Ivo of Chartres was among the scholars who pressed for this distinction. Kings might be called upon as the representative of the people to give assent

---

the whole notion of sacral kingship was disavowed in principle and practice by the outcome of the campaign against lay investiture. The aura of sacredness attached to kingship in the Old Testament, then with Constantine and other Christian emperors, and again with Charlemagne and German successors was to fade from here on. No longer in the West was the king to be viewed as having religious functions or roles. See Oakley, *Kingship*, 113.

17. Manegold of Lautenbach, *Ad Gebehardum*, quoted in George Sabine, *A History of Political Theory*, 4th ed., revised by Thomas Thorson (Hinsdale, IL: Dryden Press, 1973), 229.

18. This argument did not directly support the position that the pope might depose a king, since the argument that the ruler was dependent on the people might also be used to argue that the ruler was not dependent on the pope. Manegold's theory did not serve those papalists who believed that the coronation of Charlemagne by the pope implied that spiritual authority gave legitimacy to the temporal one. Manegold underscored his view on Henry by a historical analysis of the earlier deposition of the corrupt Merovingian king in favor of Pepin, Charlemagne's father. Manegold argued that the king had really been deposed through the consensus of the German nobility's disapproval of the king and their support of Pepin as the new ruler. Pope Zachary I simply approved the result.

to the selection of a new bishop, and if the king so chose might give substantial land holdings and powers of jurisdiction. But these material goods and temporal powers were not essential to the episcopacy, and the bestowal of them ought not be integrated into the ceremonies of episcopal consecration. The symbols of religious office should be reserved to the pope or his representative to grant.

The dispute between the German emperor and the bishop of Rome eventually spread to France and England. There were various parries and feints made by both popes and kings, but the issue was not finally settled until the Concordat at Worms in 1122.

The treaty was a compromise that gave something to both sides. Bishops in Germany were to be named by ecclesiastical authority, and the emperor would no longer invest them with the symbols of office. However, the emperor was to be present at the appointment of a bishop and was to be paid homage by the newly selected bishop. The emperor could refuse the homage and in so doing exercise a veto over any appointment. Practically, secular rulers continued to have a good deal to say about episcopal appointments for centuries to come.

Outcomes of the Confrontation

Tierney has noted several significant results of the Lay Investiture Controversy: (1) neither of the great protagonists had won, "royal theocracy had been defeated without papal theocracy becoming established"; (2) the papal right to depose an emperor was left an open question; and (3) the idea that subjects could resist an unjust ruler grew in public consciousness.[19]

One final matter noted by Tierney is that a submotif among some church reformers began to develop. Defining the proper relationship between the religious office of the bishop and the temporal wealth and power attached to the office was at the heart of the dispute. Both sides assumed that the temporal wealth and power associated with the office of bishop was a good thing. The dispute was over who should control appointments to the office.

A minority voice among church reformers, however, proposed a solution to the investiture dispute that was not adopted; namely, bishops should disavow all temporalities attached to their office. The belief was that the church should become poorer, less engaged in political and economic matters, and more focused on fostering holiness. This would become a constant theme from here on when there was discussion about church renewal. This proposal was not meant as an antipapal or anticlerical broadside; many of the proponents

---

19. Tierney, *The Crisis of Church and State*, 86. I have relied on much of Tierney's account of the Investiture Controversy throughout this entire subsection.

of such reform were staunch supporters of the papacy who simply wished to see the office less entangled in matters temporal. As the years would pass this theme was to be used again, though not always by reformers sympathetic to the papacy.

THE POLITICAL IDEAS OF AQUINAS

Thomas Aquinas (d. 1274) is not comparable to Augustine in the influence cast over Christian political thought during his own era, but his influence grew within Catholicism as centuries passed. He did not focus on politics in most of his writing, but political topics are woven throughout many of his theological and philosophical writings. Aquinas was part of a generation of scholars who lived at a time when many of the works of Aristotle were being translated into Latin and "rediscovered" in western Europe. Profoundly shaped by this intellectual revolution, Aquinas sought to reconcile Christian theology with the philosophy of Aristotle. And this project explains why Thomas has had such a lasting effect on Christianity and politics.

By his use of Aristotle, Thomas altered the predominantly negative view of the state that had been the legacy of Augustine. For Thomas, temporal life has its own proper end, and the state is seen as a necessary and positive means to attain human well-being. For Aquinas, the state is not only necessary as an enforcer of peace (as for Augustine) but also because it is an expression of humankind's social nature. Thus, its existence is not due mainly to sin but to God's plan for creation. The state is a "natural" institution in the sense that it assists human beings to achieve their proper fulfillment in the order of nature, just as the church enables humans to attain their fulfillment in the supernatural order.

Thomas is less troubled than Augustine by the risk that people will seek their earthly good at the expense of their heavenly one; for Thomas, our final fulfillment is not put in sharp tension with our temporal happiness. Put simply, grace builds on nature; it does not contradict nature, according to Thomas.[20] Of course, as a Christian theologian, Thomas has a belief in a final end that Aristotle does not envision; but Thomas did not think Aristotle was wrong in his philosophy of a rational and ordered creation that had goods to which humans should aspire. Though these goods may be secondary they are worthy of pursuit, and they need not be seen as distractions to our true fulfillment in God.

---

20. Thomas Aquinas, *Summa Theologiae* I, 8:2, *gratia non tollit sed perficit naturam,* that is, "grace does not abolish nature but perfects it."

Zōon Politikon

Thomas agreed with Aristotle's axiom that humans are political animals and also rational ones. For Thomas these two qualities mesh: because humans live by their use of reason they are naturally social. Unlike other animals who live by their instincts, human beings must furnish for themselves many of the necessities of life—food, shelter, clothing, security. Other animals function well with limited experience and nurturance, but humans must be nursed, taught, and helped to a great degree. As a result, sound reasoning leads to the insight that collaboration with others is necessary; and so, too, a division of labor is wise. Thomas cites the gift of speech as evidence that humans are meant to communicate with others and to convey ideas. We are naturally social and rational.

The communities of families or small villages offer insufficient resources, however, to satisfy human well-being. These communities must be joined with others into a greater society that is capable of providing for people's temporal goods. For Aristotle this was the city-state; for Aquinas it is best realized in a kingdom. The purpose of a political state is to bring about the proper conditions such that all members of the community can attain their temporal well-being or happiness. This is the good that all rational persons seek; it is the common good of humankind, and the state is the primary institution that exists to promote it.

Because we are guided in the pursuit of the good by reason more than instinct, it is possible to consider multiple ways to seek human well-being. Due to human finitude and ignorance we do not always know for certain which path to choose in our pursuit of the good. That is why we need wise and prudent governance, so that we can individually and corporately be directed toward the good and organized to work cooperatively in attaining it.

Questions of Governance

According to Thomas, the forms of governance are three, and they reflect the possibilities of rule by one, by a few, or by many. Government by one is kingship; government by the few is aristocracy; and government by the many is polity (a moderate democracy). Following Aristotle, Aquinas also lists the negative versions of the three forms, thereby suggesting there are six possible forms that governance may take. Tyranny is bad kingship; oligarchy is bad aristocracy; and democracy (mob rule) is bad polity. A good government rules for the sake of the common good, while a bad government seeks a restricted, selfish version of the good that benefits only those who rule.[21] Originally,

---

21. For Aristotle, democracy was problematic if it meant direct rule by the mass

Thomas preferred kingship as the best form of government, since he saw that as reflecting God's governance of the universe. In his later writing, however, he moved closer to Aristotle by approving a mixed form that moderated kingly power with roles for an aristocracy and the general populace.

More than any risk that abuse of governing power poses is the danger of anarchy. For Thomas, nothing is more negative politically than the breakdown of social order. He prefers even tyranny to anarchy. Indeed, Thomas's treatment of tyranny illustrates his cautiousness when there is risk of social disorder. Due to his view of the positive function of the state in promoting the common good, Thomas does not subscribe to Augustine's view that a tyrannical ruler is God's just punishment on the people for their sins. Instead, he upholds the position that a king has the duty of serving the people's well-being and can be disobeyed if that duty is consistently shirked.

His view on tyrannicide is developed from his understanding of law. For Thomas, law is a fourfold reality. There is the eternal law by which he means God's will and plan for creation. The natural law is the rational creature's ability to understand some aspects of the eternal law. Divine positive law is God's law as revealed in the Bible, and human positive law is the law of the state. For Aquinas, the role of the lawmaker is to apply the natural law to particular cases—to make specific and precise what may be known only generally—and to enforce the law through sanctions.

Human law is derived, therefore, from natural law and is authentic law only insofar as it reflects the natural law correctly. A ruler or lawmaker does not have the authority to promote a law that is incompatible with the natural law since the ruler's authority comes from God and is accountable to God for the proper use of that authority. A good law binds in conscience because it is in accord with the natural law, while a law that is in violation of the natural law cannot bind an individual. There is then a clear limit to the legitimate authority of a ruler. A ruler cannot act arbitrarily or selfishly but is to provide laws that are in accord with the natural law and serve the common good. A ruler who consistently and intentionally acts otherwise loses legitimacy.

Early in his career Thomas gave indications that tyrannicide might be legitimate, but in later writing he appears less willing to countenance such action. The risk of revolution and anarchy was too great to approve of such an extra-judicial means of checking a bad ruler. What may be done is to follow legal

---

of people since he thought any such political assembly would be prey for demagogues who would forge a tyranny of mob rule. That is Aquinas's view of the matter as well. He also adopted Aristotle's approval of a moderate democracy in which the people have power but delegate it to wise leaders who are accountable to the people should power be abused. Aquinas used the Latin *politia* for this form of government; I use the English word polity.

measures against tyranny. If the ruler holds power by consent of the people, then the people may depose the king. If the ruler holds power because a higher power has delegated it to him, then appeal must be made to that higher power to remove the tyrant from office. In other words, there is a proper protocol to follow that can address the problem while maintaining social order. Resorting to private judgment and action such as tyrannicide is imprudent and to be avoided.

On the issue of the interplay of papal and kingly power, Thomas is clearly a proponent of the superiority of *sacerdotium* over *regnum*. He was in principle a papalist. Thomas maintained that a pope possesses the *plenitudo potestatis*, the "fullness of power," not only in the church but in the temporal sphere as well. Thomas stated that in matters dealing with salvation one must obey spiritual authority rather than temporal authority. And in political matters individuals ought to obey their temporal ruler not the spiritual one, except when the authority is the pope who is supreme in both realms.

Despite his strong support for the papacy Thomas did not enter into political controversies and provided little detail as to his views on how to resolve specific disputes between church leaders and political rulers. That is not the legacy he left to us. His achievement was that, more than any other figure preceding him in the Christian tradition, he gave a positive interpretation to political institutions and activity. For Thomas, politics was not simply the work of "damage control," limiting the negative social effects of human sinfulness. Rather, it was a realm where good was to be pursued and in which virtue was to be practiced. Politics involved moral responsibility; people were to be directed by right reason in making appropriate choices for the building up of communal life. Both rulers and ruled were bound to a normative order that governed life in this world, and by following it they might be faithful to their Christian vocation.

UNIVERSAL PAPACY AND NATIONAL MONARCHY

Although Aquinas's political ideas would eventually have great influence within Catholic teaching, his thought did not reflect the political agenda of the papacy at the time. The historian Francis Oakley has suggested the presence of a good deal of "political Augustinianism" in the ideas of the papacy under Gregory VII and several successors such as Innocent III (d. 1216) and Innocent IV (d. 1254). Recall that some interpreters misread Augustine in a way that led them to think that the natural order was to be absorbed into the supernatural order. By the 1200s the belief was so strong in the unitary nature of Christian society, inclusive of both spiritual and temporal, that the view of two distinct realms asserted by Gelasius was lost to many.

The papacy between Gregory VII and Boniface VIII (d. 1303) effectively denied the dualistic view of medieval society that had been promoted by earlier bishops of Rome trying to resist imperial claims of unitary authority. In its early formulations the unitary view treated the emperor as holding sway over the church, which was seen as part of a Christian empire. Now under the assertive papacy of the Middle Ages the unitary formulation tended to the other extreme, with the pope understood as the head of a unified Christian society, in which the empire was part of the church.

In the long competition between popes and emperors the papacy in the thirteenth century emerged as the stronger institution. The belief that Christ gave his own power to St. Peter and his successors and that this made the papacy superior to any other earthly authority grew in acceptance. Meanwhile, the Holy Roman Emperor had considerably weakened as the German empire dissolved following the death of Henry V (d. 1125). And throughout the twelfth century the papacy resisted, largely successfully, the Hohenstaufen dynasty's efforts to restore the authority of the emperor.

Winds of change were blowing, however. New ideas, encouraged by the discovery of Aristotle's major works, were being generated. The theoretical analysis reached something of a high point in the explosion of scholarship that took place at the close of the twelfth century, continuing on into the thirteenth. The rise of the university in sites such as Bologna, Cambridge, Naples, Oxford, Paris, and Salamanca made a dramatic expansion of learning and scholarship possible. Debates concerning the relationship between spiritual and temporal authority were to continue for decades in the writings of university scholars.

A Narrative of Conflict

New political realities were also taking shape, with national kingdoms ruled by men who acknowledged no authority within their territory greater than their own. The new kingdoms employed networks of administrators at the local level joined to centralized administration of justice and finance. Assemblies of representatives from throughout a realm were occasionally convened to forge support for the policies of the king. In addition, these monarchs established armies that were hired for pay, rather than forces rallied by traditional claims of feudal oaths of fealty. All of these developments created the need for income, which kings sought to accrue by imposition of taxes on their subjects.

Phase I: A Dispute over Taxes

It was an event at the close of the thirteenth century, occasioned by taxation, that initiated the next decisive moment in the story of Christianity and politics. It was a clash between Pope Boniface VIII and Philip IV, the king of France. The dispute began with an effort by Philip to raise money, levying a tax on the clergy as one means of doing so. Although there was a standing policy that clergy ought not pay taxes to a secular ruler without first consulting with the pope, the usual practice was that kings imposed taxes and the papacy went along with it. This was particularly true in times of war, when the clergy were expected to do their part in support of a just cause.

In 1296 the war between France and England, largely over commercial interests, was unacceptable to Boniface. As was his style, Boniface did not seek a more diplomatic strategy in resolving the matter but simply issued a document prohibiting the clergy in either country from paying any tax unless approved by the pope. Philip had no interest in a debate and responded with a royal embargo of all financial support from French territory to Rome. That was a strong financial blow to the papacy.

The stakes were set very high. Given the vast amount of church holdings, it would be difficult for any secular ruler to secure adequate funds for the state's budget if all ecclesiastical property was beyond the reach of taxation. No king could countenance having to seek papal approval of state finances, especially at a time of war. On the other hand, a ruler could set ever higher taxes to fund everything from wars to palaces and thereby cripple the ministries of the church. No pope could be indifferent to the protection of the church's financial resources. And so the clash ensued.

It so happened that Boniface not only was involved in a dispute with Philip, he was also under assault by movements inside the church. There were powerful cardinals angered by Boniface's favoritism of his own aristocratic family concerning administration of the papal states; in addition, there were spiritual reformers who were profoundly disappointed by Boniface's "worldliness" when compared to his predecessor, Celestine V. These internal critics were raising a challenge to Boniface by demanding that a general council be called to evaluate his legitimacy as pope. When Philip hinted he might support such a demand, he added additional pressure to that already imposed by the financial embargo. The result was a humiliating reversal of policy by the pope, who issued a decree that the French king, without need of papal consent, should decide when a tax on the clergy was a legitimate need.

An additional factor in the clash was the rising tide of national spirit. As in the investiture conflict between Gregory and Henry, the papal side made overtures to nobles who might withdraw their support for the monarch. This time, however, there was greater unity among the French nobility toward Philip than the Germans had shown toward Henry. In fact, Boniface discovered to his surprise that many of his own clergy were willing to pay a tax in support of their secular ruler. Thus, Philip's hand was strengthened by the allegiance that French nobles and clerics had shown in his dispute with a pope who was seen to be meddling in temporal matters that were best left to others. Now it was the papacy experiencing the weakened claims of a universal authority, much as the universalism of the Holy Roman Emperor had earlier been confronted by the rise of national identity.

No doubt the papal stance had some support among church members. It was not difficult to understand that a spiritual authority stripped of all power to control temporal resources would be hampered in its mission and lack autonomy as an institution. Yet, the supporters of Philip could not fail to see a church that claimed all manner of temporal goods to be beyond temporal authority would translate into an impoverished state. Efforts to resolve this dilemma in a more theoretical and principled way were soon overtaken by events.

Phase 2: The Document *Unam sanctam*

In 1301 Philip had a bishop arrested, tried, and imprisoned on charges that were both civil and religious. Philip then sent a detailed explanation of what he had done to Boniface, requesting that the pope validate the judgment. Boniface was not concerned by the judgment of guilt but by the French king's presumption of the authority to judge a bishop. For that was in clear violation of church law, which held a bishop could only be tried in an ecclesiastical court led by the pope. A series of letters between the papal and French courts only exacerbated the tension. Philip and his advisors engaged in a successful effort among his subjects to portray the issue not as the autonomy of the church in France, Boniface's view of the matter, but the freedom of the French kingdom from papal control.

As papal efforts to reverse Philip's actions came to naught, Boniface issued a document, *Unam sanctam*, in 1302 that has become the most famous statement concerning church and state in the medieval era. It is a decree that was, to a significant extent, a compilation of statements from various popes and scholars, although these were prone to misinterpretation by being taken out of context.

On the matter of papal supremacy, Boniface may have held a view that was shared by some of his medieval predecessors, but he asserted his position in less ambiguous and more blunt prose. Not only is the pope supreme in the church but also in the temporal sphere; both of the Gelasian powers belong to the papacy, according to Boniface. All temporal power is derived from spiritual power, and therefore temporal authorities are subject to the pope. Secular rulers can be designated to hold and use temporal power but only by permission of the clergy. The teaching of *Unam sanctam* effectively denied Gelasius's assertion there were dual powers and authorities.

Following *Unam sanctam* there was no possibility of a rapprochement between pope and king. Philip pressed his case against Boniface by calling for a general council to depose the pope, and even tried a violent assault to seize and arrest him. Boniface's health took a turn for the worse, and he died in the summer of 1303. His successor continued the papal conflict with Philip; but it was a brief reign of a few months, and the next pope, Clement V, was a Frenchman. Under pressure from Philip the new pope made a number of concessions, including nullifying many decrees of Boniface, that put an end to the conflict between the papacy and the French king.

Theories and Arguments

Defense of Boniface's claim to what was called the *plenitudo potestatis* ("fullness of power") was best elaborated by Giles of Rome, a cleric of the Augustinian order, in his treatise *De ecclesiastica potestate*. The argument reflected a hierarchical worldview that had grown in popularity with the study in the West of the writings of Pseudo-Dionysius.[22] It was Giles's writing that was the likely source for Boniface's argument in *Unam sanctam*.

Basically, Giles's claim was that the law of nature teaches that the lower is subsumed by the higher; therefore, spiritual power is not only higher than temporal power, it also includes and governs temporal power.[23] All power requires God's blessing to be valid, for all power is subject to God and derived from God. No one can be truly subject to God unless one is also subject to God's church. And the representative of the entire church is its universal ruler, the pope; so all legitimate power is subject to the authority of the bishop of Rome.

Obviously, the argument of Giles eradicated any meaningful distinction between spiritual authority and temporal authority. Presuming that the Christian church was the repository of spiritual authority and the pope was the sovereign head of the church, Giles effectively made the papacy the ultimate seat of all power, temporal and spiritual.

The radical nature of Giles's claims is further illustrated by his teaching on property, which placed all property under the pope. His reasoning was that God was lord of the entire universe, and so a sinner alienated from God could not rightfully have dominion, that is, exercise lordship, over anything of God's. All humankind is sinful, and it is only the church that can reconcile sinners with God. Therefore, persons can only acquire the ability to have dominion over property if they have first been granted that ability by the church, which holds a sort of eminent domain over all material property.

---

22. The writer known as Pseudo-Dionysius was a patristic author, wrongly identified in later centuries with a New Testament figure who was a convert mentioned in the Acts of the Apostles (17:34). His writings, which were heavily Neoplatonic, were avidly studied in the thirteenth century.

23. Giles of Rome, "On Ecclesiastical Power," in *From Irenaeus to Grotius*, 365-78, esp. 367.

On the other side of the theoretical divide, the most influential voice was that of a cleric from another religious order, John of Paris, a Dominican friar. In his work *De potestate regia et papali*, he sought to present a refutation of papal claims about the *plenitudo potestatis* and explain the proper relationship of royal and papal power.[24] John employed another aspect of Aristotle's thought to refute Giles's argument that the higher power subordinates the lower.

John made the case that civil government is a requirement for the common good of human beings. (Here he follows his more famous Dominican colleague Thomas Aquinas, who integrated Aristotle into Christian theology.) Temporal authority has a natural autonomy from spiritual authority due to its necessary and legitimate role in assisting humans to act out their social nature. The state is derived from the natural law because humans are naturally political. Temporal authority is not under spiritual authority but exists parallel to it since each has its function in one of the two distinct realms of the natural and supernatural. Spiritual authority is greater in dignity, but that does not translate into the spiritual being dominant over the temporal in the realm of politics, since that would entail a confusion of realms.

John also followed Aristotle by taking a position that the natural political community is not a universal one but simply the community that allows for the highest moral development of its members. For Aristotle the city-state was the aptly sized entity that would permit the social life of citizens to flourish. In John's case, the assumption was that the kingdom as it existed in his time was the proper political community. He accorded no great importance to the Holy Roman Emperor. Each national kingdom is autonomous and is not deemed deficient because it is not part of a larger universal community.

An additional important contribution John made was his argument for constitutional limits to the papacy as well as to the monarchy. Legitimate authority was granted by God. The specific designation of individuals to bear that authority, however, was designated not by God but by human choice. Both kings and popes were chosen in order that the common good might flourish in both the state and the church.

Kings and popes had the moral and political duty to see to it that their respective institutions served that common good. If these rulers failed in their duty to the community, then the consent of the people might be withdrawn, opening the path to deposition. A tyrannical king might be deposed by a concerted action of nobles acting on behalf of and in the name of the people. A pope who betrayed the faith of the church or misused the goods of the church might also be deposed by a general council or by the body of cardinals acting

---

24. John of Paris, "On Royal and Papal Power," in *From Irenaeus to Grotius*, 400-412.

on behalf of and in the name of the faithful. For John, the best form of govern-ment in church or state would include a representative assembly of the people.

John further delineated an approach to church property that steered between what he viewed as two extremes: that of denying any right of the church to own property or of granting the church unregulated control of any property claimed to be useful for spiritual ends. He distinguished between ownership and regulation, maintaining that a civil ruler must respect private property but also may regulate it for the public good.

Outcomes from the Confrontation

The entire dispute arose in large part because Boniface could not accept development of a French state that assumed a measure of autonomy from the papacy for the temporal realm. This development, when coupled with the col-lapse of papal claims to sovereignty even in temporal matters, forced scholars to rethink the nature of church-and-state relations. The general and vague assertions of the Gelasian formula would have to be more precisely defined and established. And so what became open for debate and scrutiny was the nature and extent not only of secular authority but religious authority as well. In a real sense the questions that erupted into the Protestant Reformation of the sixteenth century first began to be posed in the dispute between Boniface and Philip.

In his history of political theory, George Sabine suggests that the contro-versy between Boniface and Philip was important for several reasons.[25] First, it occasioned the boldest expression of papal claims to power, both absolute within the church and trumping all secular authority in the realm of temporal politics. In the work of Giles of Rome as well as the papal bull *Unam sanctam*, the Gelasian formula was cast aside, and the case was made for a union of the two powers in the person of the pope.

Second, such claims provoked important rejoinders challenging the papal claims. Theorists such as John of Paris made the case that spiritual authority did not extend into the distinct realm of temporal matters and that secular authority was independent of ecclesiastical rulers. Papal authority, however it played out in the life of the church, did not extend beyond matters of religion and morality. The legacy of this school of thought was dualism in authority and constitutionalism in its exercise.

Yet another group of theorists developed the line of argument concerning constitutional authority within the church, providing a third reason for the importance of the controversy. The movement known as conciliarism chal-

---

25. Sabine, *History of Political Theory*, 268.

lenged the idea of any sovereign ruler, including the pope, exercising authority that claimed divine foundation and, therefore, unquestionable exercise of power. The conciliarists, perhaps best represented by the theologians Jean Gerson (d. 1429) and Nicholas of Cusa (d. 1464), argued for the necessity of representation and consent in the exercise of church authority.

The nub of the argument between the conciliarists and their opponents was whether the pope should reign absolutely even within the church or was he bound to rule in concert with church councils, which were broadly representative not only of clergy but of laity as well, including women. Many of the conciliarists were members of religious communities that functioned with democratic processes, or church reformers who were upset with a clerical hierarchy that resisted efforts at ecclesial renewal.

The conciliarist movement failed in its aim of changing church governance. Indeed, it inspired a counterattack within the church that enshrined many of the claims to absolute papal authority that defined medieval institutions and practice. Important for purposes of this study, however, is that much of the conciliarist debate about papal power would eventually shift to the realm of secular power. The ecclesiastical debate about papal authority and power would be replayed in debates about the divine right of kings. Opponents to royal supremacy believed in a model of free cooperation of powers throughout the society rather than the centralizing tendency of models that saw all authority descending from a single supreme ruler.

The conciliarists wrote at a time when the papacy was undergoing what has been called its "Babylonian Captivity," a period when it was seen as being incapable of independent action. The result was a significant decline in the cogency of the papal claim to universal authority and a corresponding upturn in the strength of monarchical nationalism.

THE AVIGNON PAPACY

Pope Clement V, the pope who took office in 1305, just two years after Boniface VIII, moved the papal court from Rome to Avignon in southern France. Beginning with Clement and in the ensuing decades, the next six popes were all of French descent. This occasioned much criticism that the French monarch had undue influence over papal activity. It was also a period in which the papal court began to ape the manners of the French court, leaving itself open to charges of luxury and excess regarding the lifestyles of popes, cardinals, and other ecclesiastical officials.

One of the Avignon popes, John XXII, intervened in the 1323 election of the emperor Louis of Bavaria. The resulting controversy went on for more than twenty years, involving not only John but also his successor. In the end, the papal insistence that it was the overseer and arbiter of imperial elections was rejected. A vital factor was that, even among those who were devout, there was considerable suspicion about the papacy's reliance on the French king. In addition, there was a measure of nationalism among the German nobility that led to resentment over any outside interference in the election of the emperor.

When the papacy pressed its side of the dispute, relying on arguments that were similar to those of Giles of Rome, important new voices were heard critical of the papal position. One such voice was the Franciscan, William of Occam, an Englishman. Unsurprisingly, as a member of a religious order that upheld the centrality of voluntary poverty as the path to Christian discipleship, William was critical of the Avignon papacy and its governance of the church. More to the point, he was also a critic of papal claims in the realm of politics.

Standing squarely within the Christian tradition as summarized by Gelasius, William emphasized the distinction and independence of the temporal and spiritual realms. Like Gelasius, he was not precise in his delineation of the scope of the respective powers; but William was certain that in the case of John XXII the papacy had strayed far beyond the proper bounds of distinction between temporal and spiritual matters. For William, the idea that the emperor derived his authority from the pope and that papal coronation was essential to the legitimacy of imperial authority was wrong.

Marsilius of Padua (d. ca. 1343)

A more radical voice than William's was that of Marsilius of Padua, a physician, philosopher, and former rector of the University of Paris. His interest in the dispute between John and Louis was not primarily to defend the imperial position but to demolish any papal claim to sovereignty over the temporal realm. It is in the writing of Marsilius that one can find the clearest statement of the argument that the temporal realm was to be independent of any spiritual authority.

Like Thomas Aquinas, Marsilius was Aristotelian in his political theory. Unlike Aquinas, Marsilius adopted a thoroughly naturalistic reading of Aristotle, excluding Christian revelation from any influence on his philosophical reasoning. Faith's claims may well be true, but they are not demonstrable by reason and have no place in philosophy. For Marsilius, theology contributed nothing to rational knowledge.

In his greatest work, *Defensor pacis* (The Defender of Peace), Marsilius focused on the topic of the church's relationship to temporal governance, an issue that did not engage Thomas's detailed attention. Marsilius's goal was to challenge the church's assertion of temporal power. He followed Aristotle in viewing the state as a living organism composed of several parts, each of which must do its part for the proper functioning of the whole. When that is done the result is peace. Strife is introduced when one part fails to satisfy its responsibilities or hinders another part from fulfilling its duties. For Marsilius, the papacy was the great cause of strife in political life.

In accord with Aristotle, the state is understood as a perfect society, not in the sense that it is without flaw, but in the sense that it has within itself the means necessary to attain its end or purpose. The purpose of a state is attainment of the common good so that its members can live their lives in a manner that is humanly fulfilling. Marsilius does not deny that there is a supernatural goal that will ultimately fulfill persons, but he treats that as a matter of faith and of no significance for the state. The state's job is to secure the peace by regulating and guiding all social actors in their respective tasks that build up the temporal common good. The fact that these means and ends are natural, or this-worldly, does not make them less than worthwhile. Marsilius, like Aquinas, rejected a "political Augustinianism" that demeaned natural goods.

Marsilius sees the work of the clergy as satisfying supernatural duties—preaching and teaching the truths that lead to salvation. Such duties are matters of faith and therefore beyond the concerns of political reasoning focused on attaining the common good. He can, thereby, affirm the value of Christianity and even of a clerical class, yet this acknowledgment does not affect his politics. The clergy are subject to the authority and laws of the state in the same way as any other group. Granted, there are matters of faith over which the clergy preside, but in temporal matters no church official is exempt from the authority of the state's ruler(s). Here in Marsilius's writing one finds the most secular view of all medieval political theorists.

The End of Medieval Political Theory

Marsilius died before the Avignon papacy came to a close amidst the chaos that ensued from multiple claimants to the papacy. This debacle, known as the Western Schism, is also called the Papal Schism. By any title it was a sad chapter in the history of the papacy and added to the skepticism surrounding the authority of the papal office. The rising tide of nationalism in political life raised further doubts that fourteenth- and fifteenth-century Europeans had about papal assertions of universal authority. And the failure of the conciliar movement to bring about reform in the exercise of church authority was yet another factor contributing to the dissatisfaction of many with church governance.

Marsilius's writing touched on an array of topics—the centrality of the New Testament, canon law, the role of church councils, forgiveness of sin and the sacrament of penance—that were ecclesiastical in nature and extraneous to his political theory. His views on these matters demonstrated his skepticism about clerical rank and ecclesiastical authority, and reflected a bias toward religion as an interior experience over institutional organization and expression. One finds in Marsilius a range of themes and ideas that would be picked up and refined in Protestant reformers of the sixteenth century. But in the fourteenth century it is Marsilius who stands as an early voice pointing toward the secularization of politics and the end of medieval assumptions about the political order. Indeed, he can be seen as a precursor to the figure who embodied a dramatic and new vision of political life. For if Marsilius sought to restrict Christianity to a nonpolitical role, it was Niccolò Machiavelli who would argue for a change from theologically based norms to a secular foundation for politics.

THE MEDIEVAL HERITAGE

In order to understand modern models of government it is important to have a sense of the interaction of church and state in the medieval era. Throughout a series of disputes and arguments, kings and popes jockeyed for the upper hand in their relationship. It is not surprising, given the long history of sacral kingship in many cultures, that the roles of ruler of the state and that of high priest of the people's religion would be merged in the imagination of individuals.

Seeking supreme authority in both temporal and spiritual affairs is a common pursuit in human history. What makes the Western medieval era so significant is that there were always at least two claimants to the role of theocratic monarch and that neither one ever successfully eliminated the other. Thus, dualism persisted and eventually was translated into the theories of later political thinkers.

The dualism of two competing sources of authority also profoundly influenced the development of constitutionalism in Western politics. The ongoing competition between pope and king created space for individuals to experience choices about values, principles, and loyalties. At the level of theory, it forced scholars to formulate and refine arguments about the limits of papal and royal power.

The simple fact was that no king or pope could rule without the support and cooperation of others. The nobility or aristocracy, abbots and bishops, merchants and traders in the rising towns and city-states all had some power to hinder or frustrate the ambitions of popes and emperors. It was in this context that the conciliarists sought to implement reforms that would institutionalize the need for collegiality and consensus within the church. That effort failed; but in secular politics the various early attempts at parliaments and aristocratic councils reflect the medieval experience of competing levels of authority that sought limits on unilateral rulers.

With the rise of national monarchs the argument concerning secular authority was to enter a new phase as the medieval era ended, but the issue of papal power within the church had already been settled, or so it was thought. Yet the greatest challenge to papal power was not to come from secular rulers or political theories; rather, it was the test that was posed by the corruption of the papal office in the fourteenth century and the theological dispute set off by the Protestant reformers of the sixteenth century.

QUESTIONS FOR REFLECTION/DISCUSSION

1. What factors led to the papacy emerging as a temporal as well as a spiritual power?
2. What were the implications of the idea of *rex dei gratia* ("king by the grace of God")?
3. What were the circumstances that provided the context for the development of the practice of prince-bishops?
4. Can you summarize the central dispute that led to the Investiture Controversy? In your opinion did the pope or the emperor have the stronger case?
5. What were the outcomes of the controversy?
6. Why did Aquinas's appropriation of Aristotle lead to a different assessment of political authority than that of Augustine?
7. How did the rise of a sense of nationalism transform the dispute between Philip and Boniface?
8. What were the main features of the theories of John of Paris and Marsilius of Padua about temporal power? About papal power?

6

The Age of Reform

The papacy that survived the medieval era was one that had endured serious declines in moral authority and political respect. The papacy had to scale back its ambitions from the days of Innocent III or Boniface VIII and so gave more attention to shoring up its temporal power in central Italy than to making universal claims of authority throughout the continent.

The popes of the second half of the fifteenth century and early sixteenth century may have been largely unimpressive as religious leaders, but they were impressively successful as political ones. During this time period the area we think of as Italy was divided into five independent states: the kingdom of Naples in the south, the duchy of Milan in the northwest, the republics of Venice in the northeast, and Florence, along with the Papal State, in the center. Of the five, the Papal State was the most unified and stable, a remarkable achievement after the disarray of the Avignon years.

Today the best-known political theorist from the early sixteenth century is Niccolò Machiavelli (d. 1527). He was convinced that the papacy was a significant political problem. Machiavelli longed to see a unified Italy taking its place among the emerging European powers. He viewed the church in Rome as the major obstacle to a unified Italian nation-state; the papacy was too weak to unify the Italian people but strong enough to prevent another ruler from achieving that goal. For Machiavelli this sorry situation was exacerbated by the papacy's tendency to engage in an array of foreign alliances that over the course of centuries had prompted numerous interventions by outsiders in Italian politics.[1]

Machiavelli was a diplomat for the Florentine republic who had been forced into retirement by a change in government. The two major works for which he is remembered, *The Prince* and *Discourses on the First Ten Books of Titus Livius*, were written during this period of reflection and political isolation. Evident throughout these writings is a new voice; there is a lack of interest in ecclesiastical affairs and even in the role of the deity in political matters. The medieval idea of Christendom is not so much refuted as ignored, and the ancient past

---

1. George Sabine, *A History of Political Theory*, 4th ed. revised by Thomas Thorson (Hinsdale, IL: Dryden Press, 1973), 315–17.

that is mined for wisdom is not the biblical world but that of pagan Rome. The focus of concern is neither church nor revelation nor God but human beings and their worldly goals.

The Prince is blunt in its defense of power and conquest and straightforward in its argument that a ruler must be willing to break the customary norms of morality. Yet the *Discourses* reveals a Machiavelli less indifferent to questions of justice and the common good. One point of consistency, however, is that Christianity is portrayed as insufficient as a basis for political life. Machiavelli frequently appeals to pagan Rome's military ethos as an alternative to Christianity's morality of service and self-sacrifice. He is skeptical about much of Christian revelation and sees religion's role largely in utilitarian terms.

Because of his disillusionment with the papacy and the institutional church Machiavelli developed a truly secular political theory. Yet, there were others, also fed up with Rome, who were not at all secular in their interests. Because of his preoccupation with the Italian context, Machiavelli had no awareness of the coming controversy in northern Europe that would unite Christianity and politics in a drama of substantial social upheaval and violence. Machiavelli's vision of a basically secular politics would play out in the long run, but it was a profound misreading of the spirit of his own time.

RELIGIOUS AND POLITICAL CHANGE

Throughout the period traced in the preceding chapter secular rulers—emperors or kings—learned to interact with a church in the West that was essentially united through its allegiance to the bishop of Rome. On the other hand, the church had to adapt to a variety of secular rulers, including periods when the church itself was the strongest temporal power and provided the most viable institutions of governance and order. Constantine, Charlemagne, Frankish kings, Holy Roman Emperors, national monarchs—all sorts of rulers and modes of rule had come and gone, but the bishop of Rome remained the centerpiece of the Christian church.

In the sixteenth century that reality was to undergo dramatic and permanent transformation through the great movement of reform associated with Martin Luther. In this chapter we will examine some political ideas of Luther and other religious reformers as well as the overall political significance of the Protestant Reformation and the Catholic reaction. The aim of this chapter is not to convey the broad impact of the emergence of Protestantism within the Christian tradition but merely to highlight how certain leaders and events of the Protestant Reformation affected the relationship of Christianity to the political order.

When Martin Luther, then an Augustinian priest, formulated his ninety-five theses in Wittenburg in 1517 his aim was to foster reform of church practice on a number of discrete religious practices. Chief among these was the practice of granting indulgences for monetary contributions and the popular understanding of penance and conversion that formed the background for indulgences. Soon the dispute escalated far beyond this initial protest, and by the time the church set its course for serious reform the broken unity of Western Christianity was beyond repair. Theological and ecclesiastical disputes were accompanied by political and military conflicts that marked the sixteenth century as a period of grand social upheaval.

The two key issues that bedeviled the medieval experience of Christianity and politics was the interference of religious clerics in matters of secular politics and the meddling of secular leaders in matters of church life. Neither of these issues would be resolved immediately by the Protestant Reformation or the eventual Catholic reaction. In truth, the reformers could not make any advance on these issues because they were drawn deeply into the political conflicts of the time since the fate of reform in the Christian church became more dependent than ever on the political fortunes of various supportive secular leaders.

Despite the divisions within Christianity that erupted in the 1500s, one thing that continued to be held in common by European leaders was the assumption that unity in religion was necessary for social order and that such unity in faith was possible to achieve. From neither the Protestant nor the Catholic side was there much support for toleration of religious pluralism. Instead, those spiritual and temporal leaders engaged in the religious controversies of the sixteenth century were convinced that government should uphold religious truth and that unity in matters religious was vital to societal well-being. Because the bishop of Rome's authority to resolve doctrinal and moral disagreements was precisely one of the items in dispute, there was a vacuum in decision making. It should not be a surprise that secular rulers stepped into the vacated space, sometimes acting in good faith and in other cases for the sake of self-aggrandizement. Hence, one upshot of the Protestant reform, as we shall see, was growth in the power of national monarchs who might serve as rallying points for social unity.

This growing importance of national monarchs did not come without concerns. One problem that arose was what to do when a secular ruler embraced a particular expression of Christian faith not shared by some segment of the population. Holding the "wrong" faith, that is, a faith different from that of the monarch, might bring about persecution or second-class status for the nonconformists. Despite it being a matter of sincere conviction, adherence to a different creed could be interpreted as a political protest or statement of opposition to the ruler.

Although a Catholic believer subject to a Catholic king might be a strong supporter of monarchy, a Catholic believer subject to a Protestant king might have a different view of monarchy. Consequently, a new question moved to the center of political debate: could an individual resist a king who did not hold the true faith? In the medieval period the conciliarists and other church reformers argued that a pope who was guilty of heresy could be resisted. Now in the sixteenth century the question became, could one resist a heretical king?

Recall that the idea of political obedience as a virtue was deeply entrenched in the Christian tradition. St. Paul in the thirteenth chapter of his letter to the Romans was widely cited throughout patristic and medieval literature. During the early centuries, even prior to Constantine, a standard defense of the Christian faith against its critics had been that Christians were loyal and obedient citizens of the Roman Empire. From the fourth century on, support for the emperor and empire was widely encouraged by Christian writers and preachers. With the breakdown of Christian unity a new situation had arisen, and the settled question of the obligation of political obedience now had to be revisited.

There was another question standing behind the question of political obedience: what gave legitimacy to the rule of monarchs in the first place? Supporters of obedience as an absolute obligation could appeal to a theory of the divine right of kings, political authority derived directly from God. Opponents of absolute obedience and supporters of a right of resistance to a king based their response on the theory that the authority of kings was derived from God indirectly, as it is mediated through the people. That is, God gave to human beings the authority to govern themselves, and the people then vested a monarch with the right to rule. Should a king rule in a manner against the best interests of the people, thereby violating God's purpose in granting political authority to others, then the people had the right to seek a change in rule.

The issues were not new, but the context in which they were being discussed was novel. The movements for church reform that swept across Europe in the sixteenth century had markedly altered the unity of Christendom. The impetus for religious change became closely connected to new debates in the realm of politics. Depending on place and time, a Catholic might be a rabid defender of a king or support deposing a monarch. The same could be said for the other families of Christian belief. Amidst the dramatic changes, the person identified as the protagonist was a German theologian whose remarkable life brought on revolutionary transformations, both intended and unintended.

MARTIN LUTHER (D. 1546)

Luther's ninety-five theses attacked the entire framework of indulgences that was accepted by most people at the time. An indulgence is a favor whereby the punishment due to a sinner is lessened or removed completely. It is closely linked to the Catholic belief in purgatory as a place where those whose sins have been forgiven undergo the just punishment that is incurred as the result of earthly sins. An indulgence might lessen the amount of time to be spent in purgatory or exclude the need for purgatory at all before entering into life with God in heaven. The Catholic Church was using the promise of indulgences as a motivation for performance of good deeds, for example, giving alms to the poor, making a pilgrimage, or participating in a crusade. Another use was to encourage financial contributions to Rome to support a variety of papal projects.

Whatever the subtleties of the theology of indulgences, they were surely lost on most common folk as well as on many of the preachers promoting the practice. In Luther's view indulgences seemed to be little more than church-backed promises of divine favor in exchange for financial gifts. In his attack he scorned the extravagant claims concerning indulgences, including the power of the papacy to affect life in purgatory. Beyond the challenge to papal authority, Luther also challenged the underlying idea of God's grace and salvation. The debate he set off forced him to address his understanding of the sacrament of penance and the relationship of divine forgiveness to human activity and sacramental practice. The controversy helped Luther to sharpen his understanding of justification, grace, divine action, and human sinfulness. As his thinking developed and he engaged his critics it became evident that he was moving closer toward excommunication from the Roman Church.

On January 3, 1521, Luther was officially excommunicated. Because of the close links between church and state at the time, a judgment of excommunication had legal and political consequences. One result was that Frederick, Elector of Saxony, Luther's prince and protector, was now put in the position of harboring a heretic.[2] Rome pressed Emperor Charles V to force Frederick's hand. According to law Luther had a right to a hearing in Germany, and this was granted by Charles. In April at the Diet of Worms[3] he was called before the emperor and the assembly of clergy and nobility, who were largely hostile, to be examined. Following the hearing, at which Luther refused to recant his views, the emperor formally banned Luther from the realm. To protect him, Frederick arranged that he disappear and go into hiding in Wartburg castle.

For several years Luther's situation remained ambiguous even as he returned to public life. While the emperor was occupied with other matters the movements for reform, both ecclesial and social, inspired by Luther continued

---

2. The title of elector was given to those nobles from various regions who had a vote in the selection of the Holy Roman Emperor.

3. The Diet was a general assembly of representatives of the territories that constituted the Holy Roman Empire. It could be convened for a variety of reasons. Members might be from the secular nobility or holders of important ecclesiastical office. The city of Worms was the site of several meetings of the Imperial Diet.

to grow. Throughout the 1520s Luther entered into public debates with an extensive list of publications, sermons, and speeches. He was the most widely read author throughout the Germanic kingdom.

Eventually, support for Luther among the German nobility led to a break between the Protestant princes and the Catholic emperor with his supporters. The split resulted in a standoff that wound up forestalling any action by the emperor and which, in effect, permitted each prince to determine what religious practice would be permitted within his territory. Luther lived the remainder of his life under the protection of Lutheran nobles.

Theology and Politics

When assessing the writings of Martin Luther on questions of politics it must be remembered that he was foremost a religious leader and thinker. Like many previous authors in the Christian tradition, his intention was often pastoral, writing to address a particular situation. As such, it is not difficult to find in his corpus of writing various passages that do not agree with one another. Time and circumstances differed when he did his writing, and so did his conclusions. In short, on the topic of politics Luther was not a systematic thinker but more an occasional writer, often addressing even fundamental questions with a specific situation in mind.

His political convictions, while necessarily entailing certain practical observations and judgments, were largely shaped by, and remained consistent with, his theological beliefs. Three religious doctrines in particular demonstrate what might be called the indirect influence of Luther's theology on the politics of the time.[4]

Justification by Faith

Justification through faith taught that divine grace overcame a person's alienation from God, and this gave the Christian freedom from anxiety over how to earn or merit salvation. The "slavery" of doing good works or satisfying duties imposed by human authority was overcome. And justification by faith renders unnecessary a variety of ecclesiastical disciplines and duties imposed in order that believers might be deemed worthy of God's favors mediated through the church. Christians experienced the inner freedom of faith despite their external circumstances. People might be expected to live morally good lives, but this was in grateful response to God's grace, not a means of obtaining God's favor.

---

4. For this treatment of key Lutheran ideas I am indebted to J. M. Porter, "The Political Thought of Martin Luther," in *Luther: Selected Political Writings* (Philadelphia: Fortress, 1974), 1-21, esp. 4-7.

Priesthood of All Believers

The priesthood of all believers meant that each individual had the same direct experience of God's grace and love; there was no need for a special intermediary class to dispense divine grace through sacraments or other religious measures. In place of the Catholic emphasis on the role of clergy and the sacraments as mediators for a person's experience of God there was a new emphasis on the individual believer standing alone before God. Abolishing the distinction between a clerical class and the rest of society, since all believers constitute a true priesthood, refuted claims of clerical freedom from civil authority and laws.

Biblical Authority

The primacy of the Bible as an authority for Christians, the teaching on justification through faith, and the priesthood of all believers were the theological underpinning of Luther's political views. Brushing aside the authority of scholastic theology and philosophy, canon law, and ecclesial authority, Luther argued that the meaning of God's word was readily apparent to the believer and that no authoritative interpreter was needed to translate biblical teaching for Christian conscience. If all can interpret Scripture, then papal claims to be the definitive arbiter of the Bible's meaning is undermined. This, in turn, undercuts the assertion that religious authority trumps temporal authority.

According to Troeltsch, one outcome of these core beliefs was a rise in religious individualism, a sense of intimate communion with God that did not require a clerical hierarchy.[5] The political effect of these beliefs was to upend much of the medieval world's social order. In sum, the monarchical powers of the papacy were challenged, and the very notion of hierarchy in the church questioned. This, in turn, suggested that other hierarchies in society might be challengeable as well.

Other doctrines central to Luther's theology illustrate a more direct or intentional influence on the politics of his situation.

Human Sinfulness

Due to the influence of Augustine, Luther believed that sin must play a large role in political and social relationships. Luther was not a populist who esteemed the mass of people. His profound sense of human weakness and sin made him doubtful that the majority of people had the wisdom or virtue to make proper judgments about governance. Indeed, when discussing the need for government to restrain sinful humankind Luther used the metaphor of "a savage wild beast" that had to be "bound with chains and ropes so that it can-

---

5. Ernst Troeltsch, *The Social Teaching of the Christian Churches*, vol. 2 (Louisville: Westminster/John Knox Press, 1992), 470.

not bite and tear as it would normally do."[6] Luther had an instinctive aversion to social disorder, and he saw society as always at risk of collapsing into chaos.

Consequently, the office of temporal ruler was divinely sanctioned to establish domestic peace and quell potential anarchy. The function of the state was largely negative. It had the task of limiting public wrongdoing more than the positive role envisioned by theorists of the Aristotelian/Thomistic tradition. There is only a faint sense in Luther's writing that there can be a progressive transformation of the social order toward justice. Although true Christians may do much good in their public roles as heads of households, church ministers, and government officials, they are inevitably too small a minority to counter the sinfulness of the mass of humanity.

Freedom

Because the grace of salvation comes from God alone without any human relationship or action making it possible there is the experience of utter dependence on God and absolute freedom from any created authority. The paradox, however, is that "a Christian is a perfectly free lord of all, subject to none. A Christian is a perfectly dutiful servant to all, subject to all."[7] Because of one's faith in Christ a believer is free from temporal authority; because of one's obedience to Christ a believer willingly becomes a servant to all.[8]

This attitude of freedom and service in Luther pertains to how Christians should think of their role in the body politic. In Luther's thinking Christians were a minority of the population; even among the baptized the number of true Christians was small. It is important to distinguish, therefore, between Luther's ideas about how Christians would engage political life and his views on politics in the wider society.

No achievement in political life could be salvific in itself; there could be no hint of "works righteousness," of people earning their salvation. Yet political activity could be an illustration of "faith active in love," whereby Christians serve others in gratitude for the grace of God in their lives. Luther identified three "orders of creation" or webs of relationships that characterized family life, church ministry, and political governance. By faithful service to one's neighbor in these realms of life, Christians witnessed to God's graciousness and compassion. So for Christians the political realm can incarnate faith active in love.[9]

Christians, however, do not need the state for themselves. "If all the world

---

6. Martin Luther, "Temporal Authority: To What Extent It Should Be Obeyed," in *Luther: Selected Political Writings*, 51-69 at 56.

7. Martin Luther, "The Freedom of a Christian," in *Luther: Selected Political Writings*, 25-35 at 25.

8. John Shepherd, "The European Background of American Freedom," *Journal of Church and State* 50 (2008): 647-59 at 650.

9. Carter Lindberg, "Luther's Struggle with Social-Ethical Issues," in *The*

were composed of real Christians, that is, true believers, there would be no need for or benefits from prince, king, lord, sword, or law."[10] The state exists in order to restrain the wicked and protect the vulnerable from those who would prey upon them. Christians, therefore, can serve as magistrates and in other roles of governance for this is to provide a service of love to others: maintaining order, providing for rule of law, and avoiding exploitation of the poor. The freedom of the Christian is the freedom to serve the other.

Although Luther's freedom was spiritual, for Christians who had experienced the grace of Christ it did give rise to other ways of talking about freedom. These did not always meet with Luther's support. He was troubled by calls for political freedom because he was wary of equating Christian freedom with external or material conditions. Nonetheless, Luther's condemnations of the corruption of the Catholic hierarchy led others to ask why the corruption and violence of secular nobles was any less worthy of opposition. Luther might have drawn a clear distinction between spiritual oppression and material oppression, but the German peasantry was less willing to maintain the distinction.[11] Perhaps unwittingly, Luther's religious reformation opened a door for others seeking political, economic, and social reforms within the German territories.

Two Kingdoms

Since church and state were so interlaced in late Christendom, it was imperative that Luther present his understanding of the relationship between the church and civil government. Perhaps no aspect of Luther's theologically grounded politics is as well known as the two-kingdom theory, in which he "divided humanity into two kingdoms under two distinct governments."[12]

Non-Christians belong to the earthly kingdom and are bound by its laws. Christians do not require temporal authority or law in order to live rightly[13] but accept these realities for the sake of being of service and assistance to one's neighbors. Since true Christians are a minority and most humans are of a sinful and depraved character, temporal authority is needed to restrain evil and must use violence and coercion to rein in evildoers.

Cambridge Companion to Martin Luther, ed. Donald McKim (Cambridge: Cambridge University Press, 2003), 165-78 at 174.

10. Luther, "Temporal Authority," 54.

11. Shepherd, "The European Background," 651.

12. Scott Hendrix, "Luther," in *The Cambridge Companion to Reformation Theology*, ed. David Bagchi and David Steinmetz (Cambridge: Cambridge University Press, 2004), 39-56 at 49.

13. "[I]t is impossible that the temporal sword and law should find any work to do among Christians, since they do of their own accord much more than all laws and teachings can demand" (Luther, "Temporal Authority," 54).

Closer to the pessimism of Hobbes than the optimism of Aquinas, Luther was inclined to see human beings after the Fall as selfish, violent, and prideful. Order must be imposed, and it is the task of political authority to do so. This is the way things are in the earthly kingdom; it is governed not by the Word of God but by the ruler's sword. Christians respect that necessity and willingly obey temporal authority for the sake of order in society, an order that protects people from the most violent and least scrupulous. For that reason Christians may hold public office to maintain and enforce social norms as well as to serve as soldiers to protect society from outside aggression.

The obligation to obey the ruler is near absolute for Luther, since the state is, according to Romans 13 and other biblical passages, divinely willed to bring a measure of order from what would otherwise be chaos. Even if the ruler is unjust, the subject must obey. There are two important caveats to that rule. First, the subject ought not obey a ruler in matters that violate true religion. Even in such a case, however, the recommended response is noncompliance rather than resistance. Second, in the case of a prince who engages in a war that is known to be wrong, one can refuse to participate rather than do harm to another and compound the wrongdoing of one's prince. Employing these two caveats in the treatise "Dr. Martin Luther's Warning to His Dear German People," he provided a justification for the Protestant princes to refuse to capitulate to the emperor's demand that they return to unity with Rome. He also maintained that the princes might resist any unjust act of aggression should the emperor try to force his will on them.[14]

Because of the distinction between the inner and outer person, political rulers are accorded wide authority in worldly matters, for these do not affect the inner individual. Religious leaders should encourage rulers to be fair, just, and peaceful, but there are no effective restraints on temporal rulers such as the medieval church employed to check a ruler's power. Indeed, temporal rulers have more power over the church than vice versa.

Belief in the priesthood of all believers led to an ecclesiastical polity that emphasized the consent of the faithful rather than a church hierarchy as the means of governance. However, Luther became troubled by the pluralism that began to develop, and his solution was to invite the Elector of Saxony, his most important protector, to examine the situation and make suggestions for order and discipline. The government also had the right, according to Luther, to expel from the realm anyone who upset the civil order by espousing dissident religious views. In sum, the temporal ruler was given a special role in maintaining the unity of the visible, institutional church. In this way Luther's

---

14. "Dr. Martin Luther's Warning to His Dear German People," in *Luther: Selected Political Writings*, 133-48.

approach foreshadowed the eventual practice of *cuius regio, eius religio*.[15] As noted earlier, that was the practical outcome of the standoff between the Protestant princes and the Catholic emperor.

The Peasant Wars

A series of uprisings by peasants, mainly in southern Germany, over their economic plight and lack of political power became an occasion for several important essays by Luther. Beginning in 1525 his initial statement, the "Admonition to Peace," expressed sympathy for the peasant's suffering but warned all parties concerned about the risks of violence.

A complicating factor that was to figure significantly in Luther's position was the role played by Andrew Karlstadt and Thomas Münzer. Both men were religious reformers of a more radical bent who incited violence by promoting their conviction that the kingdom of God was allied with efforts to overcome certain political, economic, and social complaints of the peasants. Rebellion became identified with the establishment of God's kingdom. To Luther this smacked of works righteousness that denied the absolute gratuity and mercy of God in granting the gift of faith and experience of salvation in Christ.

In response Luther insisted that the political activity of humans cannot bring about God's salvation and emphasized the distinction between the kingdom of God and any temporal kingdom. Because the freedom of the Christian was spiritual and internal it was not to be identified with political freedom. The same could be said with the spiritual equality of Christians and societal equality. Peasants, even slaves, could enjoy Christian freedom and equality without any disruption of the existing political and economic orders.

The publication of the "Admonition" came too late to stop the rebellion, and a second essay, "Against the Robbing and Murdering Hordes of Peasants," was then published. The tone of this work was far harsher and one-sidedly judgmental about the crisis. Luther accused the peasants of three sins: violating their oath of obedience to legitimate authority, initiating rebellion that introduced the evil of warfare, and blaspheming God by presuming to act in the name of the Christian gospel. He then called on the rest of society to do whatever was necessary to kill the rebels.

In fairness to Luther, the essay was meant as an attack on those peasants who were "robbing and murdering." It was not intended to be a fully adequate treatment of the peasants' cause. That point was lost on most people, how-

---

15. Translated literally from the Latin it is, "whose region, his religion." Paraphrased for the sake of clearer understanding, it means, "the religion of the prince is the religion of the people."

ever, and Luther was criticized not only by his enemies but by many support-ers. When the peasants were brutally crushed by the vastly superior military strength of the nobility, it only added to the sense that Luther had sided with the powerful against the needy.

Finally, a third essay, "An Open Letter on the Harsh Book against the Peas-ants," contained Luther's rebuttal to the criticism. He was unrepentant about his views and argued that his polemic was dictated by his theological convic-tions. To a great extent, this was correct. The end result, however, was that the Lutheran reform never advanced in southern Germany the way that it did in the north.

Luther's Political Legacy

Without question, Luther recovered important theological insights that had been slighted over the development of the Christian tradition. His personal courage and integrity are also beyond question. At the Diet of Worms, before the emperor and an assembly of clergy and nobility, on April 18, 1521, he refused to recant and spoke his famous words: "Here I stand. I can do no other. God help me. Amen." It was a historical moment that Luther in all likelihood would have understood as obedience to Christ and the Word of God but which subsequent generations have viewed as a great testimony to the freedom and dignity of conscience.

When considering the legacy of Luther for politics there are several points to note. First, there is Luther's appreciation for the role of power in politi-cal life. The political scientist J. M. Porter suggests that Luther is in a line of thinkers like Machiavelli, Jean Bodin (d. 1596), and Thomas Hobbes (d. 1679). They were precursors to modern political theorists in the under-standing and justification of power for securing order and peace.[16] This is a dif-ferent approach than what we have seen in patristic and medieval authors. As a consequence of the two-kingdom theory, Luther stressed that the rationale for the state was its ability to secure civil order and avoid chaos rather than its relationship to the kingdom of God. And at the same time, Luther marked a limit to state power by his witness and teaching regarding the sacredness of conscience and the inner spiritual freedom of the individual. In his apology for resistance to the emperor he made the case that imperial law acknowledged a right of resistance and that the resistance was not rebellion but self-defense against imperial aggression.[17]

---

16. Porter, "The Political Thought of Luther," 18.

17. David Whitford, "Luther's Political Encounters," in *Cambridge Companion to Luther*, 179-91 at 188.

For all his vigor in asserting the freedom and equality of Christians in the spiritual realm, Luther was not a great advocate of freedom and equality in the temporal realm. The priesthood of believers might suggest support for widespread participation in a decision-making process aimed at consensus, but this was only in church affairs. Luther's writing on the rebellion of the peasants was shaped, in part, by his acceptance of dramatic social inequalities as natural and necessary. He was a defender of the privileges of rank and nobility in political and economic matters.

Theologically, Luther's emphasis on the interior experience of God's justifying grace led to a lessened emphasis on the significance of political institutions; and, additionally, as a religious reformer his interest in temporal politics was understandably secondary. It is ironic, therefore, that he wound up promoting the authority of the state in religious matters. Not content to make a personal statement of disagreement with Rome, Luther sought to lead a movement for reform. When he was not successful in persuading the bishop of Rome to bring about church reform, Luther looked to temporal leadership for assistance in bringing about the changes in church life that he advocated. That led to Germany first, and then other places, becoming a battleground (in words and actions) between defenders and opponents of the reforms.

As an opponent of papal authority Luther had to face the issue of how to resolve disagreements within the life of the institutional church. In the end he turned to temporal leadership to exercise authority in a way that drew Lutheranism into a semidependent relationship with the state. Coupled with the deference he showed to temporal authority in matters beyond religion, the independence, power, and prestige of political leaders vis-à-vis the church grew considerably.

Along with the diminution of papal and episcopal authority, the seizure of monastic establishments and privileges, and the diminished role for courts of canon law, all conspired to weaken restraints that the medieval church had been able to employ against temporal rulers. Consequently, despite Luther's sincere desire to bring about a reformed church, most of the Lutheran churches in northern Europe evolved into state churches. The Lutheran break with Rome may have been total, but the alliance with secular rulers became more intimate.

JOHN CALVIN (D. 1564)

John Calvin was a generation behind Luther, and the movement toward reform had already spread beyond Luther's influence by the time Calvin was in his university studies. A native of France who studied classics and theology at Paris and law at Orleans, Calvin possessed a precise and logical mind.

He wrote in a lucid style with clear organization of his material. This partly accounts for his wide influence, as he was a thinker who made himself accessible to readers who were not as well educated as he was.

In 1536 Calvin traveled to Geneva, a place of refuge for French Protestants. Independent city-states such as Berne, Geneva, and Zurich were leading centers of what we have come to think of as the reformed tradition of Protestantism. Figures such as Ulrich Zwingli in German-speaking Switzerland, along with Theodore Bucer and William Farel in French-speaking Switzerland, believed that Luther had not gone far enough in his reforms. This was especially true in the areas of ecclesiology and worship, where leaders of the reformed tradition were committed only to those practices that had direct New Testament support.

Calvin was invited to stay in Geneva, and, except for three years of exile from 1538 to 1541, he did so until his death. Although some popular histories portrayed him as a virtual dictator of the city-state, that is far from the truth. Calvin did involve himself in the city's governance, civil and ecclesiastical, but he neither sought absolute control nor was he given it.

Authority was an issue of concern for Calvin. Luther had successfully overcome the dominant authority of the papacy within Christianity. However, when disagreements broke out, among even those allied with him, Luther found himself appealing to civil authorities for help in resolving disputes. To Calvin's way of thinking what was needed was to reestablish the authority of the ministry in accord with New Testament evidence. This meant he sought greater independence from civil authority and more authority for Christian ministers acting in God's name.

In Calvin's plan, written up in his *Ecclesiastical Ordinances*, the pastors as a body were in charge of appointing their fellow pastors. The city council, made up of elected civil leaders, had a right of veto over a proposed pastor. The pastors, who were to meet weekly for study and reflection, chose the teachers, though the council again claimed the power to ratify or reject names.

Besides the pastors, the other key ecclesiastical group was the elders. These individuals were appointed by the city council upon consultation with the pastors. The elders had a disciplinary role and met regularly with the pastors in a consistory, at which time all issues of order within the church were examined. The consistory could impose discipline on those not attending church, those living scandalous lifestyles, and those holding heretical views. In some cases, such as banishment or exile, the consistory would inform the chief civil magistrate who would enforce the discipline.

Throughout his lifetime Calvin never was able to implement the *Ordinances* exactly as he wished. The Geneva city council was reluctant to give too much authority to Calvin or other pastors, one indication being that the consistory was presided over by a civil magistrate from the council. Nonetheless, the consistory was quite persistent in its work and very exacting in its attention to the behavior of Genevans.

Much of the moralism that marked Geneva in Calvin's time, along with the charge that it was a theocratic regime, was due to fuzziness in drawing a line of distinction between church and state. Calvin himself proposed ideas on secular topics such as public sanitation or the defense of the city. The consistory, composed of pastors and church elders, also offered proposals on banking, trade, and the court system. From the other side, the city council examined the length of sermons, controlled publication of theological works, and corrected pastors who neglected obligations such as visiting the sick. In sum, church figures engaged issues that were outside their jurisdiction, and civic officials meddled in matters that ought to have been considered beyond their authority. There was also the fact that some individuals sat on both the consistory and the council and might not always be clear about which hat they were wearing at a given moment.[18]

Precisely because the lines of jurisdiction were blurry, a talented individual in either the council or consistory might exercise indirect power in areas that extended beyond the person's office. Calvin, being a man of great self-confidence, strong personal character, and possessing a sharp intellect along with a forceful personality, exercised authority in Geneva that exceeded his official role. It is also why Calvin encountered opposition that effectively blocked full implementation of his program; his authority was more personal and moral than legally or politically official. Without question, Geneva was a place where the Reformed Church held great sway over public life; yet Calvin was no dictator, nor was the church in direct control of government. Still, in most matters, there was a practical unity of spiritual and temporal authority that approximated a form of theocratic governance.

Theology and Politics

If Luther's thought was guided by the great themes of justification by faith and the priesthood of all believers, the direction of Calvin's theology was determined by his belief in the sovereignty of God and the lordship of Jesus. No part of creation was immune from God's absolute rule, and disciples following Jesus could carve out no realms of life that were not subject to Christ.

Calvin believed God's providence guided all worldly existence and that this providence was not to be understood as some vague, general oversight of the laws of creation. Rather, God was intimately involved in the details of each

---

18. Owen Chadwick, *The Reformation* (Grand Rapids, MI: Eerdmans, 1964), 86-87.

creature's life. What might appear as fate or happenstance to an unbeliever was the unacknowledged guidance of the divine will directing each event. Thus, God was to be praised in the moments that brought good fortune to a person, and an individual was to repent for ill fortune since this was divine chastisement.

Among those things that God directed was the course of salvation. The question of whether one was saved could not be treated as an open one, as if God had not already determined each person's fate. To suggest otherwise would be to propose that God was not sovereign over the most important aspect of existence. Many theologians prior to Calvin wrestled with the issue of how God's all-powerful will was to be understood in relation to human freedom and responsibility when discussing human salvation. Was one's ultimate end determined by God, regardless of anything that a person did? Although others had considered the question, no one put it in such bold relief as did Calvin, with his emphasis on God's sovereignty and divine providence directing all human experience.

Calvin was forthright in his teaching. God did not will to save all, only those who have been divinely elected. There can be no complaint that God is unfair in this since no one deserves to be saved; all humans are sinners and deserve condemnation. Christ came to suffer and die in order that some might be saved, not through their own merit but due to the mercy of God who has chosen to give eternal life to the elect. Why Christ came for some and not all is nothing that humans can understand; God's justice is beyond human comprehension.

For Calvin, the doctrine of election was the great consolation in the face of a potentially fearsome teaching about predestination. It transformed the language of predestination into a way of expressing the assurance that believers feel in the security of God's gracious gift of grace. Christians, therefore, might be reassured of their salvation by certain experience of God's favor.

For Calvin and his followers the doctrine of election was not a teaching that encouraged smugness, laziness, or presumption about the promise of salvation. Quite the opposite, true Christians would be disciplined, faithful, hardworking, and modest in their use of material goods as an expression of gratitude to God. Thus, did the popular image of Calvinists become one of austere, sober, earnest people who would endure significant hardships with a quiet confidence that God stood with them in their sacrifices on behalf of the faith.

Nature and Form of Government

As we have seen, Luther inclined to a view of temporal government as largely negative; it existed primarily to restrain sinners from creating societal chaos. Calvin, however, for all his criticism of Catholic ecclesiology, spirituality, and liturgy, was closer to the Thomistic view derived from Aristotle. The emphasis was on human beings as essentially social and created for community. The natural law, despite the reality of sin, still meant that human reason might know something of God's purposes for creation. Such reason demonstrated the necessity and nature of civil government.

As a resident of Geneva, Calvin experienced a polity that brought faith and politics together. In his approach to the two kingdoms he emphasized mutual cooperation rather than the sharper distinction of Luther's two kingdoms. The state may have to play a role in restraining people from acting on sinful tendencies, but more so it was meant to be an institution that enabled people to live together in relative peace with a measure of justice and security. The state can even assist the work of the church by protecting true religion and guaranteeing freedom for church ministers to continue their activities. Although the state should not try to be the church it could and should protect the church as the latter carried out its ministry.

For Calvin, the realm of politics was a sphere of life, like any other, subject to God's sovereignty. To be engaged in politics was not to take up work that was tolerated as a necessary evil. Instead, Calvin, although he held to a distinction between the spiritual and temporal orders, considered civil government to be noble work for Christians. Further, he considered the role of the magistrates to be a sacred calling more honorable than other worldly vocations.[19]

Given his positive assessment of the nature of the state, it is no surprise that Calvin followed the long tradition of affirming the divine authorization of the state. Christians were to support civil rulers, assisting them in the proper functioning of government. Like so many before him, Calvin taught that Christians had a duty to obey civil authority. Yet, Calvin opposed absolute monarchy, be it that of pope or king. Absolutism was an affront to the sovereignty of God and the lordship of Christ. He did not endorse the notion of a national church, for a temporal ruler could never lead the church.

Calvin thought that any government must respect the moral law and that it served as the foundation for civil law, but he did not develop the relationship between the moral and civil laws at length. Instead, he maintained that a good government would need to work out the practicalities of the relationship according to circumstances of time and place. Calvin thought that the form of government was not specified by Christian revelation. He did, however, have an antipathy toward hereditary monarchy due to the likelihood that such an arrangement would create social hierarchies that led to arrogance and disdain for the common people.[20]

Geneva and other Swiss city-states were locales where elements of demo-

---

19. Much of Calvin's viewpoint on the political order is presented in "On Civil Government." See book IV, chapter 20 of the *Institutes of the Christian Religion*.

20. William Stevenson, Jr., "Calvin and Political Issues," in *The Cambridge*

cratic governance had been established, and Calvin favored a form of government that contained aspects of both democracy and aristocracy. In "On Civil Government," he advised, "the vice or imperfection of men therefore renders it safer and more tolerable for the government to be in the hands of many." There was the positive reason that broad participation in governance encouraged "mutual assistance." But the involvement of the many also assured "that if anyone arrogate to himself more than is right, the many may act as censors and masters to restrain his ambition."[21]

Resistance to Authority

Of course, rulers were expected to govern in a just manner. If they did not, divine punishment was certain. While awaiting final judgment, however, did the Christian citizen have any recourse against an unjust ruler? Calvin held the standard view that Christians had a duty of obedience to proper political authorities. This was directly related to his doctrine of providence, for government was a sign of God's ongoing care for creation, establishing security, peace, and justice in what otherwise would be social chaos. To rebel against government was to mistrust the providential care of God, who was the founder of civil government.

Along with Luther and many others, Calvin insisted on the distinction between the office and the officeholder. A given ruler might be less than just, but the duty of obedience was not founded on the virtue of the ruler but on the divinely ordained office of temporal authority. Rebellion against even unjust rule was an offense against God's will. A bad ruler was to be endured for such a monarch was viewed as God's punishment on a people for their sins. God's providence allowed for use of bad government to chasten and instruct a people in need of patience and humility. Calvin's strong belief in divine providence at work even when government might be oppressive is evident in a series of letters he wrote cautioning against those who too quickly moved to rebellion. For example, he opposed the views of his follower John Knox, who had written a denunciation of Mary, Queen of Scots, exhorting Protestant reformers to depose her.[22]

Calvin was as much an opponent of resistance to a king and as much a supporter of passive obedience as Martin Luther. As with Luther, the exception was if a temporal ruler enforced a law or policy that directly contravened one's religious conscience. Then one might refuse to obey, as long as one was willing to suffer the penalty. Calvin went a bit further, however, with the implication

---

Companion to John Calvin, ed. Donald McKim (Cambridge: Cambridge University Press, 2004), 173-87 at 179.

21. Calvin, *Institutes of the Christian Religion*, IV, chap. 20.
22. Stevenson, "Calvin and Political Issues," 182-83.

that a believer might look on the ruler in such a case as no longer a duly constituted authority.[23]

What might follow from that is addressed in a famous passage from the *Institutes*:

> For though the correction of tyrannical domination is the vengeance of God, we are not, therefore, to conclude that it is committed to us who have received no other command than to obey and suffer. This observation I always apply to private persons. For if there be, in the present day, any magistrates appointed for the protection of the people and the moderation of the power of kings, such as were in ancient times ... I am so far from prohibiting them, in the discharge of their duty, to oppose the violence or cruelty of kings, that I affirm that if they connive at kings in their oppression of the people, such forbearance involves the most nefarious perfidy, because they fraudulently betray the liberty of the people, of which they know that they have been appointed protectors by the ordination of God.[24]

This passage endorsing the right of duly appointed public officials to restrain and even resist a king became a subject of much commentary. It is famous because this modest exception to the general prohibition of resistance to a king led to far broader claims by Calvin's disciples John Knox in Scotland, Johannes Althusius in the Netherlands, and the influential author of the anonymous *Vindiciae, contra tyrannos* in France. Over time the right to resist was not restricted to major political officials acting out of public duty but became a general right of all to resist rulers who fell out of favor with the general population. In this development one must distinguish Calvin from the Calvinism of his later followers.

Calvinism

Similar to Luther, Calvin was faced with a situation in which the success of his religious movement was predicated on the cooperation of secular rulers.

Calvin had experienced opposition from temporal leaders, particularly in his native France and during his early years in Geneva. Eventually, however, he became the crucial leader of civic life as well as the unquestioned leader of

---

23. In a remark about the commandment to honor one's parents, Calvin discussed the case where parents encourage behavior contrary to God's will. "If they instigate us to any transgression of the law, we may justly consider them not as parents, but as strangers who attempt to seduce us from obedience to our real Father. The same observation is applicable to princes, lords, and superiors of every description" (Calvin, *Institutes of the Christian Religion*, II, chap. 8).

24. Ibid., IV, chap. 20, sec. 31.

spiritual reform in the city. Thus, Calvin's Geneva was a setting where talk of resistance to a temporal ruler had little resonance.

The situation for Calvin's followers outside of Geneva was dramatically different. In places where the Calvinist interpretation of the Christian tradition had significant support among the population, there were Catholic monarchs who were willing to use state power to punish the reformers. It was in these regions where Calvinists altered their leader's teaching.

As George Sabine summarizes it, "Calvin's political theory was a somewhat unstable structure, not precisely because it was illogical but because it could readily become the prey of circumstances." Calvin taught the wrongfulness of resistance to constituted authority; he also taught the duty of the church to proclaim correct doctrine with the support of secular authority. "It was practically a foregone conclusion, therefore, that a Calvinist church, existing in a state whose rulers refused to admit the truth of its doctrine and to enforce its discipline, would drop the duty to obey and assert the right to resist."[25] At least that was the likely outcome if there were little reason to hope the state's ruler might be converted. Such was the precise case in Scotland, the Netherlands, and France.

The revised theory developed in two steps. In Scotland the Calvinist preacher John Knox found himself under a death sentence issued by the Catholic bishops with the agreement of a Catholic monarch. Yet, he was popular at the grassroots level and had significant support among the lesser nobility. The choice was clear: passively accept the judgment of a king and church deemed in heresy or call for a change of leadership. Knox issued his call for resistance on the ground that the higher duty is not obedience to a king but the duty to bring about religious reform.

With Knox there was a dramatic alteration of the ban against rebellion, yet the basis for the change was an appeal to religious duty. It was in France that the second step would be taken, when the basis for rebellion became not religious duty but the people's right to rebel. It was a right claimed because the monarch was viewed as answerable to the people from whom the king's power was derived. Once that second step was taken the scene was set for the social disorder that Luther, Calvin, and the Catholic papacy so feared to set loose in Europe.

RELIGIOUS WAR AND ITS CONSEQUENCE

The political situation varied importantly from locale to locale. Strong Catholic monarchs in Spain and England maintained national unity and suppressed

---

25. Sabine, *History of Political Theory*, 344.

any movements toward rebellion. In Germany, given its political fragmentation, the religious strife was essentially a battle between princes of differing regions, not a battle between rulers and ruled. In the Netherlands the rebellion took on the character of a struggle for independence from a foreign ruler in Spain who was Catholic. In Scotland the revolt led by Knox eventually succeeded in neutralizing the authority of the Catholic queen regent and establishing a Calvinist church and sympathetic secular government.

It was France where the most chaos and violence occurred, including one of the most infamous incidents in an age of intolerance, the St. Bartholomew's Day Massacre in April of 1572. Actually, it was not a single event but a series of killings spread over weeks in a number of locales resulting in the deaths of leading Huguenot (French Calvinist) figures. When all the violence was over, the upshot was a victorious Catholic monarchy that was also strongly nationalist. The nationalist fervor was evident as well in the French church, which rejected the view of those who trumpeted papal authority over a universal church. What emerged was a theory of the divine right of kings, used to rebut both the political advocates of limited monarchy and the religious advocates of papal supremacy.

The Theory of Divine Right

The appeal of divine-right kingship hearkens back to the traditional view that civil authority had divine sanction. That claim could find both biblical warrant and support from centuries of Christian teaching. David's attitude toward Saul was cited as an example of the obedience owed to even a bad king. And both Augustine and Gregory I were referenced as figures who, at least in some of their writings, confused the divine institution of the state with divine authority of the one who governs. Influential as these examples were, however, it was clear that the theory of the divine right of kings was not the mainstream position supported by the Christian tradition. By the time of the great medieval theologians it was a theory that was largely ignored.

As a theory the divine-right argument opposed the view that government was founded on popular rights. But it was not the theory that explained the appeal of a divine-right monarch. The retrieval and revision of the idea in France gained adherents because of its attractiveness amidst conditions of social disunity, coupled with breakdowns in the political and ecclesiastical orders. It was this confusing reality more than any persuasive theory that brought the claim of divine-right monarchy back into popularity. Supporters of divine right included an alliance of those who shared the religious creed of the monarch and wished to deter rebellion, people who feared the violence and destruction of ongoing religious wars, supporters of a nationalist spirit, and individuals who believed in the necessity of strong central government in such fractious times.

Defenders of divine-right monarchs challenged anyone who would rebel on the basis of religious differences. To quell religiously motivated rebellion, the divine-right theorists argued in favor of the medieval view that subjects had a duty of passive obedience. The theory also was employed to squelch claims by the papacy that it had the power to depose a monarch. The king, it was claimed, ruled as sovereign over a nation as much by God's direct authority as the pope ruled over the church.

As one can readily imagine, there were counterarguments on both fronts, those who defended the rights of the people to rebel and those who defended the authority of the papacy to depose. It was the Huguenots who produced many of the arguments for a limited monarchy on the basis of the power of the people, and it was the Jesuits who argued against the absolute sovereignty of national monarchs for the sake of defending the authority and powers of the papacy.

A Right of Rebellion

Arguably, the most famous example of the brief for the right to rebel was found in the document *Vindiciae, contra tyrannos* (Vindication, against Tyrants), a work that has never been definitively ascribed to a particular author. It was representative of many Huguenot thinkers opposed to the policies of the French monarchy in the late sixteenth century. Utilizing examples of biblical covenants, the unknown author developed not so much a general theory of the state as a treatise on religion and politics. The text addressed four questions: Must subjects obey a prince in violation of God's law? Is it lawful to resist a prince who is destroying God's church, and by what manner of resistance? Is it permissible to resist a tyrant destroying the commonwealth? Should a monarch assist the rebellion in another kingdom where there is religious and political oppression? The answers to all four questions were provided with much argument from biblical theology mixed with natural-law philosophy and Roman legal theory. The upshot was an impressive synthesis of ideas to make a case against divine-right theories of absolute monarchy.

First, God had entered into a covenant with the king who was, in effect, a trustee of God's possession, the people. Such trusteeship required the king to rule rightly, and failure to do so cancelled the people's obligation to obey. Second, both king and people are, as a result of their covenant with God, duty bound to uphold and protect the church; if one of the parties should falter in this regard the other party must fulfill the covenant obligation. Relying on earlier medieval conciliarist thinking, the author did not vest private individuals with the authority to act in resistance; rather, it was the official agents of the people—magistrates, council or parliament members, lesser nobles—who had the responsibility to act.

Concerning the third question, the author introduced a different form of covenant that directly placed ruler and people in relation to each other and not in relation to God. It is the people who are the party to charge their rulers with the obligation to secure their well-being. The people put themselves into the care of rulers, and those who accept the obligations of rule must meet the demands that are established or else be guilty of treason against their covenant partner. Borrowing from the biblical accounts of Hebrew monarchs, the king may be chosen by God, but the people then must confirm the divine appointment. With regard to the final question, the author asserts that the unity of the church suggests that each ruler has an obligation to defend true doctrine and practice throughout the church. No ruler can shirk that duty on the ground that the offense against the church is outside his realm.

The *Vindiciae* was not without its internal inconsistencies and twists of logic. And it presumed a situation of church unity and of a popular majority in union against a monarch that was not at all descriptive of the actual situation in France. Yet its argument served as a clear harbinger of the emerging theory of popular rights and the belief that a monarch might be overthrown in the name of the people.

Jesuit Opposition

Another source of criticism regarding the claims of absolute monarchs came from the Catholic sector, specifically the Jesuits, the religious order founded by Ignatius of Loyola in 1534. Like their Protestant counterparts, Catholic thinkers were well versed in the medieval practices that provided precedents for constitutionalism, representative government, and limits on absolutist claims. Where the distinctively Catholic element of the critique arose was in the use of a theory of papal supremacy to counteract the power of national monarchs. Not all Catholics were of equal intensity in promoting these papal prerogatives, but the Jesuits played a large role in doing so.

In 1545 the Catholic Church convened an important council of its bishops that met for most of its sessions at the city of Trent in northern Italy. The bishops met on numerous occasions over the span of eighteen years, during which they fashioned the church's response to the Protestant Reformation. There were pronouncements made at the level of doctrinal teaching, but also significant reforms approved at the level of practice. The somewhat misleadingly called Catholic "counter-reformation" was a concerted and largely effective effort not simply to rebut Protestant complaints but also to revivify the spiritual life of the Catholic community. In that sense it is properly seen as a Catholic reform rather than a counter-reform movement.

An important piece of the reform was a renewed papacy that would be an agent of church renewal rather than an obstacle to it. It was the Jesuits who played a major role in assisting the papacy to carry out the renewal. The situation in Europe by the second half of the sixteenth century was an emergent order of nation-states, with secular rulers increasingly independent of any church control in secular affairs. Most Europeans still thought of themselves as Christian, though the Christian church was no longer a unified institution under the bishop of Rome. Jesuit scholars were realistic enough to accept the independence of political rulers in matters that were secular, but they sought to preserve a unique and special role for the papacy in spiritual matters. It was hoped that such a spiritual leader might continue to exert authority over issues of doctrine and morals across the breadth of Christian Europe.

The general position attributed to the Jesuits is well represented by the thinking of Francisco Suarez, a Spaniard. His political theory was worked out as part of a comprehensive theory of law. Suarez systematized and updated much of the medieval heritage of natural law, providing a precursor of constitutional and international law. He acknowledged that the papacy had no temporal authority, except over the Papal States in central Italy. Yet, he maintained that the pope does have authority over all spiritual matters, and this implies a measure of indirect temporal authority insofar as temporal matters affect spiritual concerns.

Furthermore, no king serves by divine right, if by that it is meant a king receives authority directly from God. Only the pope, as vicar of Christ and spiritual head of the church, has authority directly from God. Temporal power comes from the community of people who possess it, in order to attain the legitimate ends of social existence. Secular authority has no direct mandate from God in the exercise of power. Temporal rulers receive their power as designates of the community with the authority to act on behalf of the people and in accord with the natural law. Therefore, no secular ruler can expect absolute obedience from the people since the ruler's authority ultimately is founded on being the vicar of the people, acting on their behalf to promote the goods of social life that add to human well-being.

Because the papacy has its spiritual authority directly from God it trumps secular authority whenever a spiritual end is at stake. So there may be cases when a pope can depose a ruler, for example, if the ruler is leading his subjects into heresy and suppressing the legitimate freedom of the church. As might be expected, Suarez encountered critics. His theory displeased secular rulers who resisted claims that they ruled on the basis of the people's delegation rather than divine right; the Jesuit approach also displeased Protestants for it asserted the supremacy of the papacy in all matters spiritual.

Despite the battle of ideas, at the practical level the Catholic Church was largely compliant during the age of absolutist monarchs. The more powerful a monarch was, even if Catholic, the less influence the papacy was capable of exerting. And so, in actuality, even national episcopacies often looked to their king more than the pope for leadership and support.

The Onset of an Idea

A shared feature of both the Jesuit and Calvinist theories was that the church must be independent from the control of a national monarch whose only authority lay in the secular realm. The significance of the Jesuit argument, like that of the Calvinist position, is how it moved the argument incrementally toward the separation of the spiritual and secular realms, though neither of these two groups wished that to be the case.

In the sixteenth century almost all the disputants in the religious controversies still harbored the hope that society could achieve consensus on the proper understanding of the Christian faith. A century later, as the divide between Catholic and Protestant became wider and more bitter, the idea that religious unity was unattainable would gradually take possession of the European imagination. Faced with a fractured church, convinced that the state was a secular institution, and firm in the conviction that political rulers did not have the authority to intervene in church affairs, there would come a time when Catholics and Protestants confronted the new reality.

Then would arrive the idea that the best a secular ruler might do is allow each Christian community to advance its teaching and practice of the faith, so long as the various churches did not disturb the social order. Though that conclusion would emerge eventually, it was still not the prevailing view in the sixteenth century.

OTHER TRADITIONS OF REFORM

There were additional Christian voices in the sixteenth century that provided alternatives to the Lutheran and Calvinist critiques of Catholicism. Basically, there were those who faulted Luther and Calvin for not going far enough in their reforms, and others who faulted the classical reformers for going too far in their criticism of the Catholic tradition. Those who found Luther and Calvin too mild represented what has been called the radical or left-wing reformation; those troubled by what was seen as Lutheran and Calvinist excesses reflected the views of the Anglican tradition.

Anglicanism and a National Church

The English Parliament declared the Tudor king, Henry VIII, to be the Head of the Church of England in the Act of Supremacy in 1534. The act of Parliament drew a line between those who hoped for reform from within the existing Catholic Church and those who accepted the idea of a national church removed from papal jurisdiction. The Act of Supremacy also reflected a period in English history when concerns about succession to the throne profoundly influenced ecclesiastical loyalties.

Although historians continue to debate aspects of the founding of the Anglican Church, the prevailing view is that the Catholic Church in England was not in a state of crisis in the decade prior to Parliament's action. The uproar accompanying Luther, Calvin, and other reformers on the continent had not significantly affected Christianity throughout the English realm.[26] While there were indications that religious reform was a concern, it was not the key factor in the break with Rome.

The decisive element was more political, both civil and ecclesiastical, than theological. Henry needed an heir to avoid any danger of civil war after his death, and in order for that to occur it was thought that he must have his marriage annulled and take a new wife. When the pope resisted this course of action, Henry sought to have himself named head of the church within his realm so that he might exercise supreme jurisdiction in matters spiritual as well as temporal.

Because Henry's dissatisfaction with Rome was more about church governance and practice than matters theological, he did not institute many changes in doctrine or liturgy. Opponents of the Supremacy Act were dealt with, but he also punished those who took up the causes of Luther or Calvin. Upon Henry's death in 1547, his son Edward VI came to the throne, but Edward was both underage and sickly. In this situation proponents of religious reform, who had bided their time under Henry, now sensed greater liberty to promote their views. Thomas Cranmer, the archbishop of Canterbury, was sympathetic to the Protestant reformers, and was open to Protestants who had come to England to avoid persecution on the continent. Initially, Lutheran and then Calvinist reformers influenced the changes put in place by Cranmer. In 1549 and again in 1551, editions of the *Book of Common Prayer* were published, with the second edition expressing a definite sympathy for a Calvinist approach.

The Elizabethan Settlement

After Edward died, his half sister, Mary, who was Catholic, came to the throne. She rescinded many of the religious reforms and restored union with Rome. Her reign of five years was a time of unrest and violence; she was followed by another half sister, Elizabeth I (d. 1603), whose long reign of forty-five years gave stability to the nation and also to the religious reform. A second act of

---

26. Eamon Duffy, *The Stripping of the Altars: Traditional Religion in England 1400–1580* (New Haven: Yale University Press, 1992).

supremacy was passed, and what is called the Elizabethan settlement gave a relatively fixed form to Anglicanism. Yet another edition of the *Book of Common Prayer* was issued that sought to strike a balance between Catholic and Protestant, especially Calvinist, worship.

Elizabeth's via media did not satisfy everyone. The Anglican approach was to claim that the church was both Catholic and reformed. It was Catholic in its maintenance of apostolic succession through the episcopacy, acceptance of the early ecumenical councils, and rituals of worship. It was reformed in the place it gave to Scripture, its opposition to practices of medieval spirituality, and its rejection of papal supremacy within the church. Those English Calvinists we call Puritans thought Elizabeth's approach too Catholic, while dissident Catholics faulted Anglicanism's rejection of Rome and aspects of Catholic teaching.

Richard Hooker (d. 1600)

The Anglican priest Richard Hooker took upon himself the task of defending the Elizabethan "middle way" in his multivolume *Laws of Ecclesiastical Polity*. Hooker was especially concerned to rebut the Puritan criticism of Anglicanism. If Hooker's work were only an apologia for the Elizabethan settlement it would still merit study by those interested in understanding Anglicanism. But his work is far more than that because it is a work of political philosophy that examined law and authority, as well as church and state.

Hooker's method demonstrates the Anglican effort to hold the Bible, later Christian tradition, and reason as complementary authorities. Unlike the Puritans who attacked those elements of Anglicanism deemed nonbiblical, Hooker argued for the legitimacy of historical development after the New Testament and the use of human reason in matters religious. For the Puritans, unless the Bible permitted something it ought not be done; whereas for Hooker, unless the Bible prohibited something it might be done, as long as the experience of Christians throughout history and the use of right reason did not direct otherwise.

In keeping with his Anglican outlook, Hooker borrowed from both Calvin and Aquinas. In his view of the human condition, he was closer to Calvin, being more pessimistic than Thomas about the ability of individuals to know the truth and to do the good. The consequences of "the Fall," or original sin, were more extensive and harsher than Aquinas acknowledged. In his treatment of law, however, Hooker drew heavily on Thomas.

Recall from the previous chapter that the medieval Dominican proposed a quadripartite division of law. First was the eternal law, which is the law of divine reason. The ability of humans to know something of God's law, to participate through our reason in the eternal law, is the second part of law, the natural law. Third is divine law, that part of the eternal law that has been revealed to humans expressly through biblical revelation. Divine law does not contravene the natural law but supplements and clarifies it. Finally, there is human law. Law in this sense is only true law insofar as it accords with natural law. The authority and binding power of human or civil law is directly related to our best reasoned effort to express the eternal law.

Hooker's exposition of the law is in fundamental agreement with Aquinas. However, he is more skeptical of people being able to formulate sound law because of his belief in the innate fallibility of reason and the intellectual sloth of individuals. For this reason, tradition is important for it provides potential insight from wisdom accumulated through the centuries and is able to stand the test of time. Civil law is simply the specification and application of the law of reason, the law of nature, to the particulars of time and place.

Political and Ecclesiastical Authority

The treatment of human or civil law extends to his discussion of the state. Hooker, again in accord with Aquinas and Aristotle, holds that humans are naturally social. To be in communion with others is necessary since we are not self-sufficient. We need others both for the sake of fellowship but also because the division of labor permits individuals to acquire particular skills in some areas without having to be omnicompetent. Various individuals, therefore, contribute differently to the attainment of the commonweal.

Just as Hooker maintained against the Puritans that what may be permissible in the church is what is not explicitly prohibited in the Bible, so too he maintains that what is permissible in political institutions is whatever is not opposed to the natural law. Human law can admit of a variety of schemes for governance, so long as these do not violate the law of reason. Thus, the binding authority of law or government is not that it fully expresses the preferences of an individual but that it does not contradict the law of reason. Tradition plays an important part here, since, he argues, it can fairly be presumed that a society's established institutions and laws are acceptable to reason. One ought not challenge or defy them unless they are demonstrably not in accord with the law of reason.

In following this train of thought, Hooker predictably makes several arguments. Since human law is grounded in natural law and natural law is reason's ability to understand something of divine law, it is unsurprising that Hooker opposes any notion of absolute monarchs placed above the law or as laws unto themselves. Consequently, he is a supporter of constitutional monarchy. Note his indebtedness to medieval political theory, however, in that he cites the authority of a higher law, the law of reason, as the check on a monarch's power rather than the modern era's use of a parliament, the terms of a social contract, or a bill of individual rights to restrain a ruler.

In his discussion of the power of the monarch over the church in England,

Hooker again sets boundaries for the ruler's authority. As a defender of the Elizabethan settlement, he endorsed the Act of Supremacy that threw off the papal claims to jurisdiction over the universal church, but Hooker did not interpret supremacy to mean that the monarch was absolute in the church. Here again, the law of reason, abetted by the revelation of divine law, placed limits on any exercise of ecclesiastical power. The importance of tradition, and the authority of continuity with the early church, also had to be considered. In this way, he argued for the role of the episcopacy, the importance of apostolic succession, and the central creedal affirmations of councils such as Nicea and Chalcedon. These help form a set of "constitutional limits" on the monarch's authority within the church.

Sabine described the *Laws of Ecclesiastical Polity* as "the last great state- ment of what might be called the medieval tradition" of political thought.[27] Similar to other medieval theorists, Hooker assumed Christianity was coex- tensive with society. In his case, as an apologist for the Anglican position, he argued that the English Church and the English nation were one, identical in membership. Since the laws of the church cannot offend the law of reason, they have the same binding force as the civil laws of the land, also formulated in accord with reason.

In criticizing the Puritans, Hooker argued that they were as duty-bound to accept the ecclesiastical laws of the English Church as they were the civil laws of the English realm. For him the Puritans (and the Roman Catholics) sought to make the church and state distinct, with the implication that they sought the supremacy of the church. To these groups, the idea of a national monarch as supreme head of the church was unacceptable, undercutting the spiritual autonomy of the body of Christ.

Catholics believed that papal authority was necessary to preserve both the unity and the freedom of the church; some espoused the more radical claim that popes were above monarchs. The Puritans also held that spiritual freedom was at risk with a national monarch heading a national church. If anything, Calvinism had a tendency to endorse church control of the political realm, not secular control of the church. Hooker retrieved the unity of church and state from the era of Christendom, but with the novel twist that it was a church defined along national boundaries.

The Radical Reformers

Early on in the Protestant Reformation one segment of the reformers came to be known as the Anabaptists, that is, the re-baptizers. Actually, it is a misno-

---

27. Sabine, *History of Political Theory*, 409.

mer, for this group of believers held that only the baptism of freely consenting adults is true baptism. Each believer had to make a personal commitment in freedom and out of conviction to request baptism. Therefore the baptism of infants or young children was no baptism at all. So adult baptism was not a re-baptism but actually the first baptism.

The movement has also been called the "left-wing Reformation," emphasizing its religious-political view about church and state; and it has also been called the "Fourth Reformation," distinguishing it from Lutheranism, Calvinism, and Anglicanism. The church historian George Hunston Williams proposed the "Radical Reformation" as a particularly apt designation.[28] Groups included under the rubric of radical reformers were a disparate lot, but they shared the aim of freeing the church by cutting away at the accretions of tradition in order to reach the root (Lat. *radix*) of faith and the source of divine authority.

To focus on the Anabaptist segment of the radical reformation, while not representative of all, still affords an understanding of the general orientation that the diverse groups share. The radical reformers believed Catholicism to be corrupted and the other reform movements too insufficient in their efforts at purifying the Christian faith.[29] The only true reform was to return to the model and experience of the church in the New Testament.

Essential in this regard was the conviction that the New Testament revealed a new form of life that had to be retrieved by rejecting the compromises and misjudgments following the apostolic era. Before the name Christian was used to describe the followers of Jesus, the early disciples were understood as followers of "the Way." Recovering that sense of Christianity as a different way of life was at the heart of the Anabaptist reform. Therefore, the focus of reform was not the teaching of justification by faith but the experience of the Holy Spirit enabling people to adopt a new way of life in Christian discipleship. One might say that ethics trumped doctrine for the Anabaptists; what was important was not correct teaching about God's revelation in Christ so much as right living in accord with the experience of the Spirit of Christ. To use modern terminology, orthopraxis was valued over orthodoxy.

Anabaptists read the history of the church as the narrative of a "fall" from the pristine New Testament experience of what it meant to be the church. Various moments might be seized upon as the epitome of this fall, but for many it had to do with the changes that took place as the early church interacted with classical pagan culture. The translation of New Testament experience into the

---

28. George Hunston Williams, "Introduction," in *Spiritual and Anabaptist Writers*, ed. George Hunston Williams and Angel Mergal (Library of Christian Classics 25; Philadelphia: Westminster Press, 1957), 19-38 at 22.

29. Ibid.

philosophical categories of Greece and Rome, the adoption of Christianity as the official religion of the empire, and the assimilation of Christian discipleship with the mores of Roman or Greek society were all cited as critical moments in the decline of Christianity. In each case the lesson was the same: the church of Christ had lost its way and the goal of reform was to return to the foundation of New Testament living.

Another lesson was that the church had lost its way as membership became too easy, too undemanding. People were incorporated into the church before they could understand what the gospel asked of them. Individuals could live far less than wholesome lives and still remain church members. A church open to the masses was a church that watered down the meaning of Christianity. To assure that these mistakes were not allowed to continue, there must be Baptism only for those already committed to live the way of Christ, and there must be disciplines employed to assure no backsliding or compromise by believers. As a result, there was a strategy whereby the church became a community of people who were set apart, a people who witnessed to the truth of the Christian message by the distinctiveness of their lifestyle.

Because of their indifference to certain doctrinal debates, their view of the church as a voluntary society, the rejection of clerical leadership, and their wariness of any authority beyond the experience of the Spirit, the Anabaptists found themselves opposed by Catholics, Lutherans, and Calvinists. They encountered persecution and violence in just about every region of Europe. Although there were exceptions, the majority of Anabaptists endured these sufferings without recourse to violent self-defense. Persecution, suffering, even death were to be expected, after all, if one were living as Jesus and the early disciples did.

The opposition that they encountered confirmed Anabaptists in their belief that the Christian church was a minority community; it was the voluntary association of those fully committed to live in accord with the model of New Testament discipleship. The idea of Christendom or a national church was unthinkable. Anabaptist experience of persecution from other believers encouraged them to embrace the idea of religious freedom; each person ought to be permitted to live as one's conscience dictated. The role of public officials, both in promoting one Christian creed or another and in persecuting those who dissented from the approved religion, encouraged Anabaptists to support the separation of church and state. They believed that the union of church and state led to minimalist expectations for church membership, the intrusion of political authority into church life, and the temptation to employ coercion and violence when dealing with minority dissenters.

Thus, hallmarks of Anabaptism became the conviction that the state might have to be reckoned with, but it should not be embraced as a partner with the church, and violence must be rejected as a means of dealing with conflict among people. A noted church historian offers a reflection on the Anabaptist reform:

> The Anabaptist contribution to history is comparable to that of the Norsemen who visited America prior to Columbus. They found what he found and they found it first. Their intrepidity was no less and possibly greater than his. But they do not occupy the same place in history because their deed was without sequel. Not they, but he opened up the trek from Europe to the New World. Similarly, the Anabaptists anticipated all other religious bodies in the proclamation and exemplification of three principles which, on the North American continent, are among those truths which we hold to be self-evident: the voluntary Church, the separation of Church and state and religious liberty. From the days of Constantine to the Anabaptists these principles, to us so cardinal, had been in abeyance. They were not, however, transmitted to us by the Anabaptists, but rather by the Puritan revolution and the French Revolution.[30]

The impact of the Puritans in the new world was evident in the American Revolution and its aftermath, the founding of the United States, and the creation of its Constitution. In the old world, the French Revolution, of course, unleashed a seismic change for Christianity in Europe. Both of these Revolutions will be discussed in the next chapter.

THE POLITICAL LEGACY OF THE REFORMATION

The era of reform brought about an array of changes; some were intended but many serve as an example of history's law of unintended consequences. Whether wittingly or unwittingly, by the beginning of the seventeenth century the face of Europe had changed dramatically as a result of the Reformation.

One obvious consequence was that the hope of one Christian commonwealth spread across the boundaries of western Europe was no longer tenable. Many parts of northern Europe (Scandinavia and much of Germany) were predominantly Lutheran. The Netherlands and Scotland were Calvinist, as were areas of Switzerland, England, and eastern Europe. Anglicanism was the established religion of England, and Anabaptists, while always a minority, were dispersed almost everywhere on the continent. Ireland, Spain, France, Italy, eastern Europe, southern Germany, and Austria remained heavily Catholic, in some places almost completely so.

---

30. Roland Bainton, "The Anabaptist Contribution to History," in *Studies on the Reformation* (Boston: Beacon Press, 1963), 199-207 at 199.

- With religious unity throughout Europe out of the question, there was a political movement toward unity built upon national identity. Newly emergent nation-states became the center of gravity for loyalty and power.

A second development, in those few cases where the religious demographics permitted, was the establishment of a national church with government having an extensive influence over the church. Other situations presented rulers with such religious diversity that the only solution was a fair measure of toleration for dissenters from the ruler's religious preference, at least for the larger minorities.

- While early arguments for religious toleration may have been rooted mainly in political expediency it was not a very far leap of the political imagination to develop arguments based on the dignity and rightful freedom of individual conscience. The American constitutional principle of separation of church and state has its origins in the aftermath of the Protestant Reformation.

Third, Protestant reformers rejected monasticism and the clerical system of privilege and power in Catholicism. This was done in the name of Luther's priesthood of all believers, the godly nature of all professions according to Calvin, the radical equality of all disciples among Anabaptists, and similar convictions among other reform movements. One need not retreat to a monastery to find true holiness; the active life was also such a path. Appreciation for this-worldly aspects of human experience encouraged Christians to give expression to their religious convictions in their everyday lives. This was not done in order to earn or merit grace, but as a way to give thanks to God for being saved (the Lutheran emphasis), to bear witness to God's activity in the world (a Calvinist theme), or to be faithful to the new way of living that the Spirit of Christ made possible (the Anabaptist focus).

- Even though no individual was justified by "works," human activity in the realms of family, economy, education, and politics was given new and important significance by the reformers. Believers could see their labor as a true vocation, a godly calling that was to be taken seriously. Thus, the importance of secular (nonecclesiastical) activity grew, precisely because it was not seen as profane (nonreligious) activity.

The promotion of secular action included the realm of politics and was particularly encouraged among Calvinists. As with Luther, Calvin saw the importance of good governance and social order. More than Luther, however, Calvin saw a positive role for the state and desired to bring the temporal and spiritual together in the project of creating a Christian commonwealth. In this area, Calvin was more medieval than Luther. As in Geneva, Calvin desired to see both church and state governed by biblical authority as a normative standard.

- Secular government might serve as an agent for bringing about a godly society. Although the Calvinist project was unsuccessful in Europe, the desire to transform the world and not just the church would inspire the Puritans' understanding of their mission in the new world of North America.

Both Luther and Hooker rejected the papal claims of universal jurisdiction over the entire church. This left both men to devise an alternative form of ecclesiastical polity. In Hooker's case the defense of the national monarch as head of the national church is clear. Although Luther did not espouse such a structure in theory, his deference to political authority and his reliance on it for adjudicating ecclesiastical disputes place him close to Hooker in risking the subordination of the church to the state.

Calvin was a strong critic of the national church idea and an opponent of all monarchical claims to absolute sovereignty. In that sense he could be read as one who wished for a clear distinction between church and state. Yet, as noted above, Calvin carried forward the medieval notion that temporal power should be used to promote and enforce church teaching and practice. Therefore, in practice, he could be interpreted as making the state the temporal arm of the church.

Anabaptists saw the need for separation of church and state, but nowhere were they influential enough to enact such a practice, nor were they sufficiently clear as to how the two entities should interact once separated.

Catholic reform held onto the autonomy of the papacy as a guarantor of the freedom of the church. The more extreme defenders of papal power also continued to ensnare the church in controversies of church and state with their claims of the superiority of papal authority over all political authority. In addition, the pope's role as ruler of the Papal States required the bishop of Rome to exercise temporal authority as a head of state. This frequently put the Catholic Church in a position of unfortunate alliances, with the papacy playing power politics to ensure control of its temporal realm.

- In the area of church and state relations the Reformation era left a mixed legacy. There were a variety of outcomes, either directly or indirectly shaped by the theological beliefs and practical choices made by the great reform movements.

QUESTIONS FOR REFLECTION/DISCUSSION

1. Why was the governing assumption of all sides throughout the era that unity in faith was necessary for social order?

2. Why was obedience to rulers such a central tenet in the pre-Reformation era? How was the issue transformed by the impact of the Reformation?

3. How did Luther's theological views shape his political judgments?

4. How would you explain the irony that Luther's ambition for a reformed church led to closer ties between church and secular rulers?

5. What was the influence of Calvin's emphasis on divine sovereignty and providence for his political ideas? What was the difference between Calvin and Luther on the idea of two kingdoms?

6. How did later Calvinists interpret Calvin on the question of resistance to authority? What accounts for the change in teaching?

7. What were the main features of the debate about divine-right monarchs?

8. What was the Elizabethan settlement? How did Richard Hooker articulate his criticism of Puritan dissenters?

9. For the radical reformers what were the political consequences for the church due to the "fall" from New Testament norms?

7

An Age of Revolution

The Wars of Religion on the continent end with the Peace of Augsburg (1555) and with the Edict of Nantes (1598). In England, they were brought to a close with the Elizabethan settlement (1559). The Peace of Augsburg established the principle of *cuius regio, eius religio*.[1] A Lutheran prince could establish Lutheranism as the official religion of his realm while a Catholic prince was free to establish Catholicism within his region of rule. The immediate aim was to end what were religious civil wars within the Holy Roman Empire, France, and England. The long-term goal was to solidify the idea of the nation-state.[2]

Even after the formal treaties and settlements the conflicts involving religion continued to simmer, and strong rulers often employed ruthless measures in order to quell disturbances. In 1618 war broke out again in central Europe, initially for religious reasons, but European balance-of-power concerns soon overshadowed the religious conflict. Indeed, the new conflict was not a series of civil wars as in the previous century but a true European war of nations.

Questions of trade dominance were acute with the onset of colonialism in the New World. Also there were geopolitical concerns such as the competition between the Bourbon and Hapsburg dynasties that fed the flames of war. One illustration that reveals the Thirty Years War was only superficially about religion is the case of Cardinal Richelieu (d. 1642), who served as France's secretary of state before the onset of the war until his death.

The cardinal provided assistance to the Dutch Protestants in their battle against the Spanish branch of the Hapsburgs, who also controlled the Netherlands. He also provided assistance to Swiss Protestants opposing the Austrian Hapsburg emperor. For Richelieu, undercutting the power of the Catholic Hapsburgs on the northern and southern borders of France as well

---

1. See chap. 6 n. 15, above.

2. An early example of the nation-state goal may be seen in the late 1400s with the marriage of Ferdinand and Isabella, a union that united the divided Spanish kingdoms. The Spanish monarchy then sought further social unity by the harsh treatment and expulsion of Jews and Muslims. A unified nation with the state holding a monopoly on the use of force within the territory became the ambition of monarchs throughout Europe.

as weakening the Hapsburg emperor to the east was the crucial aim of French foreign policy. That pursuit of such a policy meant assisting Protestants fight against Catholics was not a source of concern to him.

The Thirty Years War was less about religion than it was about nationalism and the desire to overcome Hapsburg power and control. The other key motive was the beginning of incipient capitalism and the move away from land-based economies to the importance of trade as the key to wealth. That is another reason why one sea-faring nation, France, was willing to assist Dutch Protestants in weakening the naval power of Spain.

THE END OF THE RELIGIOUS WARS

The Peace of Westphalia was the result of conferences and treaties that brought to a close the various conflicts grouped under the heading of the Thirty Years War. The settlement was a milestone in the history of European diplomacy that put in motion the emergent system of nation-states and modern international law. It was also the marker for a new era in the relationship of Christianity and politics in the West.

The accord was founded on three essential principles. First was the recognition of state sovereignty, the belief that a ruler had the right to exercise authority within a defined territorial region without deference to any other person or institution claiming superior authority. The second crucial element of the new order was the principle of nonintervention, barring coercive interference by outsiders in the internal affairs of a state. And the third piece of what has been called the "Westphalian synthesis"[3] was the removal of religion from the realm of international politics. The religion of the prince and his people was no longer to be a factor in calculations about justifiable resort to arms between states.

Of course, an agreement on paper is not automatically translated into actual practice. There have been challenges aplenty to sovereignty and to nonintervention in subsequent years. And religious tensions persisted long after 1648, but Westphalia did signal a new era, and part of the change was that religion was increasingly viewed as peripheral to international politics.[4]

---

3. The expression is Daniel Philpott's in his essay "The Challenge of September 11 to Secularism in International Politics," *World Politics* 55 (October 2002): 66–95 at 71.

4. It is ironic that the role of religion in political life became somewhat marginalized due to Westphalia since, arguably, the major figure in the negotiations was a Catholic cleric, Cardinal Jules Mazarin, the protégé of Richelieu. During Louis XIV's childhood while his mother served as regent, Mazarin functioned as the chief minister of France in title and, effectively, as co-ruler of France. It can fairly be concluded that through

Basically, the terms of Westphalia affirmed a revised version of the Peace of Augsburg, which had ended the conflict among the German princes at odds over Catholicism and Lutheranism. Westphalia did expand the agreement to include Calvinism among the interpretations of the Christian tradition a ruler could adopt as the established religion.

The second element of the Westphalian formula for religious peace guaranteed that if some inhabitants of a realm did not share the faith of the prince, then they were free to practice their preferred religion in private as they wished, and in public under regulated times and conditions. The established religion of the region might benefit from certain political and economic privileges, but the other expressions of Christianity were to be permitted, although under constraints. Sometimes these constraints were modest and in other circumstances quite difficult, depending on the commitment to toleration upheld by the monarch.

Among the significant outcomes of Westphalia were two that may or may not have been intended by its signatories. The desire to remove religion as a cause of political strife also strengthened the voices of those who considered religiously inspired moral constraints in the realm of international politics to be unnecessary. According to this line of thinking, political leaders should act simply on the basis of reasons of state. Within a fractured Christian Europe the decline in the moral authority and prestige of the papacy meant there was no effective spokesperson for the claims of a universal morality that might temper or override the will of a national ruler.

Westphalia not only encouraged a secular international politics; it also empowered the absolutist claims of rulers within the domestic sphere. After all, the treaty gave to political rulers the right to determine the preferred church of the realm and to establish the public rights and duties of nonestablished churches. Even in areas ruled by Catholic leaders, a weakened papacy was at a disadvantage in resisting the claims of a prince or king who sought influence over the church's personnel and activity.

Strong rulers who could enforce order and impose civil peace on an area were welcomed after the lengthy conflicts and disruptions characteristic of the fifteenth and early sixteenth centuries. It was a period when absolutist regimes emerged claiming authority over all aspects of life in a region. One key instance of such change was the Catholic Church's waning influence on universities when compared to the medieval period.

The actual shape of absolutist rule varied from place to place as individual states managed to hold onto some features of representative government that had begun in the late medieval era. For example, England, with its Parlia-

---

his role in the peace process Mazarin advanced the interests of France far more than those of his church.

ment and tradition of common law, was different than what was experienced in Spain or France. Characteristic of all the strong political rulers of this age, however, was a willingness to challenge religious authority coupled with a desire to bend the churches to serve the purposes of the state.

Within decades after Westphalia, the Gallican movement emerged within the French church. The movement, which had its early roots in the controversies between Philip IV and Boniface VIII in the medieval period, involved a variety of ideas and practices that essentially asserted (1) that French monarchs could exercise ecclesiastical authority on a variety of matters within their temporal realm, and (2) that the universal authority of the papacy was limited by the rights of the local church.[5] The diminution of papal power was integral to the rise of royal absolutism.

Most political thinkers of the period who explicitly appealed to the Christian tradition were skeptical of divine right, maintaining that although political authority came from God it was mediated through the people. Such an understanding usually was accompanied by the claim that there was a right to rebel against a manifestly unjust ruler. There were a variety of disagreements about the exercise of such a right, ranging from who might authorize a rebellion to whether it extended to tyrannicide. The central point, however, was that many Protestant theorists, particularly Calvinist, as well as Catholic thinkers, saw limits to the absolutist claims.

On a practical level, church leaders often found ways to reconcile, or at least work, with absolute rulers. In some cases this was due to the fact that a monarch supported a particular church; in other situations a given church was in no position to resist the claims of a powerful king. One church's officials might acquiesce to a ruler's claims because they sought to coax support from a monarch in efforts to limit the growth of a rival church or to gain assistance when expanding to the newly discovered lands of the Americas.

Owing to a belief in the universal authority of the pope and the existence of a natural moral law, Catholicism might seem to be especially at odds with an absolutist theory that recognized no authority beyond the monarch. Yet, the seventeenth and eighteenth centuries were a time when Catholic monarchs waged a persistent and largely successful battle to control the church within their realms. During this era the pope no longer had sway over the choice of a king, but monarchs had the ability to thwart the election of a would-be pope if the candidate was judged unsympathetic.[6]

---

5. Variations on Gallicanism appeared in other European lands in subsequent decades: Erastianism in Switzerland, Febronianism in the Netherlands and Germany, Josephism in Austria.

6. This situation, of course, was hardly a historical novelty. The role of cardinals in the election of the pope was not established until 1059. Long before and after that

FRENCH CATHOLICISM, THE REVOLUTION, AND AFTERMATH

Perhaps nowhere was the development of absolutism more advanced than in the French monarchy of the sixteenth and seventeenth centuries. French kings exercised a supremacy over the church "that was as real as that exercised by Henry VIII in England," but it was acquired more through negotiation than outright seizure of power.[7] Nonetheless, the position of the Catholic Church within France was strong.

The Catholic liturgical calendar provided a rhythm for the lives of most French people. The church regulated marriage; its religious orders had authority over much of education and social charity, and possessed substantial wealth. Catholic clergy were evident at all major public ceremonies and exercised a quasi-governmental function, often communicating government pronouncements at church services.[8] Catholicism had no real rival among any Protestant church. In 1685, under Louis XIV, there had been a revocation of the Edict of Nantes, a decree of religious toleration, and subsequent Protestant emigration was significant. As a result, the overwhelming majority of the resident population were baptized Catholics.

Despite these indications of institutional prominence and strength there were evident problems. Local parish priests were pastorally engaged, but many religious orders and bishops were removed from the lives and concerns of people, especially the poor. The hierarchy was drawn from the aristocracy; at the time of the Revolution there was only one bishop out of 135 who was not a member of the nobility. Some hierarchs functioned as absentee lords of their dioceses, rarely visiting them. The wealth of the church was dramatically skewed, with many parish priests living simply while their ecclesiastical superiors had huge incomes. The wealth of some monasteries and convents was a source of widespread envy.

Still, among the laity "the overwhelming majority of the popular classes closely identified with a Catholic religion which continued to frame the central moments of their lives and their work."[9] This was especially true in rural

----

date the emperor held a right of veto over the papal candidate. In the 1600s the kings of France and Spain joined the emperor in claiming a right of veto via their cardinal designates at the conclave. It was not until the twentieth century that those claims were formally annulled by Pope Pius X. See John O'Malley, *A History of the Popes* (Lanham, MD: Sheed & Ward, 2010), 222.

7. Michael Burleigh, *Earthly Powers* (New York: HarperCollins, 2005), 28.

8. Ibid., 24.

9. Timothy Tackett, "The French Revolution and Religion to 1794," in *Enlightenment, Reawakening and Revolution 1660-1815* (Cambridge History of Christianity 7; ed. Stewart Brown and Timothy Tackett; Cambridge: Cambridge University Press, 2006), 536-55 at 538.

areas, where more than three-fourths of the population lived. Catholic publications—lives of the saints, devotional works, liturgy of the hours—were numerous and sold well in areas outside of Paris.[10]

There were also signs of change and increasing spiritual indifference—church leaders had little interest in theology or moral reform while upper-class laity in urban areas were influenced by the centrality of rationalism in the various movements associated with the Enlightenment. The number of ordinations was in decline among city dwellers, while the vast majority of hard-working parish priests came from rural areas with modest educational training. In sum, a seemingly powerful church showed signs of entering a state of decline.

In 1789 a financial crisis led Louis XVI to call together the representatives of the long-dormant Estates General. The three estates of clergy, nobility, and commoners met as a representative body with their total number amounting to approximately 1,300 individuals. Among the interests represented were obviously those of class, but also those of region and profession, especially lawyers, many of whom were sympathetic to Jansenism.[11] The Jansenists also reflected the outlook of the new mercantilist bourgeoisie. The agenda of the Estates General included reform of abuses in both the state and the church. With regard to the state, a particular concern was the skewed system of taxation and other social obligations that placed heavy burdens on those least well off.

Although it was expected that the nobles of the second estate would provide the leadership of the assembly, that role shifted to the bourgeois members of the third estate. This development came about because of the divide between higher and lower clergy in the first estate. Because the former were largely nobility and the lower were drawn from the working class, an alliance formed between the parish clergy and representatives of the third estate. When the king sought to end the assembly as the agenda developed in ways he opposed, the third estate and its supporters in the other estates refused to cede. Eventually, the Estates General morphed into a National Assembly, and the nobility were absorbed into a more representative unitary body where their power was largely broken. With the advent of the Assembly new voices came to the fore, and these were more radical in calls for change.

A series of popular uprisings and riots in different regions of the nation also pushed members of the National Assembly to opposing extremes. Those fear-

---

10. Ibid., 539.

11. Jansenism was a Catholic religious movement that arose in the mid-1600s in support of the writing of Cornelius Jansen, a theologian and bishop of Ypres, whose writings criticized Catholic Reformation theology, particularly the Jesuit school, on a number of doctrinal points. By the late 1700s, however, the term Jansenism had become equated with a rigorist mentality on issues of spirituality and morality, along with opposition to both royal absolutism and papal supremacy.

ful of anarchy defended the monarchy and sought social stability, while others heard the calls of popular outrage and the demands of the many living in miserable economic conditions. Overall, the Assembly moved toward endorsing dramatic change rather than defending the existing social order.

During the early days of the National Assembly there was a recognition that social reform would require accompanying changes in the institutional church. Just about all the major political actors were Catholic, and the tone of the Assembly was not one of opposition to the church but more a desire for its renewal. Due to the Gallican ethos of the time, however, there was little inclination to look to Rome for leadership in this regard. Instead the National Assembly created a committee, including clergy and laity, to draw up a charter for church reform. The report of that committee was the basis for what was to become the Civil Constitution of the Clergy. That document determined the course of events for the Catholic Church in France during the ensuing years of unrest and violence that marked the revolutionary period.

The Impact of the Clergy Constitution

The Clergy Constitution was a part of the larger writing of the French Constitution, and the mandated ecclesial changes reflected the overall reform project of the nation. For example, dozens of dioceses were suppressed so that the number of remaining dioceses and their geographical boundaries coincided with those of the civil departments that were established as the regional administrative units of the French state. Bishops were expected to be the resident pastors of their cathedral churches and were to be elected by all the qualified electors within the department. Priests serving a local parish were elected in a similar manner by the electors within the parish boundaries. Bishops could only act with the support of a diocesan council. The pope was to be informed of the election of a bishop, though not asked to approve it. In effect, the papal role in leading the episcopacy would become mainly symbolic, having no juridical power over the church in France.

For those French Catholics who had imbibed the mix of ideas associated with Gallicanism, the Civil Constitution of the Clergy did not seem particularly radical or provocative. The changes had to do with institutional organization and administration, not religious doctrine or practice. In the minds of the majority all the Clergy Constitution did was put in place reforms that were deemed necessary and desirable given the failings of the clergy and organizational problems in the church during the preceding decades. Indeed, proponents of the Constitution could with justification claim that all over Europe there were monarchs, including Catholic ones, who had sought similar state control over the institutional church on matters that touched on the wider society.

There was a fatal error, however, in the French reform plan. At no point did the drafters of the Constitution make a conscious effort to sway the viewpoint of the bishops. Undoubtedly, many among the lower clergy were sympathetic to the reformist agenda, as, in all likelihood, was a good percentage of the laity. But not trying to win support from the French hierarchy left a potential fissure that was soon to grow into a wide and deep divide.

Particularly hard hit by the reforms were members of the religious orders who resisted the loss of feudal privileges. The land and wealth of many of these religious communities were taken away, and the orders themselves were forcibly disbanded. The resistance of the religious orders, as well as that of the episcopal nobility, to these events was one of the provocations to the anticlericalism of the revolutionaries.

The destruction of monasticism was a particularly telling attack on the traditional religious system of Western culture. The monasteries were the epitome of the land-based economy. Many monasteries held massive tracts of land that were the central element of local and regional economies. Once these monasteries were destroyed, religious institutions as an organizing principle of society and economy ended. Add to the dissolution process the seizure of the estates of prince-bishops, and the economic dislocation of the church was near complete.[12]

Among those who made the case for seizure of the church's wealth was Charles Talleyrand, still a bishop at the time and one who had taken the oath to the Constitution. He argued that the church had wealth not for its own sake but to enable its performance of various ministries. Since the state not the church would henceforth be responsible for caring for the poor and educating youth it was entirely appropriate for the state to take over the assets of the church.[13] Members of religious orders who engaged in education or health care would be salaried by the state as payment for their work; more contemplative or monastic orders were viewed as useless burdens and dissolved.

Under pressure from the National Assembly the king called upon all clergy to take an oath of obedience to the new Constitution. Louis XVI was personally devout and did not wish to damage the church. However, because the pope had been delayed in his response to the developments in France, the king went ahead with his call for an oath without knowing the papal reaction to the proposed reforms.

In retrospect it is now apparent that the proposed constitution was a major trauma for the church but that is because we view it with the knowledge that the monarchy would collapse after fleeing and being caught at Varennes in

---

12. The French experience was surprising by its delay; Henry VIII pursued the policy of dissolution about 250 years earlier in England.

13. Burleigh, *Earthly Powers*, 52-53.

the early summer of 1791. But in 1790 the right decision was less obvious to Pius VI. After all, the right of appointing bishops had already been conceded to rulers in Austria and the kingdom of Naples/Sicily. So to do the same in France would not be disastrous for the papacy. In 1790 there was still a French Catholic monarch and the idea of a constitutional monarch, as in England, was still possible within the proposed Constitution of 1791. The pope, therefore, deliberated over whether he could work with the Clergy Constitution.

When the deadline for taking the oath arrived at the end of 1790 there was still no word from Rome. This left the entire Catholic clergy in the uneasy position of having to act without knowledge of the papal position. The oath was to the state to the exclusion of any other authority, a striking example of the end of the old order. The state in the new order would have a monopoly of power. Although it is not possible to know with exactness the clerical response to the obligation to take the oath, one respected church historian has written, "the most reliable estimate seems to be that approximately fifty per cent swore and fifty per cent did not."[14] When the pope finally did speak and made known his strong opposition to the ideas of the Clergy Constitution the battle lines were clear. Almost the entire French hierarchy had refused to take the oath, although enough did swear to allow the reform wing to carry on with a valid episcopacy.

What led the pope to adopt a hard line in the matter was the decision to replace the nonswearing bishops with clergy who had taken the oath. In keeping with the new Constitution elections were held, and Talleyrand, who by now had already resigned his episcopal position for the sake of a secular post, agreed to consecrate the newly elected as bishops. In Rome's eyes this amounted to the creation of a valid but illicit hierarchy and revived old memories of investiture battles.[15] Now the opponent was not an emperor or monarch but a republic founded on popular sovereignty; yet the cause was similar. Would the papacy have the authority to oversee the episcopacy or would secular authority assume that role? To make his point Pope Pius VI broke off diplomatic relations with the French government.[16]

As opposing viewpoints hardened, the voices of those wishing not to reform the church but do away with it grew more powerful. The pope was viewed as an enemy of the Revolution, and refractory clergy loyal to him were treated as traitors to a noble cause. Any sense that there might be principled opposition

---

14. Alex Vidler, *The Church in an Age of Revolution* (Penguin History of the Church 5; London: Penguin Books, 1990), 17. I have relied upon Vidler's narrative throughout this section of the chapter.

15. See chap. 5.

16. Burleigh, *Earthly Powers*, 62-63.

to various aspects of the Revolution was now lost. Initially, the sworn and nonswearing clergy were both allowed to practice the ministry, sometimes in awkward competition; now, as the Revolution grew more extreme, those who refused to swear the oath were identified as counterrevolutionary and suffered for it. Although in some areas removed from Paris there might remain considerable support for those clergy loyal to Rome, there were also many examples of forced exile or massacre.[17]

Revolutionary Aftermath

At its most extreme stage the French Revolution sought to de-Christianize French civilization and put in its stead a cult of Reason, which failed miserably to win the hearts and minds of the masses. Once the Reign of Terror and the worst excesses of the Revolution had subsided, it was possible to return to public practice of the Christian faith. "[B]roadly speaking, religious policy had two distinct phases: first, a gradual return to *partial* freedom of worship from February 1795 to autumn 1797; second a two year return to the de-Christianization campaign between the left-wing *coup d'état* of September 1797 and Napoleon's coup in December 1799."[18] Rather quickly in the first phase, it became apparent that a substantial segment of the French people had remained devout and loyal to Catholicism.

The central element in the first phase was for Catholics to recover their churches and materials used in worship, to free priests from prison, or welcome them back from exile in order to reinstate public ritual. This was done through constant lobbying and petitioning of local officials. Those Catholics who were republican in sentiment sought to align the reestablishment of public religion with moderate republicanism. Those Catholics who were embittered by the Revolution's assault on Christianity and allied with counterrevolutionary activities took more dramatic steps in reasserting the right of religious practice, including guerilla violence, against the Republic.[19]

What both groups found, however, was a different experience of religion than before the Revolution. The Catholic Church was made up of dioceses that were coextensive with the Republic's own state divisions, and parishes that were the locales for baptisms, marriages, burials, and Sunday services. The records for marriages and deaths were maintained at town halls, not the parish church, and the clergy, significantly reduced in numbers, were civil servants

---

17. Ibid., 95-102.

18. Suzanne Desan, "The French Revolution and Religion, 1795-1815," in *Enlightenment, Reawakening and Revolution*, 556-74 at 557.

19. Ibid., 559.

paid by the state. Religious practice was to be focused on the parish church and local clergy.

Gone were the monasteries and convents that provided charitable assistance and medical care. The religious orders and their allied confraternities of lay members were disbanded. Abbeys and monasteries that once held libraries and art treasures serving as cultural centers had disappeared. With them went pilgrimages, religious festivals, and fairs that marked the rural calendar. This was religion on its way to struggling to avoid being a private affair practiced on Sunday (by some) and on life's special moments if so desired. It was no longer the prerevolutionary experience of Catholicism as a pervasive and comprehensive belief system that provided a worldview incarnated in an institution that was the central reality in social life.

Another feature of the new Catholicism was that it was a polarized church, especially among the clergy. One bitter divide, quite naturally, was between those priests and bishops who had taken the oath of allegiance to the Constitution and those who had refused. Yet, even among those who resisted the oath, there was division between supporters of the traditional political arrangement of the *ancien régime* and those who embraced the egalitarian ideals of the Republic. In addition, there remained a significant number of anticlerical, even anti-Christian, members of the population. As Alec Vidler summarized the postrevolutionary situation, "the future of Catholicism in France looked anything but bright."[20]

By 1795 church and state had formally separated, and religious groups were expected to refrain from any political activity. But the idea of "political" activity extended into what might more accurately be called "public" activity. Processions, steeple bells, festivals to honor saints, clerical garb, and open-air worship were all prohibited. At the same time the government still promoted the festivals of the civil religion adopted by the Revolution's leadership despite the new religion's failure to win over the imaginations of the general population.

Although there were attempts by some Catholics not wedded to royalist strategies and some revolutionary figures practical enough to want a rapprochement between church and the government there was little success in narrowing the chasm between church and state. When a new oath of allegiance to the state was formulated it now required not only a profession of loyalty to the existing government but also hatred of royalty. This was too much to ask of those who might not be active in counterrevolutionary efforts yet who had residual affection and respect for the old order.

To further add to the divide between Catholics and the French state there was continued tension between the papacy and the revolutionary government. It began with the Clergy Constitution and the condemnation of the

---

20. Vidler, *Age of Revolution*, 18.

Revolution by the pope. The situation grew worse by the creation of bishops without Rome's approval and the attacks on the refractory clergy, followed by the breaking of diplomatic relations. The culmination came in 1798 with the invasion of Rome by French troops, which effectively ended the temporal authority of the papacy. Pius VI was taken into custody and exiled from Rome; he died a year later.

A major consequence of the French Revolution was that Catholicism became identified in many minds with the forces of political and economic conservatism. Various reasons account for this. Resistance to the overthrow of the old social order by a hierarchy made up of nobles was one factor. The opposition of religious orders to the loss of monasteries and convents was another. Catholicism simply by virtue of being both hierarchical and international was out of step with liberalism's abolition of hierarchical privilege and the absolute sovereignty of the state. In addition, when the Revolution became associated with anti-Christian activity it did push a sizable number of the religiously devout over to the views of aristocratic counterrevolutionaries. Some of the counterrevolutionaries suggested that the Revolution was inspired, in part, by virulent Protestant hatred of Catholicism's position in France, while other arguments maintained that the Revolution was the project of urban intellectual elites who despised religion.

In reaction to the excesses of the Revolution a substantial number of French Catholics came to view Rome as the necessary defender of the faith against a state that might tilt toward antireligious hostility. And even those eager for church reform viewed Rome as the sole authority capable of leading a genuine renewal that would not descend into chaos. The upshot was the transformation of a "staunchly Gallican Church into what would emerge as one of the most fiercely ultramontane Churches in nineteenth-century Europe."[21]

Church and State under Napoleon

What radically altered the contentious situation of church and state was the rise of Napoleon to power. Beyond his success as a military leader he was also

---

21. Burleigh, *Earthly Powers*, 56-57. The word "ultramontane," literally "beyond the mountains," was a term used to describe the viewpoint of those Catholics in France, Germany, and other European nations who looked to the leadership of the pope, a figure who lived on the other side of the Alps. An ultramontane perspective is one that gives great significance to papal authority and jurisdiction. What should be remembered is that ultramontanism originally was a liberal movement promoted by young clerics who opposed both the old Gallicanists and those who were too accommodating to Napoleon. The early ultramontanists wanted the church to be independent of the state, and they believed their elders had sold out Catholicism's independence.

a most able public administrator. Under his rule France developed a highly centralized government that brought order and efficiency to the postrevolutionary chaos. This was done not only politically, economically, and legally, but also in the realm of religion. On this latter topic Napoleon approached the matter in a utilitarian way. Quite apart from personal devotion or belief in the truth of its creed, Catholicism was useful to him because it could foster social unity and cohesion.[22]

Napoleon knew, of course, that religion had been a source of great social conflict in the recent past, but he also saw the great reservoir of stability and order that religion might provide. For that to happen it was imperative that religious unity itself be reestablished, and that meant that the schism promoted by the controversy over the Clergy Constitution must be healed. Unlike the Gallicans, Napoleon recognized there would be no unity among Catholics if the papacy was overtly dismissed or opposed. And so he actively sought to win over the bishop of Rome by proposing a new set of terms to govern relations between his imperial state and the Roman Catholic Church. At the same time, the new pope, Pius VII, had hinted that French Catholicism was not wedded to the restoration of the Bourbon monarchy.

In order to bring about ecclesial unity Napoleon proposed that all the clergy, both those who took the oath and those who remained loyal to Rome, be joined. Furthermore, all the bishops, on either side of the controversy, should submit their resignations to Pius VII voluntarily or be removed by the pope if necessary. Napoleon would then submit to the pope for approval a list of nominees for the new episcopal appointments. Despite the reluctance of Pius to accept terms that, in effect, gave no more preference to those who had been loyal to Rome than to those who had disavowed papal authority, an agreement was signed. Part of the pact that was central to the papal side was Napoleon's willingness to reestablish the pope's temporal sovereignty over a reduced papal state. Known as a Concordat, the agreement signed in 1801 governed church-state relations in France on into the twentieth century.

Other significant elements of the Concordat included papal acceptance of the loss of property in France that had occurred during the Revolution, a loss

---

22. Vidler, *Age of Revolution*, 19, quoting from Paul Droulers, S.J., *Action pastorale et problèmes sociaux sous la Monarchie de Juillet* (Paris, 1954), 117, provides a telling quotation of Napoleon that illustrates his attitude toward Christianity: "I hold . . . that apart from the precepts and doctrines of the Gospel there is no society that can flourish, nor any real civilization. What is it that makes the poor man take it for granted that ten chimneys smoke in my palace while he dies of cold—that I have ten changes of raiment in my wardrobe while he is naked—that on my table at each meal there is enough to sustain a family for a week? It is religion which says to him that in another life I shall be his equal, indeed that he has a better chance of being happy there than I have."

of massive proportions that was the foundation of the church's wealth. In turn, the clergy would be on the state payroll, given a stipend for their services. While there was fear that this would make the clergy more dependent on civil government, it led in the longer run to many French clergy looking to Rome when defending their rights in a conflict with the state. Also Napoleon's strategy of forcing resignations to the pope and allowing him to remove a sitting bishop was an acknowledgment of papal jurisdiction over the French episcopacy that no Gallican monarch would have approved. These elements gave further impetus to the rise of an ultramontane segment within the French lower clergy, who would disdain the ultranationalist Napoleonic episcopacy after 1815.

The Concordat did not return Catholicism to the status of the established religion of the state. Calvinists and Lutherans were given legal status, but not so for smaller Protestant groups such as Methodists or Mennonites. Jews were also given legal recognition. Catholicism was acknowledged to be the religion of the majority of the French people, but this did not translate into the system of privileges that had existed prior to the Revolution.

Shortly after the Concordat was signed, Napoleon issued a document specifying the manner by which it was to be implemented. The document greatly offended Pius and undercut much of what the papacy thought it had gained by the agreement. Eventually, the rift with Pius VII would contribute to Napoleon's downfall. Despite his cynicism in dealing with the papacy, however, Napoleon legitimated the Catholic Church's role in French society. The freedom he granted to public practice of the Catholic faith and his stabilization of a divided institution following the Revolution gave the Catholic Church an opportunity to live up to its sobriquet as "the eldest daughter of the church."[23] The difficulties that followed in the ensuing decades were due less to Napoleon's Concordat than to the church's own failings. And so a majority of the French, including many clergy, saw Napoleon as a ruler who helped save the French Catholic Church.

Manifold changes in the religious landscape of France came about as a result of the Revolution. It had led to a schism with the Catholic Church, "a state-sponsored assault on Christianity itself unlike anything in the European experience since the early Roman Empire," and brought about the "first full separation of church and state in modern times."[24] The church was no longer

---

23. The "eldest daughter of the church" is an honorific title bestowed on the French church in 498 when Clovis I, king of the Franks, was baptized into the Catholic faith as opposed to the Arian form of Christianity that was also present in Gaul. The title was deemed appropriate because of the early presence of Christianity in the region and the loyalty of many to Catholic Christianity.

24. Tackett, "The French Revolution and Religion," 536.

the First Estate. French laity now owned much of the wealth that formerly was in the control of clergy. Almost the entire monastic culture of France was destroyed. The secular power of the Catholic hierarchy was eradicated. And the scholarly arguments and intellectual disputes concerning Gallicanism and French Catholicism's independence from the papacy were overshadowed by the rise of ultramontanism. Finally, citizenship and Catholic identity were no longer tightly interwoven.[25]

The Trend to Restoration

Both in the reaction to the Revolution and then to Napoleon's imperial ambitions, other European nations experienced a "fusion" of counterrevolution, nationalism, and religion.[26] After the Revolution's excess and the demise of Napoleon's project there was widespread disenchantment with the Enlightenment's exaltation of reason over religion and tradition. Christianity was restored as a source of wisdom, and a Romanticist movement swept over Europe that looked back on the medieval order as an age of faith, unity, and social order. For those leaders who came to power in 1814-1815 attacks on Christianity were understood as assaults aimed at government, authority, and morality.

As a consequence there was an alliance between throne and altar, because they both served as the basis for authority and as bulwarks against anarchy and mob tyranny. Thus it was that Protestant England served as a safe haven for many French Catholic refugees during the period from 1792 to 1820, even to the point of state support for exiled Catholic clergy. Such examples of cooperation by powerful supporters of a more traditional social order led a conservative papacy of Gregory XVI to teach that rebellion against a temporal sovereign was never permissible because temporal authority was from God.[27] This, of course, was a view that, as prior history demonstrated, many previous popes and Protestant church leaders would not have endorsed.

The need for a new political order after Napoleon and the desire to forestall future revolutionary programs in Europe led to the Congress of Vienna in 1815. In what was really a series of meetings held at various levels of government the major European powers—Austria, England, Prussia, and Russia—decided on the redrawing of the map of Europe. While jealously eyeing one another, the four powers restored the Bourbon monarchy to France, dictated terms to lesser European nations, and balanced their own competing interests

---

25. Burleigh, *Earthly Powers*, 110.
26. The well-chosen word is Burleigh's, ibid., 112.
27. Ibid., 112-18.

with the hope of establishing a balance of powers that might be maintained into the future through diplomatic means.

The papacy was represented at the Congress by its Cardinal Secretary of State. In keeping with both the interest in returning to a prerevolutionary order and supporting monarchical power, the region of central Italy was restored as the Papal States, and the pope, once again, became a temporal ruler. Concerning the other major branches of Christianity, the Restoration basically left in place the practice of secular rulers determining the status of a church. This usually meant the establishment of one expression of Christianity receiving preferential treatment while other Christian churches might experience full tolerance or something significantly less.

There is no small irony in the Restoration movement that dominated Europe during these decades. For one, it had been the emergence of absolutist monarchs that led to the destruction of many of the traditional local, regional, and subsidiary authorities that made up the medieval social order. Long before the French Revolution it was the quest for power among national monarchs that swept away those intermediary institutions embodying tradition and authority in Europe.

So, too, in regard to the church, it was the action of monarchs that led to the English Reformation, Gallicanism, Josephism, Febronianism, and Erastianism—all movements to assert a sovereign ruler's right to govern the church within a nation's boundaries. The moderate supporters of the Revolution in France simply had argued that a government of popular sovereignty had the same authority over the Catholic Church that a monarchical government claimed.

And, finally, it was the call of nationalism and the encouragement of a self-conscious sense of citizenship among European peoples that helped the governments of the Great Powers to mobilize and defeat Napoleon. Once that was accomplished, however, the newly restored sovereigns sought to tamp down any sense of active citizenship that might lead to calls for change along the lines of a democratic republic.

THE AMERICAN REVOLUTION

The Revolution in France was a harsh experience for Christians, especially Catholics, the vast majority of the nation's population. Indeed, the avowed aim of the more extreme revolutionaries was to displace Christianity with a deism that worshipped a God who was little more than a prop for the revolutionaries' agenda.

The story of Christianity and the American Revolution, however, was a very different tale. The Revolution in the New World was to prove a boon to organized Christianity, especially branches of the Protestant family, which made up the overwhelming majority of the new nation's population. To understand the religious background of the American Revolution it is necessary to know something of the situation of English Protestantism since it was the dominant factor that shaped the religious beliefs and practices within the American colonies.

English Protestantism in the Sixteenth and Seventeenth Centuries

After the reign of Henry VIII, the English Crown went through turmoil as each of his children from multiple marriages had support as the rightful heir to the throne. The disputes had a religious dimension since support for Roman Catholicism or the Church of England waxed and waned under different monarchs. Throughout the period there also was a steady and growing presence of "dissenters," those Protestant believers who thought the Anglican reform was insufficient, leaving the English church too "popish," or Catholic, to deserve support.

Henry's only son, Edward VI, ruled for a few years followed very briefly by his cousin, Lady Jane Grey. Henry's first child, Mary, his daughter with Catherine of Aragon, then ruled and supported Catholicism while persecuting Protestant reformers. Mary died of natural causes in 1558, leaving no heir, and her half sister, Elizabeth, came to the throne. Elizabeth I's reign lasted forty-five years until her death in 1603. Upon assuming the throne she asserted her support for an English Protestant church.

In 1559 two acts of Parliament were passed, the Act of Supremacy and the Act of Uniformity. Together they constituted what has been called the "Elizabethan settlement." By the first act the Church of England's independence was reestablished, and Elizabeth was named as supreme head of the church, undoing Mary's reconciliation between the English Crown and Rome. By the Uniformity Act the form and practice of the English Church was put in place, an ecclesiology that broke with many aspects of Roman Catholicism yet did not endorse all the reforms sought by the dissenters. During the long Elizabethan era the Church of England sought the "middle way" between Roman Catholicism and its Protestant critics. Nonetheless, the Anglican dominance within the Church of England would not go uncontested.

Because Elizabeth's reign was so long the settlement she embraced took root among the majority of the English people, although a Catholic minority continued to hope for a return to unity with Rome. An even larger group dissatisfied with the Elizabethan approach was Calvinist in outlook. During persecutions under Mary, many English Calvinists sought refuge on the continent, especially in Geneva. When they returned to England during Elizabeth's reign they generally held dissenting views, politically and religiously, from the established Anglican mainstream. The Puritans who would come to America in the 1600s stemmed from these Calvinist dissenters.

Upon Elizabeth's death in 1603 the religious tensions in England contributed mightily to what would eventually become a civil war. James I, not a Tudor but a Stuart, succeeded Elizabeth and had a variety of differences with Parliament. Religiously, many members of Parliament were close to the Calvinist view that the Church of England needed additional purging of its Catholic traits. James disagreed. Economically, the king needed to raise revenue, but Parliament was not disposed to approve taxes without concessions from the king in a number of areas. Politically, James subscribed to the theory of divine right and was unwilling to concede such power to Parliament.

When Charles I succeeded his father James in 1625 the simmering tensions between monarch and Parliament soon broke out into open hostility. Charles married a Roman Catholic, which greatly disturbed the Puritan wing of the Protestant community. He also engaged in several failed foreign wars, which depleted the royal treasury. Parliament consistently denied Charles the means for increasing his revenues, and, as a proponent of divine-right monarchy, he found this intolerable. He dissolved Parliament and for many years ruled without calling it into session. During this period he devised a variety of measures for raising funds, almost all of which angered the urban merchant class, the very group that had been represented by the House of Commons in the dissolved Parliament.

Many of these merchants were also religious dissenters, and the king's support for William Laud, initially bishop of London and then archbishop of Canterbury, only heightened hostilities because Laud was a fierce opponent of the Puritan outlook. The actions of Charles and Laud led to violent conflict first in Scotland, where Calvinist Christianity was strong. The king was unable to quash the Scottish resistance, but by his military actions he incurred additional expenses he could no longer afford. In order to raise revenue he was forced to restore Parliament, and, thereafter, both Charles and the House of Commons committed a series of polarizing decisions that led to a civil war in 1642.

Led by Oliver Cromwell and in alliance with the Scots, the parliamentary forces defeated the royalists after a four-year struggle. But the apparent end of the war was really just the finale of the first installment, for Charles made a deal with the Scots, who switched sides, and war ensued once more. Despite being called the English Revolution the conflict was more the last of the European wars of religion than the first revolution of the modern age.[28] In the second

---

28. John Coffey, "Puritan Legacies," in *The Cambridge Companion to Puritanism*, ed. John Coffey and Paul Lim (Cambridge: Cambridge University Press, 2008), 327-45 at 330.

stage of the war the parliamentary army, largely Puritan in makeup, decided that no settlement with Charles was possible, and upon a second defeat of the royalists the king was executed in 1649. The monarchy, along with the House of Lords, was abolished.

A period of more than ten years followed when the army was the real authority in the land and Cromwell the head of state. A variety of efforts were made to reconstitute some form of Parliament, but the political situation remained unsettled. Charles II, in exile, offered a plan of reconciliation two years after Cromwell's death that would secure religious liberty, pardon all but a small number of those involved in the civil war, and return England to a mixed government of monarchy and Parliament, with Houses of Commons and Lords. The offer was accepted.

The reign of Charles II witnessed continued religious tensions and bickering between king and Parliament. During the period of the early 1660s Parliament issued a number of rules aimed at regulating the many independent churches that had arisen during the preceding interregnum. These new laws made life difficult for Protestants who were not members of the Church of England. Historians believe Charles II was sympathetic to Catholicism, the religion of his wife, but he was not a particularly devout man regarding religious practice. Upon his death in 1685 he was succeeded by his brother James, who was an openly practicing member of the Roman Catholic Church.

James gave several royal appointments to Catholics and rescinded the laws that penalized Catholics and nonconforming Protestants. After his second wife gave birth to a male heir, concern grew that the Catholic monarchy would continue beyond James. Consequently, a group of Anglican nobles invited James's Protestant son-in-law, William of Orange, a Dutchman, to come to England and seize the throne. James lacked widespread support, and he fled England when William arrived. Parliament declared the throne to be vacant, and William and his wife, Mary, an Anglican born to James's first wife, were then declared monarchs.

The ouster of James and the ascension of William and Mary in 1688 is often referred to as the Glorious Revolution. As part of the agreement between the new monarchs and Parliament, a bill of rights was approved in 1689 that brought about greater cooperation in democratic freedoms and governance. The agreement also entailed forbidding any Catholic from being monarch or for any monarch to marry a Catholic. A law of toleration was also passed that permitted Puritans to have their own churches, ministers, and practices. One historian of the movement has said the toleration act "drew the curtain on the heroic age of Puritanism, and ushered in the rather more prosaic era of Protestant Nonconformity."[29] The nonconforming church members were

---

29. Ibid., 333.

discriminated against, however, by being barred from government positions and attendance at universities.

Puritans in the early 1600s were steeped in both the theology of Calvin and the political philosophy of Calvinism. Emphasis on divine sovereignty, coupled with a sense of the insignificance of humanity before God, encouraged in Calvinists a sense of defiance toward temporal rulers who overreached in their exercise of authority. And one area where authority could overreach was to interfere with a believer's freedom to read and interpret the Bible. A ruler who came into conflict with the sacred rights of a believer could be dismissed.

Of course, Calvin himself leaned toward autocracy in the governance of Geneva, but because the entire social order of Geneva was deeply influenced by Calvinist ideals the tension between religious liberty and temporal authority was not sharply experienced. In seventeenth-century England, where Calvinists were a minority in disfavor, the tensions were evident. The authority of the monarch was at odds with Calvinist belief, and the continued support of rulers for the Anglican reform, or even worse, for returning to Roman Catholicism left the Puritan conscience deeply troubled. The war led by Cromwell was a Puritan struggle, one in which the cause of religious liberty became entwined with political freedoms. No monarch should oppress the freedom of the individual to believe, to worship, to profess, and to practice the true gospel. It was the authority of the Bible that must be relied upon, and without a pope or bishops to interpret that text, it was left to the sincerity of the believer's conscience to find the truth.

In this way one can discern an underlying alliance between the Puritan and the Enlightenment worldviews. Both outlooks shared a profound respect for the mind of the individual. Although, as we shall see below, American Puritanism placed great emphasis on conformity, there remained the bedrock conviction that the Bible was the revealed Word of God and that the individual believer had the right and duty to read and interpret the text. Reliance on the individual's well-trained and well-disposed mind to grasp the truth was a shared starting point for both Puritanism and the Enlightenment.

In order to defend their religious liberty throughout seventeenth-century England the Puritans continually preached the political liberty that was the right of English people. They rallied to efforts by Parliament, particularly the House of Commons, to delimit the authority of a monarch. Since the Commons was largely sympathetic to Calvinism, giving to Parliament a greater role in governance was also a method to advance the Puritan cause. To suggest that there were limits to what a ruler could do without the consent of the people was to clear the political ground for making a case concerning religious freedom for a dissenting minority. No longer would the religion of the ruler dictate the religion of the people.

Christianity in the New World

America was deeply tied to a sense of newness for Europeans. For the Europeans who arrived on the Atlantic coastline of North America there was the hope that this land would permit the creation of a new society. The old world of Europe would be transformed; it would be a *new* Hampshire, a *new* Jersey, a *new* York, not just a nostalgia for those places in England. The newness was not limited to political society but included religion.

Puritans who arrived in 1630 wanted to remake the church.[30] They had rejected what they viewed as the corrupt practices of the English Church led by Archbishop Laud. The Church of England was too Catholic and insufficiently "pure" in its fidelity to the biblical message. Fired by a religious imagination that envisioned another chance at reliving the biblical drama, these Protestant dissenters would be the new Israel, a new chosen people. Their emigration from Europe had been a new exodus.

Arrival in America offered the promise not only of a new church but the creation of a holy commonwealth that would be built on Christian revelation. True to their Calvinist heritage, the Puritans sought to remake the temporal order as an enactment of their religious beliefs. The Massachusetts Bay Colony was to be a demonstration of how a Christian commonwealth should work. Following their leader John Winthrop, the Puritans believed that if they were good and faithful their religious-political project would succeed. And so there was great emphasis on conformity within the group because any individual sinner might undercut the example of the entire community. (In this regard the Puritans shared the anxiety of the earliest Christian communities who were concerned about distorting a corporate witness to the gospel and failing to show the distinctiveness of the Christian way of life.)

One characteristic that the immigrants to America brought with them from Europe was their sense of militancy regarding the faith. As participants in the religious conflicts in the Old World, the Puritans brought with them the conviction that there was but one true path and that their version of Christianity was it. The new settlers came to America in order to have the freedom to practice their faith, but they did not see it as necessary to extend religious freedom to those of other viewpoints. For all intents and purposes the Puritan faith

---

30. Scholars today suggest that Puritan does not represent a distinct group as much as a theological and political tendency among Protestant dissenters. The more traditional language using "Pilgrims" to describe the Plymouth Colony in 1620 and "Puritans" for the 1630 settlers in the Massachusetts Bay Colony reflects a now questionable view of clear divisions among those English colonists. It is better to see them as a movement with various strands rather than a neatly categorized group with all holding the exact same views.

was the established religion of the new colony, and the force of civil authority (Governor Winthrop) was committed to enforcing religious conformity.

Of course, the stress on conformity came into tension with another Calvinist belief, that of individual conscience and the freedom of each believer to read the Bible without external authority dictating the right interpretation. How that tension was managed is illustrated by two test cases that involve charismatic dissenters from the Puritan majority.

Roger Williams and Anne Hutchinson

Both Roger Williams and Anne Hutchinson came to the colony of Massachusetts Bay after the first cohort of Puritan settlers had arrived. Williams, who first landed at Plymouth Colony, arrived in the Massachusetts Bay Colony in early 1631 and was quickly established as a significant voice in the community. He was an ordained clergyman, a gifted linguist, and studied at Cambridge University where he underwent disillusionment with the Church of England under Archbishop Laud. Drawn to the Puritan outlook he was known to many of the first colonial settlers from contacts back in England. By the time of his arrival in America, however, his viewpoint had evolved to the point where he was dubious about the union of government and church authority in the new colony. The Puritan colonists in Massachusetts Bay Colony, although their ecclesial organization and form of worship had evolved in quite different ways than the Church of England, still understood themselves as being in union with the national church back home. Williams was critical of the reluctance to renounce the Church of England and never joined the church in Massachusetts Bay.

Williams's study of church history had convinced him that an alliance of Christianity with political power, in whatever form, was a mistake. He believed that not only the recent religious wars in Europe but also the entire pattern of allying church with state since the age of Constantine showed the folly of a union of spiritual and temporal power. For Williams the state was responsible for enforcing the second tablet of the Ten Commandments (do not kill, do not steal, etc.) but should have no role in enforcing the commandments of the first tablet (acknowledging God and observing the Sabbath, banning idolatry and blasphemy). Religion was a matter of the interior life of the individual, and no government official had authority over that realm. True Christianity required a voluntary acceptance of the gospel message, and any government inducement or coercion undermined the freedom of the individual in making a conscientious choice.[31]

Criticism by Williams of the colony's organization was not limited to ques-

---

31. See Edwin Gaustad, *Roger Williams* (New York: Oxford University Press, 2005), for a concise and informative biography.

tions of church and state.[32] He also launched an attack on the validity of the colonial charters that had been granted by the English Crown, saying that they were unfair to the Native American residents of the land. Williams had become a student of the languages and culture of the local tribes of Native Americans and befriended many during his time in the colony. His criticisms were not well received, however, and he came to be viewed as a provocative malcontent by colonial leaders. So Williams left Massachusetts Bay Colony for the Plymouth Colony to the southeast. In a short time he vexed William Bradford, the governor of that colony, and returned to Massachusetts Bay. The church in the settlement of Salem was led by a more indulgent pastor than other Massachusetts Bay congregations, and for a time Williams was able to preach and live in that locale. Indeed, in 1634 he was chosen to lead the congregation after the death of the former pastor.

Williams may have been welcomed in Salem, but his selection as pastor raised a variety of concerns among the majority of colonists outside Salem. Despite several interventions by other ministers he stood firm in his beliefs about a strong separation between matters of civil governance and church concerns. Although the other churches in Massachusetts Bay Colony had no right to overrule the choice of the Salem church, they did have the right to decide whether they would continue to associate with the Salem congregation. And so the Salem church soon found itself excluded from any fellowship with the rest of the colony's churches because of its support for Williams.

Eventually Williams denounced all those who disagreed with him, including those members of the Salem church who would not join in his public denunciation of the rest of the colony. Finally, in 1635, the General Court, an assembly that was the highest authority in the colony according to the royal charter, instructed Governor Winthrop to banish Williams. And so Roger Williams left Massachusetts for a new settlement to the south that he was to call Providence.

Even as the controversy over Williams was working itself out, another major dispute was about to begin. A bedrock conviction of Puritan theology, drawn from the writings of Calvin, was that all people were sinners undeserving of salvation. Yet there was hope that some would be saved due to God's gracious election of that minority of true believers. The perennial question for Christians of this persuasion was whether one could know that one was among the elect. The usual response was that one should look to the quality of one's life, not in the sense that one earned one's salvation but in the belief

---

32. Williams is reportedly the first person to use the metaphor of a "wall of separation" in matters of church and state, although his imagery was of the garden of Christ separated from the wilderness of the world.

that if you were saved there would be signs of godly behavior in one's character and deeds.

However, other Puritans feared that such an approach smacked of the "works righteousness" they opposed in Roman Catholicism and the Anglican mainstream of the Church of England. They offered a different solution to the anxiety of those seeking assurance about election. Their approach was to emphasize the experience of the Holy Spirit who brought consolation and peace to those who were saved. A person should look to an inner feeling or sensation of the Spirit's presence in order to know if one was saved.

This debate became a dominant issue within the Boston church as many of the new arrivals, led by John Cotton, one of the church's ministers, and Anne Hutchinson, an articulate and educated laywoman, supported the "spiritual" method for gaining knowledge of salvation. The discussions within the local congregation soon became known outside of Boston, and, in time, many colonists throughout Massachusetts weighed in with their opinions. Several ministers from outside Boston were particularly critical of the Cotton/Hutchinson camp. As is so often the case when a dispute moves beyond those who personally know and engage one another, the various figures in the debate and their positions became caricatured. The idea that there might be common ground between the two viewpoints was lost as both sides described the other in the most extreme guise.

The controversy continued for several years, and some leaders of the "spiritual" faction were either banished or left the colony on their own. In November of 1637 Hutchinson was put on trial. She had come to hold a position that seemed to go even beyond Cotton's preaching. Hutchinson was confident she was one of the elect because God had directly communicated this to her. Her assurance of salvation based on personal revelation clashed with the uncertainty and humility about being elected that the majority of Puritans thought proper. Beyond the theological controversy, her position put her at odds with civil authorities such as Winthrop who promoted self-discipline and persistent effort as the means to the colony's success as a new "holy commonwealth." The governor feared Hutchinson's perspective could lead to a too-easy confidence that God would take care of the material needs of the elect, quite apart from human activity.

Because she was a woman, there was little public record of Hutchinson's beliefs; she had never preached in public nor signed petitions on behalf of the spiritualists. Thus, it was not easy to resolve her case. At one point in the trial, however, she turned on Winthrop and the other members of the General Court and warned them that they were to be cursed for their actions and that this had been revealed to her by God. The Court decided to banish her from the colony. Then in a second trial before the Boston church, Hutchinson was found to hold views that were unorthodox, and she was excommunicated. By the spring of 1638, along with several close supporters, she left Massachusetts and settled in the same region as Roger Williams, the future Rhode Island.

As one commentator has written, the banishments of Williams and Hutchinson were not surprising, given a fundamental premise of Puritan belief.[33] The colonists of Massachusetts Bay had entered into a covenant with their creator, and believed in all sincerity that if they did not live in accord with God's will the fate of the colony was doomed. Thus, Winthrop as governor and the religious leaders of the various Massachusetts congregations saw their obligation to correct the errors of individuals who put not only their own souls in danger but the success of the entire commonwealth. When, despite correction, individuals remained adamant in their error they had to be punished. The last resort was exile; it was a way to remove the infection from spreading to the rest of the body.

The Legacy

The stories of Williams and Hutchinson point out an ongoing tension within Christianity between, on the one hand, the personal faith commitment of each man and woman and, on the other hand, the need for the church to maintain a sense of community (common unity) that demarcates the boundary limits of a religious body. The tension has been present from the beginning of Christianity and had been resolved in various ways, but the tension was sharpened by the Protestant Reformation. No longer could one appeal to a pope to settle disputes. In some cases the reformers held onto the model of an episcopacy that would serve as the authority (e.g., Anglicans). In other cases, church elders or presbyters would play an authoritative role (e.g., Presbyterians). For others, a general assembly or synod of delegates from the various congregations might play that role (e.g., Lutherans).

The Puritans, however, gave independence to each local congregation. With thinkers like Roger Williams or Anne Hutchinson, the dynamic of the Reformation continued as the individual's conscience was set against the views of the congregation. Puritans drew a line that settled the boundary between orthodoxy and that of the individual conscience in a manner that was true to their congregationalist ecclesiology: if the individual could not be reconciled with the local community's viewpoint, then the person was to be excluded. Although in their method of deciding who determines the bounds of orthodoxy the Puritans may have been different than many earlier Christians, there is a sense in which they were very much like all the Christians who had

---

33. Francis Bremer, "The Puritan Experiment in New England, 1630-1660," in *The Cambridge Companion to Puritanism*, 127-42 at 136. This essay by Bremer, a leading scholar of Puritanism, has been an important source for the material on Williams and Hutchinson.

preceded them: that was their assumption that religious unity was essential for social unity.

The disputes with Williams and Hutchinson forced the Puritans to work out their approach to religious freedom. Those dissenting from the mainstream were to be opposed and, if necessary, driven out of the area. In truth, Hutchinson was as religiously intolerant as those who opposed her.[34] But in Roger Williams and his Providence settlement something new was encountered. His argument was that civil authority should play no role in religious matters. Believers should be free to follow their conscience in matters of faith without fear of penalty imposed by civil government.

It was Williams who pressed the case for the freedom of religious conscience before the state. For Williams, religion was mainly internal and individual and, therefore, not a matter for interference by public authority. This legacy, though put in place in his colony, would not be fully realized in the New World until almost 150 years later. During that interim period the alliance of church and state would continue in a majority of the colonies. Nine of the thirteen colonies had some kind of church establishment, which meant that all citizens subsidized the privileged church through taxation and that the official church provided a minister to speak at public ceremonies and special occasions.

The Puritans, who became the Congregational Church, were the established church in the colonies of Massachusetts, Connecticut, and New Hampshire. Other Protestants—Presbyterians, Baptists, Lutherans, and Quakers—found little toleration and moved on from the New England colonies. Maryland, Virginia, Georgia, and both Carolinas established the Anglican Church, although they generally practiced greater tolerance than the Congregationalists in the north. Rhode Island, New Jersey, New York, Delaware, and Pennsylvania had no established churches.

The Great Awakening and the Virginia Statute

The next significant chapter in the narrative shifts to the south and the colony of Virginia and reflects the significance of Anne Hutchinson's religious experience. In the middle of the eighteenth century an Anglican clergyman, George Whitfield, promoted a form of religious identity that echoed ideas of Hutchinson. Whitfield accepted the radical sinfulness of humanity and the consequent need of people to be redeemed in order to be saved. Also, like Hutchinson, Whitfield sought to reassure people about their being among the elect. He maintained that people had to experience a spiritual awakening enabled by the Holy Spirit. True Christians should have an immediate experi-

---

34. Ibid., 137.

ence of God, and such revelation is not notional but affective, a felt sense of the presence of God rather than a clear idea about God.

Whitfield promoted these themes to a broad audience. Although unwelcome in many Virginia churches because his evangelical style did not sit well with most Anglican clergy or the civic leadership, Whitfield practiced open-air preaching at outdoor revivals up and down the Atlantic seaboard. A charismatic preacher who could move his audience to great emotional heights and depths, Whitfield became popular among the Virginia colonists. His influence was immense, in no small part due to his engaging preaching style, but also because of his extensive travels. It has been estimated that as many as one of every four Americans heard Whitfield preach. His appeal was ecumenical, reaching a diverse Protestant audience.

Other leading clerics, notably Jonathan Edwards, joined with Whitfield in the religious renewal that came to be called the "Great Awakening." Historian Edwin Gaustad has written that "The Awakening was 'Great' because it was general: none escaped its influence or avoided its controversy."[35] Indeed, its influence was evident as "the first true inter-colonial intellectual and spiritual event."[36] It was at this time that historians find "the rise of talk not about this or that colony, or about His Majesty's colonies, but, for the first time broadly 'the American colonies' or the nation."[37]

The controversy over the movement was that it led to divisions within existing denominations. People started to challenge their regular clergy as they heard a different message from itinerant revival preachers. Local congregations split between the reform enthusiasts and those who supported a more traditional theology and spirituality. Throughout the colonies there were schisms and a redrawing of denominational boundaries. One outcome was a sense that people had the rightful liberty to choose their own churches, which, of course, undercut support for the idea of government-established churches.

The influence of the Great Awakening was not only religious. As time went on, the idea of religious liberty would become connected to political liberty. If an individual was capable of exercising freedom in the realm that determined one's salvation, why ought not that same individual be capable of exercising freedom in the realm of politics? The conviction that the Holy Spirit directed a person in the rightful use of freedom became a way to merge religious and political liberty.

---

35. Edwin Gaustad, *The Great Awakening in New England* (New York: Harper and Brothers, 1957), as quoted in William Grimes, "Edwin Gaustad, Religious Historian, Is Dead at 87," *New York Times* (April 4, 2011), B9.

36. Martin Marty, "The American Revolution and Religion, 1765-1815," in *Enlightenment, Reawakening and Revolution*, 497-516 at 499.

37. Ibid., 500.

The Great Awakening also encouraged a spirit of egalitarianism that made colonists less deferential to their English rulers. The familiarity of laymen challenging clergy, of minority dissenters questioning religious establishment, of lower-status colonists being told that their religious experiences were no less significant than that of social elites—all this would erode ideas of status and class stratification, which eventually led ordinary colonists to believe they could challenge the laws and policies of the English Crown and Parliament.

A Debate within Virginia

In 1773 a Baptist minister, Jeremiah Moore, was arrested in Fairfax, Virginia, for preaching without a license to function as a clergyman. He and other Baptists had migrated from Pennsylvania, where they had been tolerated, to Virginia, where Anglicanism was the established religion. Moore and other Baptists had some success in preaching their message of the need for spiritual rebirth and the practice of adult baptism. The Anglican establishment tried to stifle the message and opposed public preaching by the Baptists.

As was still commonly believed by the majority of colonists, despite the earlier arguments of Roger Williams and his followers, religion was seen as an essential unifying force in colonial society. The Baptist message of believer's baptism and adult conversion threatened that by suggesting that one might leave the Anglican fold and join another church.

Virginia may have been the most highly structured society among all the colonies, and a strong, established Anglican Church was viewed as a pillar of that order. The Baptist message of adult conversion was dangerous to the tight alliance of religious and political elites in the Virginia colony. Yet any effort at repressing the activity of the Baptist missionaries only seemed to further energize them. In October of 1773 Moore, along with thousands of other Baptists, petitioned the Virginia assembly for the freedom to preach and practice without interference or persecution from civil authorities.

Thomas Jefferson became their advocate in the Virginia assembly. Jefferson was not a Baptist in his personal beliefs, but he agreed with their strategy of no state establishment of any religion. Jefferson thought that religious establishment amounted to government abuse of individual liberty; his preference was for a free market of ideas, including religious ones. Jefferson drafted a bill supporting religious liberty that was opposed by a majority in the assembly. It was not until January of 1786, three years after the Treaty of Paris secured American independence, that Jefferson's bill would pass the Virginia legislature.

The eventual success of Jefferson's cause was due in large part to his young friend James Madison, who was elected to the Virginia assembly in 1784. Madison was a strong advocate of religious liberty. Patrick Henry had offered an alternative bill that would have brought about not disestablishment of the Anglican Church but establishment of multiple Christian churches. Henry's proposal was opposed by many minority churches—Lutherans, Quakers, Presbyterians, and especially the Baptists. For the Baptists, the idea of non-establishment was not a matter of expedience given their minority status but a matter of principle. State control or state legitimation of religion was deeply offensive to their ideal of religious liberty.

Madison drew up his "Memorial and Remonstrance," a protest aimed at Henry that argued the lesson of history was that state support for religion only led to violence and strife, the corruption of religion, and the undermining of personal freedom. For Madison and many others, the idea of religious establishment was a betrayal of America's Revolution. Henry's bill stalled, and Madison brought Jefferson's bill for religious freedom to the floor. Debate ensued, and some of Jefferson's original wording was altered; but the bill was passed under Madison's leadership while Jefferson was living in Paris as U.S. ambassador to France.

In the next year, 1787, the delegates to the Constitutional Convention met in Philadelphia. Jefferson and Madison hoped that the Virginia statute would provide the approach to be endorsed in the new Constitution, but that was not the case. Because the prevailing view of the delegates was that they were drawing up a legal document for a civil state there was little attention given to religion anywhere in the text. The colonies were religiously pluralistic, and it seemed highly unlikely that the churches would overcome their differences and come to agreement. The safe and sane course was to avoid religion as far as possible if the delegates were to develop a constitution that would create the unity that the weak Articles of Confederation could not.

The sole mention of religion in the text was the exclusion of any religious test for holding office under the Constitution. When the document went to the various state conventions convened to ratify the proposed Constitution there was concern about the lack of any religious consideration for office as well as unhappiness over the absence of any mention of God anywhere in the text.

Even greater dissatisfaction arose over the lack of any explicit list of rights that guaranteed the personal freedoms that many Americans viewed as the main rationale for the Revolution. Jefferson, who was not present in Philadelphia, wrote to Madison from Paris expressing his disappointment. He was hardly alone in his reaction, and Madison pledged that the first order of business in the new Congress would be a bill of rights.

The proposed first amendment concerned with religious liberty was received differently in the various colonies. Those states that had no established church had little difficulty, but those colonies with established churches struggled with the question. As he had argued so persuasively during the earlier debate in Virginia, so now James Madison again became an important voice in support of the amendment during the debates on the Constitution and Bill of Rights.

And so in September of 1789, at the first session of the newly instituted Congress, a bill of rights was approved by both House and Senate. In 1791 the First Amendment to the U.S. Constitution, along with nine others, was ratified by the necessary number of states.

The full text of the first amendment reads, "Congress shall make no law respecting an establishment of religion, or prohibiting the free exercise thereof; or abridging the freedom of speech, or of the press; or the right of the people peaceably to assemble and to petition the Government for a redress of grievances."

The first phrase, the establishment clause, secured that the federal government cannot favor any religion over another, while the second phrase, the free-exercise clause, guaranteed that the federal government cannot suppress any person's religious belief. Never before had a nation failed to guarantee religion's central place in public life through a state-supported church. "For 1,400 years, since the age of Constantine in the Roman Empire, wherever Christians were a strong presence they favored and often held a monopoly or at least a privileged status at the hands of a complicit government."[38] That period came to an end with the First Amendment. And so, with government favor and repression both ruled out, a great experiment began about how church and state would interact in the new nation.

A Constitutional Commitment

The First Amendment, as the late Christopher Mooney suggested, "involves a three-fold commitment: to religious pluralism, to religious freedom, and to government neutrality."[39] Religious pluralism was a fact about the New World long before any constitutional convention was convened. The dissenting heritage of Hutchinson and Williams foreshadowed the diversity of religious belief that came to characterize religious practice in the colonies. This situation made it evident that no one Christian church would be in a situation to dominate the public space and control all other religious traditions.

In a very real sense the First Amendment gave legal recognition to what was already undeniably true: without religious freedom that acknowledged the existing religious diversity there could be no public peace or hope for

---

38. Ibid., 512.

39. Christopher Mooney, *Public Virtue: Law and the Social Character of Religion* (Notre Dame, IN: University of Notre Dame Press, 1986), 21. In what follows I am indebted to chap. 2 of Mooney's book for his analysis of the threefold commitment.

national unity. In that sense the religion clauses of the First Amendment, as John Courtney Murray pointed out, were not articles of faith but articles of peace;[40] they expressed not the sanctity of dogma but the rationality of law.[41] The commitment to diversity held out the hope that a citizenry of varying religious beliefs could live and work together.

Religious freedom was a sensible extension of the commitment to religious diversity. In drawing on a distinction prevalent in the patristic and medieval eras but lost during the age of absolutism, the commitment to religious freedom differentiated between the religious and the political realms. Much as the Anabaptist tradition warned against the corruption of the church when it was allied too closely with the state, the founding generation of the American nation worried about the corruption of the state if allied too closely to the church.

The distinction between the institutions of church and state did not extend, however, to the realm of public philosophy and values. In that area the Christian religion had a pervasive and influential role in shaping the public life of the new nation. Also, it was not until the mid-twentieth century that the First Amendment norms were made applicable to the individual states. This permitted state and local governments to work out a variety of ways whereby religion was accommodated in everyday life. As we shall read below, this explains the nineteenth-century controversy over public education in New York City.

The third commitment entailed by the First Amendment was to government neutrality regarding religion. The framers of the Constitution never provided any detail for how to balance the promotion of religious freedom (the free-exercise clause) with the non-promotion of religious belief (the nonestablishment clause). The principle of government neutrality "is not self-elucidating," according to Mooney; its meaning must be surmised from what the Court does in its name.[42] And what the Court has done has not always been consistent, and certainly it has not been a settled matter. As will be explained later in this chapter, there have been shifts in the general approach of the Supreme Court toward the First Amendment cases in recent decades as it seeks to strike the proper balance between the two religion clauses.

---

40. John Courtney Murray, *We Hold These Truths* (New York: Sheed & Ward, 1960), 56.

41. Ibid., 49.

42. Mooney, *Public Virtue*, 36. Or as he puts it, "The meaning of the concept . . . has to be drawn from Supreme Court decisions, rather than the meaning of the decisions from the concept."

CHURCH AND STATE IN THE U.S. CONTEXT

Any fear that nonestablishment of religion would lead to a decline in America's religious fervor was allayed in the first decades of the new political order. A second period of Protestant evangelical fervor began in the early decades of the nineteenth century that continued until mid-century. As settlers moved farther west into areas that are now Kentucky, Tennessee, Ohio, Illinois, and Indiana, a form of religious revivalism accompanied the growth on the western edge of the original territory that was the United States after the Revolution. When the Louisiana Purchase in 1803 opened up territories west of the Mississippi River, a variety of Protestant missionaries spread the Christian message into the new frontier. What would eventually become the states of Missouri, Kansas, Iowa, Nebraska, Arkansas, and other states of the Great Plains saw a huge growth in Baptist and Methodist denominations, along with Presbyterians, Disciples of Christ, and other Christian churches. The growth of the Methodist Church provides a particularly dramatic example. In 1776 it is estimated there were fifteen thousand Methodists in the thirteen original colonies, and by 1850 there were as many as one million in the United States. Much of the growth was due to the success of itinerant missionary preachers in the region we now think of as the Midwest.

In addition to the success of this "Second Great Awakening" there also was the arrival of the first great company of European immigrants. In the 1820s large numbers of German and Irish immigrants came to the United States, and immigration from those two nations would continue throughout the nineteenth century. After 1840 the sources of new immigrants expanded to include Italy, Poland, French Canada, and other nations. Many of the new immigrants looked to religious bodies not only for assistance in their transition but also for stability and constancy in identity, values, and folkways. The new Americans did not forsake their Christian faith even as they settled into their new and challenging homeland. The waves of immigration brought growth in the Catholic, Lutheran, and Orthodox churches. In the 1840s with the addition of Texas and the land annexed after the Mexican War, a large number of settlers with Spanish Catholic backgrounds were also included in the U.S. population.

A result of both the Protestant evangelical spirit and the increased number of immigrants was that the numbers of those who claimed membership in a Christian church grew dramatically in the first half of the nineteenth century. What became clear was that the guarantee of religious freedom was sufficient to ensure the expansion of Christian belief in the new nation even without the support of religious establishment. The great experiment inaugurated by the First Amendment, that religion could flourish under a secular state, seemed to many as demonstrably true. Whether the other half of the equation was also true, that a state could flourish without the social legitimation and "glue" of religious unity, was going to be sorely tested in the second half of the century.

By the middle of the eighteenth century, two-thirds of Americans belonged to Protestant churches shaped by evangelicalism. One political consequence was the widely held desire, hearkening back to John Winthrop's Massachusetts Bay Colony, to make America a Christian nation by building a society that would embody the ideals of Christ's kingdom. In the nineteenth century this led to social movements with various aims—temperance, abolition, public education, provision of social services—that were linked by the religious fervor that inspired them.

There was a concern, however, about this project of Christianizing America. The rise in numbers of immigrants that began in the 1820s meant Roman Catholicism, the very church that evangelical Protestants feared and disliked, was a growing presence by mid-century. For many Americans, Catholicism was inextricably linked to historical memories of oppression in Europe and resistance to freedom and progress. Catholic immigrants were viewed as a threat to the Protestant vision of the American nation.

From the Catholic perspective, the animus toward Catholicism undercut the claim that the United States practiced religious freedom or that it did not have an established religion in fact, if not law, namely, Protestantism. This clash of views led to one of the earliest controversies bearing upon the interaction of church and state in the nation. While Protestant America was increasingly dividing over abolition, Catholics, who were largely urban in their settlement patterns, found education and social services to be the vexing issues.

For many Protestants the influx of immigration posed the question of how the new nation might be held together. What would be the point of unity amidst the growing diversity within the population? One answer that struck many as necessary was civic education that would teach people the history and theory of the American republic. The aim was to make sure that new immigrants would enter into the larger society as productive and responsible citizens. The logical place to start was with children in the school system. Given the dominance of the Protestant ethos it is unsurprising that the ideas and values transmitted within the system reflected Protestant Christianity. And that was what gave rise to the New York City schools controversy.

The Public Schools Controversy

The public school system in the city was controlled by the Public School Society, a private group of civic leaders who operated on the assumption that schools should reflect the broad Christian tone of their culture. While Protestant denominations had differences with one another, there was a cultural Protestantism that included Bible instruction, prayer, hymn singing, moral education, and nonsectarian creedal instruction. It was assumed that lessons in history, literature, and geography would include comments about the foolishness and errors of "Romanism."

Due to the bias of the teaching, many immigrant children were not going to school, and the limited number of Catholic schools could not expand their services without financial assistance from the School Society. John Hughes, archbishop of New York, called for such support and the governor of the state, William Seward, agreed with the request. The state assembly, however, was not amenable because of strong opposition from representatives of New York City.

Hughes then decided upon a dramatic strategy. Although he was not a member of the party himself, Hughes realized that most Irish Catholics in New York were Democrats, the party that appealed to urban immigrants and unskilled wage laborers. Yet it was the Democratic Party that was resisting his appeal for financial support. At the time of the 1841 election of state legislators, Hughes entered his own ticket of candidates. Ten of those on his ticket were Democrats who had supported his request for school funding. Three other incumbent Democrats who had opposed Hughes's appeal were not endorsed and found themselves running against Hughes-backed independent candidates. Although none of the independent candidates won election they attracted enough Catholic votes to allow the underdog Whig Party candidates to defeat the three Democratic incumbents opposed by Hughes. All of the ten Democrats whom Hughes endorsed won election.

Democrats in the state assembly got the political message; Hughes might not be able to lead a third party to victory, but his people could play the role of spoilers, defeating a nominee if Hughes so chose. The state assembly voted to take control of the New York City school system away from the Public School Society. However, the victory for Hughes was hardly complete; he never attained state funding for Catholic schools. What he did accomplish was to end the Protestant control of public schools. When educational reformers such as Horace Mann promoted the advent of secular school systems Hughes found a new foe. Seeing the growing popularity of Mann's approach, Hughes decided to build a parochial school system for his own flock.

Hughes's attacks on the public school system further solidified a sensibility among Catholic immigrants that they were a distinct subculture within an often hostile society. The result was the formation of a group consciousness adopted by immigrant Catholics to defend their interests by supporting "their own" in elections and public policy debates. Most Catholics did not resist the process called "Americanization," that is, becoming inculturated in their new land. Yet they were determined not to let the process be controlled by forces that did not respect their Catholic faith and morals.

Of course, the example of a Catholic bishop organizing and leading his people in a political election was precisely the sort of activity many Protestants feared in regard to Catholics, that they would form a religious voting bloc controlled by a hierarchy loyal to a foreign leader, the pope. From Hughes's perspective, however, he was challenging Americans to be true to the proclaimed right of religious liberty by fair treatment of minorities who did not subscribe to a Protestant interpretation of the Christian tradition.[43]

The issue of Catholics and public education would remain a continuing source of controversy, both among Catholics and in the larger culture, yet it is just one among many possible illustrations of a truth that was evident about the United States. The American republic was a country that was remarkably diverse in religious belief. The influence of Roger Williams and Anne Hutchinson lived on in the new nation; as the number of inhabitants grew, so too did the range of religious creeds. While Christianity was the dominant faith by far, there was great diversity among the churches that took root in the American soil. And the ground rules for interaction among the diverse communities of belief left much room for interpretation.

The First Amendment guaranteed there would be room for religion to grow in the nation with state protection but not promotion. It also determined that the state should refrain from interfering in the beliefs and practices of its citizens. Beyond the broad strokes laid out by the constitutional mandate the issue of church-state relations would require that much greater detail be filled in to complete the picture. Much of that detail has been developed in the history of Supreme Court rulings on the meaning of the First Amendment.

Making Sense of the First Amendment

The federal Constitution serves as the touchstone for reflection on matters of church and state from the governmental perspective. And two clauses—no establishment and free exercise—of the First Amendment provide the key formulation: "Congress shall make no law respecting an establishment of religion, or prohibiting the free exercise thereof."[44]

It is the interpretation of these two clauses and their interplay that is at the heart of public policy arguments on matters of church and state. Can governments give tuition vouchers, drawing upon tax money, to parents who then may use them to pay parochial school tuitions? Can legislatures have chaplains lead prayers at official sessions? May employees sue employers who do not

43. For more on the schools controversy as well as the formation of a distinctly immigrant style in American politics see David O'Brien, *Public Catholicism* (New York: Macmillan, 1989), 44-61.

44. In a number of decisions the Supreme Court has indicated that the Fourteenth Amendment incorporates the provisions of the First Amendment and applies them to the individual states as well as to the federal government.

provide for time off to meet religious obligations? Can smoking peyote or use of a controlled substance be permitted in the context of religious rituals? May animal sacrifice be permitted in religious rituals? Can public monies be used to set up religious symbols on public grounds? May the armed forces forbid distinctive religious clothing or grooming among its members? Can religious agencies receive government funding for provision of public services? Can the courts require public disclosure of church personnel files in cases of criminal or tort law occasioned by clergy malpractice or sexual abuse? All of these questions have been argued in the nation's court system.

Traditionally, the Supreme Court viewed religion and religious commitment as something special, touching on the most intimate aspects of the person. Therefore, government had to provide a compelling reason for imposing a burden or restriction on free religious expression; a "compelling reason" being a higher legal standard than just a good reason.

By the end of the twentieth century, the Supreme Court seemed to lessen the significance of the free-exercise clause, viewing religious motivations as something to be respected but no more seriously than, say, other sincere motives or causes. Whereas in the past those cases involving the free exercise of religion were subject to the strict scrutiny test by which the Court requires the presence of a compelling reason to restrict behavior it now suggested a less rigorous standard. In doing so the Court allowed the government wider latitude to regulate religion, just so long as religion was not singled out but merely treated like other institutions.

The 1990 case of *Employment Division v. Smith* is an important marker in the development of the legal argument. The case involved an individual denied unemployment benefits after being fired for smoking peyote. The individual claimed that he was being penalized by the state for freely exercising his religious beliefs since it was in the context of a Native American religious ritual that the peyote was ingested. The state of Oregon claimed that its drug laws against smoking peyote generally could include restrictions on religious use as well. In other words, the right of religious expression ought to get no special respect that would grant an exemption to the general prohibition. In effect, the argument was that the standard for judgment should not be the presence of a "compelling reason," for a rational basis was sufficient as a reason to regulate religious practice. The Supreme Court majority agreed with the state's case.

The Oregon case serves as a reminder that there has been a persistent public debate over how much regulation of religious groups constitutes violation of the free exercise of religion, and how much state cooperation with religious groups constitutes violation of the no establishment of religion clause. Throughout American history different emphases on these questions can be seen in court decisions, legal documents, as well as in religious and historical literature.

Some in the religious community view a strict separationist position as prejudicial, reflecting an antireligious bias. It is impossible, of course, to deny that could ever be a motive of some separationist positions. After all, the secular mind is as prone to bigotry as any other outlook.

Restrictions placed on the churches by strict separation, however, should not automatically be viewed as antireligious. People may rightly worry about the fragility of a pluralistic society such as the United States. Certainly, religion can be a source of societal division. Consider the situations in Northern Ireland, postcommunist Yugoslavia, the Sudan, or East Timor, to cite just a few different instances.

The dangers that strict separationists perceive are real: religion can breed intolerance toward others who see things differently. Believers can be so committed to the rightness and justice of their views that they will pursue their ends without regard to democratic processes. Democracy requires compromise, yet some religious people may see compromise as evil. Pluralistic societies require overcoming certain differences to create a common identity, yet religion can be used to emphasize the deep differences citizens have in fundamental worldviews.

It must also be remembered that some citizens stress strict separation because they worry not about American democracy but about the risk to true religion. This had been the traditional view of Baptists, carrying on the idea of Roger Williams. Pursuit of power can be a great temptation. The churches and their leaders may be tempted to surrender or water down essential convictions in order to acquire or maintain political clout or financial support. Political favoritism and economic privilege can tarnish religious witness and encourage both personal and institutional arrogance.

Still another danger that might discourage the church from an alliance with the state is a fear that Christianity will become too closely identified with the secular aims and values of American life. The risk is that Christianity will be transformed into a form of domesticated religion used to prop up the culture and lend it legitimacy, thereby losing any prophetic ability to preach a dissenting word to the society.

Clearly, a review of the history of church and state involvement provides a number of arguments for strict separation that do not stem from bias or prejudice. Rather, people concerned with maintaining a fragile unity amidst sectarian passions or folks who worry about the corruption of faith by excessive entanglement with secular political concerns have legitimate worries. When interpreting the First Amendment there are reasonable voices both in and outside of the church, in the past and in the present, who take a strict separationist stance in understanding the two clauses of free expression and no establishment.

Without question, there is a constitutional basis for the separation of church and state. Yet several important clarifications are in order.

- The Constitution limits governmental action; it does not prohibit religious groups from speaking or acting in public.

If the churches choose not to act publicly, then those limits are self-imposed for theological, strategic, or other reasons. They are not legally imposed limits.

- The Constitution separates church and state, not church and society, nor religious and moral values from public life.

Organized religion is free to speak and act in public. Whether a religious leader or community is heard or noticed is another matter, owing to the quality and persuasiveness of the words and actions. Generally, the more sectarian the issue the less persuasive it will be to the wider public. For example, church leaders speaking out over racial injustice have gotten wide attention, whereas clergy calling for "blue laws" and Sunday store closings have gotten much less support.

- The use of the metaphor of a "wall of separation" is not found in the Constitution but comes from Thomas Jefferson's private writings. Judges of the Supreme Court have used the metaphor in their decisions, but it is an interpretation of a constitutional principle, not the principle itself.

The metaphor of "wall" may well be appropriate; yet if we think of a wall as solid and unmoving it may be misleading. The relationship of church and state is complex and time conditioned; it is not a clear and settled matter once and for all. Perhaps the metaphor of "border" or "boundary" is more apt, especially if we realize that the boundary shifts from age to age and that we occasionally have border raids where one side arguably crosses the line. Metaphors like border or boundary suggest that the exact line of church-state separation is a disputed question and is not fixedly settled like the placement of a brick wall between properties.

AN ONGOING CONVERSATION

There are several reasons why the demarcation between church and state is disputed. First, there is the matter of free exercise, since the distinction between the spiritual and social mission of the church can be blurry. If the mission of the church is to witness to the gospel of Christ, then such witness will inevitably entail actions as well as words in order to be credible. Questioning the involvement of a church in its support for civil rights activities or opposing war or promoting pro-life concerns may be an unacceptable limitation on a church's freedom to witness to its Christian beliefs. Yet engaging in such witness may involve the church in a range of interactions with the state, for example, lobbying, voter education, public protests, and other activities that are political in nature.

A second reason why there will be ongoing disputes over separating church and state touches upon the establishment clause, since when church and the state share a common concern it is not always easy to discern if cooperation between the two is actually a form of establishment. The state's action to provide relief from a natural disaster may include using a church-sponsored charitable agency to deliver services or provide material goods. In the case of such funding is the state aiding a church or seeking a legitimate secular purpose that also happens to correspond with the interests of a church? Other examples where a public good and a benefit to a church might coincide are provision of a public health nurse or social worker in a religious school or the funding of religiously inspired programs for treatment of addictions.

It is important to remember when discussing such cases that what determines whether something is too sectarian to be supported with public resources is not the nature of the motive (does it have religious inspiration?), but rather its content and effect (does it serve a useful societal goal? does it create a situation that reflects favoritism for or bias against religion?). This helps to determine whether the state should enact policies that may happen to correspond to a particular church's teaching on issues such as divorce, civil rights, abortion, school prayer, human cloning, or school vouchers.

To assist in making the determination as to what is or is not acceptable constitutionally, the Supreme Court in a 1970 case, *Lemon v. Kurtzman*, devised three tests for judging whether a policy violates the First Amendment:

- the legislation must have a legitimate secular purpose;
- the *primary* effect must be to neither advance nor inhibit religion;
- government must avoid "excessive entanglement" with religion.

A policy must "pass" all three tests if it is to be constitutional. In later years the guidelines came under attack on the grounds that, in effect, they made the no-establishment clause of the First Amendment the primary concern. Critics of the *Lemon* guidelines maintained that a rigidly strict separationist position errs not by preventing the state from expressing religion (which it should) but by preventing individual citizens from expressing religious convictions in public places (which it should not). The charge was that the court's focus had so fixed on the idea of no establishment (and its extension to barring personal expression of religion in public) that the free-exercise clause of the First Amendment was under attack. The courts, it was claimed, through the *Lemon* tests and their interpretation of the non-establishment clause, were inhibiting religious exercise by an overly strict rendering of the separation of church and state. For the critics, many court rulings in the period from 1950 to 1990 did not reflect state neutrality toward religion but discrimination against it.

Commentary on Supreme Court rulings suggests we may be entering a third stage in our national church-state debate. Stage one was the era during which mainstream Protestant beliefs and values dominated public discourse. Legal decisions tended to reflect that prevailing mindset, being broadly supportive of a public presence for Protestant Christianity. The first stage carried on from the early days of the nation until well into the middle of the twentieth century.

The second stage, reflecting the decline in mainstream Protestant influence over the culture, saw the emergence of strict separationist arguments and the subsequent uproar over rulings involving school prayer, Christmas displays, and programs on public property or in public schools, as well as the use of the Bible in moral education. Critics of this second stage of Court rulings complained that strict separation discriminated against religion and promoted secularism, requiring a "naked public square."[45] Many aspects of the so-called culture wars[46] of the last quarter of the twentieth century involved differing reactions to the evolving second stage of church-state debates.

An emerging third stage in the evolution of the Court suggests a movement to balance the principle of strict separation with a principle of equal treatment of religion. A significant case in this regard was *Widmar v. Vincent*, a 1984 Supreme Court ruling. Lower-court rulings had upheld a University of Missouri decision that no religious group could use campus facilities for meetings, even though other student groups, including political activists, could have such use. The lawyer for the plaintiffs, Michael McConnell, argued that any public institution that opened its doors to private nonreligious groups had to do the same for religious groups. The reasoning was that religion is not to be treated as exceptional, and therefore whatever is available to the nonreligious is also to be provided for the religious. The university was blamed for treating religion as less than equal to other concerns and therefore showing bias against free exercise. The argument was successful.

Then in 1995 the Court in *Rosenberger v. University of Virginia* overturned a policy whereby the school subsidized student journals for secular purposes but not student publications for religious purposes. The argument was made that equal treatment trumped strict separation, since the latter actually led to discrimination against religion when compared to treatment of other groups. The Court's acceptance of the equal treatment argument in these cases suggests a need to renegotiate the boundaries between church and state.

---

45. Richard Neuhaus, *The Naked Public Square* (Minneapolis: Eerdmans Publishing, 1984).

46. James Davison Hunter, *Culture Wars* (New York: Basic Books, 1992).

What appears to be happening is that the period of strict separation created a backlash among people, including legal theorists, who believe that religion was being singled out in a manner that hindered free exercise of religion. The new goal is to ensure that religion has the same freedom in the public square as permitted others. There are three risks in negotiating this third stage. One is that we slip from religious equality in public life to religious supremacy in public life. A second risk is that the state will exercise greater regulation of religious activities since it is no longer a "special" realm; this reflects the significance of moving from "compelling reason" to "rational basis" for approving state regulation. The final risk, also reflective of the view that religion is no longer special, is that the state will see no particular reason to make special accommodation for religion in matters such as granting exemptions to religious institutions in personnel practices, eligibility requirements for government grants, or taxation.

What to make of the debates over interpreting the First Amendment? Certainly the case law is complicated, and it can be difficult to see a consistent trend in court decisions. Yet several conclusions can be drawn from the way that U.S. courts have understood the First Amendment. First, organized religion should expect neither favor nor obstruction by the state in its practice. Second, the churches as institutions must be separate from the state as an institution, but there should be no separation of religion or the churches from society. Third, a democracy the size of the United States requires the existence of vital voluntary associations, a variety of intermediary institutions that foster participation in public life and a diverse social life. Churches serve society in that role.

So a socially active church does not violate the U.S. Constitution more than any other activist voluntary group does. The church ought not be treated with more or less favor than other groups. The idea of the separation of church and state is not meant to be a "gag rule" on religion in public life. Separation is not equivalent to exclusion. More accurately, the constitutional requirement is designed actually to protect religion by providing a space for each religion to speak and act in public. Separation means religious communities should expect neither favoritism nor discrimination concerning whether their words and actions are persuasive to all actors in the public square.

Here one can see the significant difference between the European and American approaches to religious toleration. The European experience, given the wars of religion, understood toleration as taking religion out of the public sphere so people could live together. The American view of toleration was born not of hostility to religion but of respect for it. There was a clear sense of the limits of any government's competence to intervene in religious matters.

QUESTIONS FOR REFLECTION/DISCUSSION

1. What is meant by the "Westphalian synthesis"? What were the key outcomes of Westphalia for the role of religion in politics?
2. How would you describe the impact of the Clergy Constitution upon the Catholic Church in France?
3. What was the state of Catholicism in France during the immediate aftermath of the Revolution? What do you see as the most significant long-term impact of the Revolution upon the French church?
4. How would you describe Napoleon's attitude toward Catholicism? The Catholic Church's attitude toward Napoleon?
5. What is meant by the term "Restoration" as a post-Napoleon development? What part was played in the development by the Congress of Vienna?
6. How did developments in English Christianity influence the early Protestant colonists in seventeenth-century America?
7. Who were the Puritans? What was at stake in the controversies involving Roger Williams and Anne Hutchinson? What was the lasting impact?
8. What was the Great Awakening, and what was its influence on American Christianity?
9. What was the issue in the debates over the Virginia statute? What role did Thomas Jefferson and James Madison play in the debates?
10. What is the point of the nonestablishment clause of the First Amendment to the U.S. Constitution? Of the free-exercise clause?
11. What was the public schools controversy? Who was John Hughes, and what was his significance in the controversy?
12. Do you think a "wall of separation" is the most apt metaphor to describe the American practice of church-state relations? How would you characterize the relationship?

Part III

CONTEMPORARY PERSPECTIVES

8

The Nature, Purpose, Role, and Form of the State

Over the course of the centuries the Christian churches have encountered many different political systems and have interacted with these systems in widely varying ways. Because of this diversity of political systems, as well as different theological frameworks, it cannot be claimed that there is a uniform understanding of the political order within the Christian tradition. As the previous chapters have illustrated, the historical narrative of Christianity and politics is a story with multiple subplots and digressions along with a variety of heroes and villains. It is difficult to formulate agreed-upon lessons from the history that would be acceptable to all current Christians.

In this chapter I will not attempt to draw conclusions that are beyond dispute by one or another branch of the Christian family. Instead, I will present the prevailing view of one major strand within the historical narrative on the important topic of a Christian view of the state. It should not be thought that this one strand captures all the narrative elements within the Christian tradition on how to view the state, or that an understanding of the state resolves all the questions involved in a comprehensive treatment of Christianity and politics. Yet the view of the state is a central topic for any examination of Christianity and politics, and so in this chapter we shall look at how one significant tradition, Catholic social teaching, has come to understand a particularly important topic—the nature, purpose, role, and form of the state.

THE CATHOLIC SOCIAL IMAGINATION

The sociologist Andrew Greeley has made the point that the formal documents of the modern era of Catholic social teaching are examples of what he calls the "high tradition."[1] These statements of the church's hierarchy are basically an articulation of the "low tradition," reflecting the fundamental Catholic viewpoint on human nature and human society. The low tradition has been formed by stories, images, parables, and metaphors that make up the Catholic

---

1. Andrew Greeley, *No Bigger Than Necessary* (New York: Meridian Books, 1977).

social imagination, an outlook that is different from that of Buddhists, Marxists, Muslims, or even other Christians. This social imagination, or low tradition, informs and underpins the articulated high tradition that comprises the written documents of official Catholic social teaching.

Greeley suggested four characteristics of the Catholic social imagination: (1) an optimism about human nature; we are more good than bad; (2) individuals live in an organic society that does not limit but enhances freedom; (3) there is an importance—theological and social—to "rootedness," to a sense of tradition, local community, and historical ties; (4) a bias is held in favor of decentralization, mediation, person-centered not bureaucratically structured organizations. This worldview is formative for how Catholic social teaching approaches specific issues.

Similar to the Greeley thesis is Drew Christiansen's suggestion that the "deep theory" of Catholic social teaching is a communitarian vision of human life.[2] That is, embedded in the Catholic imagination is a social vision that undergirds and inflects thinking about a just society in such a way that the accent falls on the relational or communal context of social issues. Attention is given to the responsibilities, conditions, and elements necessary for community life to flourish. The formal expression of Catholic social teaching derives from and offers further reinforcement to the communitarian vision.

While the Catholic imagination predates the modern era, the body of teaching that is commonly labeled "Catholic social teaching" is directly tied to its historical situation in the nineteenth through twenty-first century. Important to realize is that Catholic social teaching often is a reaction *against* some troubling social development as much as a constructive argument *for* a particular political or economic agenda. The social teaching expressed in the documents issued by the church's pastoral leaders is frequently focused on the social ills accompanying the onset of economic modernization, especially industrialization. That is why the topic of economic justice looms larger than politics in the early documents. Yet, given the close connection between politics and economics one can still find in this formal teaching a description of the nature, purpose, and form of the state.

THE NATURE OF THE STATE

In Catholic social teaching the nature of the state is developed within the broad context of political anthropology and the image of society. At the very heart of the Catholic social tradition is the conviction that the person is defined

---

2. Drew Christiansen, S.J., "On Relative Equality: Catholic Egalitarianism after Vatican II," *Theological Studies* 45 (1984): 651-75 at 668.

relationally—by the relationships he or she has with God, other persons, other creatures. The relationship with God is grounded in the belief that each person is created in the divine image. By virtue of this claim there is a fundamental personal dignity of each and every person that must be respected. A deepening insight into what respect for that dignity entails is part of the story of the evolution of Catholic social teaching. The uniqueness, freedom, equality, and historicity of the person were all qualities that received growing attention in magisterial teaching over the course of time.

Another important aspect of the claim that we are created in the divine image is the fundamental theological conviction that God is Trinitarian. "The revelation in Christ of the mystery of God as Trinitarian love is at the same time the revelation of the vocation of the human person to love."[3] The dignity of the person and the freedom of the person are shaped by their Trinitarian source. To be created in the image of a God who is Trinitarian love means that to be human is to be in loving relationship. At root we are profoundly social, created for relationship, called to give ourselves away to the other in love. As the bishops at Vatican II wrote, there is "a certain likeness between the union of the divine Persons, and the unity of God's children in truth and charity."[4] If the inner life of God is loving communion so too must the life of creatures made in the divine image be characterized by loving union. The human person cannot achieve authentic selfhood except through a sincere gift of the self to the other.

Not only the relationship with God but our relationship with the rest of creation underscores the belief, at the heart of the Catholic worldview, that personhood entails relationality. "Sociality is as essential to human nature as rationality."[5] It is not possible to address the human condition apart from the truth that the person is in the world with others. The isolated individual is an abstraction. Thus, Leo XIII, the pope whose writings are commonly cited as the first documents of modern Catholic social teaching, did not see society as a human creation but rather as divinely ordained, for without it the person could not satisfy elemental human needs and achieve authentic development.

In accord with the theological foundation of the dignity and sociality of the human person, the Catholic social tradition then relies heavily on human reason to develop its view of the state as a natural community. Human beings are made to be social, destined to live in community. However, community

---

3. Pontifical Council for Justice and Peace, *Compendium of the Social Doctrine of the Church* (Vatican City: Libreria Editrice Vaticana, 2004), no. 34.

4. Vatican II, *Gaudium et spes* (Pastoral Constitution on the Church in the Modern World, 1965), no. 24.

5. Henri Rommen, *The State in Catholic Social Teaching* (St. Louis: Herder Book Company, 1945), 138.

cannot exist without structure, some ordering and governing mechanism that provides for the proper functioning of the community. The political community is a necessary association that allows humans to attain fulfillment of their social nature. In sum, the state is necessary for well-ordered community, and community is necessary for human well-being. Thus, the state is an institution that is part of God's created order.

This understanding of the human—as having a unique and personal dignity and as being fundamentally social due to the *imago Dei*—and view of the state—as being both natural and necessary—set Catholic social teaching on a path that would distinguish it from two great rival political theories of the nineteenth century.

Classical liberalism's emphasis on the unencumbered individual, freely calculating the benefit of entering into a social contract, was judged to be neither empirically accurate nor morally desirable. While upholding the dignity and uniqueness of the person, the Catholic social tradition understands that the development of the self is realized only in community. Human beings achieve their true self through involvement in a dense web of overlapping relationships that creates a variety of communal experiences for the person. Within the communitarian perspective of Catholicism, the classical liberal model of society as a contract between autonomous individuals is rejected in favor of a viewpoint that emphasizes reciprocity and mutuality as inherent to the human situation.[6]

Socialism's bias toward a collectivist vision is also judged unworthy by the Catholic social tradition. Without denying the communal nature of the person there is also the emphasis on the dignity and uniqueness of the person in Catholic teaching. Because of this aspect the Catholic vision is not easily reconciled with any collectivism that reduces the person to a cog in the wheel of the political community. Treating humankind as one great mass of people, without attention to the uniqueness of personal existence, is not an acceptable alternative to the failings of liberal theory. The communitarianism of Catholicism requires that the individual person be given attention within his or her concrete situation, thereby demanding a healthy respect for the particular relationships and communities that nourish a unique human personality.

The commitment to a religious vision of how God has created humankind undergirds the Catholic articulation of a social theory critical of both liberal individualism and socialist collectivism. As one commentator on the Catholic social tradition puts it, at the center of the tradition is a "theologically inspired communitarian ethic."[7] Such a social ethic sees society neither as

---

6. Ibid., 123-28.

7. Michael Schuck, *That They Be One* (Washington, DC: Georgetown University Press, 1991), 180.

one great collective nor as a voluntary choice by those rationally maximizing self-interest. Instead, each person must be treated as equal in dignity with any other, always remembering society exists for the sake of the person. Yet, as the bishops of the United States stated in an important pastoral letter, "human dignity can be realized and protected only in community."[8] The human was made for community, and society is a community of communities organically related to one another.

Society, Community, and the State

The point about society is important because it limits the nature of the state. Important as the state is for social life, society cannot be equated with the state. Society is made up of many groups and institutions, and a healthy society embraces a wide array of communities that stand between the individual, the family, and the state. The essential pluralism and diversity of communities are a central feature of communitarian thinking.

Society is not just one body, the error of collectivism, but a number of groupings, each with its rights, duties, and roles. In the Catholic version of communitarian theory two communities are fundamental, the family and the state.[9] For Leo XIII, "the family was the original human society, the foundation of all others, and the instrument for developing the virtues needed for the existence of all social groups."[10] The state also was given high standing for it is the "highest and most comprehensive" form of social life.[11] Other forms of association exist in addition to the state and while they can be regulated by the state they should not be abolished by it.[12]

Life in various communities enlarges and perfects the individual. To develop as a person, participation in community is necessary, for communal life provides the opportunity to give oneself away to another and by so doing the person becomes more fully realized. Giving of oneself, in relationships of mutuality, permits both parties to grow toward their full humanity. Participating in the dynamic of giving and receiving within the community leads both to the person's well-being and the good of others.

In modern Catholic social teaching the word used to convey this communitarian outlook is solidarity. Solidarity seeks to transpose "pre-modern understandings of natural law, of human being as essentially social, and of society

---

8. United States Conference of Catholic Bishops, *Economic Justice for All* (Washington, DC: United States Conference of Catholic Bishops, 1986), no. 14.

9. Rommen, *The State*, 136.

10. Richard Camp, *The Papal Ideology of Social Reform* (Leiden: E. J. Brill, 1969), 30.

11. Rommen, *The State*, 123.

12. Leo XIII, *Rerum novarum* (On the Condition of Labor, 1891), no. 38.

itself as organic and cooperative" into our contemporary context of popular democracy and market economics.[13] Solidarity is more than what we think of as interdependence. The fact that we are linked to one another in a variety of ways is the experience of interdependence, but individuals may acknowledge this fact while being resentful or indifferent toward it; some may even take advantage of the others with whom they are interconnected. In short, interdependence does not rule out domination or exploitation.

Solidarity, on the other hand, moves interdependence to another level for it promotes not just acknowledgment of interdependence as fact, but shapes the response we should have to that reality. Solidarity is a virtue, not a feeling of vague compassion but a "firm and persevering determination to commit oneself to the common good." As a virtue, solidarity shapes the character of a person so that mere recognition of interdependence is transformed into a dedication to the common good. It is solidarity that enables the person to devote him- or herself "to the good of all and of each individual, because we are all really responsible for all."[14]

It is impossible for something to be called a virtue in Catholic moral theology if it does not lead toward human flourishing and perfection. Thus, to commit oneself to the common good cannot be understood in a way that undercuts the good of the person for then solidarity could not be a virtue. By calling it a virtue the Catholic social tradition highlights the conviction that human persons realize themselves only by participation in community life.

The theory of the state in Catholic social teaching is an outgrowth of the communitarian vision of the human person and society. The state is intimately related to the social nature of the person for it is a key institution that gives shape and form to community. The state establishes public order for the multiplicity of social groupings—families, professional associations, religious communities, economic corporations, social clubs, and others—that make up society.

The existence of the state is not simply voluntary, enacted out of self-interest and limited to the utilitarian aims of individuals. From the perspective of Catholic social teaching the state "proceeds by inner moral necessity from the social nature" of the person "for the sake of the more perfect life," and to achieve the "fuller realization of personality for all its members" in an "order of mutual assistance and mutual cooperation."[15]

The "inner moral necessity" of the state indicates that in the Catholic tradition the state has a divine sanction, but not the state in any specific concrete

---

13. Matthew Lamb, "Solidarity," in *The New Dictionary of Catholic Social Thought*, ed. Judith Dwyer (Collegeville, MN: Liturgical Press, 1994), 908.

14. John Paul II, *Sollicitudo rei socialis* (On Social Concern, 1988), no. 38.

15. Rommen, *The State*, 137.

manifestation or form. In the particularity of history any specific state is a creation of human will and reason. Human beings create a state in freedom even if the idea of the state's role in serving the common good provides a norm for guidance.

Although an ordered society requires political authority, the form of such authority is not divinely dictated. There have been developments within Catholic social teaching in determining what specific forms of the state satisfy the normative idea. Monarchy, aristocracy, democracy have all been suggested as acceptable, and at different times one or the other has been deemed preferable. Leo XIII in his major political encyclicals *Diuturnum* (On the Origin of Civil Power, 1881) and *Immortale Dei* (On the Christian Constitution of States, 1885) made clear that although the papacy might be monarchical that was not to be understood as the only appropriate model for secular government. Leo maintained that as a product of historical evolution, the state would necessarily take on a variety of forms and there could be no single paradigm for its structure.[16]

Sovereignty and the State

Irrespective of the preferred form of the state, all the modern popes wished to clarify the foundation of state power. Sovereignty can be understood as the assertion that someone has supreme and decisive power within a political unit. Some of the most common appeals to sovereignty have made claims on behalf of God, a king, the papacy, the nobility, a parliament, or the people.

In Catholic teaching sovereignty has never been accorded the pride of place it was granted in the writing of international lawyers and political theorists. As a way of resolving the Thirty Years War the principle of *cuius regio, eius religio* (the religion of the prince is the religion of the people) was an expression of the idea that states should respect the autonomy of domestic order within other states. Sovereignty was upheld in order to maintain some limitations on the constant provocation for states to meddle in the internal life of other states in an age of religious intolerance. It was also a restraint on the political or economic ambitions lurking beneath the pretext of zeal in defending religious faith.

The principle of *cuius regio, eius religio* was a corruption of sovereignty according to Catholic theory, however practical it may have seemed at the time in the effort to end the protracted violence. A subsequent effect of such an expansive understanding of the authority of the prince was to extend the

---

16. Jay Corrin, *Catholic Intellectuals and the Challenge of Democracy* (Notre Dame, IN: University of Notre Dame Press, 2002), 64.

state's authority into areas where it lacked competency, namely, religion. Once approval of religion was made subject to the prince there was no possibility of distinguishing between the law of the state and any higher moral law. Lost was a traditional theme in Catholic social thought: the limited role of the state and the restriction of its sovereignty to certain areas of social life.

Important in Catholic political thought is that sovereignty was understood as supreme with "regard to certain matters and to a certain content."[17] That is, Catholic political theory understood sovereignty within the context of divine and natural law that limited the scope of sovereignty to supreme power within boundaries. There were limits to the exercise of political authority set by God's intended order for creation and the moral norms known by reasonable people of good will. Thus no political authority—individual or collective—can ignore fundamental rights of the person, the family, the church, and other communities that exist for their own purposes and are not simply creations of the state. The state, in whatever form, may have sovereignty within its order of the temporal common good, but other entities exercise sovereign authority within their own orders.

After the revolutions of the eighteenth century, sovereignty was no longer embodied in the monarch but transferred to the collective will of the people. No higher authority was recognized in France's *Declaration of the Rights of Man and of the Citizen*. It was this version of continental liberalism that Leo XIII opposed in his assertion that all authority comes from God. For Leo, a social-contract theory that suggests the state's authority is solely based on the power granted by the citizenry is inadequate. "This is not to suggest that the people cannot designate their ruler through whatever means proves effective, but only that the conferral of authority to rule comes from a higher source."[18]

Regardless of whether an author followed the "translation" or "designation" school, a major point in the Catholic tradition was to insist that all authority ultimately rests on God. God grants power to citizens who then may transfer their power to a ruler (translation) or select a ruler to act in their name (designation). But the authority is both originally and finally God's, not that of the citizenry.[19] In sum, the people may have final say about the mode of governance, but the authority to govern, the moral right to exercise civil power, comes from God alone.

The sovereignty of the state, when understood according to Catholic theory, meant that within its legitimate realm of competency the state was the final arbiter. With respect to the purpose of government the state is supreme, but as we shall see below, the purpose of government is not all-encompassing.

17. Rommen, *The State*, 398.
18. Corrin, *Catholic Intellectuals*, 67.
19. Rommen, *The State*, 440–73.

There are areas of human existence that are beyond the proper activity of the state. Thus, a state's sovereignty is exercised only in regard to those matters that fall under the rubric of public order, a part of the common good. From the Catholic perspective, the Hobbesian notion of the state as leviathan distorted the meaning of sovereignty.

THE PURPOSE OF THE STATE

The Catholic view of the state as a natural association in accord with the nature of humankind suggests a positive function for the state. Because of human sinfulness the state does have the task of restraining evil activity and punishing wrongdoers. But that is not the main purpose of the state. Thomas Aquinas gives expression to the traditional Catholic idea that even if there had been no sin there would still be a need for the state. This is because the purpose of the state is positive not merely negative; the state should "direct people to the common good of the group as well as to their own good."[20]

There may be nothing so clearly expressed in Catholic social teaching as the view that the state is to protect and promote the common good. Every pope of the modern era has emphasized that basic statement of purpose. Pius XII made the point that "the state, then, has a noble function; that of reviewing, restraining, encouraging all those private initiatives of the citizen which go to make up national life and so directing them to a common end." This common end is not something of human invention for "it is determined by the duty of aiding man to the attainment of the perfection which is natural" to persons.[21] Because God has created human persons as social there is an obligation to contribute to the common good that benefits each and every person. Furthermore, this common good requires a political institution to protect and promote it. So it is in that sense, of the state as a necessary institution that orders society for the individual and common good, that we can say the state's existence is ordained by God.

This way of thinking about the state's purpose is readily distinguished from classical liberalism. The anthropology of liberalism with its idea of a "fully self-sufficient, perfect being, autonomous in itself, a being for which sociality is only accidental, an external relation, useful but not essential for its internal perfection and a higher form of good life" makes it difficult to recognize the political end of an objective common good.[22] Hence, the duty to contribute to

---

20. Charles Curran, *Catholic Social Teaching 1891-Present* (Washington, DC: Georgetown University Press, 2002), 140.

21. Pius XII, in *The Major Addresses of Pope Pius XII*, vol. 2, ed. Vincent Yzermans (St. Paul: North Central Publishing, 1961), 433.

22. Rommen, *The State*, 124.

such an end or purpose is dimly perceived since the state's role is interpreted as merely a convenience that facilitates the individual pursuit of self-interest.[23]

In the liberal framework it is hard to allow any positive role for the state interfering in the economic sphere beyond that of enforcing commutative justice, enforcing individual rights and duties. The Catholic tradition, however, emphasizes distributive, legal, and social justice as well as commutative. The first addresses the person's rights to share in the goods of the community; the second, the duties of the person to the community; and social justice requires that societal institutions be structured and organized in such a way that the demands of commutative, distributive, and legal justice can be adequately met. State intervention in the various spheres of public life, such as the economic order, is based on the obligation that when the "true form of the common good has been distorted" the situation must be rectified.[24]

The Common Good

It is the twin aspects of participatory community—it provides for the good of the individual as well as the good of others—that frames the Catholic understanding of the common good. One of the foundational themes of Catholic political theory, the common good has been described as "the sum of those conditions of the social life whereby persons, families and associations more adequately and readily may attain their own perfection."[25] The common good pertains to the condition of a particular group. Most often the term is used in reference to a nation, but the term also may refer to smaller groups as well as larger, the international or global community.

Note that the common good has to do with the "sum of" social conditions, or the state of the whole not simply its parts. Not that it ignores the individual, for the common good includes the good of each member of the community, and all aspects of personal well-being—that is, "the good of all people and of the whole person."[26] Unlike the classical liberal tradition, however, the common good does not mean merely the sum total of the distinct goods of discrete individuals.

Rather, the Catholic tradition sees the common good of the society as including the organic relations of individual members. To belong to a flourishing society is itself a good and one that is included in the common good. To contribute to the common good is neither self-interest nor a denial of the self but a common interest that enriches both the self and the other at the same

---

23. Ibid., 125.

24. Ibid., 148.

25. *Gaudium et spes*, no. 74.

26. *Compendium of the Social Doctrine of the Church*, no. 165.

time. "Belonging to everyone and to each person" the good "remains 'common,' because it is indivisible and because only together is it possible to attain it."[27]

In its proper understanding, the common good is not something that can be achieved alone, nor is it something attained at the expense of the individual person. A good community exists, therefore, to secure a person's rights *and* to locate a person's duties. Both the rights and duties of a person point to the common good for it is both by means of sharing in the benefits and contributing to the maintenance of the common good that human flourishing occurs.[28] By the inclusion of a person's rights and duties in its understanding of the common good the Catholic position is distinguished from an individualism that exalts personal rights but de-emphasizes the duties of the individual to others. The Catholic view is also to be differentiated from a collective approach that ignores personal rights for the sake of claims by the group.

Understanding the common good as including all members of the community raises another central idea in Catholic social teaching, the preferential option, or love, for the poor. In democratic theory each person's voice and vote count, but in democratic practice the access to government leaders is often unequal. Some groups and individuals within a society have greater power and influence than others. This often translates into such elites setting the agenda for public policy, and wielding disproportionate impact on a government's decisions.

To correct for the inequality that can occur even in democratic politics, it is helpful for public officials to have a special concern that the poor and other marginalized people have their interests and needs represented in public discussion. In *Rerum novarum*, Leo XIII made this point, and subsequent popes have endorsed the idea that special account is to be taken of those in society who may be excluded in the deliberations of the elites.[29]

An Evolving Idea

Two further comments about the state and the common good should be added. First, the Catholic tradition's grasp of what exactly constitutes the

---

27. Ibid., no. 164.

28. Perhaps the most sophisticated treatment of the common good as understood within the Catholic tradition can be found in David Hollenbach, S.J., *The Common Good and Christian Ethics* (New York: Cambridge University Press, 2002).

29. Leo observed that it is the duty of the ruler to use his power in order "to benefit every class in the State, and amongst the rest to promote to the utmost the interests of the poor" (no. 32). For a detailed and thorough treatment of the development of the preferential option for the poor in Catholic teaching, see Donal Dorr, *Option for the Poor and for the Earth: Catholic Social Teaching* (Maryknoll, NY: Orbis Books, 2012).

common good continues to undergo development. Popes have cited various items encompassed by the common good:

> creation of just law, maintenance of criminal justice, oversight of public morality and spiritual well-being, coordination of social institutions, care of the poor and minority groups, monitoring of national population growth, support for education, protection of human rights, promotion of world peace and international social improvement, and encouragement of global structures of governance.[30]

Of late, a number of statements by church officials have specified environmental issues as being part of the common good.[31] John Paul II wrote that it is "the task of the state to provide for the defense and preservation of common goods such as the natural and human environments, which cannot be safeguarded simply by market forces."[32] Previously, the environment was not explicitly included within the common good, undoubtedly because it was taken for granted as a precondition of the common good. Sustainability would have been presumed in the past, but as the environment has become threatened it became necessary to specifically acknowledge the environment as part of the common good for which the state has a responsibility.

A second remark about the common good is that because it is so multifaceted it cannot be assumed that any one community can satisfy its achievement. While the goods of political community are essential, they are insufficient to encompass all that the common good entails. There remain the goods of family, friendships, religion, and other key components of human life. To presuppose that one undifferentiated community of humanity is adequate to realize the good of each person is to run the risk of creating what Pius XII called "the masses," whose "de-personalization" leads to the growth of the bureaucratic state.[33]

While the state is a highly prized institution of community within the Church's social teaching, it cannot be understood in a totalitarian way. Here the contribution of liberalism to Catholic social teaching ought to be acknowledged. Liberalism's emphasis on individual freedom and its concern for avoiding state encroachment on legitimate areas of liberty have had an impact, as is evident in Catholicism's increased appreciation for the limited constitutional state.[34] Lessons drawn from the experience of both the paternalistic states

---

30. Schuck, *That They Be One*, 183.

31. See Drew Christiansen, S.J., ed., *And God Saw That It Was Good* (Washington, DC: U.S. Conference of Catholic Bishops, 1996), for a collection of such statements.

32. *Sollicitudo rei socialis*, no. 40.

33. Pius XII, in Yzermans, *Major Addresses*, 42.

34. Paul Sigmund, "Catholicism and Liberal Democracy," in *Catholicism and*

of eighteenth- and nineteenth-century European monarchies, as well as the totalitarian Fascist and Communist states of twentieth-century Europe, have impressed on the Vatican the benefits of liberal democracies with their constitutional limits. At least since the papacy of Pius XII the preference of Catholic social teaching is clear in this regard.

THE ROLE OF THE STATE

It was Leo XIII who most obviously drew the line of demarcation between classical liberalism and Catholic communitarianism. He did it in two ways: first, Leo declared that justice was the first norm of the economic order, thereby ruling out the liberal exaltation of the free market; and second, he insisted on the right of the state to intervene in the economic order. It was the plight of the poor and the cause of economic justice in the late nineteenth century that directed papal attention to the state's responsibility to intervene in economic life.

Leo's concern was the failure of governments to act responsibly in the face of threats to the common good.[35] His argument in *Rerum novarum* was rather sweeping, calling on the state "in general to do everything necessary for the general welfare which could not be handled as well by private interests."[36] The state bears a particular responsibility to care for those who are most in need. As Leo wrote, "when there is a question of protecting the rights of individuals, the poor and helpless have a claim to special consideration."[37]

The papal assertion that there is a general right of government to intervene "rests upon the duty of the state to protect the true interests of the citizens. Such intervention is not to be looked upon as something to be tolerated, but as something which is indispensable."[38] There are three aspects of the right that deserve additional comment. First, and briefly, the right is not something newly minted and added to the Catholic theory of the state. Rather, the right flows from the very nature of the state: "the principle of this intervention is that the prosperity of the community and its members is an immediate part of the end which the state ought to be seeking."[39] The purpose of the state is to promote the common good, of which economic prosperity is an integral part.

Liberalism, ed. R. Bruce Douglass and David Hollenbach (New York: Cambridge University Press, 1994).

35. Camp, *Papal Ideology*, 138.

36. Ibid., 141.

37. *Rerum novarum*, no. 29.

38. Jean-Yves Calvez and Jacques Perrin, *The Church and Social Justice* (Chicago: Henry Regnery, 1961), 317.

39. Ibid., 319.

So state intervention in the economic order is, in Leo's mind, in full accord with the Catholic theory of the state. Indeed, it is a direct corollary of that theory. That much should be clear from the comments above about the meaning of the common good and the purpose of the state.

The second and third rationales for state intervention require more extensive comment. The second rationale has to do with justice and government intervention in the economy. The third rationale addresses how the state should exercise its right to intervene; this concerns what the Catholic social tradition calls the principle of subsidiarity. Each of these rationales will be addressed in turn.

Justice and State Intervention

In the Catholic tradition justice is intimately linked to the common good. If the common good is, indeed, common, then all members of the society are expected to contribute to building it up and to enjoying the benefits that flow from it. With regard to economic life each person has the duty, as far as one is able, to contribute to the economic prosperity of the community, as well as making a claim to a fair share of the economy's output.

Justice is of fundamental importance to understanding the role of the state in society. To make that observation does not imply that what constitutes justice is easily agreed upon. Defining justice has been a centuries-old debate in political life. The most common description of justice is that it has to do with rendering to each what is their due. Justice is concerned with treating people rightly or appropriately.

Perhaps the first implication of such a statement is that people ought not be dealt with arbitrarily or capriciously. There should be consistency in the way that people are treated since, barring a significant reason, equal respect for persons precludes rewarding one person and punishing another for doing the same thing. Thus, "acting justly is so often a matter of following *rules* or applying *laws*, since these guarantee consistency."[40] Justice requires that we treat similar cases similarly.

This leads to a consideration of when are cases dissimilar. Some differences do not appear relevant for the determination of justice, while others do. There was a time when American civil law treated race or gender as significant for determining whether a person had the right to vote. We no longer see these factors as relevant. Yet we still see age or citizenship as having significance

---

40. David Miller, *Political Philosophy, A Very Short Introduction* (Oxford: Oxford University Press, 2003), 76 (italics in original). I have utilized a number of Miller's ideas in the presentation of this subsection.

when deciding whether to grant a person the right to vote in a national election. So the question of relevance has to do with whether a particular difference between two people justifies different treatment; if the difference is deemed not relevant the expectation is that people are to be treated the same way.

Benedict XVI has observed that one form of justice in the tradition, distributive justice, is particularly important for market economies.[41] Modern Catholic social teaching developed in an era that witnessed fundamental changes in social institutions because of industrialization, urbanization, new class structures, and the theories of capitalism and socialism.

From the outset, Catholic social teaching was hostile to what it saw as the excesses of the age, particularly the economic suffering of the working class and indigent along with the false ideologies propounded in the name of those suffering. When the newly industrialized economies of the West began to produce great wealth there was a clear failing in the distribution of the benefits within the new economic order. Large numbers of people were living in economic misery while others amassed vast fortunes. Leo XIII challenged the new economic system for its lack of distributive justice.

As already noted, equality is one important consideration in determining just distribution. People expect to be treated with equal respect due to the fundamental moral equality of persons. Yet equality does not stand alone as a determining factor in justice. Another candidate as a rule or canon for distributive justice is need. In Catholic social teaching the idea of distributive justice has entailed satisfying the basic material needs of all in a society. By basic material needs are meant those requirements that must be met in order for persons to live decent lives in the society to which they belong. Such needs "are socially relative, to some degree, but they are not merely subjective."[42] An economic system that consistently fails to provide for people's fundamental needs must be reformed so that the essential needs of all are addressed prior to some receiving far more than what is necessary.

Ordinarily, the expectation is that participants in a market economy will be able to meet their basic needs through the rewards of labor, either by making a profit or earning a wage. Due to infirmity, age, or other hindrance, individuals may not be able to provide for their own needs. Or, due to some failing in the economy, people may be prevented from providing for themselves. The state as the promoter of the temporal dimensions of the common good has the responsibility to intervene in the economic realm when the ordinary working of the economy is unable to satisfy the norm of a just distribution for all. In

---

41. Benedict XVI, *Caritas in veritate* (Charity in Truth, 2009), no. 35.
42. Miller, *Political Philosophy*, 82.

such cases, the state may draw on the resources of the common good to meet the basic needs of all in the political community.

Securing for any group of persons what is their due is simply another way of promoting the common good by making sure it is shared in by all.[43] This conviction is what gave rise to Leo's teaching that "[t]he richer population have many ways of protecting themselves, and stand less in need of help from the State; those who are badly off have no resources of their own to fall back upon, and must chiefly rely upon the assistance of the State."[44] Satisfying the basic material needs of those unable to meet those needs in the marketplace is an important role for the state. By making sure distributive justice is adequately taken into account the state is not favoring one group over another but merely guaranteeing no one is denied their rightful share of the temporal common good.

In keeping with its strong sense of the social nature of the person, Catholic teaching on justice talks not only about the goods to be derived from the common good but also the duty a person has to contribute to the common good. Put differently, there is not just the issue of a fair distribution of the benefits of the common life but also a fair distribution of the burdens of living in community. Individuals have a duty in justice to contribute to the common good.

One of the key dimensions of the economic burden that contributes to the common good is that of taxation. It is widely accepted within the Catholic social tradition that taxation is governed by distributive justice, and that in the case of burdens as distinct from benefits the important canon is that of the ability to pay. As a knowledgeable commentator on the tradition succinctly put it, "[t]he very general criterion governing distribution is that goods or advantages are to be distributed according to needs and necessities while burdens should be distributed according to capacities."[45] This means there should be a graduated or progressive system of taxation whereby the well-to-do pay a higher percentage of their financial resources for taxes than is expected from those with fewer resources.

Free-market economies produce many positive outcomes for society, and the Catholic tradition endorses market approaches. Yet the tradition has always been sensitive to the potential negative effects of free markets that lack adequate oversight, regulation, and restraint. One of those negative effects is that some people will not be able to provide for their basic material needs through normal market exchange. An important role for the state is to intervene in such situations to ensure that everyone is provided with a fair share of

---

43. Rommen, *The State*, 322.

44. *Rerum novarum*, no. 29.

45. Charles Curran, "Just Taxation in the Roman Catholic Tradition," *Journal of Religious Ethics* 13, no. 1 (Spring 1985): 113-33 at 120.

the common good through adequate provision to meet basic needs. There is a floor or minimum of material well-being that should support every member of the society.

Because of distributive justice, the tradition also endorses an approach to taxation that places a larger burden for care of the least well off upon those who have the greater share of economic resources. State funding of social assistance programs through a system of progressive taxation is a crucial form of state intervention in the economy for the sake of the common good and the ability of all to share in it.

Subsidiarity and State Intervention

A third comment about intervention concerns the reasoning behind limiting the state's role in economic life. Leo's defense of the state's right to intervene was straightforward, and no subsequent pope has disagreed with the argument laid out in *Rerum novarum*. What has occurred in later teaching is an examination of the extent of the state's right.

Since Leo's argument was made in the face of liberal free-market resistance to an activist state it is understandable that his focus was to establish a government's right to intervene. It was left to later popes to articulate more precisely the boundaries of that right. For instance, there is Pius XI's formulation of the principle of subsidiarity. Subsidiarity, as explained in *Quadragesimo anno*, can be easily paraphrased as "no bigger than necessary, no smaller than appropriate." Although the basic insight of the principle of subsidiarity is not difficult to grasp, it can be misunderstood when taken out of the context of the social tradition that precedes and continues on after Pius's formulation.

By the time Pius XI wrote *Quadragesimo anno* in 1931 "the 'night watchman' state of the liberals was disappearing in Europe, but an apparition even more sinister, to him, had taken its place in some nations: this was the omnicompetent state."[46] Pius wanted to avoid Leo's argument for a right to intervene being turned into a brief for the state overwhelming all other forms of human association.

Recall the point that the common good is richer than any one community can encompass. The political community is but one realm of experiencing the common good, and the state but one social institution, albeit a crucial one. Subsidiarity appears in Catholic social teaching precisely as that norm meant to prohibit reducing the richness of human association to one form—the state. Between the individual and the state there are an array of intermediate communities—the family, neighborhood or town, and voluntary associations

---

46. Camp, *Papal Ideology*, 145.

formed for diverse aims including religious, recreational, professional, cultural, and philanthropic purposes. Subsidiarity was cited by Pius XI as a way of providing a guideline to nuance the argument espoused by Leo that the state had the right, even the duty, to intervene in the marketplace.

Subsidiarity distinguishes Catholic social teaching from any collectivist or totalitarian outlook that allows the state to dominate all other forms of communal life. Catholic communitarianism requires a rich variety of associations that give life and color to communal experience. Subsidiarity maintains that the state's role is to help these smaller communities achieve their proper aim whenever they are unable (or unwilling) to make their distinct contribution to the overall well-being of the person or the larger community.

In effect, subsidiarity seeks the proper fit between the task and the competence, so that groups are asked to do neither more nor less than they should. Subsidiarity, then, warns against a state assuming too great a role in public life, but it also warns a state not to fail in fulfilling its duties to promote the common good. Subsidiarity regulates the institutions of society, especially the state, so that participatory community is possible. The aim of multiple associations, after all, is to permit persons to realize the variety of goods that make for human flourishing by fostering participation in communal life.

The story of higher education in the United States offers an example of subsidiarity in practice. The primary responsibility for education rests with the individual and family. Churches and private groups soon took upon themselves the role of providing higher education. When these resources were insufficient to meet the need, local governments entered with state colleges. This was followed by the federal government's support for land-grant colleges under the Morrill Act of 1890, which provided federal resources for states to initiate schools devoted to agriculture and mechanic studies for industrial classes pursuing a variety of occupational fields. Then government started the so-called normal schools to train elementary grade teachers. Following World War II there was a new need for broadening educational access, and local governments at the city and county levels created community colleges. Important to note is that in doing all this government at the federal or state level did not take away the role of smaller groups but simply added to what smaller entities could not supply. Indeed, both federal and state governments provide help in a variety of ways to private institutions of higher education rather than competing against such schools.

Viewed in the above way, subsidiarity is an instrumental norm meant to serve the foundational values of community and the common good that make for personal well-being. Subsidiarity serves two purposes—pluralism and participation. Pluralism is the maintenance of a vast array of nongovernmental associations that contribute to public life and the common good. Participation entails the ability to enjoy those fundamental rights and to act on those basic duties that the person has as a result of sharing in the common good. Subsidiarity serves these twin aims of pluralism and participation not by being interpreted as anti-state but by being understood as pro-involvement in the diverse richness of society.

A Balancing Act

In a society as complex as ours it is apparent that more than the state is necessary for realizing the common good; it is equally clear, however, that we do need the state. John XXIII was sensitive to the latter point when he introduced the term "socialization" in his 1961 encyclical *Mater et magistra*, translated in the English text as "an increase in social relationships." John described socialization as a more complex interdependence that introduces "many and varied forms of association in the lives and activities of citizens, and to their acceptance within our legal framework."[47] The process both arises from and evokes increased state intervention in the socio-economic realm. The encyclical gave a cautious but clear approval to this increasing role for the state because of the new complexities of modern economic life.[48]

A matter of debate today is what level and extent of state involvement are proper. Necessary for formulating an answer is the ability to assess what forces threaten the basic goods held up by the social teaching of the Catholic Church. Surely, Pius XI was right that the state can endanger social goods, but other forces and institutions also may block participation in communal life and thereby deny a person's ability to partake in the common good. For example, long-term unemployment can effectively undercut a person's ability to participate in the economic life of society, which, in turn, can mean the inability to fulfill basic material needs and frustrate the full realization of a person's talents and skills. The psychological and emotional damage of unemployment can undercut proper self-esteem and hinder the full maturation of the human personality.[49]

When considering the strategy for addressing obstacles to the common good it is not possible to rely upon a single ideological premise. While local grassroots activity is often necessary, indeed essential, it is unwise to think that all social ills are resolvable at neighborhood, city, or county levels. Some tasks

---

47. John XXIII, *Mater et magistra* (Christianity and Social Progress, 1961), no. 59.

48. At Vatican II the bishops of the world also noted the process of socialization as "reciprocal ties and mutual dependencies increase day by day and give rise to a variety of associations and organizations, both public and private." They further observed that socialization, "while certainly not without its dangers, brings with it many advantages" (*Gaudium et spes*, no. 25).

49. See *Economic Justice for All*, nos. 137-43.

require the competence of the national government and international actors, such as policies to address migration, climate change, foreign trade. Subsidiarity is not an expression of ideological bias against the state, for a serious analysis of the issue at hand must precede a determination of what is the proper level of government action to handle adequately a problem.

In some situations John Paul II noted that even well-intentioned state activity may undercut the role of other communities such as family, neighborhood, and voluntary associations. He saw a risk that "the social assistance state leads to a loss of human energies and an inordinate increase of public agencies which are dominated more by bureaucratic ways of thinking than by concern for serving their clients." The pope went on to say, "it would appear that needs are best understood and satisfied by people who are closest to them and who act as neighbors to those in need." His conclusion was that many people in need "can be helped effectively only by those who offer them genuine fraternal support, in addition to the necessary care."[50]

Evident in the papal warning is the persistence of the communitarian outlook. First, there is the claim that large bureaucratic structures are alienating and that governmental bureaucracy is no more humane than the bureaucracies of other large social structures. More desirable is an approach to social action that is planned on a human scale. A second communitarian theme is the value of locally based service agencies. It is quite possible that organizations closer to the grass roots than large governmental departments are better able to deliver services that address the concerns of people. A third communitarian theme is that more than material needs must be addressed. People in any society do not live by bread alone, even if bread is necessary. The values that humans cherish include those found in the experience of being in relationship with others.

It is important to notice that the papal reservation about some state activity is because the mechanisms of the state may not always be the best way to care for people. The obligation to care for people remains. It is a mistake, therefore, to think that subsidiarity is a principle to be invoked to limit care. Rather, subsidiarity is concerned with how care is to be provided. Benedict XVI, John Paul's successor, underscored this point when he wrote that subsidiarity is "first and foremost a form of assistance to the human person."[51] Therefore, it must not be understood in a manner that prevents the provision of social assistance. (The Latin word that is the basis for the English subsidiarity is *subsidium*, which means "help" or "assistance.") In short, a legitimate objection to state activity on the grounds of subsidiarity cannot be an effort to trump

---

50. John Paul II, *Centesimus annus* (One Hundred Years of Catholic Social Teaching, 1991), no. 48.

51. *Caritas in veritate*, no. 57.

the fundamental obligation of solidarity, but merely a caution about the most effective means to implement solidarity with those in need.

Subsidiarity serves to remind us that how a larger entity intervenes in the life of a smaller entity can take various forms. For example, the federal government may provide block grants to individual states for programs devised and implemented at the state level. Or funds may be given to implement programs mandated by the federal government. Or the federal government may set norms concerning the quality of a service and provide enforcement of those norms in state or county programs. The federal government may provide training and education for caregivers. Or the federal government may administer and run a program directly. Intervention can take many forms, and not all involve large bureaucracies or extensive government activity.

The essential nature of human life as social and of society as an organic community of communities determines the appropriate response. Participation in a wide array of communities allows a person to experience social life through "interrelationships on many levels," and it is "intermediate communities" that give human scale to mass society, offering an alternative to the person who is "often suffocated between two poles represented by the state and the marketplace."[52]

Once again, it is important to recall that subsidiarity does not entail an anti-state stance, but it does encourage strategies to maximize participation. By developing a variety of opportunities for participation the reality of our interdependence can be elevated to the experience of solidarity; we come to see the other not simply as someone with whom we are linked but a person with whom we can join in the pursuit of mutual goods and shared goals. Due to its sheer size and bureaucratic structure the state may not always provide the best way to implement mechanisms to promote solidarity in each case, but we ought not presume the other extreme that nongovernment strategies are always to be preferred, for in many cases they may not be up to the magnitude of the task.

To properly understand the role of the state it must be remembered that subsidiarity is an instrumental norm; it is not an end in itself. Subsidiarity is a way to foster participation, and the experience of participation can develop a sense of solidarity as people give of themselves in service to others and the common good. Subsidiarity without solidarity is unworthy of the Christian community. Subsidiarity is a vital strategy to encourage the existence of a multiplicity of institutions that offer the means to respond to the call to solidarity. Government, local and national, constitute some of those institutions, but they should not squeeze out all other social institutions such as churches, schools, labor unions, professional associations, humanitarian agencies,

---

52. *Centesimus annus*, no. 49.

charitable organizations, and other vehicles that recruit and empower people for building better societies. Pluralism reminds us that a rightly ordered society will have a wide variety of intermediate groups whereby a person may participate in the common life. The extent of the pluralism of social institutions provides a means to assess the health of a society, for the fewer the number and weaker the power of intermediate associations the more endangered is the social fabric.

Within Catholic social thought these three elements—the virtue of solidarity, the strategy of subsidiarity, and the test of pluralism—are constitutive of participatory community, or the communitarian vision of a good society. All three elements are subordinate to the master theme of the common good. The state in Catholic social teaching has as its purpose service to the common good. The role the state fulfills in attaining that purpose is to be shaped by the elements of solidarity, subsidiarity, and pluralism.

DEMOCRACY AS THE FORM OF THE STATE

It has been said that discussion of "the best form of government constitutes philosophically a negligible part in Catholic political thought."[53] The main explanation for this is that any judgment about the best form a state should assume is more a contingent judgment within a historical context than a principled determination of a universal nature. That is, the question is how best to realize the common good in the particular circumstances of a given time and place. The best form of government should be determined by that determination rather than "an abstract idealizing of one of the traditional forms of government"—monarchy, aristocracy, democracy.[54]

Certainly it is true that Christians have lived and functioned within a wide array of political institutions. Empires, monarchies, republics, dictatorships, tyrannies, oligarchies, aristocracies, democracies, theocracies, revolutionary regimes have all come and gone within the history of Christianity. From Nero to Stalin, from Charlemagne to Oliver Cromwell, from Napoleon to John Winthrop, there have been all manner of political leaders functioning at the head of any number of political institutions, and the Christian community has prospered and suffered, dominated and tolerated, opposed and supported, these leaders and institutions. So in the sense that Christians can endure and persist despite the grand parade of human politics, it can be said that Christianity is philosophically "indifferent" to the different forms that the state may take.

---

53. Rommen, *The State*, 479.
54. Ibid., 480.

Yet, as the above implies, history not only shows that the church can be faithful under various political conditions, it also demonstrates that some forms of governance are preferable to others. After all, it makes a considerable difference for human dignity and well-being if one lives under a political regime that practices ethnic cleansing or one that secures the equal rights of all citizens. Contingent judgments must be made, but it is vital that such judgments be informed by prudence. Nondemocratic states cannot be presumed to be bad, for there have been wise and benign monarchs. And there have been instances of democratic governance that amounted to little more than mob rule with majorities oppressing minorities. So "indifference" in the sense that no one system should be identified as *the* Christian political system is not the same as moral indifference to what form of governance should be preferred in a specific society. Prudential judgments do matter.

Democracy and Catholicism

In December of 1944, as the Second World War was drawing to a conclusion in Europe, Pius XII delivered his annual Christmas radio address. In the course of his remarks he stated that democracy is the form of government that is seemingly most in keeping with the dignity of persons today.[55] The statement by Pius might well have surprised many of his predecessors.

Gregory XVI (d. 1846) was an avowed enemy of democratic movements, and his successor, Pius IX (d. 1878), may have begun his papacy with greater openness to democracy but changed after the revolutions of 1848. Throughout the nineteenth century much of the French episcopacy was monarchist in loyalty. In addition, many Catholic writers commenting on the politics of Europe after the French Revolution were unsympathetic to democracy.

Why was the papacy uneasy with democracy and why was Catholicism slow in coming to endorse democracy? No single reason or person but a number of factors explain the skepticism toward democracy.

Questionable Theories
The experience of the French Revolution and its aftermath appeared to many Christians, especially French Catholics, as a time of mob rule, of "the people" claiming political power without any acknowledgment of the boundaries of sovereignty. So, too, the claims of Parliament during the English Revolution were, for Roman Catholics, an assault on the proper limits of political authority over religious matters. Thus, the language of democracy and belief in the

---

55. Pius XII, "1944 Christmas Address," in Yzermans, *Major Addresses*.

sovereignty of the people did not resonate as favorably within the Vatican as it did in other locales.

The liberal revolutions of 1848 in Europe were not only about democracy, for they also drew on support for other liberal tenets that were not always well grounded. Freedom of religion, a fundamental right that the Catholic Church came to endorse only in the mid-twentieth century, was not always defended in the nineteenth century with arguments that might persuade a skeptical Catholic hierarchy.

Freedom of religion was supported by some people on the grounds of relativism, and by others on the basis of what was called "indifferentism." The relativists were those who thought there was no such thing as truth, at least not religious truth, and that it was necessary, therefore, to dislodge any ecclesiastical claims to authority based on possession of the truth. Since truth was unattainable it was left to each person to decide what religion, if any, should be followed.

Among the indifferentists the claim was not that truth was impossible to grasp but that religious truth was too insignificant to matter, and, therefore, the state should simply ignore religion and let people do as they wished in such matters. No surprise, therefore, that when freedom of religion was presented as a corollary of either relativism or indifference those who took religion seriously would find it hard to endorse.

Democracy and Romanticism

Besides opposition to some of the theories espoused in support of democratic structures and culture there was also a second concern, that the benefits of democracy were not all that evident, at least not for many people. Catholic writers and leaders of an aristocratic background were troubled by a democratic culture that appeared overly materialistic and destructive of traditional communities and their values.

Without question, part of what informed the conservativism of nineteenth-century European Catholics was the influence of the Romantic movement and its idealization of a medieval culture washed away by the liberal revolutions of democratic politics, free-market economics, and cultural individualism. Democracy was not simply a political cause but was also linked to economic and cultural changes that alienated large numbers from traditional lifestyles.

For many classical conservatives their opposition to democracy was accompanied by their anticapitalism as well. Beyond the widespread material suffering of the poor in the early decades of laissez-faire capitalism there was also criticism of a situation in which many uneducated workers and their families were uprooted from rural villages and towns. Resettled in the new surroundings of crowded urban areas, people might experience themselves less a democratic citizenry than an anonymous mass bereft of their traditional culture offered a sense of identity and meaning. Although not a satisfactory response, the conservative Catholic approach of a benign paternalism toward these victims of the social upheavals of nineteenth-century Europe might seem more humane than what the new democratic culture provided.

Institutional Self-Interest

A third concern about the liberal democratic revolutions was the impact on the church's institutional life. This concern embraced a variety of possible consequences, all viewed with reserve within the Vatican. For example, the call for democracy in politics could be extended to calls for democratization within the life of the church.[56] And there were reformers who sought the popular election of bishops, greater oversight of clerical decisions and performance by the laity, and a lesser role for the papacy in church life.

Having experienced the abuses and the divisiveness occasioned by the Clergy Constitution of the French Revolution, Rome was unsympathetic to institutional changes that weakened the Vatican's role in the selection, appointment, and oversight of the higher or lower clerical ranks. As history attested, there had been a long struggle to achieve and maintain independence for the church from the power of monarchs and princes. Rome was not interested in surrendering its autonomy to a new secular power, "the people" or the democratic state.

Accompanying the movement to democracy across Europe was the cause of nationalism. The liberal revolutions were aimed against the old imperial powers and were inspired by movements to translate cultural nationalism rooted in ethnicity, language, and custom into political nationalism that saw the nation as the foundation for a democratic state. From the Vatican perspective such nationalist sentiments raised several risks.

As noted in chapter 7, the Catholic Church was well integrated within the old political order and was able to preserve a variety of institutional privileges that the church enjoyed due to its relationship with Catholic rulers. The forces of nationalism would threaten such arrangements and nowhere more than on the Italian peninsula.

The spirit of nationalism sparked the *Risorgimento*, or movement to Italian unification. Success in this drive would entail dissolution of the Papal States, and the Vatican reacted in a predictable way, calling on Catholic rulers in Europe to defend its territorial sovereignty. Such reliance on foreign rulers

---

56. Such calls, of course, were not modern inventions. The conciliarist movement (see chap. 5) was an effort to restrain the monarchical papacy and situate ecclesiastical authority and power within a more democratic, though not egalitarian, understanding of the church as a community.

and their troops only further angered those committed to ridding the Italian territory of outsiders and creating a unified Italian state.

Italian nationalism was a major threat to the cherished autonomy of the papacy. Pius IX and his advisors did not see how the freedom of the church could be preserved if the church had no territorial independence. Of course, one could ask if the church had not over the centuries entered into compromising alliances and arrangements precisely because of the Papal States and the desire to protect them. Nonetheless, for the hierarchy in the nineteenth century a nationalist movement resulting in the demise of the Papal States was a force to be opposed.

Coupled with the loss of papal territory that put papal autonomy at risk, there was the threat that nationalism posed for the universality of the church. The long competition with Gallicanism and the subsequent experience of other national church movements were part of the historical memory of the Vatican. A vision of the church splintered into numerous national churches, with the papacy functioning as little more than an ineffectual sign of unity among the churches, was a future to be resisted with vigor.

Missing the Difference

As a result of the concerns noted above, the Catholic Church during the nineteenth century came to be seen as an avowed opponent of the emerging democratic order. Following the death of Pius IX in 1878, Leo XIII in 1881 and 1885 issued encyclicals that made clear democracy was compatible with Catholicism. He also began making overtures to indicate his support for the French Third Republic, a regime that French Catholic monarchists had stoutly resisted. Nonetheless, the general impression remained that Catholicism resisted democracy, in part because in his writings Leo did not distinguish between the liberal democratic theory found on continental Europe and that of the Anglo-American approach.

Continental liberalism was influenced by the writing of Jean-Jacques Rousseau, whose *Social Contract* was key to the 1789 *Declaration of the Rights of Man and of the Citizen* that expressed the philosophy of the French Revolution. This political outlook acknowledged no authority higher than that of the collective will of the people and saw the state as the source of personal rights. Leo, like his predecessors, considered this a serious error and sought to preserve the view that all authority comes from God and any temporal authority, democratic or otherwise, was subject to divine and natural law. For Leo, this did not mean all forms of democratic theory and popular sovereignty were wrong, but he did not attend adequately in his writing to the democratic theory that had developed in England and America. Consequently, the bridge that might have been built between Catholicism and democracy was not constructed, and the reputation of Catholicism as antidemocratic continued on into the twentieth century.

In the 1930s there continued to be evidence that Catholicism, at least in some settings, was cool toward democracy. In Spain and Italy there were Catholic clergy who took the side of fascist regimes, often because of the belief that the worse alternative was communism. Even in Germany and Austria there were early sympathizers who thought Hitler, while excessive in rhetoric and tone, was a reasonable alternative to those on the extreme left whose enmity toward Christianity was evident. The sorry story of the misreadings and misjudgments that led clerical leaders of the Catholic Church to think that enemies on the left were always more real and much worse than enemies on the right is complex, but as a result Catholicism too often appeared uneasy with democracy until recent decades.

A New Context for Democracy

The reasons for the shift in the Catholic position are both theoretical and practical. Concerning the latter, the bitter experience of Nazism and fascism in the decades of the 1930s and 1940s prodded the church to ally itself with those states that opposed Hitler and Mussolini. That, with the exception of Russia, these nations were democratic cast the strength and vitality of such systems of government in a new light. Many of the concerns about anti-Catholicism, religious indifferentism, mob rule, and ineffective leadership were dissolved.

Following the war, the transformation of Russia into the leader of a Soviet bloc, which adopted totalitarian measures and which systematically oppressed the Catholic Church, pushed the Vatican into a closer working relationship with Western democracies. In the political struggles throughout postwar Europe, the Vatican approved and encouraged the formation of various Christian Democratic parties in order to provide an alternative to the Communists.[57]

At the theoretical level one can see the development of the Catholic position reflected in a remark of Paul VI's from 1971 that "two aspirations persistently make themselves felt" in the modern age, "the aspiration to equality and the aspiration to participation."[58] For Paul VI these aspirations are forms of human dignity and freedom.

During the twentieth century important dialogues with liberalism and socialism took place that led to revisions in Catholic thinking about the state and democracy. Catholic social teaching had long defended the moral equality

---

57. For the story of this period, see Tom Buchanan and Martin Conway, eds., *Political Catholicism in Europe 1918-1965* (Oxford: Clarendon, 1996); and Martin Conway, *Catholic Politics in Europe 1918-1945* (London: Routledge, 1997).

58. Paul VI, *Octogesima adveniens* (A Call to Action, 1971), no. 22.

of all persons due to the doctrine of the *imago Dei*. However, the affirmation of moral equality did not immediately lead to an appreciation of equality's relevance in other areas. In time, the recognition dawned that political equality was an important expression of moral equality and that any relationship involving authority over another required justification; no person was naturally superior to another.

It is widely acknowledged that the call for overcoming social and economic inequalities forced societies to confront the way that poverty and marginalization undercut human dignity. However, the emphasis on equality also led to calls for political change whereby a basic equality in the civil rights of citizens and the exercise of fundamental political powers could be experienced.

If all are equal, then no person's vote should count for more than another person's ballot. Thus, the votes of a majority count for more than a minority. Nonetheless, equality applied to the political order also suggests equal rights of political expression, equality before the law, and equal access to the political process. Even minorities retain those rights when outvoted by a majority.

The aspiration to participation highlights the movement of people to seek a role in exercising self-determination. All persons should be able to express their preferences for public policies that will affect their lives. Participation underscores the norm that people ought to be allowed to speak and act for themselves rather than assume that others know what they want or need.

This way of thinking about the import of participation strikes against paternalistic views of government whereby the monarch was viewed as the *paterfamilias* of the nation, responsible for directing the nation's "children" toward the common good. The traditional view identified the leader of a state as the embodiment of the nation as well, and this allowed the state to assume a role in directing the lives of citizens that could be intrusive and overbearing even if benevolently intended.

In a time characterized by widespread illiteracy, acceptance of social hierarchy, and extensive poverty, the idea of a ruler functioning as a parent toward immature children may have resonated with the lived experience of people. In the contemporary era, the underlying social conditions that lent feasibility to such an authoritarian approach to the political order have undergone decline. When self-determination and self-governance become the conventional wisdom of the age, participation in the processes of democracy is established as the desire of men and women.

Evident in the changes of the "high" tradition's teaching on democracy is a shift in the social imagination or "low" tradition of Catholicism. The metaphor of society as an organic body had been foundational to Catholic political theory. In the body there are different roles, some higher than others. Each person had a defined role, and fulfilling the obligations of one's role was the expectation for a person seeking to obey God's purposeful plan.

Modern Catholic social teaching relies on a view of society as a community of communities. Political community calls for a shared purpose, the common good. But unlike the predetermined role and duties of the members of an organic body, the teaching of Vatican II states, "many different people go to make up the political community, and these can lawfully incline toward diverse ways of doing things." Of course, it is the role of political authority to organize and direct citizens in promoting the common good, but "this authority must dispose the energies of the whole citizenry toward the common good, not mechanically or despotically, but primarily as a moral force which depends on freedom...."[59] The Catholic social imagination has embraced a new metaphor for the nature of society, one that is less congenial to a paternalistic state and more suggestive of a limited state that shares the traditional purpose of the state in the tradition but follows a different approach to its role and form—a limited state with a democratic polity.

Democracy and Protestantism

It is important to recognize that many Protestant Christians came to embrace democracy prior to Catholic leaders. Of course, even among Catholics, including their bishops, there was considerably more enthusiasm for democracy in the nineteenth and early twentieth centuries in the United States than in Europe.[60] Still, the reason American Catholics supported democracy was that they had first-hand experience of its benefits.[61] And democracy in the United States was directly connected to the religious and political world of English Protestantism.

So before ending this chapter the importance of Protestant thinking on democracy ought to be acknowledged. Since the story of English and American revolutions has been related in chapter 7, the material in this chapter will consider how an influential twentieth-century Protestant made the case for the compatibility between democracy and Christian beliefs.

In the preface to one of his books the American Protestant theologian Reinhold Niebuhr wrote a much-quoted statement as a Christian assessment of democracy: "Man's capacity for justice makes democracy possible; but man's inclination to injustice makes democracy necessary."[62] Niebuhr was often

---

59. *Gaudium et spes*, no. 74.

60. See Gerald Fogarty, *The Vatican and the American Hierarchy from 1870 to 1965* (Wilmington, DE: Michael Glazier, 1985).

61. For an excellent overview of the American Catholic experience of living and working within the U.S. democracy, see David O'Brien, *Public Catholicism* (New York: Macmillan, 1989).

62. Reinhold Niebuhr, *The Children of Light and the Children of Darkness* (New York: Charles Scribner's Sons, 1944), xiii.

a critic of theologies and political theories that were overly optimistic because they did not take seriously the human propensity to evil.

Whether it was due to excessive confidence in human reason, good will, or moral perfectibility, Niebuhr argued the history of theology and political thought offered multiple examples of thinkers who underestimated the pervasive power of sin to corrupt human hearts and institutions. Therefore it is always essential that those entrusted with political authority and power should be held accountable to others. There must be a system of checks and balances within a political system to ensure that power is used for the common good and not simply for the interests of those in authority.

At the same time, Niebuhr was aware of the possibilities of grace transforming human hearts and societies. Taking sin seriously did not mean being cynical about working for justice, nor did it mean we should expect nothing in the political order but the dogged pursuit of self-interest. Humans were capable of transcending narrow self-interest, and social institutions could be open to reform and improvement. Therefore, the ability of people to reason together, to undertake cooperative efforts at social change, to use their skills and resources for the sake of shared goods, suggests that a political system ought to create space for broad participation, open debate, and free consent. A political system should call forth and channel the nobler aspects of human character and not merely protect us from the darker side of our natures.

The subtitle of Niebuhr's book was *A Vindication of Democracy and a Critique of Its Traditional Defense*. Niebuhr argued in favor of democracy and against the threats of tyranny and totalitarianism that he saw in Europe. The antidemocratic forces were those of the children of darkness and were to be resisted. At the same time, Niebuhr rebuked those supporters of democracy who built their theory on a misguided theological or philosophical anthropology. The children of light create a good deal of suffering when they introduce utopian and naïve views into the political order. Personal freedom and self-governance were to be encouraged, but history taught that even democracies will use the power of the state to advance the interests of some but not all of its citizens.

For Niebuhr, the traditional defense of democracy was too closely linked to an economic ideology of free markets and individual rights that undercut the democratic project of freedom and equal justice. The failure to restrain economic power adequately meant that political power would inevitably become undemocratic. Defending democracy on the basis of an optimistic reading of the harmony of human interests along with the easy reconciliation of economic self-interest and the common good was the traditional error. For Niebuhr, the danger was the very real challenges posed to order and justice that a naïve exaltation of freedom overlooked.[63]

---

63. This theme remained a constant in Niebuhr's writings. Twenty years after *The*

Niebuhr's Theological Basis for Democracy

Niebuhr's aim was to examine the moral standards that made democracy viable and necessary. To do such an examination required a grasp of the religious foundations of these moral standards. Made in the image of God, the human person is drawn to goodness and possesses a capacity for justice. People can reason together and cooperate to attain social goods. The reality of human sinfulness does not totally eradicate the *imago Dei* nor completely diminish people's aptitude for acknowledging and pursuing the good.

Complementing the Christian understanding of creation there is also the conviction that in Christ humankind has been redeemed. God's healing and sanctifying grace allows individuals and communities to move beyond self-centeredness and anxiety so that a measure of social unity and cooperation can be achieved through trust and solidarity. Coercive power is never fully absent in political life, but there is a degree to which good will and concern for the other is also evident in society due to the grace of Christ at work in history.

Democracy, therefore, can be understood as in keeping with Christian affirmations of human dignity, freedom, and participation. People want to exercise their God-given ability to reason and seek out the good that beckons to them; they require an appropriate sphere of liberty in which to act on the life plans they develop and pursue; and they want to exercise self-governance through participation in the decision-making processes of the institutions that direct and order their lives.[64]

Children of Light and the Children of Darkness he wrote, "All the realities of power and interest are obscured in our idealistic eyes by the myth of 'freedom.' Not that actual freedom is a myth. What is mythical is our venerating it apart from the context of social processes involving interest and power. Open societies are not merely political devices for choosing rulers by the 'free consent of the governed.' They are fluid communities in which interests and powers can compete with each other and displace one another as dominant or cooperative forces in society." See "Johnson and the Myths of Democracy," in *Faith and Politics*, ed. Ronald Stone (New York: George Braziller, 1968), 245-52 at 247.

64. The contemporary political theorist Francis Fukuyama has noted the continuing importance of the theme of human dignity for understanding political movements.

In the Anglo-Saxon world, there is a tendency to see politics as a contest of economic interests and to define rights in utilitarian terms. But dignity is the basis for politics everywhere: Equal pay for equal work, one of the great banners of feminism, is less about incomes and more about income as a marker for the respect that society pays for one's labor. There are no interests that gays could not protect through civil unions, but same-sex marriage has become an issue in American politics because it signifies recognition of the equal dignity of gay and heterosexual unions. One can understand the rights enumerated in the U.S.

Also present in the Christian tradition is the conviction that human beings are the inheritors of original sin. Sin is found not only in people's deeds or inactions but also within each person—darkening human reason, weakening the will, and corrupting the heart. Humans can live comfortably with illusions, avoiding the truth and convincing themselves that a partial view is, in fact, the full perspective. Even when people can acknowledge a good, they may lack the courage, the discipline, or the zeal to embrace what is the correct course of action. And, as Augustine taught so insightfully, the human heart can fall in love with lesser rather than greater goods. The doctrine of human sinfulness is a reminder that there is no sphere of human existence not marred by the manifestation of sin.

A consequence of the above for politics is the danger that power may be inadequately distributed. Vesting any individual, class, or group with too much power in a society creates a strong temptation for the powerful to identify their interests with the general interest, their private good with the common good. The legitimate pursuit of recognition of a group's rights or liberty is often pursued at the expense of another group. The injustices that in-groups inflict upon out-groups are frequently reprised when those formerly on the margins come to power themselves. This temptation to use power to seek partial rather than universal ends was a constant theme of Niebuhr's political ethics.

Creating a system of governance that permits alternative viewpoints to be voiced, invites open debate about public matters, and forces decisions to be explained and examined through reasoned argument may significantly lessen the risk of power being abused by an elite. Requiring a majority of the governed to approve of their leaders and policies also increases the likelihood that rulers will not seek goods that are beneficial only to a small group.

Yet, the risk of majorities abusing minorities is ever present, and, therefore, there is need for mechanisms that protect the well-being of those not in the majority. Dividing political powers—executive, legislative, judicial—into different and independent branches of government is another way to diffuse power and avoid its abuse. Instituting methods of accountability such as terms of office and popular election, a free press, and rights of redress are additional measures that keep the powerful accountable to those in whose name they rule.

Constitution, as well as those in the basic laws of other liberal democracies, as mechanisms for formally recognizing the rights, and therefore the dignity, of the citizens to whom they are granted. (Francis Fukuyama, "The Drive for Dignity," *Foreign Policy* (January 12, 2012): 1-3 at 2. See http://www.foreignpolicy.com/ articles/2012/01/12/the_drive_for_dignity?print=yes&hidecomments=yes&page =full).

Niebuhr knew that the doctrine of human sinfulness meant self-interest was a deeply rooted flaw in human nature and that it was not easily countered. Thus, it was best if government was not set up on the presumption that only the virtuous would govern. Since even the virtuous were tempted to vice, a better system of government would have checks and balances that limited the negative aspects of power while still permitting the exercise of power for the good of society.

The separation of powers that is enshrined in the U.S. Constitution reflects the skepticism that the founding generation of American leaders had about permitting too much power to accrue in the hands of any one person or organ of government. The three branches of government—executive, legislative, judicial—each with the ability to check or reverse decisions by the other two, are an institutionalization of skepticism or doubt about power becoming too concentrated in a democracy.

A Presumption for Democracy

History provides examples of hereditary monarchs or noble oligarchs who have governed with wisdom and a commitment to the common good. And history is replete with examples of democratically elected leaders who have engaged in widespread corruption, inflicted unnecessary violence, and shown indifference to the suffering of others. Democracy is a human system of governance and cannot be considered immune from the legacy of sin. Yet, although democracy offers "no guarantee of good results, . . . it does keep things open. It does provide channels for criticism and for change. . . . Indeed, the most corrupt periods in the histories of democratic societies seem also to be those times when people are least interested in exercising their opportunities and responsibilities."[65]

As the term is widely understood today, democracy means more than a set of techniques or rules for government. Without dismissing such practices, democracy also includes what might be called an ethos or moral culture that embraces ideals about human dignity and derived rights, equality before the law and due process, equal protection of personal freedoms to worship, association, assembly, free expression, and justice in the protection of rights and exercise of duties. Understood thus, it is no surprise that the Methodist theologian Philip Wogaman has proposed there is a "Christian 'presumption' for democracy."[66]

---

65. J. Philip Wogaman, *Christian Perspectives on Politics*, rev. ed. (Louisville: Westminster John Knox Press, 2000), 219.

66. Ibid., 220.

What Wogaman means by presumption is that democracy should not be seen as a moral absolute in the Christian tradition. For "much depends upon the actual development of the history of a society and the character of the challenges it faces."[67] Yet, the presumption is that democracy is the preferred form of the state unless there is good reason to the contrary. The language of presumption suggests that the case against democracy must be made, and that barring such an argument the democratic system is the "default position" in the present age.

This thinking is akin to the way jurors operate with a presumption of innocence in our criminal justice system. The accused does not have to prove innocence; rather, the prosecution in the case has to prove beyond a reasonable doubt that the accused is guilty. Of course, if there is adequate evidence and testimony provided by the prosecution the jurors may reach the conclusion that the presumption of innocence should be overridden and the accused found guilty. But the burden of proof rests with the prosecution to make the case. If the evidence is not sufficiently compelling, then the jurors must presume innocence.

So the language of presumption does not mean that democracy is always and under all circumstances the best form of government. It does mean that one starts with the conviction that democracy is the appropriate and preferred form of government and that a different conclusion must be argued for with persuasive reasons.

CONCLUSION

The interpenetration of church thought and practice with secular political thought and practice is extensive. What one finds today in the various movements throughout the globe concerning human rights, individual freedoms, democratic culture and processes can be linked to themes (theoretical and practical) within the Christian tradition. At the same time these global developments have entered into the mainstream of Christian thought and action. For much of Christianity, developments within temporal politics have influenced the way the church has organized itself and explained its own authority and power.

Throughout the history of Christianity's engagement with the political order, one of the perennial issues is how individual believers as well as the church will interact with the institution of the state. Throughout the preceding chapters there have been narratives of cooperation, confrontation, and coopta-

---

67. Ibid., 221.

tion between church and state as well as between individual disciples and the state.

In this chapter there has been a presentation of how one significant interpretation of the Christian tradition, Roman Catholicism, has developed a theory of the state—its nature, purpose, role, and form. Other interpretations of the Christian tradition will differ with some or much of Catholic political theory. This is due not only to theological differences within Christianity but also to different experiences of secular politics and state activity.

If nothing else, such differences point up the important lesson that a Christian view of the state is more than a matter of developing a theory from abstract first principles of theology. There has been much trial and error during the course of history that has shaped and reshaped the way that the tradition thinks about the state. In the following chapters we will consider two important questions for Christianity: why is the church engaged in temporal politics and how ought the church be engaged? No surprise that historical trial and error will be a prominent method for addressing the questions.

QUESTIONS FOR DISCUSSION/REFLECTION

1. How does the view of the human person as created in the image of God provide an alternative perspective on the nature of political life to that of classical liberalism or socialism?
2. How would you describe the difference between society and the state?
3. What is the importance of solidarity for a proper view of the state? How should the sovereignty of the state be understood?
4. What is the purpose of the state? How do you understand the meaning of the common good?
5. Can you summarize the role of the state in society? What is the meaning of distributive justice? What is meant by subsidiarity in Catholic social teaching?
6. In your opinion, is democracy the best form of government? Are there any other forms of government that are acceptable from a Christian perspective?
7. How did Catholicism come to terms with modern democracy after the French Revolution?
8. Do you agree with Reinhold Niebuhr that the human capacity for justice makes democracy possible but that our inclination to injustice makes democracy necessary? Why?
9. What are the key theological elements that Protestant scholars have proposed to defend democracy?

9

Why the Church Is Engaged in Politics

The Christian church is a social institution with customary patterns of authority, decision making, and activity. There is also an underlying theology to support these patterns. The branch of theology that is concerned with the nature and mission of the church is called ecclesiology. So in this chapter we are examining the church as a corporate or institutional agent, not the deeds of individual believers.

In this chapter we will examine one of the ecclesiological issues occasioned by the church's activity in political life. As preceding chapters have shown, the Christian church has often been intensely involved in the political life of the societies in which it finds itself. Faced with the historical record, one can still ask whether the church *should* be involved in temporal politics, and, if so, why? In short, is there a theological rationale to justify the church's political activity? Or has the church engaged in politics for purely pragmatic or self-serving reasons that betray its religious identity and mission?

This chapter has as its goal, making the case that the mission of the church, correctly understood, includes a necessary engagement with temporal politics. In the following two chapters the question of *how* the church should engage politics will be considered. In this chapter we will address the reason *why* the church should engage the political order.

In the three major sections to follow I will first present the approach that Vatican II adopted in its explanation of the church's self-understanding about its mission in the world. Then I will provide an interpretation of what the Council taught about the relationship of the church to the particular dimension of worldly existence that we think of as political. The final section of the chapter will look at several important theological themes and how they relate to the church's involvement in political life.

What explains the church as a corporate body, as an institution, getting involved in the political order? Over the course of the centuries various rationales have been provided, but one particularly important way of formulating a brief for the church as a political actor can be found in the deliberations of the hierarchy of the Roman Catholic Church at the Second Vatican Council.

VATICAN II ON THE CHURCH IN THE TEMPORAL REALM

Obviously, the Second Ecumenical Council held at the Vatican did not establish the tradition of socio-political engagement. But this gathering of the Catholic hierarchy, often referred to as Vatican II or simply as the Council, did initiate a distinctive era in the story of Catholicism and politics. As one Protestant commentator put it, "the Second Vatican Council (1962-1965) expressed a sea change in Catholic thinking about church-state relations, religious liberty, and issues of political participation in the modern world."[1]

To explain the nature of the "sea change" it will be helpful to understand some of the elements of the Council's wider effort at renewing the church in the middle of the twentieth century. Most of the themes that became dominant during the four autumn sessions of the Council beginning in 1962 were preceded by work that began as early as the mid-nineteenth century. During that span of time an array of "intellectual, organizational and pastoral movements in the church"[2] laid the groundwork for what transpired during the sessions of Vatican II. Renewal in the area of biblical studies, the development of a liturgical reform movement, a call to retrieve the social meaning of Catholic doctrine, the beginning of Catholic ecumenical conversation—all these had started prior to Vatican II. What the Council did was bring these ideas "in from the cold" where they had marginal impact on the everyday life of the church to the warm center of Catholic theology, spirituality, and practice. Due to the Council, ideas and themes that small numbers of committed Catholics in a few locales discussed and hoped to someday implement became widely shared commitments that were given papal and episcopal legitimation and encouragement.

Three important aspects of the biblical, liturgical, and theological renewal brought on by Vatican II was that it (1) offered the church a rich array of images and metaphors for ecclesial self-understanding; (2) urged a reconsideration of the church's relationships with the state and with society; and (3) suggested the possibility of a different method for addressing social questions. The second and third items will be addressed in the next major section of the chapter. Here we will take up the array of images used for ecclesial self-understanding.

One way to describe the effects of Vatican II is that at the Council the church underwent an identity crisis. That is, more important than any specific change in teaching or practice was the larger transformation pertaining to the

---

1. Philip Wogaman, *Christianity and Politics*, rev. ed. (Louisville: Westminster John Knox Press, 2000), 46.

2. J. Bryan Hehir, "Forum: Public Theology in Contemporary America," *Religion and American Culture* 10, no. 1 (Winter, 2000): 20-27 at 23.

church's self-understanding. Crisis is not used here in a negative sense, but as a moment of choice and transition; a familiar identity was being reconsidered in favor of a new self-image shaped, in part, by a retrieval of metaphors drawn from the biblical and theological tradition that supports Catholic faith and practice. A brief review of some of these new, yet traditional, images of the church will suggest how the renewal of Vatican II affected the Catholic approach to political life.[3]

Church as Sacrament

In the opening paragraph of the document *Lumen gentium*, the Dogmatic Constitution on the Church, we find the statement, "the church is a sign as well as an instrument of salvation."[4] Prior to the sacramental rituals familiar to Christians, such as Baptism or Eucharist, the church itself is a sacrament. There are two points to underscore about this claim.

First, a sacrament "causes" grace by signifying, that is, incarnating the reality of grace. For example, the act of lovemaking by a married couple is not simply an indicator of the love between them but is the very embodiment of their love. Sexual intercourse is their love given visible expression, and by that expression their love for each other deepens and is made more real. The grace of married love comes to be incarnated, made flesh, in the act of conjugal intimacy. Sacraments do not simply point to grace "over there somewhere" or found in another event. The sacrament itself is the "bodying forth" of the graced reality. Sacraments make the graced reality present to us by giving it visible expression. So sexual intimacy can be seen as a sacramental expression of human love.

Similarly, if the church is a sacrament, it must be capable of incarnating or "enfleshing" the reality it seeks to communicate. Like the other sacraments, the church does not bring grace to a situation that is wholly profane or void of grace; rather it illuminates the presence of grace in situations that we only imagined to be profane, but which were already graced by God's presence. Put differently, the church assembly is not "more holy" than other assemblies of people; rather, the church is the assembly of people who are conscious of the gracious presence of God whenever two or three gather in the Lord's name. The church is the place where people make explicit what is always going on implicitly: God's gracious ongoing presence permeates the world and is always being made available.

---

3. I borrow the images, though not their explication, from Richard McBrien, *The Church: The Evolution of Catholicism* (New York: HarperCollins, 2008), 162-81.

4. Vatican II, *Lumen gentium* (Dogmatic Constitution on the Church, 1965), no. 1.

The second point that follows in this framework is that to be a sacrament requires of the church that its own internal life be an adequate expression of its message to others. The Christian community must live in such a way—by its devotion to love and forgiveness, justice and compassion, freedom and truth— that when others look at the church they are reminded of God's grace at work in the world.[5] It is for this reason that the bishops of the United States pointed out in a pastoral letter on economic justice that "All the moral principles that govern the just operation of any economic endeavor apply to the Church and its agencies and institutions; indeed the Church must be exemplary."[6] Therefore, church reform is important not just for the membership of the church but for the sake of the external mission to witness to others. The sacramental witness of the church is betrayed when its internal life embodies something radically other than the gospel message it wishes to proclaim.[7]

Church as Servant

The church understands itself as having a religious mission, but that religious mission entails a commitment to serve the rest of humankind. Drawing upon the claim about its sacramental character, the church is portrayed by the bishops at the Council as the "universal sacrament" of God's salvation.[8] The church does not exist only for its own members but for all of humanity. Just as Christ came to save all people, so, too, the church cannot accept a narrower mission of catering only to those in formal membership.

The church must be wary of what Protestant theologian James Gustafson has called "the sectarian temptation," since the church has the responsibility to

---

5. As the episcopal synod held in 1971 stated, "everyone who ventures to speak to people about justice must first be just in their eyes" (1971 Synod, *Justitia in mundo* [Justice in the World], no. 40).

6. National Conference of Catholic Bishops, *Economic Justice for All* (Washington, DC: United States Catholic Conference, 1985), no. 347.

7. This last point indicates an ongoing tension in the life of the Catholic community. Is the church to be a church of the masses, accepting within its walls many people only partially or hesitantly committed to the gospel message? Or, is the demand on the church to be a faithful witness such that those admitted to membership must consistently show themselves as a sacramental community capable of signifying the presence of divine grace in the world? In other words, how distinct from the rest of humankind must disciples be if their witness is to be noticed as more than a pale reflection—and their voice is to be heard as something other than a mere echo—of the wider society?

8. *Lumen gentium*, no. 48, quoted in *Gaudium et spes* (Pastoral Constitution on the Church in the Modern World, 1965), no. 45.

assist in the transformation of the world, not simply tell its message to itself.[9] The Pastoral Constitution situated the church within the world, as a part of the human community, not set apart from it. In its opening words the Pastoral Constitution described disciples not as separate from the rest of humankind but as devoted to serving others: "The joys and hopes, the griefs and anxieties of the people of this age, especially those who are poor or in any way afflicted, these too are the joys and hopes, the griefs and anxieties of the followers of Christ."[10]

The Synoptic Gospel accounts of Jesus' ministry make clear that the core of his preaching was the coming of the reign of God, and the challenge to his listeners was to respond appropriately to the good news of the in-breaking of God's reign in history (Mark 1:15). The bishops at the Council understood that the mission of the church must be in conformity with the ministry of Jesus.[11]

According to the Council, the reason for the church's existence is to continue the work of Christ, "the mission of proclaiming and establishing among all peoples the reign of Christ and of God." Furthermore, and in keeping with the sacramental view of the church, the bishops declared that the church is "the seed and the beginning of that reign."[12] Although remaining incomplete on this side of history, the church is called to be an anticipatory presence of God's reign in the midst of humankind. Human beings can create communities that effectively point to the goal of history—the fulfillment of creation through the establishment of God's reign over all historical realities, including human hearts and minds.

In accord with the Catholic principle of mediation[13] the bishops at Vatican II maintain that it is not divine action alone that brings about God's reign but God acting through, with, and in us. Human activity, therefore, has significance and meaning because we can cooperate in God's plan for creation or seek to frustrate it by pursuing our own designs. The church, for its part,

---

9. James Gustafson, "The Sectarian Temptation," in *Proceedings of the Catholic Theological Society of America* 40 (1985): 83-94. Within Catholic theory and practice the sectarian impulse has been incorporated through certain theologies and spiritualities that characterized the life of vowed religious. There have been times when religious life was interpreted as a flight from the world, a refusal to sully one's hands with the world's work.

10. *Gaudium et spes*, no. 1.

11. "[T]he Church seeks but a solitary goal: to carry forward the work of Christ himself" (*Gaudium et spes*, no. 3).

12. *Lumen gentium*, no. 5.

13. Richard McBrien's explanation of the principle of mediation is a standard one: "The theological principle that God is available to us and acts upon us through secondary causes: persons, places, events, things, nature, history" (*Catholicism*, vol. 2 [Oak Grove, MN: Winston Press, 1980], xxxvi).

must always place itself at the service of God's reign, helping to establish it in history, pointing to its fulfillment beyond history, seeking to embody it in its own internal life and external ministry. Yet, the fullness of God's reign is in the future, and even the best of human activity falls short of that future. Therefore, the status quo can never be sacralized and placed beyond scrutiny or considered immune from the necessity of ongoing reform.

Church as Communion

The communion of churches implies that the universal church is composed of many churches that are united in faith, worship, and mission. This means that the church catholic is not only realized as one, large universal church but also locally and regionally in the many individual churches that exist. "The Church of Christ is really present in all legitimately organized local groups of the faithful, which, insofar as they are united to their pastors, are also quite appropriately called Churches in the New Testament."[14]

Without question the church is transnational, but it is also national and with deep roots in particular cultures and histories. This accounts for the distinctive experience of Christians in Poland, Rwanda, Brazil, South Korea, and the United States. Though the church professes "one Lord, one faith, one baptism" (Eph 4:5) a legitimate diversity is found that permits differences in issues and strategy when the church turns to the political realm. Local, national, and regional expressions of church will give rise to a variety of goals and methods for church engagement with politics.

Two examples that can be cited here are the work of the Latin American episcopate (CELAM) and of the bishops of the United States (USCCB). The Latin Americans were not a particularly powerful or influential force at Vatican II. Compared to the Europeans, the Latin American bishops had not found their collective voice at the time of the Council. However, the experience of the Council led the bishops to increased communication among themselves and a desire to match their experience with the teaching of Vatican II. The Latin Americans returned to their own continent not content simply to apply the teaching of Vatican II to their situation. Instead, they sought to interpret the teaching so that it spoke to a situation they knew was far different from the history and culture of European Catholicism.[15]

In the United States one notable consequence of the Council's vision was

---

14. *Lumen gentium*, no. 26; see also *Christus dominus* (Decree on the Pastoral Office of Bishops, 1965), nos. 36-38.

15. Among the many accounts of the early years of Latin American church life after Vatican II and the rise of liberation theology one clear treatment is Edward Cleary, *Crisis and Change* (Maryknoll, NY: Orbis Books, 1985).

the gradual willingness of the episcopacy to assess its own national experience and begin an effort to develop a new pastoral agenda. This agenda moved the church beyond the strategy that had guided the pastoral care of the tens of millions of immigrant Catholics who came to the United States in the nineteenth and twentieth centuries. No longer was the American Catholic Church best understood as urban, ethnic, and working class. By the middle of the twentieth century substantial segments of the American Catholic population had become suburban, assimilated, and with members in the managerial and professional classes.[16] In this new situation the bishops, after some fits and starts, eventually hit on a process of formulating pastoral letters that became notable contributions to the political life of this nation.

In both of these cases it was the conciliar support for episcopal leadership in the local church and the initial encouragement given to national and regional bodies of bishops that made possible the important Medellín and Puebla documents of CELAM as well as the pastoral letters on war and peace and economic justice by the USCCB. The ability of a local church to name its own reality and devise a pastoral strategy in response accounts for the development of various initiatives that have had political significance in particular locales, for example, the Philippine church and the Marcos government, the South African church under apartheid, the Nicaraguan church with the Somoza dictatorship first and the Sandinista regime later, the Polish church and the communist regime.

Church as People of God

Both in chapter 4 of *Lumen gentium* and in another Vatican II document, *Apostolicam actuositatem*,[17] there is clear and emphatic support for what *Gaudium et spes* called the layperson's "own distinctive role." Further, the bishops acknowledged that secular life and its activities belong "properly" to the laity. This suggests an appropriate degree of autonomy from clerical oversight and direction. As the bishops made clear, laypersons should follow their own well-formed consciences in seeking to live the faith in everyday life. There should not be the presumption that "pastors are always such experts, that to every

---

16. I do not, of course, wish to deny the importance of the new wave of immigration, composed largely of people of color from continents other than Europe, that is currently transforming the Catholic and general population of the United States. My point is that a major shift in pastoral strategy occurred as the Catholic population in the United States was affected by public policies like the immigration act of 1924 and the G.I. bill after World War II. These measures altered the social characteristics of American Catholicism in several ways by the mid-twentieth century.

17. *Apostolicam actuositatem* (Decree on the Apostolate of Lay People, 1965).

problem which arises, however complicated, they can readily give" to the lay-person an answer. Indeed, to play that role is not the mission of the clergy.[18]

In the Council documents there is a turn away from a model of lay activity known as Catholic Action.[19] Identified especially with Pius XI's papacy (d. 1939), this model presumed that laypeople participated in the ministry of the church in a manner akin to infantry serving in the church's army under the command of clerical officers.

It was the universal call to holiness articulated in the Dogmatic Constitution on the Church that reasserted a different understanding of the Christian life. According to the Council, all persons of "whatever rank or status are called to the fullness of Christian life,"[20] and "one and the same holiness is cultivated by all who are moved by the Spirit of God."[21] Laypersons were encouraged to see their baptismal commitment as a true vocation, one that encouraged taking responsibility for the quality of witness to the world that was given by the community of faith.

The image of the church as the people of God undercut the abuses of clericalism and emphasized the significance of family life, the workplace, secular culture and its organizations as the locale for where laypeople work out their salvation. In accord with the Decree on the Apostolate of the Laity, no person in the church can be understood as passive because each person has a part to play in the work of the church. In a particular way, laypersons are charged with "penetrating and perfecting the temporal sphere of things through the spirit of the gospel."[22] This is done through a committed effort to witness to the truth of gospel values while functioning in a variety of roles, including spouse, parent, neighbor, worker, manager, employer, consumer, and citizen.

Recapturing the vital importance of laypeople's worldly activities and its connection with Christian witness has forced the church to see the world of politics as an important sphere of concern. Politics is not prized because the church can pursue its institutional self-interest but as an important realm for faithful witness and as a way of living the mandate to love the neighbor, especially the distant neighbor who will be aided not by personal contact but through the instrumentality of just institutions.

---

18. *Gaudium et spes*, no. 43.

19. Pius XI defined Catholic Action in a letter dated November 18, 1928, as "the participation of the laity in the apostolate of the hierarchy." Note that the laity had no distinctive role to play in the church's mission. Ministry was the domain of the ordained and/or professed member of a religious order. In fairness to Pius XI it should be noted that he inherited from the papacy of Pius X an "integralist" tendency in the church that sought clerical control over all lay Catholic organizations.

20. *Lumen gentium*, no. 40.

21. Ibid., no. 41.

22. *Apostolicam actuositatem*, no. 2.

Church as Ecumenical

Among the signal moments of the Council was the promulgation of the Decree on Ecumenism, which reads in part, "all who have been justified by faith in Baptism are incorporated into Christ; they therefore have a right to be called Christians, and with good reason are accepted as brothers and sisters by the children of the Catholic Church."[23] This opening to the movement of unity among Christians was widened by the Decree on Non-Christian Religions[24] to the point that subsequent documents of Catholic social teaching have followed the lead taken by John XXIII in *Pacem in terris*[25] and been written for all people of good will. Encyclicals, originally sent as circular letters by the bishop of Rome to other bishops, now routinely address a wider audience when they concern topics of social teaching.

Catholic leaders, on any number of occasions, have professed their willingness and desire to work with others on issues that touch on the common good of a society, be that local or global. Behind that commitment is the Catholic belief in human dignity as the foundation for moral reasoning on matters of politics. In short, there is no claim that there is a "Catholic" solution to arms proliferation or drug trafficking, no body of Catholic teaching that constitutes a "third way" between capitalism and socialism when thinking about the role of the state in a free-market economy. The goal is not to establish a Catholic political party or Catholic state but a humane set of social institutions that serve the human dignity and well-being of all.

In this way the Council disavowed a triumphalistic approach in favor of a dialogical partnership when engaging social questions. Indeed, the bishops go so far as to state that the church "has greatly profited and still profits from the antagonism of those who oppose or persecute her."[26] Even more common has been the assistance the church has received from people of good will who have helped the church learn through "the experience of past ages, the progress of the sciences, and the treasures hidden in the various forms of human culture."[27]

Martin Marty, a Lutheran historian, has written of what he calls the emergence of a "public church" in American society. He means by this an ecumenical alliance of churches that share three commitments. First is the willingness of a church to accept a measure of responsibility for the temporal good of society. This was clearly affirmed in both *Lumen gentium* and *Gaudium et spes*.

---

23. *Unitatis redintegratio* (Decree on Ecumenism, 1965), no. 3.

24. *Nostra aetate* (Declaration on the Relation of the Church to Non-Christian Religions, 1965).

25. *Pacem in terris* (Peace on Earth, 1963).

26. *Gaudium et spes*, no. 44.

27. Ibid.

Second is the church's acknowledgment of the legitimate autonomy of other social institutions to develop and act on their self-understanding and mission. It is not for the church to control or dominate other areas of social life such as law, the arts, or business. This is a consequence of secularization and is clearly approved by *Gaudium et spes* and *Dignitatis humanae.*[28] Finally, there is a commitment by the church to work with all others of good will to promote the common good of a society. The Decree on Ecumenism and Declaration on Non-Christian Religions, along with *Gaudium et spes*, affirm this principle. In sum, the teaching of Vatican II supports the framework of what Marty calls the "public church."[29]

THE COUNCIL ON CHURCH AND POLITICS

All of the above elements in the shift of ecclesial self-understanding provided grounds for the way the Council discussed the relationship of the church with the modern world. The effort to describe that relationship resulted in the Pastoral Constitution on the Church in the Modern World, a document in two parts. The first part provides a synthetic statement of the theological foundations for why the church is engaged with secular questions of politics, economics, culture, and family life. The second half of the document takes up certain questions of "special urgency," among which are the life of the political community. Taken together, the first half (nos. 1-45) and the specific section on politics (nos. 73-76) offer a reflection on how the church understands its rightful place in the world, the competence it possesses in worldly affairs, and the manner in which it comports itself in the world.

Engagement with politics falls under the heading of the social mission of the church. Throughout the modern era there was always an implicit assumption that the church could and even should involve itself with political affairs. *Gaudium et spes* moved the social mission beyond being an implicit assumption to a theological framework that integrates the social mission with the rest of ecclesiology. It does this in a way that both repositions the social mission and preserves the integrity of the church's religious identity and the secular independence of the political realm.

A Religious Mission with Political Implications

The work of the church is directed to humankind. After all, it is humanity that must be renewed by the Christian message; it is the human person who

---

28. *Dignitatis humanae* (Decree on Religious Liberty, 1965).
29. Martin Marty, *The Public Church* (New York: Crossroad, 1981).

is redeemed by Christ. And it is the whole person, "body and soul, heart and conscience, mind and will," that is of concern.[30] There is no effort to ignore the earthly, historical person for the sake of an other-worldly spiritual being.

Rather, the bishops chose a humanistic norm for their teaching since Christ is understood as the embodiment of true humanity: "it is only in the mystery of the Word made flesh that the mystery of the human person truly becomes clear."[31] Thus, the bishops maintained it was precisely because of its faith in Christ that the church could speak to the human situation, including social questions of political life. "The Church believes that the key, the center and the purpose of the whole of human history is to be found in its Lord and Master. . . . And that is why the Council, relying on the inspiration of Christ . . . proposes to speak to all people in order to unfold the mystery that is the human person and cooperate in tackling the main problems facing the world today."[32]

The Pastoral Constitution is clear that there is no proper political mission for the church; rather, its mission is religious.[33] That religious mission is to proclaim the reign of God. God's reign penetrates human existence and connects with human history in a variety of ways: defense of human dignity, protection of human rights, promotion of unity within the human family, and assistance for people to find meaning in their daily activities.[34]

Part of the good news of the gospel message is the affirmation that humans are creatures of dignity. This belief is rooted in the doctrine of creation (the *imago Dei;* the human creature is made in the image and likeness of God) and incarnation (the human is *capax infiniti;* capable of receiving or being home to the infinite). Protecting and promoting human dignity are religiously significant therefore, since the church must serve as a "sign and safeguard" of the transcendent dignity of the person.[35]

Protecting the dignity of the person entails respecting the nature of the person, and humans are social beings necessarily. Consequently, the human person "ought to be the beginning, the subject and the object of every social organization."[36] Since the person is both sacred and social a common life must be established that preserves and promotes human well-being. The cause of human rights is to establish those basic conditions whereby persons can live in communion with others while enjoying a basic measure of freedom, truth, justice, and love. The church's efforts to defend human dignity and human rights, promote human unity, and help people find meaning in life are all part

---

30. *Gaudium et spes*, no. 3.
31. Ibid., no. 22.
32. Ibid.
33. Ibid., no. 40.
34. Ibid., nos. 41-43.
35. Ibid., no. 76.
36. Ibid., no. 25.

of its religious mission to serve God's reign. In doing those things there will be points of contact between the religious mission of the church and the realms of politics, economics, and culture.

The church, it is claimed, does not engage these realms in the quest for power, wealth, or prestige, or on behalf of any ideology. Rather, the desire to be faithful to its religious mission of witnessing to God's reign requires of the church an indirect vocation to transform the realms of social life to serve, rather than threaten, the human person. The duty of the church to engage the political order is a consequence of its religious mission to be a sacrament of God's reign.

The competence of the church in matters political is not based on technical knowledge but due to the insights provided by faith as to the meaning and goal of human life. It is the mission of the church to anchor what is authentically human against all tides of opinion that may threaten human beings. The earthly ministry of Jesus as well as his passion, death, and resurrection reveal the true nature of human existence: the values that affirm our humanity and the end for which our lives are destined.[37] On the basis of that revelation the church claims a limited competence to teach and act on matters political; it is a competence that extends to the moral dimension of political life. Even that competence, however, is a matter of degree as one moves from greater certainty regarding matters of basic principle toward considered judgments about social matters that are based on contingent realities.

Due to its self-understanding the church opts for a style of presence that is dialogical. The church must learn as well as teach, listen as well as speak. *Gaudium et spes* makes clear that the church, "by reason of her role and competence" is not to be identified with any political system or movement.[38] The political realm has a legitimate autonomy from the church. There is no desire to establish a theocracy.

Acknowledging the many contributions made by other Christians, people of faith, and nonbelievers the church admits it has not always been faithful to the message it preaches and that this is a cause for repentance.[39] There is a modesty of style envisioned by the bishops as they comment on how the church should teach and act in the political realm.

In sum, what the bishops did in *Gaudium et spes* was (1) explain why the church cannot be indifferent to politics, (2) explored what competence it has in the area, and (3) set a tone for the manner in which it will engage the political realm.

---

37. Ibid., no. 41.
38. Ibid., no. 76.
39. Ibid., no. 43.

The Council on Church and State

As important as the Pastoral Constitution was for the topic of Catholicism and politics it must be coupled with another conciliar document, *Dignitatis humanae*, the Decree on Religious Liberty. It would have been impossible for the bishops to take up the question of church and world had they not also agreed to deal with a question that had bedeviled Catholicism throughout the modern era and which still had not been satisfactorily addressed prior to Vatican II.

For centuries the Catholic Church struggled to adapt to the rise of nation-states and the claims of monarchs, as well as the emergence of territorial churches that were a consequence of the "Westphalian synthesis."[40] Part of the dilemma, of course, was the acceptance by both popes and monarchs of the paternalistic role of the state in society. When the secular state arose in the European situation, often brought in on the tide of anticlerical and even antireligious forces, the ecclesial reaction was defensive and hostile. This reaction held true even in the case of secular states like the United States that were not hostile but constitutionally limited in their role within pluralistic societies. Coupled with this reaction was a longing for the *ancien régime* that was at least familiar, if not always friendly. Hence, even well into the twentieth century, Catholic leaders failed to grasp the import for church-state relations of the transition from paternalistic monarchies to limited, constitutional republics.

In the older context of paternalistic states, the church employed what was called the thesis/hypothesis method for assessing church-state relations. The thesis was that the Catholic Church, as the institutional expression of the one, true religion, ought to be given a privileged public role in the life of a nation. The hypothesis was that exceptions to the thesis could be made if implementation of the thesis would lead to civil unrest and severe animosity toward the church and its members.

For many Protestant observers, "the traditional Roman Catholic viewpoint [meant] that the church should use the state for its own institutional enhancement and to secure cultural victories over competing religious bodies."[41] It was this traditional approach that was discarded by the arguments found in *Dignitatis humanae*. The document articulated the view that a right of religious liberty ought to be enshrined in any political community and that states lacked the competence to determine true religion from false. As a result, the state's

---

40. Daniel Philpott, "The Challenge of September 11 to Secularism in International Politics," *World Politics* 55 (October 2002): 66-95 at 71. See chap. 7 for more on the Treaty of Westphalia.

41. Wogaman, *Christianity and Politics*, 51.

interest in regulation of religious practice was simply the protection of public order, not the promotion of one religious creed over others.

The importance of the Decree on Religious Liberty is that it created the condition for a new kind of relationship to develop between Catholicism and the constitutional state, one that did not expect the state with its coercive and regulatory powers to secure the public presence of any church. Indeed, as the Pastoral Constitution on the Church in the Modern World stated, "the Church utilizes temporal realities as often as its mission requires it. But it never places its hopes in any privileges accorded to it by civil authority; indeed it will give up the exercise of certain legitimate rights whenever it becomes clear that their use will compromise the sincerity of its witness, or whenever new circumstances call for a revised approach."[42]

The new model of public Catholicism discussed above became possible as a result of changing the dialogue partner for the church. Jose Casanova has observed that the role of a church in public life is largely determined by the "structural location any church accepts between state and society."[43] *Dignitatis humanae* broke traditional linkages developed in history between Catholicism and the state and by so doing allowed a reconceptualization of how Catholicism and society might be related in the present era.

Vatican II was the watershed event when the church shifted its emphasis from a church-state dialogue to an appreciation of a new partner—civil society. *Dignitatis humanae* made the switch in partners possible, no longer expecting an alliance between state and church that bestowed privileges on the church. *Gaudium et spes* made the dialogue with the new partner of civil society far different than it otherwise would have been. This was one of the landmark contributions of Vatican II, providing a theologically coherent account for why the Christian church must engage the political order as well as how it might do so without sacrificing its religious identity or mission.

OTHER THEOLOGICAL THEMES
FOR THE CHURCH'S POLITICAL ACTIVITY

The way that the mission to the world is expressed in the documents of Vatican II was of great importance for Catholics and many other Christians since it helped many believers articulate the faith that motivated their commitment to service and social reform. As powerful as that contribution was, it was not the only way to describe the linkages between Christian belief and a concern

---

42. *Gaudium et spes*, no. 76.

43. Jose Casanova, *Public Religions in the Modern World* (Chicago: University of Chicago Press, 1994), 70.

to engage the political order. Within the Christian tradition there are a number of classic themes that have proven powerful in their ability to encourage and sustain political activity by those who understand themselves as disciples of Jesus. In what follows we shall consider a few of these themes.

Evangelization and Human Development

At the center of the mission of the church is the work of evangelization. The church understands itself as charged with the task of spreading and proclaiming the message of Jesus that God's reign is near at hand and people ought to respond to that reality by changing their lives, that is, by undergoing conversion. From the New Testament era forward, Christians have always believed that those who have heard the good news of the gospel message must also bring that message to others. The narrative of the life of the early church found in the Acts of the Apostles testifies to the importance of evangelization by the Christian community. So the ministry of proclaiming the good news of Jesus can never be neglected in any theological rendering of the church's mission.

Yet it would be an error to completely identify the process of evangelization with the verbal announcement of the gospel message. Recall in the first part of this chapter the suggestion that multiple metaphors are needed to grasp the nature of the church. Certainly, the church must be a proclaimer, but ecclesial self-understanding must adopt the images of sacrament, servant, and community as well as other metaphors that disclose diverse aspects of the rich nature of the church.

In a 1975 apostolic exhortation concerning evangelization, Pope Paul VI observed, "the modern person listens more willingly to witnesses than to teachers, and if he does listen to teachers, it is because they are witnesses."[44] Without question, proclamation of the gospel is an essential ministry, but it is also vital that the message be lived, that evangelization not be done solely through words but be translated from words into actions. Evangelization, therefore, involves a process that is more complex than proclamation alone.

In addition to his comment about witnesses and teachers, Paul VI also mentioned that among the elements to be included in the process of evangelization was "entry into a community of believers."[45] It is not enough for people to be preached or lectured to on beliefs or doctrine; they must be brought into a community of faith. The entrance into community membership is a nec-

---

44. *Evangelii nuntiandi* (On the Evangelization of Peoples, 1975), no. 41; available at http://www.vatican.va/holy_father/paul_vi/apost_exhortations/documents/hf_p-vi_exh_19751208_evangelii-nuntiandi_en.html.

45. Ibid., no. 23.

essary part of the conversion experience. Furthermore, the community must have a distinct pattern of behavior.

In its earliest years Christianity was known as "the Way," because it was seen to be about living a certain way of life, becoming part of a particular community. This was only to be expected since the gospel message can never be a matter of ideas alone; it must affect the way people live. Belief in the gospel must be a transformative experience. Throughout history the community of believers has never lost sight of this fact; after all, nobody denies that Christian discipleship demands a code of personal ethics. So the moral implications of Christian faith have never been disregarded in their entirety, but there have been overly restrictive approaches to Christian morality that have given short shrift to the way that the gospel must inflect social as well as personal life, including the political order.

For effective evangelization, however, it is not enough to have the gospel message. If the community of witnesses is to minister well, then every effort must be made to understand the people who are the object of the church's concern. This requires attention to people in the particularity of their historical situation, to be sensitive to people's questions and concerns in order to demonstrate how faith in Christ speaks to the issues of moment within the lived reality of people. A great obstacle to effective evangelization is the error of proclaiming a message untouched by the human situation. The danger for the church is to proclaim a religious message that implies people can ignore or dismiss worldly cares as unimportant, rather than speaking a word of faith to the needs and hopes of the historical situation in which people live. The risk is that the reign of God to which the church witnesses will be understood as if it is totally in the future, a promise to believers of a better life after death. The more biblical understanding is to view the reign of God as a reality that has both future and present significance. Neither dimension should be overlooked.

As discussed in chapter 3, an understanding of the public ministry of Jesus requires an appreciation for the theme of the reign of God. That was the dominant theme of his preaching, and his ministerial actions embodied the values characteristic of God's reign: mercy, compassion, forgiveness, love of neighbor, justice, and integrity. When Jesus sought to announce his ministry Luke tells us he read from the prophet Isaiah in the synagogue. There he told his audience that the blind will see, prisoners will be freed, and the poor will hear the good news (Luke 4:16-19). Yet his earthly ministry did not eradicate all the illness or suffering of the people of his time.

So, on the one hand, the reign of God is a warning against political utopias that promise more than is possible. Human fulfillment is beyond history and cannot be achieved by even the best political, economic, or social order. On the other hand, the church must insist that the reign of God is not the simple negation of human history but the positive fulfillment of it. The reign of God calls for action to bring about a world where each person can live in dignity with others. Service to others and the promotion of human well-being is a legitimate expectation of those individuals and communities claiming to be disciples of Christ and who follow his way of life.

Jesus' life, passion, and death remind us that the complete and final manifestation of God's reign remains in the future, and his resurrection also underscores the belief that final fulfillment is beyond history. Even so, the resurrection of Jesus anticipates the future to which history is headed. Therefore, if the mission of the church is to be congruent with the ministry of its Lord, then the church must point to the presence of God's reign, both in the way that it enters human history and in the way that it lies beyond human history.

The church, in order for it to be faithful to its Lord, must witness to both the here-and-now dimension of the reign of God as well as the future dimension of that belief. Just as Jesus in his earthly ministry was the agent of God's reign, so the church's mission in history is to be the active agent that witnesses to God's reign, even if the manifestation of that reign is incomplete.

The resurrection of Jesus was the definitive sign of the presence of God's reign when even the power of death is broken by divine love. Jesus' risen life was not understood as an act of resuscitation, the mere continuance of earthly life. Resurrection entailed the transformation of earthly life in a manner that moved beyond the limits of historical existence. Accounts of the risen Jesus in the Gospels testify to the new nature of Jesus' post-Easter existence.[46] Although the resurrection transcended historical reality, the resurrection also involved taking up the historical life of Jesus in a way that the newly risen Lord remained recognizable as the earthly Jesus known to the disciples, as the New Testament also clearly attests.[47]

It is by holding onto both aspects of the risen life of Jesus that we understand the resurrection of Jesus as providing a model for the church's own life. There was, indeed, something new done by God in the resurrection, while at the same time the risen Jesus was in continuity with the Jesus who lived, ministered, and died amidst his disciples. The resurrection did not eradicate the historical Jesus but was the fulfillment of his life that went beyond historical experience.

In an analogous way the gospel message may be seen to have relevance to life here and now, even as it points to a final end that moves beyond temporal

---

46. Various New Testament texts suggest that Jesus could travel great distances in a short period of time, appear and disappear in the midst of his disciples, walk through locked doors, and ascend into the heavens.

47. Encounters with Mary Magdalene at the tomb, Peter on the beach, and Thomas in Jerusalem are all narrated to dispel any doubt about the risen Jesus being the historical person the disciples had known.

existence. Christians must not be carried along on a wave of naive optimism for the reign of God is a trans-temporal reality. (The resurrection of the dead is a future hope.) However, we should not lapse into the other fault of ignoring the here-and-now quality of the reign of God. (The promise of the resurrection has been fulfilled already in Jesus.) Belief in Jesus entails belief in the full message of his life, death, and resurrection.

Throughout his earthly existence Jesus made clear that the reign of God was a reality at work within history, not just a goal to which history tended (Mark 4:26-32; Luke 13:20-21). If the reign of God is here and now as well as in the future, then the reign of God is to be experienced in history even if not fulfilled in history. The reign of God is more than a future promise; it has already happened in Jesus. Like Jesus, the reign of God has become incarnated and part of the human drama. The evangelizing mission of the church must help men and women to enter into the present reality of the reign of God so as to become more truly the people God desires them to be in history, even if their final fulfillment lies beyond history.

To put the matter in the form of a question: will the church's proclamation of God's reign enable or distract people from the task of building a more human world? Benedict XVI provided his answer with the statement "in evangelization it is unacceptable to disregard areas that concern human advancement, justice and liberation from every kind of oppression." Proclamation of the gospel that exhibits a "lack of concern for the temporal problems of humanity 'would be to forget the lesson which comes to us from the Gospel concerning love of our neighbor who is suffering and in need.'" For Benedict, the process of evangelization must pay "special attention to solidarity."[48]

To properly understand the mission of the church it is not sufficient to preach the gospel when people are enveloped in conditions that deny the very dignity that Christianity claims is rightly theirs. So an effective and true evangelization must be closely linked to a social mission that makes the gospel message both credible and attractive to people living in their historical moment. It must work at building communities where humanity is not broken and violated but healed and made whole.

The anticipatory aspect of the future reign serves as a reminder of the fulfillment of our humanity that awaits us. The future dimension of the reign of God will not eradicate the present partial experiences of it but bring the historical incarnation of the reign to its completion. That fulfillment embraces the human person meant to live within a social order that upholds human

---

48. Benedict XVI, "Message for World Mission Sunday" (October 23, 2011), quoting Paul VI, *Evangelii nuntiandi*, no. 34. Available at http://www.vatican.va/holy_father/benedict_xvi/messages/missions/documents/hf_ben-xvi_mes_20110106_world-mission-day-2011_en.html.

dignity and promotes the basic rights and duties of women and men through the creation of appropriate social institutions.

Sin and Conversion

The flip side of the church's primary mission of proclaiming the good news of Christ is the duty to oppose the reality of sin. The opposite of God's reign is the tragedy of human sinfulness. The Christian community must strive to resist sin and facilitate conversion. Most people are familiar with the idea of sin in an *intra*personal sense, that sin lives within each of us; our individual lives are skewed by it. The Christian tradition speaks of original sin to indicate this manifestation of the mystery of sin within the human person.

There is also the familiar notion of sin in an *inter*personal sense. That is, sin is something we do to one another. We speak of committing the sin of theft or lying or cruelty. Actual sin is the term used to name this dimension of human evil, that sin is expressed in our actions. In this sense, sin can be committed many times over the course of our lives, harming others as well as ourselves through misguided deeds.

Both original and actual sin are recognized aspects of the Christian tradition's vocabulary for the experience of evil. No one questions the idea that the mission of the church entails calling people to conversion, to move away from sin and to embrace the message of the gospel. Nor would it surprise anyone that for the church to be true to itself it must help individuals accept God's offer of grace that is transformative, bringing people out of the bondage of sin to the freedom of God's reign.

The *intra-* and *inter*personal aspects, however, do not exhaust the reality of human sinfulness. There is also a *trans*personal dimension of evil whereby we live in sin, not just individually but as a collective body. Sin characterizes the communal life of humankind, and in this manifestation it may be called social sin.

To understand social sin we need to recognize the mutual dynamism between human beings and their cultures. Humans create cultures. Consider our legal system, political institutions, business practices, religious beliefs, the Internet, and social media—all of these have been created by the activities of many people. These and other elements of our culture are more than the work of any one person, and, while they can and do change, it takes more than one person to bring about the reform of any of these cultural realities. A culture is not something we simply imagine; it is a social reality that is larger than any single individual. People experience their culture as more than personal desires and ideals; culture is a collective entity that envelops its members.

Culture may be a collective creation of generations, but it also helps to create each one of us. People are shaped by the culture in which they live; of course, they are not totally or completely determined by their cultural setting. But we are different—we think, feel, believe, and act differently—because we live in the United States of the twenty-first century rather than in seventeenth-century France or ninth-century Japan or second-century central Africa.

Now if the historical process of creating a culture has this mutual dynamism, that a culture is made by human effort and, in turn, the culture shapes the human person, the groundwork is laid to understand the language of social sin. The evil that exists within the human heart, for example, a bias against an ethnic group, will find expression in the culture we create. Political and economic institutions may discriminate against members of this group; educational institutions may give short shrift to the heritage of these people; our entertainment industry may provide stereotypical images of the group; neighborhoods or towns may be inhospitable to members of the ethnic group living or working in the area.

Such cultural practices reinforce and institutionalize the personal biases of individuals in the majority such that the issue is now not simply changing the beliefs of those biased persons but also having to change laws, customs, financial practices, educational systems, and other social realities that exist apart from the individual. A culture that is biased against an ethnic group will transmit that bias to the next generation through formal and informal channels that teach that a particular group is inferior to others, not to be trusted, to be avoided in social interaction or segregated in housing.

Even those not of the generations that created the unjust policies and structures are implicated by their unwillingness to reform the flaws in the culture they inherit. Social sin refers both to the ways in which our personal sins become embodied in unjust social structures and to the ways in which these structures, having taken on an independent life of their own, make it harder to resist the evil they embody. It is a vicious cycle where evil acts beget evil cultural beliefs and institutions, and these cultural realities encourage and promote further evil acts.

Social sin is the term used to convey the experience of being immersed in evil, not always due to conscious choice, but as the inability to overcome the moral blinders that shield members of a society from the evil resident within it. Thus, the first task to perform in overcoming social sin is to provide people with an alternative vision of their situation so that they may recognize the skewed values and beliefs they have adopted. Then it will be necessary to develop strategies to reform the cultural practices and structures that enshrine the sin. These two tasks are entailed in the process of conversion from social sin, moving away from cultural ideologies that distort human life and reforming sinful structures that are the institutional embodiment of the false ideologies.

Once we grasp the insight that sin has a social dimension as does conversion, then it becomes clear that the church must engage in the work of social change. It does so because the call to conversion must embrace all aspects of the human situation that require a movement away from sin and toward God's grace. Because the mission of the church is to witness to the power of God it must assist individuals and communities to effect the transformations that represent an authentic conversion from social sin.

Christian Love of Neighbor

People cannot experience conversion simply in their minds and not give expression to it through speech and action. People need to symbolize their interior life in order for others, and even for themselves, to know it. And so people say words and perform actions that convey what they experience in their inner life.

In the early church, symbolic expressions of inner conversion were important. Falling in love with Christ required some gestures, words, and symbols that made the interior reality visible. One quickly developed practice was prayer, personal and communal, directed to Jesus as Lord. Some prayer rituals, Baptism and Eucharist, were especially prized within the community. But other actions also came to be necessary: caring for other members of the community who were in need, holding fast to the faith despite rejection by nonbelievers or persecution from the state, refusing to be conformed to the ethos of the wider culture.

Fairly quickly a moral code arose as an expression of conversion to Christ; converted people acted *this* way. This was done with the same logic that prevails when people find it appropriate that friends act in a certain way toward one another. And so morally speaking the great expression of love of Christ is love of neighbor. The norm of neighbor-love became the pattern for how Christians should act if in fact they were who they said they were, a people who had fallen in love with Christ. To claim to love Christ apart from love of neighbor was understood to be self-deception: "Those who say, 'I love God,' and hate their brothers and sisters, are liars; for those who do not love a brother or sister whom they have seen, cannot love God whom they have not seen. The commandment we have from him is this: those who love God must love their brothers and sisters also" (1 John 4:20-21).

The New Testament provides ample evidence that the historical Jesus preached love of neighbor. Jesus is portrayed in all four Gospels as teaching his followers that they are to follow the commandment to love (Mark 12:31), even to the point of loving one's enemies (Matt 5:44). When confronted by the Pharisee about which commandment was the greatest, Jesus replied, "'You shall love the Lord your God with all your heart, and with all your soul, and with all your mind.' This is the greatest and first commandment. And a second is like it: 'You shall love your neighbor as yourself'" (Matt 22:37-39). In the famous portrayal of the final judgment Jesus goes so far as to identify himself as the needy neighbor and to state that divine judgment would be based on the care given to the alien, hungry, thirsty, naked, ill, and imprisoned neighbor (Matt 25:31-46).

The Gospel of Luke relates the question put to Jesus about who is to count as one's neighbor. In reply, Jesus tells the parable of the good Samaritan (Luke 10:29-37), where the neighbor is described as whoever is in need. This suggests the neighbor is not always in close proximity, and yet the obligation to love the one in need still stands. Most people have a sense of what loving the near neighbor may entail, but how does one demonstrate love of the neighbor who is geographically distant? That is a challenge if we think of love only in terms of personal kindness and care.

Benedict XVI has suggested another way to think about the matter. He agrees that the duty of charity or love toward others is incumbent on each Christian. But for Benedict, "if we love others with charity, then first of all we are just towards them. Not only is justice not extraneous to charity, not only is it not an alternative or parallel path to charity: justice is inseparable from charity, and intrinsic to it." The obligations of justice do not fulfill all that is asked of a disciple for "charity transcends justice and completes it,"[49] but one cannot claim to love the neighbor while the neighbor is denied justice. Love of neighbor asks for more than justice, but it never demands less than justice for the neighbor.

Benedict then describes "the institutional path—we might also call it the political path—of charity, no less excellent and effective than the kind of charity which encounters the neighbor directly, outside the institutional mediation of the *polis*."[50] By the latter term, the pope refers to the realm of public order and political life. The *polis* is the arena of social institutions, the state, and also nonstate organizations, which allow people to work together to attain collective goals and shared goods.

Working for justice through social institutions is a way whereby we enact the duty of love of neighbor in social contexts when the neighbor cannot be reached through the medium of personal contact. Charity demands justice: recognition and respect for the legitimate rights of individuals and peoples. This is not to water down the moral obligation but to recognize that the distant neighbor presents a different challenge than the near neighbor. Effective and efficient action to assist neighbors in need will often require the use of resources and institutions that are part of the political order—government, legislation, financing, regulation—at local, national, and global levels.

Christians are called to love and serve others; organized action in the policy arena is one significant way to act on that duty. Unable to be cared for through

---

49. Benedict XVI, *Caritas in veritate*, no. 6.
50. Ibid., no. 7.

personal expressions of loving concern, distant neighbors are reached through the instrumentality of social institutions that protect and promote their basic freedoms, goods, and relationships. Hence, Benedict XVI's belief that charity "strives to build the *earthly* city according to law and justice."[51]

In sum, political engagement, working for justice through government and nongovernmental organizations, can be motivated by and give expression to the Christian duty to love the distant neighbor—a duty that is incumbent on individual Christians and the entire gathered community of disciples. It is for that reason that the 1971 Synod of Bishops stated, "Action on behalf of justice and participation in the transformation of the world fully appear to us as a constitutive dimension of the preaching of the Gospel, or the church's mission for the redemption of the human race and its liberation from every oppressive situation."[52]

CONCLUSION

This chapter began with the question of why the church was involved in the political order. Taking a cue from the teaching of Vatican II on the mission of the church, the argument was made that the church necessarily must be concerned with the temporal realm of politics because the church's self-understanding is that protecting and promoting the dignity of the human person is part of its essential nature.

If the church is to proclaim the reign of God, if it is to invite people into a relationship with God, it needs to assist people in developing a way of life where they have some foretaste, some here-and-now experience, of the fruits of God's reign—peace, justice, mercy, love. The church must point out how a relationship with God transforms one's life, or at least calls for that transformation.

A second way of understanding the church's mission in the world flows from understanding the relationship of its religious mission of evangelization to the social mission of working for a just society. Absent that relationship, the church is reduced to promising a reign of God that is only future, with no element of historical presence. And as the Bishops' Synod of 1971 stated, "Unless the Christian message of love and justice shows its effectiveness through action in the cause of justice in the world it will only with great difficulty gain credibility."[53]

In addition, one can see the correlation between fundamental theological

---

51. Ibid., no. 6.
52. *Justitia in mundo*, no. 6.
53. Ibid., no. 35.

themes such as sin, conversion, and neighbor-love and the church's role in the political order. The reign of God is the experience of being in covenant with God and God's people. During his earthly ministry Jesus invited his listeners to have the same relationship with God that he had; his disciples were taught that they should address God as Father and to understand themselves as being children of God. That implies being a brother or sister to one another. The belief that we are brothers and sisters must have repercussions for our conduct toward one another or it is reduced to mere pious sentiment.

Of course, establishing that there are solid theological premises behind the church's involvement in the realm of politics is not to posit there are no limits to the church's political activity. Answering the question of why still leaves open the question of how the church ought to be involved. In the next chapter the role of the church in the domestic politics of the nation will be examined. The final chapter will consider the role of the church in international politics.

QUESTIONS FOR DISCUSSION/REFLECTION

1. What images of the church do you find most attractive and helpful for thinking about the church's role in society?
2. How would you summarize the "sea change" that Vatican II brought about in Catholic thinking on politics?
3. What is meant by "the sectarian temptation"?
4. How would you explain the political implications of the church's religious mission?
5. What is the connection between evangelization and social engagement?
6. What is meant by the expression "social sin"?
7. How would you describe the relationship of love and justice in regard to caring for one's neighbor?

10

The Church and Domestic U.S. Politics

Involvement in political life is not a new reality for the Christian churches. Earlier chapters in this book abundantly demonstrate that throughout its history Christianity has engaged the political order. There is also the record of service evidenced by the multitude of institutions sponsored by churches over the centuries: hospitals, orphanages, schools, asylums, halfway houses, poor houses, medical clinics, and a vast array of providers of social charity. These institutions have all had strategies for how they will relate to the wider social order, including the state. Add to these the various movements for social change allied with and supported by the church in different eras—labor unions, land-reform alliances, economic cooperatives, political parties, abolitionist movements, antiwar organizations—and the historical record is clear. The church in every age has had to consider how it will interact with the political order.

In this chapter a number of topics related to Christianity and the domestic politics of the United States will be considered. While not aiming at comprehensive coverage, the topics treated aim to provide an illustration of a style and method for how the churches should relate to the American political system. The topics to be considered include single-issue politics, voting, the relationship of morality and law, and the tensions facing Christians holding public office. To begin we will address the role that religion plays in American public life.

THE FIRST OF POLITICAL INSTITUTIONS

In 1831 Alexis de Tocqueville, a French politician and social theorist, visited America. Observations on his experience of the young nation were published in the now classic *Democracy in America*. There he noted that "Religion in America takes no direct part in the government of society, but it must be regarded as the first of their political institutions."[1] De Tocqueville's reason for making that claim was the pervasive sense among Americans that religion was necessary for the ongoing success of the ideals and institutions of the

---

1. Alexis de Tocqueville, *Democracy in America*, trans. and ed. Harvey Mansfield and Delba Winthrop (Chicago: University of Chicago Press, 2000).

new republic. Despite the constitutional arrangement that separates church and state this sense of religion's public significance in America has continued throughout the nation's history.

The importance of religion for the citizens and civic life in the colonies of New England is evident. The religion in question was predominantly Protestant Christianity, and this form of public religion continued throughout the life of the newly established nation. It influenced the way that Americans think about their democratic institutions as well as the substantial role given to voluntary agencies and private philanthropy in remedying social ills. During the nineteenth century, Protestant Christianity markedly influenced the idea of manifest destiny, and social movements like abolitionism, temperance drives, and women's suffrage.

The religious liberty clause of the Constitution ensured that even minority religious voices would become part of public discourse, and so nonmainline Protestantism and Catholicism could enter civic life. By the later decades of the 1800s the Catholic Church had become a vigorous participant in public debates about labor unions, social charity, immigration policy, and primary education. As the Progressive movement grew in size, supported by many Protestant leaders in the Social Gospel movement, Catholics began to find common ground for social action through ideas and groups inspired by Leo XIII's *Rerum novarum*.

During the twentieth century the public presence of Catholicism continued to grow. In the middle of the century many African-American religious leaders led in the struggle for civil rights and against racial segregation. Clergy in the black churches had traditionally been core figures in the African-American community, and from the 1950s onward these clergy became recognized figures in the wider society. Christian leaders who were also public figures became a more diverse group in the second half of the twentieth century, with mainline Protestant figures playing a somewhat diminished role as a new generation of church leaders rose to prominence. One of the major developments in this regard was the re-entry of evangelical Protestantism into public life.

Although a substantial presence in the general population, especially in certain regions of the country, evangelical Protestantism had been a muted voice in public affairs for a good deal of the twentieth century. Chastened by the wider society's rejection of their views on human evolution and prohibition, evangelicals had largely withdrawn from national politics, even as their traditional customs and folkways were confronted by the rapid changes brought on after World Wars, the Great Depression, urbanization, and industrialization. In addition, a spirituality that emphasized the moral depravity of American society suggested to many evangelicals that religion's focus ought to be on saving individuals and not reforming society.

A series of Supreme Court decisions in the 1960s and 1970s, particularly those on school prayer and abortion, led to an aroused evangelical community becoming more politically active. This was due to a perceived threat of secularism denigrating the traditional values of the nation. A variety of ministers, congregations, and church-affiliated foundations began to work together in an alliance commonly identified as the "religious right." This surge in political engagement by evangelical Protestants spurred a polarizing reaction from groups that saw the evangelical movement as promoting an unhealthy mixture of Christianity and politics.

Today, there is a wide range of church-related groups representing Christian activity in the political realm. These groups span just about the entire American political spectrum from left to right. Some of these have direct ties to church leadership, while others are less formally linked but nonetheless claim Christian beliefs as the inspiration and guidance for their activities.

In sum, de Tocqueville was correct in his observation that organized religion was not directly engaged in the institutions of American politics. And he astutely realized that separation of church and state did not translate into separation of religion and politics in the United States. First, mainline Protestantism, then Catholicism, and, more recently, evangelical Protestantism have all undertaken the task of shaping and influencing the wider public culture that is the context for politics and government in the nation.

Contributing to a Public Philosophy

Basically, Christian communities have two options whereby they can engage American society: through their ideas and through their institutions. When discussing the importance of ideas in politics it is useful to distinguish between public opinion and public philosophy. The former is important, but public opinion undergoes shifts, sometimes significant ones, in fairly short periods of time. An event—an assassination, a natural disaster, a televised speech, a rise in unemployment—can alter public opinion overnight. Public opinion is fluid and will often change with the news headlines. Public philosophy, on the other hand, refers to enduring values and ideals that characterize both a culture and its inhabitants. Public opinion will focus on the popularity of a president or congressional leader while public philosophy, for example, will uphold preserving the separation of powers in a democracy. Paramount in the political role of religion is the development of public philosophy.

An important dimension of public philosophy is the moral vision of a good society that citizens in a democracy embrace. Unless the political realm is guided by some overarching vision, a public philosophy of what a good society looks like, it will have difficulty acknowledging that politics is more than merely adjudicating among competing private interests. A view of politics informed by the Christian tradition underscores the fact that policy choices should be addressed in terms of moral values as well as other criteria. The Christian tradition reminds us that people ought to engage in politics for the sake of creating a just, well-ordered society and not simply to secure access to the public purse by private interests.

Cultivation of an informed public philosophy about value choices is a vital resource for healthy political community. In a democratic system public philosophy plays a two-sided role: at times providing support for necessary policies while at other times placing limits on the direction of a public policy. The aim in a representative democracy is not to have a simple translation of values into policy. Rather, the goal is that on key moral and political issues an atmosphere can be created, a climate shaped, within which the specifics of public policy are then formulated. De Tocqueville realized this project of contributing to a public philosophy—one that provides both direction for and sets limits on power—is a significant political role for religious communities to enact.

When moving from public philosophy to public policy it is necessary to make two major distinctions: first, between principle and policy; and second, between the audiences of church and secular society. Regarding the first distinction several things should be kept in mind when crossing the bridge from moral principle to formulating and implementing policy. There is no specific policy choice that necessarily flows from one public philosophy. There is an element of prudence or practical wisdom involved in such decisions. For example, a principled commitment to assist the working poor does not necessarily dictate that the right policy is to raise the minimum hourly wage.

When making such prudential judgments individuals and groups need to assess the resources available. Policy determinations require that attention be given to relevant empirical data of history and the contemporary situation. And prior to making a decision there should be an honest dialogue with those operating with different assumptions. Having a political philosophy is not a guarantee of wisdom, even when it is informed by one faith's tradition.

Christianity in any of its particular interpretations is not the only wisdom tradition. Including the Christian tradition in public dialogue does not mean that the Christian religious heritage must dominate all other sources for a public philosophy. Christians believe the basic foundations of morality are divinely revealed, not the specifics of public policy. When one moves to the level of specificity we ought to refrain from claiming divine approbation of our political judgments. It is one thing to describe an opposing view on tax policy or national security strategy as unfair or unwise. It is another thing, and rhetorically provocative, to describe it as sinful and a breach of one's relationship with God. We ought not claim that our prudential judgments based on a variety of contingent information have been divinely commanded.

Concerning the second distinction about the audience, church or society, it is important to understand to whom Christian believers are speaking. There is an approach for talking to Christians gathered as a religious assembly and another appropriate style of discourse in the wider public square. This raises the strategic question: how to relate religion to politics so as not to undermine democratic pluralism?

There is a danger, although much less than is often feared, of Christians imposing their beliefs on others. At the same time, passionate moral intensity is not always wrong in politics, whether its source is religious or some deeply held value. Is it realistic to ask religious people to suppress the deeply held beliefs and hopes that are the source of their political involvement? Perhaps present anxiety over the vulnerable fabric of public debate overlooks the long track record of Christianity's interaction with the American political system.

Some critics of politically engaged churches may think of abortion or gay marriage as the issues that move religious people to passionate language and zealous opposition. But focusing only on the "hot button" issues at one point in time can lead us to lose sight of the way that Christian churches have taken on political issues in another time. There was passionate engagement by religiously inspired citizens in the abolitionist movement, the Progressive Era's agenda, the civil rights movement, as well as a variety of campaigns in opposition to war and war-related concerns. Passionate speech and activity served a useful purpose in those cases. Some who are now skeptical of Christianity's political engagement applaud its political activity in the past. American democracy has seen such activity before and has become better for it. So we should not be too quick to raise alarms over Christian churches developing a political agenda.

Nonetheless, we should distinguish religious motivation and inspiration from religious approval and legitimation. When it is not a matter of motivating mass movements or inspiring activism but offering specific policy proposals, it is best to avoid inflating the rhetoric. If an argument for a policy can be made in the name of justice then it should be done by an interpretation of justice that can be understood by people of good will. Christians should not argue for public policy in the name of Jesus, as if asserting that motive settles the matter. To identify a particular political agenda with Christian faith is dangerous.

When it comes to policy debate, if we use the rich, thick, symbolic language of religion when speaking to fellow believers, how do we translate that into language understandable by others who do not share our religious belief? This is the importance of knowing one's audience. It is also important to be clear about the task or role the church is playing. Is the church speaking in the capacity of a prophet or of an analyst? Prophets see and motivate, whereas analysts research and strategize. Language and action that is appropriate in one realm may not be apt for the other realm.

Above all, the church's major contribution to public philosophy is to be a moral voice, not a partisan one. As an institution the church should give no endorsements, and individuals identified as church leaders must be wary of appearing partisan. A democratic society's deliberations will be enriched if the church can persuasively articulate a set of principles rooted in a moral vision. Cultivating a public philosophy will be easier if the church is widely viewed as committed to foundational moral values and not the advancement of institutional self-interest or the specifics of a partisan policy agenda.

Public Virtue, Public Skills, and Public Spirituality

Beyond shaping public deliberation through an insistent interjection of a moral point of view, the Christian community also makes a political contribution through the moral formation of its members. A free society requires virtuous citizens. There are not enough police officers, FBI agents, or IRS auditors to enforce honesty in the manifold activities that constitute public life. Unless most of the people in a society are honest most of the time there is social chaos. Only an aggressively invasive totalitarian state can enforce a semblance of public order if people do not voluntarily behave appropriately. It is religion as much as any other force that helps to teach and instill the necessary disciplines of self-restraint, compassion, honesty, and cooperation that make a free society possible.

This concern for public virtue is what de Tocqueville was referring to when he saw democracy's need to form citizens with certain "habits of the heart" that express a commitment to the commonweal. Christianity can serve as a resistant to the distortions and excesses that come about in the competition for power within political life.

Christian churches can provide both the skills and opportunities that broaden political participation, especially by nonelites. In the United States, interest groups representing the affluent and well educated—such as the American Medical Association, American Bar Association, Business Roundtable, and American Federation of Teachers—have enormous advantages and influence far beyond their size in proportion to the rest of the population. Church membership is far broader and more diverse than the elite membership of many political pressure groups. Religiously affiliated lobbying groups provide political access to individuals and groups that are otherwise left out of the political process. Church groups frequently champion the cause of the poor and disadvantaged, often urging citizens to consider elements beyond self-interest. Christian churches engaged in political life offer a way of involving more and different people in politics than would be the case otherwise.

It is by membership in a church that individuals can be recruited for volunteer activity within their communities. Although voluntary associations are always looking for ways to enlist greater involvement from people, impersonal efforts such as flyers, signs, and general community announcements are largely ineffective. Personal contact and invitations to join in a group activity from an associate or friend are a far more effective way to recruit new volunteers. Within the location of a Christian assembly an approach can be made to an individual by a known contact whose personal invite to join in a group's activity is more compelling than a general invite or request for assistance from an unknown contact.

Becoming engaged in a church activity also opens doors to broader involvement in social action that moves beyond the Christian community. Public life in general and the political realm in particular can appear mysterious and beyond a person's understanding and influence. Church activity can get and keep members engaged in a public world beyond the immediacy of family without confronting large impersonal bureaucracies that overwhelm and actually discourage a sense of belonging and active participation. Christian churches are among the most significant institutions of civic life, that realm of life not governed by the rules of market activity or the coercion of government power, but by moral suasion. Just as in the past it remains true today that Christian communities foster the awareness that society is more than the institutions of state or market.

Active membership in a church can equip people with the necessary skills for political participation. And this is true not only for church-based groups such as Bread for the World and Pax Christi that have an explicit political agenda, but politically valuable skills are also learned in nonpolitical church groups focused on adult education, Bible study, parish administration, or worship. In these latter settings individuals and groups learn skills such as public speaking, fundraising, organizing meetings, budgeting, determining agendas, and arranging publicity. These are transferable skills that may be first developed in a church context but can then be utilized in a political setting.

Many Americans learn the skills for political activity in their workplace but that setting tends to skew education in the skills to elites and managers, not ordinary workers. It is religious institutions that offer a counterbalance by teaching skills to a segment of the population that might otherwise be resource poor. This is especially important in an age when labor unions are weak and few political groups work with manual laborers, the unemployed, and other groups marginalized in the political system. For these people it is the churches that are often the sole social organization in which they are active participants.

The Christian community thereby functions as a significant source of equal access to civic skills.[2]

Public philosophy, public virtue, and public skills can help individual Christians build bridges between their identity as disciples and their lives as workers, citizens, and consumers. The challenge is to provide a framework for people to link their faith with their public lives. Doing this will require that efforts are made to promote a spirituality for the workplace, forums to discuss the moral dimensions of political life, and the faith dimension of social change.

One of the major contributions that the Protestant reformers made to public life was an expanded sense of vocation that encouraged believers to see the godly nature of one's life in the everyday world. Luther emphasized that believers were to be faithful in the variety of settings in which they served, be it family life, business, or politics. Calvin echoed this idea in his teaching on "social humanism."[3] More recently, Catholicism has recovered the "universal call to holiness"[4] that has encouraged the exploration of spirituality for "secular" roles since all are called to holiness of life, not only the clergy or vowed religious.

Today many Christians, because of personal prayer, spiritual direction, retreats, and other practices, recognize the spiritual foundation at the base of their personal lives; they understand that their existence is rooted in God. People also are able to see the spirituality of interpersonal relationships; that spouses and friends are mediations of God's love, and that individuals grow in grace and holiness through interpersonal love and commitment. It is precisely by loving another that one may enter into a deeper love of God. This is why in the eyes of many Christians marriage is considered a sacrament.

Needed still, however, is more attention to the spiritual dimension of working for societal transformation. Social institutions that enhance human dignity become a way of mediating God's presence: to have sufficient material goods is, as the saying goes, to be blessed. Someone blessed with food, shelter, clothes, and health care can readily experience that earthly life is good. And knowing creation to be good encourages acknowledgment that the creator is good. Transforming society by means of reforming and creating just political institutions can be a means of providing an epiphany of God for those who previously had been violated by that society.

Participating in activity that humanizes the world is also, for those with eyes

---

2. Many of the points in the above paragraphs draw upon the research of Sidney Verba, Kay Lehman Schlozman, and Henry Brady, *Voice and Equality: Civic Voluntarism in American Politics* (Cambridge, MA: Harvard University Press, 1995).

3. Andre Bieler, *Social Humanism of Calvin* (Richmond, VA: John Knox Press, 1964).

4. The phrase is drawn from the heading for chap. 5 of *Lumen gentium* (Dogmatic Constitution on the Church, 1965).

to see, a participation in the restoration that Christ brings to a world marred by sin. Establishing justice is a way of building the new creation begun by Christ. In short, there is a depth dimension, a spirituality, present in political and economic activity just as assuredly as there is in personal relations. Christian churches must keep making that point to people who may not understand how creating a more just, peaceful, and sustainable world is an activity that is in accord with a deepening of one's life with God.

As suggested in the previous chapter, it is a distortion of the Christian tradition to ascribe to the church a political rather than religious mission. That is not to deny that in the pursuit of its religious mission the Christian community will proclaim ideas and engage in actions that have clear political implications. For that reason a commentator on American politics as astute as Alexis de Tocqueville could suggest that organized religion was the first of the nation's political institutions. Such a role is not due to any explicit political mission at the heart of the church, nor is it due to a particular political agenda. Rather Christianity engages the political realm indirectly through a myriad of ways, including influencing the nation's political philosophy, as well as shaping the character, abilities, and spirituality of Christians in the exercise of their role as citizens.

SINGLE-ISSUE POLITICS

Special-interest groups have long been a staple of American politics, and single-issue groups are but a species of the interest-group genus. An interest group is any organized collective of people seeking political influence who share a concern based on a common industry, occupation, or cause. Single-interest groups are those that focus attention on one issue or type of issue.

Throughout the nation's history, a number of single-issue groups have walked across the political stage. Just a few names indicate the diversity and influence of the cast: the Know-Nothings in the 1840s, the Free Soil Movement just prior to the Civil War, the Grange movement in the 1870s, the Free Silver movement in the 1880s, the Prohibition movement in the early part of the twentieth century, along with the suffragettes of the same era. Most of these groups avoided overt partisan politics by stressing a principle or goal. At times, however, the choice between candidates or party platforms was so clear, even at the level of principle, that partisanship was inevitable.

Though single-issue politics has been around for a while, today it appears to have a restored prominence. How proper in a pluralistic democracy is single-issue politics? How wise is it for Christian churches to be, or be perceived as, a single-issue group? Before answering those questions it will be useful to understand why single-issue politics has once again become a significant style of engagement.

Causes of Single-Issue Politics

Two social issues in mid-twentieth-century American politics—the civil rights and anti-Vietnam-War movements—contributed to the growth of today's single-issue groups. The civil rights movement was not a monolithic campaign. Vigorous debates went on in the 1960s over the goals and strategies of those working for racial equality. Although in its later years the civil rights movement encompassed more than a single issue, its original emphasis was focused: the legal recognition and protection of civil rights for African-Americans. Among the things the civil rights campaign taught other groups that mobilized for political ends was the value of public demonstrations and reliance on the media for spreading one's message.

The Vietnam War's opponents were a disparate group, a loose movement with many different strategies. It copied the civil rights strategy of public demonstrations and dramatic media coverage. It also accelerated the breakdown of party loyalty in American politics. As the war dragged on, people voted for candidates on the basis of their position on the war question irrespective of a candidate's party heading on the ballot. The war issue lessened the pull of party affiliation for many people and paved the way toward a cause-oriented politics that transcended party membership.

Besides the influence of these two social movements a second factor in the renewal of single-issue politics was the advance in organizational techniques available to political actors. Phone banks, refined polling methods, professional lobbyists, media consultants, and social networking all contribute to the ability of a group to organize itself and influence others. Most important is the use of computer-based methods to solicit funds or foster rapid communication. The sophistication of a political organization's management increases its impact far beyond the dreams of an earlier generation of grassroots movements.

Most significant as a cause for single-issue politics is the decline in the influence of the two traditional parties. Among the electorate there has been growing disenchantment with both major parties and a rise in the number of independents within the citizenry. Many Republicans were upset by the Watergate scandal in the seventies and the growing uniformity of conservatives that left GOP moderates feeling unappreciated in the 1980s and later. Moderate Democrats were troubled by urban riots and the anti-American tone of the sixties movements, as well as by a strong drift toward social policies that disconcerted people who were not cultural liberals.

Other factors have influenced the parties' decline. The Federal Election Campaign Act weakened the parties' financial clout and enhanced that of political action committees. Changes in the nominating procedures—new convention rules and more state primaries—have lessened the influence of long-time party bosses. Congressional reforms that abolished the old seniority system and created new subcommittees dispersed power so that no longer can a small group of leaders control the destiny of younger legislators. Finally, television and social networking have allowed individual politicians to skirt the party apparatus and appeal directly to the public.

Historically, the major parties served as mediators between interest groups and the general electorate. Without that traditional structure a politician, less tied to the discipline of a party, is more inclined to pick and choose what planks of a party's platform to support. Candidates for office may owe more to certain interest groups than they do the national party organization. Thus, there is less pressure to moderate one's stance on an issue to fit in with the party's policy statement, one that reflects the give and take of consensus building. Getting out in front on an issue is a quick way for a politician to gain media attention. With the lack of party regimentation, politicians do not have to ask permission to speak out on an issue: the party maverick is no longer so exceptional. As one observer puts it, "A politician who thinks he's a lone wolf is finding out it's a pretty crowded prairie." On such political terrain, both individual officeholders and various issue-oriented groups can stake a claim and wield power without subjecting themselves to the strictures of a national party organization.

The breakdown of party discipline can mean the challenge of forging a democratic consensus becomes more difficult. Nonetheless, historical patterns reveal that the intensity of commitment that one issue can evoke diminishes as the group's agenda widens. If the group is to survive as a viable political movement, its agenda almost always does widen. While single-issue politics may initially undercut the consensus-building process, it cannot completely avoid the give-and-take of pluralistic democracy.

The danger inherent in single-issue politics is factionalism—a narrow-minded pursuit of one's interest at the expense of the common good. Acting in one's narrow self-interest is problematic, but a number of groups that may be labeled as "single-issue" maintain that it is precisely concern for the common good that motivates them. Certainly it is evident that an array of groups promote issues to which they are committed for the sake of a social ideal rather than narrow personal benefit.

Furthermore, such movements provide ways for people to participate in political life by making involvement manageable and comprehensible. People may feel overwhelmed by the complexity and sheer number of issues confronting them. A single issue can engage people who might otherwise stand bewildered on the sidelines of a political contest. Single-issue groups can also provide a valuable outlet for venting frustration over government unresponsiveness. Time and time again such groups have stimulated debate on topics that might otherwise have gone overlooked in political discussion. At times, the quality of the debate was not high, but the loud and shrill voices that eventually lose their strength first performed the service of calling attention to an issue.

Single-issue politics can also encourage responsible voting. Voting on behalf of a candidate deeply committed to racial equality in the era of Jim Crow legislation was quite justified if the opposition candidate was a supporter of ongoing discrimination. Such a conclusion would still be true even if the civil rights advocate inspired some reservations in voters about other matters such as defense spending or fiscal policy.

Churches and Single-Issue Voting

Should churches adopt a single-issue approach as they engage the political order? To answer the question in an a priori manner would be unwise. Suppose the Catholic and Lutheran bishops of Germany in the late 1930s had promoted opposition to Nazism as the focal point of their social mission. Or if the Anglican and Catholic bishops of South Africa selected the dismantling of the legal structures of apartheid as the predominant issue of moment in that nation in the 1960s. Choices like these might be quite defensible. Church leaders might decide to promote exclusively some ideal or oppose some evil. But such a decision would be exceptional, for two reasons. One has to do with the nature of the church, while the other has to do with the nature of politics.

As was discussed in the previous chapter, the social mission of the church encompasses the defense of human dignity, the promotion of human rights, the cultivation of human unity, and assisting people in finding meaning in their daily lives. With such a wide perspective it can be dangerously reductionistic to highlight one area of concern. For the church to reflect the whole spectrum of concerns that are entailed in its social mission, a broad array of issues must be given attention from the people of God.

Trying to isolate an issue when it has interconnections in public policy can be difficult. For instance, the abortion dilemma would be greatly eased if we, as a society, could eliminate the reasons why many women resort to abortion. Those reasons appear to be linked to significant social change. In the United States, women still find themselves caught between the work of child rearing and economic solvency. Most mothers who work do so because they are single parents or because they supplement a husband's modest income. Their work is necessary not optional for economic well-being. Yet present economic and political realities penalize the mothers of young children. If we are to create a social climate wherein abortion is not economic common sense, then we must provide better prenatal care, greater maternity benefits, reasonable parental leave that protects job security, and good but affordable child care.

An intelligible strategy for decreasing the abortion rate is to get at the causes of abortion. Thus, a progressive social agenda may arguably be a pro-life program. An effective anti-abortion position should advocate social reforms that strike at the conditions that incline women to choose abortion. Thus, issues such as poverty, labor reform, and social welfare would be included within a pro-life political stance. Issues such as job-protected parental leave and abortion are quite distinct, but they are related. For this reason single-issue politics is strategically problematic. Focusing too intently on an issue distorts a contextual understanding of the topic and obscures the array of policies needed to deal with the matter effectively. That opposition to abortion should be linked with other issues follows the historical pattern of single-issue politics and indicates that anti-abortion politics should be set within the full social mission of the church.

It is important to distinguish between applying single-issue politics to political ends or principles and applying a single-issue approach to the political strategies used to achieve those ends. Single-issue activists sometimes have focused not on a political principle but on a strategy for bringing about their aim. In such an instance the potential for polarization in the body politic and the church greatly increases. Suppose, in an election, both parties endorse policies that are aimed at making abortion less frequent. One party's strategy for lessening the choice of abortion includes creating a federal child-care policy whereas the other party thinks this approach ill advised. For the church to make the child-care strategy a matter of single-issue politics seems overly partisan and narrow-minded in its pursuit of the goal.

Single-issue politics, even when justifiable at the level of principle or goal, is highly questionable at the level of strategy. For the church to focus on the strategic level risks more than the accusation of partisanship. To advocate deciding an election solely on a judgment of strategy is political narrow-mindedness and theological trivialization; narrow-minded because it allows a disputed question to override all other matters; trivializing because it reduces the church's social message to one risky judgment on a matter several steps removed from the core elements of Christian faith.

So there are twin concerns on the topic of single-issue politics for the church. The first is whether it is appropriate to make one goal or principle the sole focus for the church's engagement with the political order. If in exceptional moments the judgment that such a single-issue agenda is legitimate, there remains the second concern that the focus should be on a goal or foundational principle and not on a strategy for attaining the goal or defending the principle.

When we move from generalities to specifics on moral questions, we of course do so with less certainty. That does not mean that church leaders cannot teach specifics, only that they should do so with a becoming modesty in their claim to final wisdom on the topic. Claiming modesty for the church is difficult if the most decisive issue in an election is whether the candidates agree with the viewpoint of church spokespersons. For that reason, single-issue politics should remain at the level of political ends or principles so that the church can assert, without appearing presumptuous, that a crucial and necessary criterion is being employed in assessing candidates. When the specifics of public policy on a topic are held up as the single most important issue in a candidate's record, the risk of divisive partisanship and arrogant intolerance is high.

A number of groups in U.S. society and in the Christian church might argue that their particular issue should be the sole factor in judging a candidate. The very fact that a number of such groups exist, each with wise and compassionate adherents, leads to the conclusion that the church must be wary about stating that a given issue is of decisive import. That is not to deny that such could be the case in another situation if what is at stake is a fundamental societal goal or principle. What will remain troubling for any time, however, is the choice of a specific strategy as a suitable rationale for single-issue politics.

RESPONSIBLE VOTING

Participation in the political life of a nation is an important responsibility incumbent on citizens. Because the realm of politics is closely tied to the establishment of an order of justice in society (sees chapter 8) it is not proper for Christians to be indifferent to political life. As was discussed in chapter 9, the church's mission to witness to the reign of God includes a commitment to defend human dignity, promote human rights, and foster solidarity among people. Because the political order and its institutions profoundly affect a society's experience of these basic goods, Christians cannot be apathetic toward the establishment and ongoing maintenance of the political order with its values, processes, and institutions.

Benedict XVI proposes that active political participation ultimately flows from the duty of disciples to love their neighbor, for "charity must animate the entire lives of the faithful and therefore also their political activity, lived as 'social charity.'"[5] Consequently, as the American Catholic bishops put it, the "obligation to participate in shaping the moral character of society is a requirement of our faith."[6] And the *Compendium of the Social Doctrine of the Church* reflects the Catholic conviction that "participation in community life" is one of the "greatest aspirations of the citizen, called to exercise freely and responsibly" one's "civic role with and for others."[7]

---

5. Benedict XVI, *Deus caritas est* (God Is Love, 2005), no. 29.

6. United States Conference of Catholic Bishops, *Forming Consciences for Faithful Citizenship* (Washington, DC: United States Conference of Catholic Bishops, 2011), no. 9. In another paragraph the bishops state, "In the Catholic Tradition, responsible citizenship is a virtue, and participation in political life is a moral obligation. This obligation is rooted in our baptismal commitment to follow Jesus Christ and to bear Christian witness in all we do" (no. 13).

7. Pontifical Council for Justice and Peace, *Compendium of the Social Doctrine of the Church* (Vatican City: Libreria Editrice Vaticana, 2004), no. 190.

The duty to be active citizens also entails the duty for Christians to be responsible in bringing their moral convictions into the political order. The goal is not to emulate or add to the partisanship, power grabs, and interest-group elements that characterize too much of political life. Rather, the responsibility of the Christian citizen is to enact "a different kind of political engagement: one shaped by the moral convictions of well-formed consciences and focused on the dignity of every human being, the pursuit of the common good, and the protection of the weak and vulnerable."[8] So political participation for Christians is a duty, but the duty entails "a different kind of political engagement," one that melds "our principles and our political choices, our values and our votes" to bring about a more just political order.[9]

One of the reasons why Catholicism has come to be a strong supporter of democracy is because it is a political system that provides important ways for citizens to participate in political affairs. And among those ways is voting. Indeed, in a democracy the political leadership of the state gains its legitimacy and support from the consent of the governed. Absent an active and informed citizenry's vote it is difficult for elected officials to avoid being indebted to small but committed segments of the population who gain disproportionate power due to the lethargy of the majority.

After weak democratic regimes in Italy and Germany failed to prevent the rise of fascism and Nazism, Pius XII sought to invigorate the reestablished democracies of postwar Europe. Through a variety of talks and writings the pope stressed that the moral obligations of citizenship in a democracy included informed voting. In 1947 Pius went so far as to label a failure to vote as a serious sin of omission.[10] Standing behind this sense of voting as a moral obligation is the Christian realization that we have a duty to care for one another and to promote the common good of the society in which we live. In a democratic nation it is possible for citizens to use their voice and vote in ways that foster solidarity among citizens, justice in public life, and accountability from political leaders.

Of course, the duty to vote cannot be understood as absolute. It may be that some voters conclude they cannot vote for any candidate in good conscience due to principled disagreement with the candidates' policies. It is also possible that a Christian citizen might reject the conventional electoral process as a protest against perceived corruption or irrelevance for the sake of another form of political activity. Finally, a voter may decide not to vote because he or

---

8. United States Conference of Catholic Bishops, *Forming Consciences for Faithful Citizenship*, no. 14.

9. Ibid.

10. Pius XII, "Allocution to International Union of Catholic Women's Leagues," *Acta Apostolicae Sedis* 39 (1947).

she has not taken the time to study the issues, learn about the candidates, or understand the referenda put before the electorate. In such a case an irresponsible vote would only compound the failure of not being an informed citizen.

Therefore, we can conclude that the church's support for the idea that voting is an obligation in a democracy presumes yet another duty. The obligation to vote entails the further obligation to be a certain kind of voter, one who is informed and responsible. The informed voter takes the time and makes the effort to learn about the candidates and the crucial issues before the electorate, as well as what are the values and principles reflected by those politicians and topics. Responsible voters then exercise the crucial virtue of prudence in determining their choices.

Conscience and the Exercise of Prudence

The "different kind of political engagement" that a Christian citizen aspires to practice involves being "guided more by our moral convictions than by our attachment to a political party or interest group."[11] For the Christian citizen, it is a properly formed moral conscience that guides voting and not simple self-interest or party loyalty. Bringing moral values into the political equation is crucial for the Christian citizen.

Having an informed conscience in regard to voting entails different kinds of knowledge. In one sense conscience refers to the inner depths of a person where individuals seek the good in the presence of God. Conscience is the internal forum where people strive to know what it is that God wishes for each of them. It is, therefore, an encounter with one's very self whereby we can live with integrity or betray the truth about ourselves.[12]

The pursuit of moral goodness is not something Christians are left to do on their own. They are assisted through study of the Bible as well as the Christian tradition, including the teaching of the church. The quest for moral truth is not an isolated journey, as Christians also find insight and encouragement in

---

11. United States Conference of Catholic Bishops, *Forming Consciences for Faithful Citizenship*, no. 14.

12. "In the depths of his conscience, man detects a law which he does not impose upon himself, but which holds him to obedience. Always summoning him to love good and avoid evil, the voice of conscience when necessary speaks to his heart: do this, shun that. For man has in his heart a law written by God; to obey it is the very dignity of man; according to it he will be judged. Conscience is the most secret core and sanctuary of a man. There he is alone with God, Whose voice echoes in his depths. In a wonderful manner conscience reveals that law which is fulfilled by love of God and neighbor" (*Gaudium et spes* [Pastoral Constitution on the Church in the Modern World, 1965], no. 16).

the formation of their conscience through participation in the communal life of the church, particularly its prayer, liturgy, and acts of service. The type of knowledge that results from such thoughtful reflection by an individual is a sound grasp of the values and principles that should guide political choices.

But a political vote cannot be a simple translation of one's moral values. Voting always requires a measure of the classical virtue of prudence. The popular understanding of prudence today may equate it with caution, even timidity. That is not the way the term is understood in the traditional literature on moral virtues. For the ancient Greeks, *phronēsis* was understood to be practical wisdom, the ability to make sagacious judgments in matters requiring discernment about what is most apt given the circumstantial realities. The common Latin word used for the Greek term was *prudentia*. In the Catechism of the Catholic Church, prudence is explained as the ability "to discern our true good in every circumstance and to choose the right means of achieving it."[13]

Prudence is crucial to responsible voting because it permits sound judgment not just about proper values and principles but also concerning how to choose the best policy and candidate to enact one's moral convictions. As the American Catholic bishops state, "prudence shapes and informs our ability to deliberate over available alternatives, to determine what is most fitting to a specific context, and to act."[14]

Prudence is related to another sense of conscience, the ability to make wise judgments about right action, to determine how best to translate one's moral commitments into support for particular political leaders and policy choices. Prudence is the virtue par excellence for this second sense of conscience; it is the ethical skill of knowing the most fitting or apt choice in a particular circumstance with its opportunities and limits.

Guidance from the Tradition

A particularly thorny aspect of voting arises in the all-too-common situation when a candidate for public office holds positions some of which are in accord with a voter's moral beliefs and some of which violate those beliefs. In short, many voters find that no candidate perfectly mirrors their preferred moral commitments. Voting for a candidate in such a circumstance will mean that voters find themselves seemingly complicit in the doing of evil.

This experience is an example of a wider problem that has long troubled thoughtful people. In a finite world populated by finite creatures with limited

---

13. *Catechism of the Catholic Church*, no. 1806.

14. United States Conference of Catholic Bishops, *Forming Consciences for Faithful Citizenship*, no. 20.

resources, it is not possible to do all the good one might wish to do. Multiple commitments, for instance, put a strain on good people who must struggle to live up to all the expectations that come with being a spouse, parent, sibling, friend, employer or employee, citizen, neighbor, church member, and other social roles. There simply is not enough time in the day, energy in our bodies, money in our wallets, or talent in our skill sets to do all the good we would like if it were possible. What to do when faced with our desire to promote the good and the limits imposed by our creatureliness? Christians have wrestled with this problem as it has appeared in various guises in human experience.

One particularly vexing variation on the challenge of finitude is that some-times we cannot attain a good without at the same time bringing about a measure of evil. In the case of voting one finds the dilemma when confronted by the fact that the candidate one supports due to his or her views on racial justice or economic fairness is also the candidate who disappoints due to his or her views on torture or drone warfare in matters involving national security. Can a voter support a candidate for the hoped-for good they will achieve while at the same time countenancing the likelihood that the same candidate will bring about evil by other policies? To address such a thorny yet common political choice the Christian moral tradition has developed the principle of cooperation to help in working through the problem.

This principle of moral guidance developed as a result of the experience of priests hearing the confessions of people who might or might not have been complicit in the sin of another person. The principle of cooperation is really a set of distinctions that help a person think through moral judgments when one is seemingly implicated in the wrongdoing of others.

Every four years the Catholic bishops of the United States issue a docu-ment on political responsibility in an election year. In the version prepared for the 2008 election and reissued for the 2012 election, the bishops state that certain wrongful acts are always evil and never acceptable. The church leaders were clear that Catholics could never vote for any candidate who supported any of the intrinsic evils.[15] Note that no voter should ever cast a ballot for a candidate *because* the candidate supported an intrinsic evil. The bishops did not rule out voting for such a candidate *despite* his or her support for what is intrinsically evil.

Consider the case of a candidate who supports the use of interrogation techniques in combating terror that constitute torture according to the norms of international law, the International Red Cross, and the broad consensus of human rights organizations. It is not permissible to vote for such a candidate

---

15. The list of intrinsic evils includes abortion, euthanasia, human cloning, destruction of human embryos in research, torture, genocide, the deliberate targeting of civilians in war or terrorist attacks, and racism (ibid., nos. 22-23).

because of that position in support of torture, an intrinsic evil according to church teaching. To do so would be to endorse the commission of the evil. In the language of moral theology a voter would be guilty of formal cooperation in bringing about the use of torture. Formal cooperation means the cooperator has an agreement of the will with the evil deed of the actor.

However, suppose voters abhor torture and wish their preferred candidate did also. Yet on a wide array of other issues of significance, their candidate upholds policies that are deemed enlightened, fair, wise, and necessary for addressing the common good. If voters support the candidate because of these latter policies and *despite* the candidate's policy on torture, they are not in formal cooperation with the evil of torture during interrogation. At most, such voters would be engaged in material cooperation.

According to church teaching, a Christian voter ought never be culpable of formal cooperation. A voter may engage in material cooperation if there are truly proportionate reasons for doing so.[16] In other words, the issue of formal cooperation always results in a negative judgment. It is wrong to so act. The question of material cooperation must be assessed on a case-by-case basis to determine if there are proportionate reasons that can be determined.

Among other factors to be considered, one key item is the length and complexity of the causal chain between one's vote and the evil that is foreseen but not desired. The closer or more proximate the connection between one's vote and the moral evil, then the higher the threshold that must be passed for claiming proportionate reasons exist. Conversely, the more remote the connection then the lower the barrier to be overcome in claiming there are proportionate reasons.

In many cases the chain of causality between a citizen's vote and an intrinsic evil is quite extended. For example, an individual's vote for a candidate who supports a pro-choice position still leaves a long list of decisions and judgments by a variety of other actors for the death of even a single fetus to occur. It would appear that a reluctant vote in support of a pro-choice candidate for the sake of that candidate's other policy stances that are morally defensible

---

16. A Catholic cannot vote for a candidate who takes a position in favor of an intrinsic evil, such as abortion or racism, if the voter's intent is to support that position. In such cases a Catholic would be guilty of formal cooperation in grave evil. (ibid., no. 34)

There may be times when a Catholic who rejects a candidate's unacceptable position may decide to vote for that candidate for other morally grave reasons. Voting in this way would be permissible only for truly grave moral reasons, not to advance narrow interests or partisan preferences or to ignore a fundamental moral evil. (ibid., no. 35)

is a case of remote material cooperation in which proportionate reasons may well exist.[17]

Considerations in Voting

In deciding who will get one's vote, it is helpful to consider a number of factors that will help to guide judgment.[18]

When voting for a candidate it is important that more than a statement of policy positions is the basis for one's vote. A voter must make a judgment about the intelligence, temperament, and character of a candidate. Political life is unpredictable, and the issues that will become dominant are hard to know in advance. For a president, of course, there are the unknowns of war or terrorist attack, as well as humanitarian crises and other events on the international stage.

Even for domestic leaders at the state or municipal level there are the unforeseen events of natural disasters, civil unrest, crime waves, and other concerns that can become the issues of moment during a public official's time in office. So it is important to assess candidates not only on their stated policies but also on the sort of leader they might be in times of crisis or sudden emergency. Despite one's differences with a candidate on one or another issue a voter might conclude that the person is on the basis of personal qualities a more reliable leader.

Issues do matter, of course, but statements of candidates or party platforms are not the same as actual priorities. Candidates take positions on a wide array of issues, and are asked questions about an even broader range of topics. Having espoused a position on an issue is not the same thing as a solid commitment from a candidate actually to do anything about the matter.

It is important to gauge whether the concern of a voter is really a high priority for a candidate. Casting a politically painless vote for a bill that has little chance of passage is quite different from a legislator who actively works on creating legislation, garners support for it, and sees it through to passage. Some officeholders may be in passive agreement with a voter's concern, but there is no passion or lively interest in making the concern a centerpiece of the elected official's agenda. Looking at a candidate's track record of activity can

---

17. Though the morality of abortion is a hotly debated and highly polarizing issue, I assume the rightness of the teaching of the Catholic Church that the deliberate killing of fetal life is an intrinsic evil in order to illustrate how the Christian tradition reasons about complicity in evil.

18. For the ideas discussed in this subsection I acknowledge my indebtedness to Clark E. Cochran and David C. Cochran, *The Catholic Vote: A Guide for the Perplexed* (Maryknoll, NY: Orbis Books, 2008), 92-113.

reveal more than reading a list of issue statements. Identifying which issues have engaged a candidate's energies and resources over the years is information that a responsible and informed voter would want to know.

Another aspect of the question of priorities has to do with the nature of public office. Not all public officials have the same mandate, responsibilities, or power. Presidents must deal with war, and candidates for that office should be closely questioned on the topic and their past actions examined regarding their views and grasp of the topic. The same cannot be said about those running for the office of town council. Voters might be curious about what a council candidate thinks about U.S. policy on nuclear proliferation, but it is not an issue central to the candidate's political role. A presidential candidate may endorse the death penalty in order to appear tough on crime, but the governor of a state has far more involvement with death penalty questions than does a president. A member of the House of Representatives might praise or criticize appointments to the Supreme Court, but a congressional representative has no role in the selection or approval of a Supreme Court justice. Voters need to consider the candidate's fitness for the office that is being sought, rather than be swayed by a candidate's opinions on questions peripheral to his or her responsibilities as a holder of that office.

Yet another factor for a voter to reflect on has to do with political timing. The French writer Victor Hugo is credited with the saying that "nothing is stronger than an idea whose time has come." However true that may be, it says little about an idea whose time has not come. A much-prized political skill is knowing when an issue has the potential to become a matter of broad public concern and when an issue has little likelihood to inspire support or arouse opposition. Lacking such skill, a public official can spend a great deal of time and effort tilting at windmills or leading crusades for which no one enlists. Sometimes it is evident that a given issue is simply not going to be on the minds of the public or the agenda of their leaders, despite a voter's interest in the topic.

It is possible a citizen may decide the issue is of such import that bringing the matter to the voting booth is a way to act prophetically, to draw attention to a concern, and to interject the topic into public debate. History attests that many matters of social justice required champions whose voice was lonely at the beginning of their efforts. So a judgment that the timing is wrong need not be decisive in every instance. Nonetheless, a public official may reasonably determine that now is not the time to introduce a given piece of legislation, or push for a policy change, or promote a cause. Voters need to consider the political context, for in a given time and place the promotion of, or opposition to, a particular policy may be highly unlikely to succeed. The candidate who makes such an unlikely policy the focus of a campaign may not be the right choice.

LAW AND MORALITY

Sometimes one of the challenges voiced to a particular law is not whether it is wise but whether the law should even exist. The very foundation of the law is questioned when the charge is made that the law simply amounts to one group "imposing its morality on us," the rest of society. Of course, sometimes that complaint is a consequence of one's preferred moral position being set in opposition to another in public debate. Opposition to enshrining a moral position in a law becomes simply a matter of whose ox is being gored.

Taking the charge seriously, however, forces citizens to reflect on the relationship of law and morality. Is the enforcement of morality a role of law? Is law open to moral criticism? Different answers to these questions stand behind the serious debates about "imposing morality."

The issue of law and morality is not the same as the issue of law and religion. Strong support for the First Amendment's nonestablishment clause can be easily reconciled with the affirmation of a close link between law and morality. That is because morality is not necessarily founded on religion, and arguments about public morality do not rise or fall on whether one is a Christian or any kind of theist.

Of course, laws regarding abortion, gay marriage, or euthanasia are often what comes to mind when people fret over "imposing morality" through the civil law. But using tax funding to subsidize a national gallery of art or public television or national parks are also public policies that are enacted with the intent of promoting some vision of the "good" society; such policies necessarily involve value judgments. So, too, are moral values involved when decisions are made to tax people in order to pay for the social welfare of others. Are such activities proper for a government? Can government encourage one set of values and regulate other values? Why and how?

It is a commonplace to describe America as a free society, a nation built on freedom. Our Constitution's preamble states the nation was founded to secure the blessings of liberty. And civil liberty is understood as the freedom of the individual to pursue a life plan without interference. The politically conservative interpretation of this outlook treasures personal freedom and discourages anything but limited government. Society is viewed as a collection of autonomous individuals connected only by free contract in a state that protects individual rights. On matters of value judgment that extend beyond individual liberty government ought to be neutral.

The politically progressive alternative reading of the nation's commitment to personal liberty affirms neutrality as the starting point but ends up supporting active government in order to remedy those obstacles that hinder people from pursuing their life plan, that is, inequalities and injuries that result not from preference or choice but luck, special need, and previous injustice. Government, in this interpretation, can intervene in society for the sake of promoting equal opportunity. The aim is to see to it that an individual really is free to pursue a personal life plan with its private goals.

So both the conservative and the progressive version of liberalism support personal liberty but differ as to the measures necessary to secure it. Yet, the proponents of both schools of thought believe they are striving for neutrality with regard to the personal values of citizens. The liberal theorist opts for value neutrality in most cases because this allows every individual to live by one's preferred values. However, one can question the foundational premise of either form of liberalism, that people form societies only in order to protect individual liberty and that liberty is diminished when society encourages certain values over others.

An alternative viewpoint, one that resonates with a good deal of the Christian tradition, posits that people seek social interaction for the sake of communal living and the broad range of benefits that result from shared life. Members of any community cannot escape the question how shall we live? And inevitably, that question is, in part, a moral inquiry. Rather than profess neutrality about values other than liberty, would it not be better to admit that political actors appeal to a broad range of cultural, social, and moral values in their policy making? Thus, scientific research, the cultural arts, preservation of nature's beauty, infrastructure for travel, and practices of education are all fit subjects for public policy because they are public goods. Viewed in this way, the question for policy making is not whether we should make value judgments but how do we make the best ones.

In the effort to make the correct choices there is no substitute for public debate. Two rules ought to be observed in the process. There must be safeguards against the majority tyrannizing a minority. There also needs to be caution and modesty in pressing for one's views, for even the wisest can be wrong and subject to correction. Still, we should admit that we do make moral judgments in our political decisions. That is unavoidable. When such judgments are made, therefore, the opposition ought not be based on "imposing morality" but on the grounds that the moral judgment is unwise or simply wrong. That is where the debate should be joined.

Different Approaches

There are a variety of ways to relate the legal and moral orders. From a Christian perspective, a particularly unappealing approach is one that overemphasizes pragmatism. A purely pragmatic view sees law's function as largely to reflect how the society operates and to codify what is widely accepted as socially normative. The aim is for people to see their existing convictions expressed by the law. The aim is not to embody what is good or bad, right or wrong, but to give legal status to the prevailing viewpoint.

Certainly a pragmatic approach is deferential to the pluralistic nature of American society, limiting law to those areas where moral consensus exists. The difficulty with this approach, however, is that the prophetic and pedagogical roles of law are slighted. For example, at different points in the nation's history, labor law or civil rights law did not simply reflect an existing social consensus but expressed moral ideals. Enforcement of the laws helped to build a societal consensus behind those ideals.

A quite different approach to the question of law's relationship to morality is associated with Thomas Aquinas. In the *Summa theologiae*, Aquinas framed the question of morality and legality in terms of a relationship between natural law and civil law. Natural law in its broadest sense refers to the view that morality derives from the very nature of human beings, not from societal custom. Morality is not a code of behavior imposed on us from without, but is intrinsic to the person. Moral truth is an expression of what leads to human well-being and flourishing.

The natural law is the human person's ability to know the moral good and to discern right from wrong using our reason. The basic moral truth of the natural law is "do good and avoid evil." In addition, there are more practical truths—render to each their due; always seek the truth; preserve life; love God and neighbor—that can be known by reasoned reflection on human activity and experience.

For Aquinas, law was defined as an ordinance of reason directed to the common good promulgated by one who has authority.[19] Civil law is something in accord with our judgment as reasoning beings. Any act judged to be morally good is an act in accord with right reason, the process of human reflection that identifies our tendencies and purposes as God has created us. The civil law, based on authentic moral values, serves to specify right action in the concrete circumstances of a given community. Civil law points out and directs the person toward the good, but civil law does not create the good. It is not the authority of the legislator that makes a law good but the fact that the civil law is an adequate expression of the natural moral law. The obligation to obey the law stems from the statute's capacity to guide us toward recognition of and performance of the moral good, that is, the flourishing of human well-being.

Despite this close association of morality with civil law in the Thomistic framework, since the two realms though related are not identical, it is possible that the laws of a particular society may differ from proper morality. At times, it is not reasonable to apply the moral law to all cases of civil law. Civil law is ordered to those matters that touch on the common good.[20] And, for Aquinas,

---

19. Thomas Aquinas, *Summa theologiae*, IaIIae, q. 90, art. 4.
20. Ibid., q. 96, art. 1.

that meant recognizing that other considerations must be factored into the determination of whether a civil law was necessary and wise.[21]

An illustration of Aquinas's reasoning in this regard is his comments on the parable of the wheat and the weeds (Matt 13:29ff.), where the servant is instructed by the master not to pull out the weeds if it will also damage the wheat. Better to wait until the final harvest, the servant is told, and then separate the wheat and weeds.[22] In short, overzealousness in eradicating evil can bring about unnecessary harm.

At another point in the *Summa*, Aquinas asks, "whether the religion of infidels should be socially permitted?" In his answer Thomas proposes that human government should imitate the divine will.

> Human government is derived from the divine and should imitate it. God, although he is omnipotent and perfectly good, permits some evils to occur in the universe, evils which he could prohibit. He does this because if these evils were removed, greater evils would ensue. Thus also in human government, those who rule properly should tolerate certain evils lest other good things are lost and even worse evils come about.[23]

Rulers of a society may tolerate certain evils to prevent even greater evil or to allow the occurrence of a compensating good. In his answer Aquinas mentions the idea of Augustine that it is better to permit public prostitution than seek its eradication since the sinful activity undoubtedly will continue even if illegal but in worse circumstances.[24]

One more passage of relevance concerns the question whether law ought to suppress all vice. Aquinas answers that law is directed to all people in society, not just the virtuous. What can be expected of the just person is not what can be demanded of the morally weak and immature. Thus, law must consider the capacities of the people to be governed and not be overly idealistic. Aquinas recommends that law ban those serious vices that make social life difficult or intolerable, for example, murder or theft; but when the vice is not directly harmful to society the law should not be involved.[25]

In Catholic moral theology this unwillingness to turn all moral norms into civil law is guided by the principle of toleration. It is an ethical guide rooted in the wisdom that, although law in the Thomistic tradition has an intrinsic con-

---

21. Ibid., q. 97.

22. Aquinas addresses the lesson of the parable in several places. Among those are *Summa*, IIaIIae, q. 64, art. 2, and IIaIIae, q. 108, art. 1.

23. Ibid., q. 10, art. 11.

24. The reference is to Augustine's *De libero arbitrio*, bk. I, V. I.

25. Aquinas, *Summa*, IaIIae, q. 96, art. 2.

nection to morality, there remains a distinction between the two realms. An attempt to translate all moral truth into civil law would be a mistake.

A Modern Thomistic Approach

A further and important refinement of the Thomistic approach can be found in an insightful gloss on the teaching of Vatican II in the Decree on Religious Liberty. In a commentary on the document, the American Jesuit John Courtney Murray, a key figure in the formulation of the conciliar decree, presented his revised, yet still Thomistic, approach to civil law. To understand Murray's treatment of law and morality it is helpful to grasp his reasons for defending a right to religious liberty.

When making the case for a right of religious liberty, Murray argued that a limited constitutional government had a narrower role in society than promotion of the entire common good. The common good includes all aspects of human life that promote the flourishing of human persons. These aspects are both material and spiritual. For instance, the common good of society will be more readily attained when all its members come to a full recognition of truth. Thus, there is a moral obligation incumbent on each person to seek the truth; but it is not the role of the state to enforce the obligation. Unlike the all-encompassing role for the institution that is seen in an earlier, more paternalistic theory of the state, the role of a limited, constitutional state is different.

For Murray the power of government ought to be restricted to preserving the basic conditions for communal life. Those conditions Murray grouped under the heading of "public order," which essentially entails an order of justice, an order of peace, and an order of morality. Public justice safeguards the rights of all and establishes a forum for resolving disputes. Public peace is not the quietude of repression but the state of domestic tranquility that comes about through the effects of justice and the establishment of institutions for orderly administrative processes.

Finally, public morality does not embrace all dimensions of the moral life nor a broad consensus on all details of a moral code. Rather, public morality entails social consensus on minimal standards of behavior that are to be enforced on all in order for social life to be maintained. Thus, there must be state enforcement of norms regulating acts of violence, theft, or bribery, for example, since these cause clear harms to others in society and to the existence of social order. But moral norms governing behavior with less clear public harm do not require state enforcement. Only when the fundamental conditions for public order are threatened should government act. Otherwise freedom is to prevail.

Murray's approach reflects the presumption in favor of liberty, which is the hallmark of societies with limited constitutional states. Citizens of such

societies expect to enjoy the freedom to pursue their life plans without interference from the state unless persuasive reasons are presented that override
the presumption of personal liberty. Law's function is to preserve that part
of the common good that constitutes public order, no more and no less. The
presumption is in favor of freedom unless the threat to public order is judged
to override it.

Besides the criteria of as much freedom as possible and the protection of
the public order, there are additional factors to be considered when deciding
whether a law is wise. Law must be enforceable. A law may be judged unenforceable for a variety of reasons. Enforcing a law against certain acts of sexual
immorality is impractical because of the intrusiveness that would be necessary.
Or enforcing a law that bans all deceitful speech would require such an extensive network of surveillance that the costs become prohibitive. Or, again, some
laws are unenforceable because the vast majority of citizens do not support the
law's aims. Perhaps the most famous example in American history of citizen
unwillingness to support a law was the attempt to ban the sale of alcoholic
beverages during the Prohibition Era (1920-1933). After the Eighteenth
Amendment banned the production, sale, and consumption of alcohol, and
this turned out to be unenforceable, the Twenty-first Amendment reversed
the policy. So unenforceability may be a matter of impracticality, expense, or
lack of popular support.

Law must be equitable. A law that is designed to single out one group of
people for different treatment is prima facie wrong. One of the advancements
of modern politics is that there is greater equity under the law for groups
that have traditionally been treated with harmful discrimination, for example, racial minorities, women, the poor, and religious minorities. Concern for
equity does not rule out laws that can be shown to discriminate for good reason, for example, laws that enact age requirements for the exercise of certain
freedoms. But the burden of proof rests on those who oppose impartial treatment and enact a law that discriminates against a group on the basis of some
shared characteristic.

Yet another consideration for the wisdom of a law is whether it will lead
to disrespect for the institution of law and the erosion of popular support for
administration of the law. This was one of the difficulties with the Eighteenth
Amendment, which banned the manufacture, transport, and sale of alcoholic
beverages. In time, despite the good intentions of the legislation, the experiment in prohibition led many to disparage law and its officers.

The concern about public attitudes toward the institution of law is related
to the political aspects of legislating in a pluralistic society. Despite the good a
law might achieve there is a need to determine whether the political context is
receptive to the proposed legislation. There may need to be significant prepa-

ration done to influence and win over public opinion, or it may be that economic or social conditions need to alter before a law will be widely supported.

All these factors—the presumption for liberty, the need for public order, enforceability, equity, respect for law, the social context—constitute what may be called the "prism of feasibility" that a proposed law must pass through if it is to become a wise law. Differing assessments of the appropriateness of a law, when viewed through the prism of feasibility, have led to tensions between church leaders and members of the church who hold public office.

CATHOLIC POLITICIANS AND CATHOLIC BISHOPS

In the fourth century, Ambrose, the bishop of Milan, wrote a tract, *De officiis*, that addressed the duties of Christians holding public office. This was a new and pressing question with the conversion of the emperor Constantine to Christianity.[26] Earlier Christian writers defended Christians as good citizens who paid their taxes and prayed for the emperor, but Ambrose considered the new theme of a public official exercising civil authority as a form of Christian service to the society. Ambrose wanted to develop a moral guide for how public persons ought to act in light of their dual identities as Christians and citizens of the Roman empire. By Ambrose's time there had arisen the expectation that the state, an institution natural to the human condition, could be held to a higher purpose: the attainment of a measure of justice in social life rather than serve as a coercive instrument for a ruling elite. And so, as full members of the empire and as significant officers in its governance, Christians would assume new social roles and take on new duties.

The early attempt by Ambrose to address the issues involved in Christians wielding civil power was important, but his work was just an opening foray into an area that has remained contested terrain throughout history. In American democracy it is no surprise there will be tensions between political figures and church leaders. The nature of partisan politics and the need for politicians to unify a number of ideologically diverse segments of the voting population make it highly unlikely that any political party will mirror the teaching of any one religious body. Consequently, as the Catholic Church teaches, "to claim that one party or political coalition responds completely to the demands of faith or of Christian life would give rise to dangerous errors."[27]

Despite that counsel, it is no secret that a variety of religious communities and leaders have publicly supported, even endorsed, political office seekers. And although such direct partisan political action threatens the tax-exempt

---

26. See chap. 4.
27. Pontifical Council, *Compendium of Social Doctrine*, no. 573.

status of religious institutions if that status were interpreted strictly, the practice is generally overlooked. For example, there is a long and widely held tradition among many of the historically African-American churches to endorse candidates in local and national elections. America's Catholic bishops have been known to indicate their political preferences even without direct endorsements through veiled remarks, photo opportunities with a candidate, and invitations to public officials to speak or receive awards at church-related events.

In recent years there has been a notable increase in the tension between Catholic bishops and Catholic political candidates or public officials.[28] For the vast majority of cases the tension has been over the issue of abortion, and the perception of many bishops that certain political leaders hold policy positions permitting ready access to abortion. In a few instances the tension has risen to a level such that bishops have announced a political figure ought not receive the Eucharist when attending Catholic liturgy. For these reasons the disputes between Catholic politicians and the bishops provide an illustration of some of the challenges involved in relating morality and public policy.

Catholics in the United States

A variety of issues, including some already discussed in this chapter, are entailed in thinking through the question of how Catholic public officials ought to exercise their roles. One factor that must be kept in mind is the location of Catholicism in the public life of the nation. American Catholics are not in the same situation as the earliest Christians, a small, disenfranchised group of outsiders within the Roman Empire. American Catholics, like Christians of the post-Constantinian era, are a powerful and sizable part of their society. With that size and power comes the accompanying obligation to act responsibly for the good of the society.

In fulfilling that obligation, however, Catholics are not in the same situation as medieval Christians because the church does not exert direct influence over the arts, law, economics, politics, education, or the professions. The United States presents a setting that is pluralistic and secular, a society within which a range of institutions have various roles to play in the maintenance of a healthy democracy. The autonomy of those other institutions, like the church's autonomy, must be respected. No church can rightly impose its political agenda on the others.

Nor can the present situation for American Catholics be compared to the

---

28. For evidence of such an increase, see Thomas Massaro, "Catholic Bishops and Politicians: Concerns about Recent Developments," *Josephinum Journal of Theology* 12, no. 2 (Summer/Fall 2005): 268-87.

experience of the immigrant church of the nineteenth and early twentieth centuries, for many church members are well established educationally, financially, and professionally. Catholics are the largest single denomination in American society and represent a broad cross-section of the population, including the poorest and the richest. Such pluralism within the Catholic demographic sector will naturally lead to political outlooks that compete and conflict.

An additional consideration is that, unlike the experience of believers in other eras, American Catholics do not live in a context dominated by absolute monarchs, paternalistic aristocracies, or totalitarian regimes. This nation's governance remains relatively open despite the forces working against participatory democracy. Candidates at all levels must still come before an electorate seeking their votes, and citizens are still free to cast their votes for whom they please, or not cast them at all. Government leaders must still convince and persuade the wider citizenry about the wisdom and fairness of a policy or it will not long prevail. Church leaders must take into consideration both the opportunities and the pressures that the changed status of American Catholicism provides, not only for church officials but also for Catholic public authorities.

A consequence of these transitions in American Catholicism is that bishops and other church leaders have less power for political mobilization and less direct influence over political activity. In the United States, the church sponsors lobbyists, legislative networks, and letter-writing campaigns; it continues to encourage justice and peace groups and social ministry organizations to advance the social mission, but these activities only sporadically demonstrate substantial political muscle. It is uncommon for church leaders to deliver a "Catholic vote" in an election or legislative debate.

Occasionally there have been instances when ecclesial leaders have fallen back on strategies that sought to exercise fairly direct political influence. In recent decades this approach has not met with great success.[29] Efforts to adopt constitutional amendments, pass referenda, or defeat politicians at election time have not been notably popular regardless of the issue involved: limiting sales of contraceptives, restricting the grounds for civil divorce, opposing war, banning abortion, or prohibiting capital punishment. The "political clout" of the Catholic episcopacy is weaker than many of those anxious about a Catholic lobby realize.

---

29. There is also evidence that direct activity by Catholic bishops in some of these areas is leading to disaffection toward the church, particularly among young adults. See Robert Putnam and David Campbell, *American Grace: How Religion Divides and Unites Us* (New York: Simon & Schuster, 2010), and Pew Forum on Religion and Public Life, *U.S. Religious Landscape Survey* (2008). The survey is available at http://religions.pewforum.org/reports#.

One Source of the Tension

It is not just church leadership that must think about its political activity. Catholic public officials must be able to articulate a more nuanced position than John Kennedy's disavowal of his faith's influence on his public role, however reassuring that may have been to non-Catholic Americans in 1960. It has taken time for Catholic public officials to work out an adequate understanding of Vatican II's call to overcome the "false opposition between professional and social activities on the one part, and religious life on the other."[30]

One example of a failed approach can be seen in the tactic employed by many Catholic politicians on the abortion question. The public official declares that he or she is personally opposed to abortion but does not wish to see abortion prohibited or even regulated in any way that would restrict a women's access to abortion services. The inconsistency between declaring one's personal opposition to abortion and the lack of political activity to limit, if not eliminate, abortion then raises questions in the minds of the bishops about the sincerity of the declaration of opposition to abortion.

One motivation for such a position is a reluctance to "impose morality" on another person. The difficulty with this approach is that it involves confusion between moral principle and personal preference. To say one is morally opposed to something because it is wrong means that it is wrong not only for the person espousing the view but wrong for the listener as well. It is a matter of moral principle. To say that I personally do not practice something but that you may very well practice it is not a statement of principle but merely of preference.

Take slavery as an example to illustrate the distinction. If I am morally opposed to slavery, then I am making the claim that no one should own another human being as legal property. However, if I say that I personally oppose slavery, but you are free to practice it if you wish, then I am only expressing my individual preference. So to morally oppose slavery is to claim that no one should practice slavery. To state that I do not own slaves is merely to indicate a preference, not establish a moral claim.

Confusion between principle and preference accounts for some of the misunderstanding between church leaders and Catholic public officials. Bishops are calling for such public officials to state clear moral opposition to abortion, not just announce that they personally disapprove of it. And in consequence of such moral opposition there would be an expectation that public officials would engage in some actions that would limit the practice of abortion, or at least prepare the political ground for eventual limitations on resort to abortion.

Now what those actions might be still allows for debate, given a public

---

30. *Gaudium et spes*, no. 43.

official's need to consider the "prism of feasibility" for proposed policy. Furthermore, it is both possible and reasonable that the action adopted to limit abortion could take the form of remedying the social and economic conditions that encourage women to consider abortion. Because of the need for the "prism of feasibility" there is no automatic requirement that moral opposition to abortion requires automatic support for specifically targeted legislation to ban abortion.

A Second Source of the Tension

Just as public officials need to overcome the "false opposition" between religious and professional roles, the bishops must acknowledge the legitimate distinctions between their religious roles as teachers and the professional competencies of public officials. That distinction is not always respected.

One helpful illustration of the necessary modesty that bishops should exemplify is evident in their teaching on war and peace. In a well-received pastoral letter written near the culmination of the nuclear arms race between the United States and the Soviet Union the American bishops made explicit reference to the different levels of moral teaching in the letter.

> We do not intend that our treatment of each of these issues [the arms race, contemporary warfare, weapons systems, negotiating strategies] carry the same moral authority as our statement of universal moral principles and formal Church teaching. Indeed, we stress here at the beginning that not every statement in this letter has the same moral authority. At times we reassert universally binding moral principles (e.g. non-combatant immunity and proportionality). At other times we reaffirm statements of recent popes and the teaching of Vatican II. Again, at other times we apply moral principles to specific cases.
>
> When making applications of these principles, we realize—and we wish readers to recognize—that prudential judgments are involved based on specific circumstances which can change or which can be interpreted differently by people of good will (e.g. the treatment of "no first use").[31]

The bishops are straightforward in acknowledging that their teaching operates on multiple levels and that treating it in a uniform manner misses the necessary subtlety and nuance that good teaching requires. Not everything

---

31. National Conference of Catholic Bishops, *The Challenge of Peace: God's Promise and Our Response* (Washington, DC: United States Catholic Conference, 1983), nos. 9-10.

that the church teaches has the same authority behind it, nor the same power to bind the consciences of believers.

In a dispute that arose years later concerning legislation that would overhaul health care delivery in the nation, the bishops appeared to ignore the distinctions between levels of moral teaching. The dispute concerned how medical services that the bishops opposed, artificial contraceptives and abortion, would be paid for according to the new health care law passed during the Obama administration. A variety of theologians and other commentators pointed out that the argument was not at the level of moral principle. Instead, it was a disagreement about what a proposed regulation meant and how it would function. By most accounts the issue entailed a prudential judgment that could not be accorded the same authority as a moral principle or be held with the same certainty as to its correctness.[32] Though there was clearly a moral component to the dispute, it necessarily involved legal, financial, and political reasoning for which the bishops could make no claim to special competence. Yet the bishops elevated the argument beyond prudential judgment by making the claim that it was a "fundamental disagreement" that constituted a "wound to Catholic unity."[33]

Of course the bishops have a right to speak publicly on moral issues and have a duty to do so by way of informing the consciences of their fellow Catholics and others of good will. But informing conscience is not the same as binding conscience. On this specific aspect of health care reform legislation the bishops could not claim to be teaching at the level of "universal moral principle" or "formal church teaching." Instead the proper understanding was that they were making a "prudential judgment" that ought to be heard and weighed by their fellow Catholics but about which people could respectfully disagree. Failure to acknowledge that fact put the bishops in the position of looking as if they sided with one side in a partisan political debate between Democrats and Republicans.

---

32. See Richard Gaillardetz, "The Limits of Authority," *Commonweal* 137, no. 14 (August 13, 2010): 9-11; Daniel Finn, "Uncertainty Principle," *Commonweal* 138, no. 6 (March 25, 2011): 18-20; Nicholas Cafardi, "Cul-de-Sac Catholicism," *America* (April 12, 2010), available at http://www.americamagazine.org/content/article.cfm?article_id=12239.

33. Cardinal Daniel DiNardo, Bishop William Murphy, Bishop John Wester, "Setting the Record Straight," United States Conference of Catholic Bishops (May 21, 2010), available at http://www.usccb.org/news/archived.cfm?releaseNumber=10-104.

Moving Forward

Both church leaders and public officials have work to do in developing a proper balance between the bishops' competency to teach on social morality and a government official's exercise of political wisdom in formulating public policy. Establishing a simple divide between the two is one unfortunate option that some public figures have chosen in the effort to establish the autonomy of politics from religion. Inflating the authority of moral teaching in complex matters of public policy is the other unfortunate option that bishops and other church leaders should avoid. Only by disavowal of these options will the relationship of religion and politics serve to benefit both realms.

Most American Catholics distinguish between the role of religion in public life, which they strongly support, and the role of religion in politics, about which they are dubious. In a sense, one can conclude that American Catholics have accepted the view that the church ought to engage society but should keep its distance from partisan debate. They want a faith that addresses issues of public life, but they do not want a Catholic political party or even a Catholic political movement. Nor are they much interested in what used to be called Catholic Action, an approach to social engagement that presumed clerical leadership and direction.

A Vatican statement, "Doctrinal Note on Some Questions regarding the Participation of Catholics in Political Life," issued by the Congregation for the Doctrine of the Faith is an illustration of a church trying to sort through the civic duties of believers in societies that are religiously pluralistic and politically secular.[34] The document acknowledges the rightful freedom of conscience and the legitimate autonomy of Catholics and others acting in the political arena. But the document laments a cultural relativism that permits one to conclude that any appeal to conscience settles matters. Following one's conscience can beg the questions of whether conscience is properly informed or if a good faith effort to be informed has even been attempted. The freedom of conscience must be respected, but freedom includes an obligation regarding conscience formation.

The document is clear in its support for the legitimate autonomy of Catholics in public life. The Congregation does not see Catholic officials as representatives of the church or as lobbyists for things Catholic. According to the document, the troubling concern for present-day political life is a spirit of relativism that undercuts a sound relationship between morality and politics.

---

34. Congregation for the Doctrine of the Faith, "Doctrinal Note on Some Questions Regarding the Participation of Catholics in Political Life" (November 24, 2002), available at http://www.doctrinafidei.va/documents/rc_con_cfaith_doc_20021124_politica_en.html.

Note that the document explicitly states the issue is one of morality and politics not religion and politics.

Due to the persistent pluralism on moral matters that we find in modern cultures, the task of relating morality and public policy will likely remain a controversial area. As the earlier section on law and morality explained, the Catholic Church cannot accept a simple separation of these two realms. The church, however, has yet to develop a fully convincing strategy for relating them when there is profound moral disagreement within a society. Catholic politicians are caught in this situation, and it has given rise to tensions between civic officials and church leaders.

CONCLUSION

American politics has always been influenced by the religious beliefs and practices of the American people. Although they have been at times, Christian churches need not be overt and direct in their political influence in order to make an impact on the nation's politics. Being a consistent voice for moral values in political discussion is an important contribution that the churches can make. Challenging the conventional wisdom of a culture is a necessary task lest the status quo is too quickly assumed to be the natural state of things. Confusing the existing political situation with the necessities of the human condition can allow political leaders and citizens to abandon the cause of ongoing social reform. In such circumstances it is valuable for a nation to be confronted by the prophetic voice that the Christian tradition can provide on behalf of ever-greater realizations of justice, peace, and the common good.

There are risks that the churches can themselves become obstacles rather than motivators to social reform. Organized religion and its spokespersons can be used to legitimate and bless social arrangements that are less than authentically human. At times, secular social movements will play the prophetic role that churches can presume is theirs alone to play. Therefore, the Christian community must engage in dialogue and be open to the insights of those outside the churches. Still, there have been abundant examples throughout the nation's history of Christian churches offering useful and important assistance to efforts for fashioning a better society.

In playing a role in the political life of the nation there are difficult shoals for the Christian churches to negotiate. Single-issue politics provides a recurring temptation; and, while not always irresponsible, it is generally unwise to resort to this approach. This is so both for theological and political reasons. Voting also is a political act that poses questions for conscientious Christian citizens. The challenge is to be an informed and responsible voter. The relationship of law and morality is a complex one, and Christian believers need to keep the two realms related without ignoring the necessary distinction between them.

Churches must continually negotiate a path between political irrelevance and political partisanship. Church leaders may and should contribute to debates over specific policies, but they should do so in a manner that acknowledges the differences in upholding moral principle and making prudential judgments about policies or public officials implementing those principles. Of course, it can happen that one major party or candidate endorses a basic moral principle or value but the other side does not, and that may leave the church looking partisan if it continues to defend the fundamental moral norm or good. The charge of partisanship in such an atmosphere should not deter church leaders if they are convinced that the basic goal is central to the well-being of society.

When the differences between candidates, parties, or policies is not at the level of moral principle or values but prudential judgments about how best to attain the good, church leaders ought not overreach. When bishops and other church officials do overreach in their claims of authority or become clearly partisan in their words and deeds they diminish the teaching authority of the church and sow seeds of disunity both within the church and the wider society.

As the history of Christianity and politics attests, there are different models for how the church will engage the political realm. In the present age it appears five things should not be lost sight of in whatever model is adopted.

- First, the church must shape politics not through coercion but persuasion.
- Second, the church should have a proper respect for the legitimate autonomy of other public institutions and actors.
- Third, the church's involvement in public life must have as its goal promotion of the common good, not primarily institutional self-interest or sectarian beliefs.
- Fourth, in matters of law and policy the church's aim should be to protect public order.
- Finally, the church ought to be able to explain its political choices using language and ideas that are accessible to all citizens of good will, relying on reason rather than revelation.

QUESTIONS FOR DISCUSSION/REFLECTION

1. Do you agree or disagree with de Tocqueville's observation that religion is the first of America's political institutions? Why?
2. What is the difference between public opinion and public philosophy? What role does the Christian community play in shaping either or both?
3. What do you understand by single-issue politics? Do you think it is ever justifiable to use such a strategy as an individual? As the church?
4. Why is prudence such an important element in responsible voting? What

is the difference between formal and material cooperation? Is it ever permissible to cooperate in evil?

5. What factors do you consider in determining whether to vote for a candidate?

6. Can you describe the relationship between law and morality? How did Thomas Aquinas understand the relationship? How did John Courtney Murray refine the Thomistic approach?

7. What is the "prism of feasibility" and how does it factor into the making of laws?

8. What do you consider the main source of tension between Catholic Church leaders and Catholic public officials? How might the tension be alleviated?

11

Christianity and International Politics

Clearly, religion and religious institutions have been involved in violent conflict, but they have also been a resource for conflict resolution and peacebuilding. Religious actors have played important roles in developing and promoting international norms, especially human rights, in a variety of areas, including migration, humanitarian intervention, debt relief, fair trade, warfare, human trafficking, and democracy. This chapter will consider the role that Catholic Christianity plays in four important areas of concern for American foreign policy: globalization, human rights, war, and peace.

At Vatican II, the assembled bishops discussed the role of the church in the modern world. Emphasizing that the church's mission was religious in nature, to proclaim the reign of God, the bishops also stated that out of the religious mission comes "a light and an energy which can serve to structure and consolidate the human community according to the divine law."[1] The bishops observed there were many worthy social movements at work in the world, "especially an evolution toward unity." Promoting unity "belongs to the innermost nature of the church," they declared; thus, they encouraged a "process of wholesome socialization and of association in civil and economic realms."[2]

Catholicism stresses the unity of the human family, because of the belief in the common origin and destiny of all humankind. The idea of humanity as a single global family is part of the "light and energy" that impels the church to oppose those realities that foster division rather than harmony among the world's population.

War is one of the clearest manifestations of disunity, and the building of peace is an important counterforce. The denial and suppression of basic human rights is another example of the threats to the unity of humankind, when some are treated as less than equal in dignity to others. And globalization has the potential to be that "wholesome process" of "socialization and of association" that the bishops commended. Of course, globalization can also be a process that fosters division through economic inequality, cultural imperialism, and

---

1. Vatican II, *Gaudium et spes* (Pastoral Constitution on the Church in the Modern World, 1965), no. 42.
2. Ibid.

political powerlessness. All four topics to be addressed in this chapter shed light on the promise and the challenge of building a world with "a very vivid awareness of its unity and how one person depends on another in needful solidarity."[3]

The social scientist Jose Casanova noted that medieval Christendom was characterized by the transnationality of institutions and activities: the papacy, religious orders, ecumenical councils, universities, and activities such as pilgrimages and feast days. All of these were then diminished to a substantial degree after the sixteenth century. The closing decades of the nineteenth century saw a reconstruction of Catholicism on a new global basis. Today, "Catholicism has been reconstituted as a new transnational and de-territorialized global religious regime."[4] As such, the Catholic Church's engagement with the process of globalization is a useful entry point into the realm of Christianity and international affairs.

GLOBALIZATION

Providing a fully satisfactory definition of globalization is difficult. One reason is that there are multiple globalizations. The word means different things to political scientists, economists, sociologists, anthropologists, social activists, consumers, diplomats, and artists. The features that unite the multiple elements into the reality we call globalization is the experience of increasing interconnectedness on a planet where distance is shrinking and time is accelerating, compared to the experience of life just a few decades ago. We might see globalization as the integration of free markets, nation-states, and information technologies so that people can reach around the world faster, deeper, and cheaper than ever before.

Globalization can be thought of as a braid with distinct yet intertwined strands. Politics, economics, communications, religion, education, environment, fine arts, technology—all are strands forming the braid. Yet each strand has its own distinctive appearance and represents a particular form of globalization.

The variety within globalization can be overlooked due to the tendency of most commentators to focus primarily on the economic strand, whose dominant form is global capitalism. This very well may account for why individuals from developing countries often have a dimmer view of globalization than commentators from industrial and postindustrial nations.

---

3. Ibid., no. 4.

4. Jose Casanova, "Public Religions Revisited," in *Religion: Beyond the Concept*, ed. Hent de Vries (New York: Fordham University Press, 2008), 101-19 at 111.

Without denying the possible benefits of economic globalization, the abiding concern of people in developing nations is that globalization in the form of neoliberal capitalism increased inequality in some places, both economically and politically. For such critics, economic globalization is a twenty-first-century form of economic imperialism that hearkens back to the laissez-faire economics of the nineteenth century.[5]

In 2001 Pope John Paul II stated, "Globalization, a priori, is neither good nor bad. It will be what people make of it."[6] That statement suggests three important points. First, globalization is not a fully formed and developed reality; it is in the process of coming to be. Second, globalization is not predetermined by impersonal forces beyond human influence; it is a reality to be shaped by human choice and action. Finally, globalization, precisely as a set of processes that are humanly guided, is subject to ethical assessment, and such evaluation does not presume globalization is inherently right or wrong.

Echoing the papal view, Daniel Groody sees globalization as an ambivalent reality, both ethically and theologically. On the one hand, it "has created possibilities for local, regional, and global integration"; on the other hand, "it has also left waves of disintegration in its wake."[7] Theologically, "globalization offers a new hope for human solidarity and interconnectedness, which coexist against the reemergence of age-old human constants like greed, selfishness, and sinfulness."[8] In sum, globalization's evolution will be a matter of value preferences by persons exercising moral agency.

While there will be different judgments about a reality as multifaceted as globalization, traditions of moral wisdom like that of Catholic social teaching can provide normative elements useful for shaping processes of globalization that will be appropriate to human flourishing. To borrow Groody's terminology, Catholic social teaching offers "ethical coordinates" that will "help steer the ship of globalization" in the proper direction.[9] The provision of evaluative criteria for globalization demonstrates the conviction that it is not a mysterious force beyond human influence. Both in the ends sought and the methods employed, globalization is subject to moral guidance and evaluation.

Developing a strategy for sustainable globalization both at home and

---

5. Clement Campos, "Doing Christian Ethics in India's World of Cultural Complexity and Social Inequality," in *Catholic Theological Ethics in the World Church*, ed. James F. Keenan (New York: Continuum, 2007), 82-90 at 83.

6. John Paul II, "Address to the Pontifical Academy of Sciences" (April 27, 2001), no. 2. Available at http://www.vatican.va/holy_father/john_paul_ii/speeches/2001/documents/hf_jp-ii_spe_20010427_pc-social-sciences-en.html.

7. Daniel Groody, *Globalization, Spirituality, and Justice* (Maryknoll, NY: Orbis Books, 2007), 12.

8. Ibid., 21.

9. Ibid., 118.

abroad is a challenge. Like any unregulated and free activity of human beings, globalization spreads its benefits and burdens unevenly. The challenge for the Christian community is to draw on the wisdom of a tradition such as Catholic social teaching to formulate a strategy for globalization, one that is respectful of the dignity of persons and supportive of human rights. In what follows I provide a list of evaluative criteria, seven "ethical coordinates" for globalization that are drawn from Catholic social teaching.

Authentic Humanism

An axiom of Catholic social teaching is that an incorrect view of the human person will inevitably lead to an inadequate theory of politics or economics. Paul VI in *Populorum progressio* gave special prominence to the risk of human development being skewed by economic reductionism, a message that is even more important today, given the emphasis on economic globalization. "Development cannot be limited to mere economic growth. In order to be authentic, it must be complete: integral, that is, it has to promote the good of every person and of the whole person."[10]

As Sri Lankan moral theologian Vimal Tirimanna summarizes the matter, the old question was "how much is a nation producing?" whereas the correct question is "how are its people faring?"[11] Of course economic growth is important, and economic well-being is crucial for development; yet economic development is not the whole story and must be integrated into a wider understanding of development that enhances the ability of people to flourish on multiple levels. Paul VI described the characteristics of a multifaceted approach to authentic development based on a complete and integral humanism: satisfaction of material needs, reformed social structures that eliminate oppression, opportunities for learning and appreciating a culture, cooperating for the common good, working for peace, acknowledgment of moral values and their transcendent source, the gift of faith, and the deepening of unity in love.[12]

It is evident throughout Catholic social teaching that any ethical coordinates proposed for assessing globalization must be based on the foundation that human persons are the primary moral reality. The principle of human dignity is the touchstone for Catholic social thought. Human dignity is rooted not in one's identity as a citizen or producer but in the conviction that humans are made in the image and likeness of their divine creator. The theology of the

---

10. Paul VI, *Progressio populorum* (On the Development of Peoples, 1967), no. 14.

11. Vimal Tirimanna, "Globalization Needs to Count Human Persons," in *Catholic Theological Ethics in the World Church*, 245-52 at 247.

12. *Progressio populorum*, no. 21.

creation narrative of Genesis provides the foundation for the commitment to the dignity of each person.

There is an ethical egalitarianism present in Catholic social teaching, for each person has an equal claim to moral respect. That claim generates other ethical coordinates, as will be suggested below, but the process of normative guidance begins with claims about the nature of the person: human beings are creatures of God-given dignity and each person has equal standing to the claim of respect. Faced with (1) an economic globalization that can reduce individuals to their value in the free market, (2) a political globalization that can marginalize persons from effective access to power, and (3) a cultural globalization that can ride roughshod over the communal patterns by which people make meaning and give expression to their values and beliefs, it is crucial that Christianity continues to espouse an integral humanism. Insisting that the moral measure of globalization is the authentic development of each person in all these areas is a major ethical coordinate that Catholic social teaching can help to establish.

The second fundamental claim Catholic social teaching makes about the human person is that we are social. Community is not an option chosen by those inclined to it; it is an affirmation of the basic unity of humankind. The creation narrative of Genesis teaches the lesson that humans were made for one another. A theological doctrine such as the Trinity suggests communion is at the heart of the divine mystery. This is expressed in the ethical claim of the unity of the human family under the loving gaze of the one God who is creator of all. These beliefs have shaped Catholic social teaching to such an extent that a consistent theme is "human dignity can be realized and protected only in community."[13] Building bonds between and among individuals and groups is a necessary condition for human beings to flourish precisely because we are social beings.

Solidarity

An aspect of communal life is the natural inclination of a group to define itself by its distinctiveness from those not in the group. That inclination gives rise to the temptation of viewing the outsider not only as different but as inferior to insiders. Being linked to others can produce annoyance at those who are strange and exotic or the linkage may provide an opportunity for the manipulation of others. The evils of racism, sexism, nationalism, religious

---

13. U.S. Conference of Catholic Bishops, *Economic Justice for All* (Washington, DC: United States Catholic Conference, 1985), no. 14. Available at: http://www.usccb .org/sdwp/international/EconomicJusticeforAll.pdf.

discrimination, xenophobia, and other patterns of marginalization in human history testify to the dark side of communal experience.

Because globalization creates new ties of interdependence and reinforces older ties, there is a danger that the empirical reality of interdependence will not be accompanied by the moral reality of solidarity. The other with whom one is brought into contact may be treated as less than equal. Globalization can heighten tensions and the likelihood of conflict if groups encounter one another with an attitude of mistrust or misunderstanding. Solidarity is Catholic social teaching's description of the appropriate response to interdependence. By solidarity is meant "not a feeling of vague compassion or shallow distress at the misfortunes of so many people," but rather solidarity "is a firm and persevering determination to commit oneself to the common good . . . because we are all really responsible for all."[14]

John Paul II discussed interdependence as "*system determining* relationships in the contemporary world" and solidarity as the "correlative response as a moral and social attitude, as a 'virtue.'"[15] He went on to state that solidarity "helps us to see the 'other'—whether a *person, people, or nation*—not just as some kind of instrument . . . but as our 'neighbor,' a 'helper' (Gen. 2:18-20), to be made a sharer on a par with ourselves, in the banquet of life to which all are equally invited by God."[16] Indifference to the plight of others or a mere utilitarian approach that attends to others only as possible trade partners or marketplace consumers falls far short of solidarity.

In the 2000 World Day of Peace message the pope further reflected on solidarity and globalization: "We cannot of course foresee the future. But we can set forth one certain principle: *there will be peace only to the extent that humanity as a whole rediscovers its fundamental calling to be one family*," a unity that precedes and overrides any distinction between people. The pope continued, "Recognition of this fundamental principle can give the world as it is today—marked by the process of globalization—a soul, a meaning and a direction. Globalization, for all its risks, also offers exceptional and promising opportunities, precisely with a view to enabling humanity to become a single family, built on the values of justice, equity and solidarity."[17]

Solidarity seeks to ensure that the emerging global order is one that will truly serve the well-being of all people and not just a segment of the world's population at the expense of the rest of humankind. In particular, solidarity

---

14. John Paul II, *Sollicitudo rei socialis* (On Social Concern, 1987), no. 38.

15. Ibid.

16. Ibid., no. 39. All italics in quotes are found in the original unless otherwise noted.

17. John Paul II, "Peace on Earth to Those Whom God Loves," World Day of Peace Message (January 1, 2000), no. 5.

calls for attention to the poor, those who are at most risk of being marginalized in processes of globalization. It is an important element of the ethical framework Catholic social teaching employs to assess globalization.

Common Good

Globalization is creating new forms of interaction and interdependence, and this ought to prod us to examine the nature and quality of human relationships as well as the kinds of communities that actually foster human well-being. Needed, David Hollenbach argues, is a communitarian perspective, one that puts "the connections among people back at the center of social and moral inquiry."[18] Consequently, a creative retrieval of the ideas of common goods (and "common bads") "in a normative framework adequate to guide response to new forms of global connection" is needed.[19]

In 1961 John XXIII defined the common good as being "the sum total of those conditions of social living, whereby people are enabled more fully and readily to achieve their own perfection."[20] Two years later, John specified that the common good (1) must take the good of the individual person into account (noncollectivist); (2) all must share in it (basic rights satisfied); and (3) it has both material and spiritual elements (holistic).[21] The common good entails interdependence and interconnections that ought to be characterized by equal respect for all the members of the society. This ensues from the earlier comment about authentic humanism requiring equal dignity and mutuality as essential claims about the human person.

When John introduced the idea of a universal or global common good in the encyclical *Pacem in terris,* he was translating the traditional language from its local and national contexts to a new setting. He noted the existence of global problems that transcend the ability of any one nation to remedy and the lack of an adequate transnational authority to promote the global common good. The pope did not call for a world-state but creative means whereby existing public authorities might address global concerns in a fair and noncoercive way. John did not develop a fully adequate analysis of the global common good, but his insight prodded social theorists to consider those shared goods and bads that must be addressed at a transnational level. His language pointed out a necessary way of thinking as interdependence became a reality in the latter half of the twentieth century.

---

18. David Hollenbach, *The Common Good and Christian Ethics* (New York: Cambridge University Press, 2002), 44.

19. Ibid.

20. John XXIII, *Mater et magistra* (On Christianity and Social Progress, 1961), no. 65.

21. John XXIII, *Pacem in terris* (Peace on Earth, 1963), nos. 55-57.

Of course a simple acknowledgment of the common good is insufficient to formulate a richer and more complex political understanding of the human person than the autonomous individual offered up by neoliberalism. As human beings find themselves living in ever more complex networks of interconnection, a schema of values that "gives primacy of place to non-interference and non-judgmentalism lacks the criteria needed to address these connections in a critical manner." Needed instead is a values framework that "can assess the relative merits of different modes of living *together*."[22] In developing this framework there must be extensive work done to resolve long-standing questions about the meaning of the common good, who defines it, and assigning responsibility for promoting and protecting it.[23]

Traditionally, the idea of the common good was associated with a hierarchical and static social order composed of a central authority that delegated to subordinates limited authority in discrete areas. The image of society was that it was unified and rather homogenous, with members contributing to the common good in accord with the rights and duties they had by reason of their station in life.

Each of those traditional elements is now fraying at the edges, if not already unraveled: egalitarian and participatory aspirations have advanced, central authority has been relativized, societies have become dynamic with social and geographic mobility, and individuals have adopted life plans reflective of pluralistic worldviews and value systems. Transposed into this new social framework, is the concept of the common good still useful? Stripped of outmoded assumptions about the social order, the main claim regarding the common good is that certain goods are basic to human well-being and necessary for persons to endure with dignity intact, for example, food, shelter, health care, relationships with God and other persons, physical integrity, and security.[24]

Precisely because of the pluralism that globalization exhibits as well as the false universalisms that history has revealed, the assertion of a universal

---

22. Hollenbach, *Common Good*, 56.

23. This way of formulating the agenda is not identical with, but is very close to, Lisa Cahill's understanding of the challenge that globalization presents to CST. I rely on a number of her insights in Lisa Sowle Cahill, "Globalization and the Common Good," in *Globalization and Catholic Social Thought*, ed. John Coleman and William Ryan (Maryknoll, NY: Orbis Books, 2005), 42-54.

24. As Cahill puts it, "basic human goods are required by human nature and known by human reason; they also define justice as social relations in which material and social goods are distributed fairly, conflicts resolved, and violations compensated" (ibid., 47).

common good or set of goods will meet with resistance. Thus, the project of naming a common good must avoid any method only suitable to a bygone model of social order. "Clearly, any approach to defining the content of the common good that will be persuasive and useful today must be inductive and dialogical."[25]

The hope is that a searching and open conversation about what goods will serve individuals and their communities can eventuate into an evolving consensus on what basic goods must be secured and what evils prevented or resisted. Pursuing such a model of inquiry will require that Christians be enriched by the insights of scholars who do not share their broader theological framework but who are committed to developing a humane world order.

Justice

Since existing relationships among people reflect inequality and marginalization, there is a need to establish normative standards to which we can hold the future processes of interaction that constitute globalization. Claims about the desirability of using globalization to build human community should be accompanied by additional ethical coordinates that address what kind of community makes the good life possible. Here the Christian tradition requires that a truly human community must provide basic justice for its members. In the case of a global community, this means justice is secured for all people and each local community within the global family.

The classical definition of justice is rendering to each what is their due. Sorting out what someone is due, however, has long been a contentious political argument. Justice is a complicated ideal since it has to do with the "allocation of goods, powers, and opportunities, about access to decision-making processes, about fundamental respect among people, and about the basic structures of society."[26] Within the Catholic tradition, justice is understood as a fundamental characteristic of what constitutes good community. Without justice, life together involves oppression, neglect, and harm.

Modern Catholic social teaching came into existence as a response to the abuses of liberalism during the early stage of industrial capitalism in the nineteenth century. As noted earlier, critics see the early stage of economic globalization being characterized, in large part, by a neoliberalism that excuses extreme inequality as an unfortunate byproduct of the freedom that must be

---

25. Ibid., 48.
26. Karen Lebacqz, *Six Theories of Justice* (Minneapolis: Augsburg, 1986), 10.

maintained in order to reap the benefits of globalization.[27] Free trade, free contract, and free movement of capital (with "free" meaning unrestricted or unregulated) are the hallmarks of economic liberalism, and they are all defended as
essential to economic globalization.

While acknowledging the new global context, Christians must not forget
the key values and principles that constitute the moral legacy of the tradition. When Leo XIII encountered the argument of liberal economics that
free contracts were intrinsic to free markets, he asserted there is "a dictate of
nature more imperious and ancient than any bargain" between persons; it is a
demand of natural justice that wages be set at a level "to support a frugal and
well-behaved wage earner."[28] Justice is crucial to Catholic social teaching as
an ethical coordinate because it is concerned with securing the basic goods to
allow all people to live with dignity.

The claim that justice trumps freedom in economics was a decisive break
with the free-market ideology of the time and separated the church's social
teaching from liberal free-market orthodoxy. For the economic liberal of the
time, the idea of a just wage was simply what a worker freely consented to
accept in exchange for labor. By contrast, Leo held that a just wage must adequately compensate a worker in order to meet conventional needs.[29] A century
later, John Paul II would declare, "It is a strict duty of justice and truth not to
allow fundamental human needs to remain unsatisfied, and not to allow those
burdened by such needs to perish."[30]

The criterion of meeting basic human needs looms large in the Catholic
understanding of justice, and this provides a different emphasis from what is
found in the neoliberal approach where a climate of meritocracy and deregula-
tion shapes the reigning model of economic globalization. The need for new
skills and new information has led to a sense of entitlement among those
populations who have acquired such skills and information first. Economists,
of course, take incentives seriously and warn against creating disincentives for
those who are breaking new paths. While some meritocratic dimension of
economic reward is useful and not offensive to Catholic social teaching the
line between considerations of merit and a revised version of social Darwinism
can be easily crossed.

To the extent that globalization advances, or is grounded in, a champion-
ing of free trade, free investment, free consumption, and free contract without

---

27. A representative critical essay is James Hug, "Economic Justice and
Globalization," in *Globalization and Catholic Social Thought*, 55-71.

28. Leo XIII, *Rerum novarum* (On the Condition of Labor, 1891), no. 45.

29. Ibid., no. 34.

30. John Paul II, *Centesimus annus* (One Hundred Years of Catholic Social
Teaching, 1991), no. 34.

adequate concern for basic justice in the form of socio-economic rights, then it must be subjected to criticism from the perspective of Christian morality.

Human Rights[31]

The understanding of justice in Catholic teaching has evolved in a substantive manner through the adoption of human rights language. While John XXIII's encyclical *Pacem in terris* is rightly viewed as the earliest extensive treatment of human rights in Catholic social teaching,[32] his approach has been ratified again and again in statements of hierarchs, scholars, and activists. This approach to human rights embraces both those rights commonly called civil and political as well as those labeled socioeconomic.[33] The rights are understood as deeply rooted in the church's teaching on human dignity. In keeping with the social as well as the sacred dimension of the person, human rights in the tradition are also correlated with a strong sense of duties and responsibilities to the community and common good.

Promotion of a set of basic human rights that ought to be universally established and recognized is a further elaboration of the idea of justice that Catholic social teaching provides for assessing globalization. While allowing for pluralism in ethical options, there is a set of basic rights that reflect transcultural values and that multinational businesses and local governments must respect. Basic human rights serve as a fundamental norm, even as we recognize the persistence of pluralism and local loyalties amidst the reality of globalization.[34]

Participation

Catholic thinking about justice has also been greatly enriched by the increased prominence given to the theme of participation. Paul VI in *Octogesima adveniens* identified participation, along with equality, as "fundamental aspirations"

---

31. The topic of human rights will be treated at greater length in the second major section of this chapter. Here I merely want to make clear the importance of human rights as an ethical coordinate for globalization.

32. *Pacem in terris*, esp. nos. 8-36.

33. David Hollenbach, *Claims in Conflict: Retrieving and Renewing the Catholic Human Rights Tradition* (New York: Paulist Press, 1979), remains among the finest and most detailed explanations for the evolution of official church teaching in this area.

34. Hollenbach, *Common Good*, 220-21.

302 *Christianity and the Political Order*

that are "two forms of human dignity and freedom."[35] For Paul, the drive to participation reflects a rise in information and education among people. It also testifies to a basic drive within human beings as they seek greater development, the legitimate wish to share responsibility for decisions that shape their individual and collective futures.

In Catholic social teaching, participation applies to many realms, but the theme has a distinct contribution for political globalization since present global institutions suffer from a "democratic deficit."[36] The expression reveals that in the processes of global decision making there are two major fault lines.

The first is that, in many of the forums, conferences, and summit meetings where rules and procedures of globalization are discussed, the viewpoint of the local communities does not get an adequate hearing. Decisions about trade, foreign debt, and capital investment are made with little or no input from the majority of people affected. While these intergovernmental organizations "are formally accountable to the states that are their members, they represent only certain constituencies within those states, frequently conduct their business in closed sessions, and operate as distant bureaucracies."[37]

Regarding the second fault line, there is not just a divide between elites and the local communities, but even entire states often lack true participation. "Votes in these international agencies are often distributed in proportion to the wealth or budgetary contributions of the member states and sometimes non-members are not officially represented at all."[38]

In sum, the "democratic deficit" of globalization is that large numbers of the world's peoples are without effective means of participating in a meaningful way in decisions that will directly bear on their well-being. This is a serious injustice to persons whose dignity entails exercising their creative moral agency.

Subsidiarity

Catholic social teaching sees globalization as a set of practices and institutions that can and should be made subject to oversight by moral agents. In order for that to happen, however, there must be mechanisms for governance and regulation that take into account the new architecture of international relations. The old building blocks of nation-states have not disappeared, but they now

---

35. Paul VI, *Octogesima adveniens* (A Call to Action, 1981), no. 22.
36. Joseph S. Nye, Jr., "Globalization's Democratic Deficit: How to Make International Institutions More Accountable," *Foreign Affairs* 80, no. 4 (2001): 2-6.
37. Hollenbach, *Common Good*, 224.
38. Ibid.

operate within a different context. States retain power, yet they must wield that power in collaboration with other nations and nonstate actors.

Globalization has taken some oversight power away from nations and placed economic actors in a more depoliticized global space. Just as with any other social space, however, there is a need for regulation to codify rights and responsibilities. Honest, reasonable regulation is not an enemy of globalization but a necessity if there is to be avoidance of a backlash against the abuses of free-market capitalism. As Aquinas and other earlier thinkers knew, wherever there is society there needs to be governance.

Attention to the multiple levels of global society and the diversity of actors to be engaged in the life of that society suggests the need for greater interest in what Catholic social teaching calls subsidiarity. This traditional theme calls for keeping the capacities to assess, decide, and act at the most local level possible while still being effective in securing the common good.

What is needed is a new framework within which forms of global authority may be conceived. The political theorist Richard Falk has written about a "Grotian moment," in which the political, legal, and diplomatic status quo is being transformed.[39] Recall that it was Hugo Grotius who provided a new language of international law to address the post-Westphalian international order.

This age of globalization requires the creation of institutions and practices for managing a different emerging world order. The challenge is to find an approach so that globalization may be regulated and directed. In his 2003 World Day of Peace message, John Paul II had his own "Grotian moment" when he wrote,

> Is this not the time for all to work together for a new constitutional organization of the human family, truly capable of ensuring peace and harmony between peoples, as well as their integral development? But let there be no misunderstanding. This does not mean writing the constitution of a global super-State. Rather, it means continuing and deepening processes already in place to meet the almost universal demand for participatory ways of exercising political authority, even international political authority, and for transparency and accountability at every level of public life.[40]

John Paul returned to the theme in another speech later that same year. After listing several negative aspects of the present state of globalization, he called for guidelines that "will place globalization firmly at the service of

---

39. Richard Falk, *Law in an Emerging Global Village* (Ardsley, NY: Transnational Publishers, 1999).

40. John Paul II, *"Pacem in terris*: A Permanent Commitment," World Day of Peace Message (January 1, 2003), no. 6.

authentic human development—the development of every person and of the whole person—in full respect of the rights and dignity of all." The pope continued by making clear that he did not see globalization in itself as the problem. "Rather, difficulties arise from the lack of effective mechanisms for giving it proper direction. Globalization needs to be inserted into the larger context of a political and economic programme that seeks the authentic progress of all."[41] He then suggested to his audience that the time was ripe for a new international order.

Benedict XVI has also observed that because of "the unrelenting growth of global interdependence, there is a strongly felt need, even in the midst of a global recession, for a reform of the United Nations Organization, and likewise of the economic institutions and international finance." He went on to note that "to manage the global economy; to revive economies hit by the crisis; to avoid any deterioration of the present crisis and the greater imbalances that would result; to bring about integral and timely disarmament, food security and peace; to guarantee the protection of the environment and to regulate migration: for all this, there is urgent need of a true political authority."[42]

The papal call for a new approach to global governance has been repeated by others, for it is widely acknowledged that "change in our social and economic realities has outpaced change in the political institutions and processes that once firmly embedded them."[43] It is important to remember, however, that these calls for new forms of governance and political authority are not equivalent to support for one world government.

Several examples of new methods of regulation and agency reflect "globalization from below."[44] These include citizens' organizations and transnational networks combating climate change, promoting human rights, or supporting microfinancing. Grassroots activism on behalf of women's rights, public health services, and fair trade has forged links through globalized communications and travel.

While subsidiarity is needed, a renewed approach to that principle does not simply refer to vertical levels of authority interacting with one another, but horizontal interactions also with an array of organizations, institutions, and community groups, as well as governmental regimes.[45] Globalization's

---

41. John Paul II, "Address to the Pontifical Academy for Social Sciences" (May 2, 2003). Available at http://www.vatican.va/holy father/john paul ii/speeches/2003/may/documents/hf jp-ii spe 20030502 pont-acad-sciences en.html.

42. Benedict XVI, *Caritas in veritate* (Love in Truth, 2005), no. 67.

43. John Coleman, "Making the Connections: Globalization and Catholic Social Thought," in *Globalization and Catholic Social Thought*, 9-27 at 14.

44. Cahill, "Globalization and the Common Good," in *Globalization and Catholic Social Thought*, 49-50.

45. Ibid., 50.

"democratic deficit" must be countered by ensuring that existing institutions are reformed and new ones designed with participation, transparency, and accountability in mind.[46] Organizations like the World Bank and International Monetary Fund "need to go through a radical change that would ensure the equal participation of both the rich and poor nations."[47] What is needed is global governance that provides the poor with access to power and voice in the regulation of globalization.

Among the new forms of governance are regimes and global policy networks. Regimes are bodies possessing "sufficient functional powers, delegated to them by states through multilateral agreements, for limited purposes to regulate, coordinate, or implement global rules."[48] For example, air safety is regulated by the International Civil Aviation Organization in Montreal, and international food safety laws are overseen by the Food and Agricultural Organization in Rome. Regimes come in a variety of formats, some purely private, some a mix of private and public, and some public but overseen by a standing IGO (intergovernmental organization).

Global policy networks are an admixture of NGOs (nongovernmental organizations), IGOs, and multinational corporations. These networks help "close the participatory gap in global governance." Their main purpose is to "place new issues on the global agenda and raise issues that have been neglected or treaties that are not being implemented."[49] In effect, they enable people to engage in public discourse.

Globalization is fostering a range of organizational approaches that include yet extend beyond the traditional categories of states and IGOs. Globalization will require some institutional infrastructure for governance and regulation. This will require openness to new institutions and procedures. What is needed is a political globalization that matches the extent of economic globalization.

Questions such as, who rules?, in whose name?, by what means?, and for what goals? are vital for the future of governance. It is clear that there are multiple stakeholders in globalization's governance, and each should be able to find some means of having input. The church will provide a genuine service if it can contribute to the formulation of an ethical framework that includes the legitimacy and usefulness of new models for subsidiarity, such as regimes and networks, just as past reflections on subsidiarity contributed to our thinking about the nature, purpose, and role of the state in earlier eras.

---

46. Hollenbach, *Common Good*, 225.

47. Tirimanna, "Globalization Needs to Count Human Persons," in *Ethics and the World Church*, 245-52 at 249-50.

48. John Coleman, "Global Governance, the State, and Multinational Corporations," in *Globalization and Catholic Social Thought*, 239-48 at 242.

49. Ibid., 243.

HUMAN RIGHTS

The idea of human rights has become among the most commonly cited themes in international politics. The topic has become central to the agenda of many involved in international affairs, both for the debates that the idea sets off as well as the hopes that human rights discourse inspires. The Catholic Church must be included among those who use human rights as a way to articulate its view of international politics. Indeed, the distinguished theorist of international affairs, Samuel Huntington, observed that the church during the pontificate of John Paul II had become one of the major human rights actors on the global stage.[50] How that came to be is a story of developments both in the internal life of the church and within the realm of international politics.

The Evolution of Rights Language

The language of rights developed within the Christian faith community in the medieval era. According to the distinguished historian Brian Tierney, rights were originally recognized by eleventh- and twelfth-century theologians and canonists who sought to articulate the proper powers and claims of popes, bishops, clergy, religious, and laity so as to describe the church's nature and life accurately. Long before the use of rights language in modern liberalism. the language of rights was used to express the proper way to interrelate the various categories of people constituting the church. Rights language was a way to describe and secure proper participation in the life of the community.

The two great personal forces in the medieval world were the pope and the emperor. This dynamic of power went through many shifts over the centuries, but perhaps no change was as significant as the fact that after the Protestant Reformation neither pope nor emperor could control the actions of individual monarchs ruling the newly formed nation-states. In time, this new political force, a monarch vested with absolute claims of sovereign power, had to be reckoned with, and the institutions of papacy and empire were inadequate to the task. The feudal system, which placed kings in a dense network of relationships with nobles, creating personal loyalties, mutual duties, and traditional privileges, was largely eroded by this period.

Eventually, a new political force, embodied in the theories of social contract, came to be: the idea of the individual possessing natural rights preceding any claim of state or monarch. This new political reality emerged as the counterweight to the monarchical claims of power. The theory of natural rights helps to create a zone of liberty against which no state can encroach.

---

50. Samuel Huntington, "Religion and the Third Wave," *National Interest* 24 (Summer 1991): 29-42 at 30.

Natural rights are spheres of immunity guaranteeing life, liberty, and property. This is the foundation of liberalism, the political theory that champions the free individual who should be able to act without interference from the state, church, or any other institution because of the natural rights that precede the social contract.

In the eighteenth century, an important transformation occurred, one that is linked to the name of Adam Smith, whose famous book, *The Wealth of Nations*, provided the intellectual foundation for a free-market economy. The natural rights of the person were identified with the "natural" workings of the free market so that private property, free contracts, and the nonregulation of business activity became identified with natural rights just as that term had been linked to the political rights of seventeenth-century liberalism. In effect, political freedom became subordinate to economic freedom.

Natural law still was seen as the rule of human existence, but the term lost its moral meaning and came to be associated with the laws of the free market, production, and exchange. The laws of the marketplace were viewed as the true natural laws. This was the theory that legitimated laissez-faire capitalism or economic liberalism. Freed from the shackles of feudal church and empire, protected from overreaching national governments by rights and natural law, and equipped with the necessary raw materials and new technology, the European states experienced a revolution of dramatically increased productivity.

But not everyone shared equally in the fruits of the Revolution. By the middle of the nineteenth century the emergence of overcrowded urban slums with a large number of unemployed or underemployed workers had led to concerns about the new economic order. The writings of Charles Dickens, beginning in the 1830s, portrayed the squalid living conditions of the poor; in 1848 Karl Marx and Friedrich Engels issued the "Communist Manifesto"; and in 1871 the Paris Commune gave expression to the discontent of the working class. A broad array of social reformers—church leaders, artists of the romanticist movement, humanitarian philosophers, democratic and revolutionary socialists—called for change in the prevailing view of political economy.

During the last quarter of the nineteenth century, liberalism split into two camps. There were free-market liberals, who held onto economic freedom as the foundation of human well-being and insisted on various aspects of laissez-faire capitalism (private property, free contracts, and nonregulated markets) as first principles. There were other liberals, utilitarians, who espoused economic freedom because they believed it promoted the greatest good for the greatest number. Theirs was an argument not from natural rights but a belief based on social utility.

The difference between the two camps was that for one, economic freedom was a nonnegotiable principle, while for the other camp, economic freedom was a strategy to promote social welfare. For this latter group of utilitarian liberals, government interference in the market was not an invasion of individual rights but an obstacle to progress. If that claim was shown to be untrue, at least in some circumstances, then the door was open to accepting government activity in economic life.

In time the various social reformers developed a number of ideas that placed limits on the economic freedoms of others: child and women labor laws, poor relief taxes, minimum work weeks, and minimum wage laws. While initially opposing such measures, utilitarian liberals came to see the good that such actions brought about and eventually joined in advocacy of such restraints on the economic freedom of capitalism. They could do this because once they saw a better strategy for achieving the aim of social welfare they were free to adopt it. But for those who professed economic freedom not as a strategy but as a principled commitment, no such endorsement of government intrusion in the market was permissible. Thus, the economic liberals remained opposed to a variety of social reforms that were supported by the utilitarian liberals.

As the nineteenth century continued, the socialist critique of capitalism grew harsher. Hard-line socialists and Marxists denied natural rights as simply ideological defenses of privilege. Democratic socialists, labor parties, and social welfare liberals were prepared to defend some rights as long as there were social and economic rights serving as empowerments, not just civil and political rights serving as immunities. As a result, the language of rights began to expand beyond civil and political liberties.

The debate continued on unresolved into the twentieth century. Following the brutal experiences of fascism, Nazism, and Stalinism, which denigrated human beings in horrific ways, there was revived interest in rights language as a way of defending human dignity against totalitarian ideologies. Due to the Cold War atmosphere of the forties and fifties, however, the argument often took the predictable form of Western nations promoting civil and political liberties, while the Eastern bloc called for social and economic rights.

An additional difficulty was that secular thinkers on both sides of the East-West divide were uncomfortable with the metaphysical background that generated the medieval language of natural rights. Consequently, in the early debates surrounding the establishment of the United Nations, the term human rights was used as a more philosophically neutral foundation, and a comprehensive list of human rights was drawn up that embraced civil, political, social, and economic rights.

Human Rights and Catholicism

Before World War II the Catholic Church was not seen as a major supporter of rights language owing to its concerns about liberalism and its preference for the social language of duties rather than rights. Following the war, Pius XII, in

line with the Vatican's support for the United Nations, encouraged cooperation in formulating the "Universal Declaration of Human Rights" that was
adopted by the UN General Assembly in December of 1948. Church leaders,
like political leaders at the time, were interested in reasserting the dignity of
human beings that had been so grievously violated during the prior decade.

John XXIII and Vatican II firmly moved human rights into the framework
of Catholic social teaching. In *Pacem in terris* John placed human rights at
the center of his global vision. He also provided the most extensive listing of
human rights to be found in Catholic social teaching, one that closely parallels
that of the U.N. Declaration.[51]

For John, human rights are linked to the common good; indeed "it is agreed
that in our time the common good is chiefly guaranteed when personal rights
and duties are maintained."[52] Because human rights flow from the person the
common good cannot be interpreted in a collectivist manner. By accepting a
full range of civil and political liberties in his list of human rights, John reassured those who worried that Catholicism's emphasis on the common good
might lead to an authoritarian political approach.

The idea of state sovereignty has been a building block of the modern world
order. Yet it is not a notion that has been understood in the same way by
everyone. One interpretation of sovereignty focuses on "the rights of states
as a collective form of their citizens' individual rights to life and liberty. The
nation-state may be seen as a pooled expression of individual rights."[53] Such an
approach places great weight on state sovereignty and self-determination by
a community since such ideas are viewed as a means for upholding the rights
of individual persons. Sovereignty would be an absolute principle, or nearly
so, in this framework since the rights of the individual to life and liberty are
highly esteemed.

By contrast, there is the cosmopolitan school's understanding of sovereignty.
This approach "stresses the common nature of humanity. States and boundaries exist, but this does not endow them with absolute moral significance."[54]
Human rights, at least certain basic rights, take precedence over territorial
boundaries. We ought not grant too much to a presumption in favor of sovereignty but rather uphold the overriding import of human rights when confronted by genocide, ethnic cleansing, and other crimes against humanity. The
concern here is that the state may not in fact serve the rights of individual

---

51. *Pacem in terris*, nos. 11-27.

52. Ibid., no. 60.

53. Richard Cooper and Joseph Nye, Jr., "Ethics and Foreign Policy," in *Global
Affairs*, ed. Samuel Huntington and Joseph Nye, Jr. (Lanham, MD: University Press of
America, 1985), 23-41 at 25.

54. Ibid.

citizens. Thus a state cannot expect that esteem for the rights of the person automatically translates into respect for territorial boundaries or governments.

Catholic social teaching expresses a preference for the cosmopolitan approach while not ignoring the insights found within the state moralist outlook. For example, throughout *Pacem in terris* there is an argument that a state's sovereignty must be restrained by structures both lower and higher than the state. Catholic social thought begins with a society of persons not a society of states. But it does not end with a society of persons, since the state is a necessary structure. Within Catholic teaching, persons in society are also citizens of states, and states are members of an international society. The state has a legitimate role in Catholic social thought but one circumscribed by the rights of persons making up a society and the place of states in the scheme of international society.

Thus, "from below" the state is bound to respect the rights of individual human beings who have basic needs, essential freedoms, and fundamental relationships that are given expression in the language of human rights.[55] "From above," the individual state is limited by the duty to cooperate with other states and institutions in creating a global order that serves the international common good. While important, the state is neither the beginning nor the end of Catholic political thought. Its value is instrumental. State sovereignty, therefore, cannot be absolute but must be tempered by the rights of the human person and the common good of the international community.

Vatican II and Human Rights

At Vatican II the assembly of bishops also affirmed the centrality of human rights for human dignity, including the right of religious freedom, a civil liberty that the Catholic Church had been slow to endorse. The hierarchy feared that religious liberty would be equated with endorsing religious indifferentism, understood as meaning that one religious creed was no more true or false than another. However, as was discussed in chapter 9, the conciliar Decree on Religious Liberty affirmed a human right to religious freedom not because of indifference to religious truth but because of the limits of the state and the importance of freedom for the human person. By endorsing religious liberty as a human right, the church cleared away the largest obstacle to its acceptance of the modern human rights agenda.

Another dimension that Vatican II provided was the experience of the uni-

---

55. "[T]he very heart of international life is not so much States as man" (John Paul II, "Address to the Diplomatic Corps Accredited to the Holy See," *L'Osservatore Romano* [weekly edition in English] 26 [January 20, 1993], 1-3 at 3).

versality of the church and the diversity the church encounters as a global institution. This experience provided the basis for an essay by Karl Rahner, S.J., often called the most important Catholic theologian of the twentieth century. He posited the thesis that the experience of Vatican II was the beginning of a new era in the history of Catholicism.[56]

From the perspective of theology, Rahner suggested that the church had known two previous eras, the brief period of Jewish Christianity followed by the long "period of the Church in a distinct cultural region, namely that of Hellenism and of European culture and civilization."[57] Obviously, this second period has many significant subdivisions, as chapters 4 through 7 of this book attest, but it was still the narrative of Christianity as preached and enacted within the context of Greek and Roman cultures and then transmitted to Germanic and other peoples throughout the continent. Even with the discovery of the Americas, it was a European Christianity brought by the conquerors and colonists to the new lands.

The experience of Vatican II signaled the transition to a new context, from "the Christianity of Europe (with its American annexes) to a fully world religion."[58] Christianity had spread across the entire globe, but it was Christianity in European language and thought forms transplanted to the foreign soils of Asia, Africa, Oceania, and the Americas. Now in the third era of the church, there is a recognition that pluralism is ineradicable; for the Christian message truly to take root there needs to be greater diversity in the way the Christian proclamation is expressed and lived. Vatican II was the symbolic passage from the second to the third eras of Christianity, just as the Council of Jerusalem in the first century was the symbolic passage from Jewish to Gentile Christianity. With Vatican II, "the world Church modestly began to act as such."[59]

Postconciliar Catholicism and Human Rights

The implications of Rahner's essay are broad, indeed, but for our purposes it suggests a rationale for the reliance on human rights language in modern Catholic social teaching. At the end of his essay, Rahner noted that a truly world church cannot be governed "with the sort of Roman centralism that was customary" in the preceding period of church life.[60] One sees a glimmer of that

---

56. Karl Rahner, "Towards a Fundamental Theological Interpretation of Vatican II," *Theological Studies* 40, no. 4 (December 1979): 716-27.

57. Ibid., 721.

58. Ibid., 722.

59. Ibid., 726.

60. Ibid.

awareness in the caution of Paul VI when confronted by the social issues of his time. In a famous passage from his letter commemorating the eightieth anniversary of Leo XIII's *Rerum novarum*, Paul first comments on the situation he sees before him. "There is of course a wide diversity among the situations in which Christians—willingly or unwillingly—find themselves according to regions, socio-political systems and cultures."[61] The significance of the pluralism is that it leads the pope to reconsider the nature of his role as a teacher.

> In the face of such widely varying situations it is difficult for us to utter a unified message and to put forward a solution which has universal validity. Such is not our ambition, nor is it our mission. It is up to the Christian communities to analyze with objectivity the situation which is proper to their own country, to shed on it the light of the Gospel's unalterable words and to draw principles of reflection, norms of judgment, and directives for action from the social teaching of the Church.[62]

The papal role in the pluralism of a world church, as Paul VI reflects upon it, is not to speak a "unified message" or to propose a response that will have "universal validity." Rather, it is for the church in various regions to develop an appropriate response. As a consequence, the decades of the 1970s and 1980s were a period of significant activism by local episcopacies. Many of the statements authorized by individual bishops or national conferences of bishops employed human rights as a means to articulate concerns about economic development, trade, immigration, poverty, and work.[63]

Another dimension of Paul VI's teaching on human rights is the interconnectedness of human rights. In liberalism the commitment was first of all to political and economic liberty, while in socialism the commitment was to equality of participation in society. In theories of development that became popular in the decades of the 1960s and 1970s there was much discussion of satisfying basic human needs. Paul, in keeping with his predecessors, championed human rights upon a vision of human dignity that included freedom, participatory community, and satisfying essential needs.

And so Paul employed the term "integral development" to capture the sense that human rights should blend together to express those conditions essential for human dignity to be experienced.[64] In Paul's writing there was a close linkage among many human rights because such moral claims reflected the

61. *Octogesima adveniens*, no. 3.

62. Ibid., no. 4.

63. For documentation and analysis of the wide variety of statements made, see Terence McGoldrick, "Episcopal Conferences Worldwide on Catholic Social Teaching," *Theological Studies* 59, no. 1 (March 1998): 22-50.

64. *Populorum progressio* is an extended reflection on the need for a wholistic

minimal conditions that any society ought to promote and protect if it was to be just. The synod of bishops held in 1971 captured the same idea with its call for a "right to development," which is described as the "dynamic interpenetration of all those fundamental human rights upon which the aspirations of individuals and nations are based."[65] Two comments are necessary about the word "aspirations." First, the word makes clear that in its human rights discourse the church was not presuming the actual existence of legal rights but making an appeal to moral ideals that ought to be in place and secured for every human person. Second, use of the word "aspirations" is not meant to signify something to be hoped for in an undetermined future, because a legitimate human right establishes a moral obligation to be satisfied in the present.[66]

The papacy of John Paul II was an era not only of increased appeal to human rights in Catholic social teaching, but increased and dramatic papal action on the topic. Through his extensive travels, John Paul II knew the pluralism of societal models firsthand. The daunting diversity of political, economic, social, and cultural institutions was undeniable, yet the pope was not as hesitant as was Paul VI in acting upon his role as universal pastor of the church. The challenge for John Paul, however, was how to formulate social teaching in a manner that permitted him to speak to widely disparate situations, for example, Poland, the Philippines, Uganda, Brazil, and the United States. The primary way became the discourse of human rights.

John Paul used his teaching on human rights as a vehicle to assess, positively and negatively, the many different nations he visited in his travels. There might be major differences between a gathering in Chicago or Manila, but in both settings the pope could appeal to basic human rights to affirm or challenge his listeners. In effect, the human rights teaching of the papacy developed as an ethical framework that set limits, while permitting pluralism, in the way that a society organized itself.

Human rights can be understood as establishing a picture frame surrounding a canvas. Every society has the freedom to draw on the canvas in a way that is most suitable given the history, culture, values, resources, and beliefs of the society. In fashioning a political system or economic system there is no single right way to do it, anymore than there is only one way to draw a picture. However, whatever economic and political institutions and arrangements are fashioned, they cannot violate human rights. The drawing cannot extend

---

approach to human development, not just economic. See paragraph 21 for the papal understanding of integral development in outline.

65. 1971 Synod, *Justicia in mundo* (Justice in the World, 1971), no. 15.

66. Pontifical Council for Justice and Peace, *Compendium of the Social Doctrine of the Church* (Vatican City: Libreria Editrice Vaticana, 2004), no. 446.

beyond the canvas and ignore the picture frame. There is legitimate pluralism within limits, and for matters of social life those limits are set by the framework of human rights.

Early in his papacy John Paul II attended a meeting of the bishops of Latin America that was held in Puebla, Mexico. In his opening speech at the conference he gave a preview of his approach to social teaching.

> Perhaps one the most glaring weaknesses of present day civilization lies in an inadequate view of the human being. Undoubtedly, our age is the age of various humanisms, the age of anthropocentrism. But paradoxically it is also the age of people's deepest anxieties about their identity and destiny; it is the age when human beings have been debased to previously unsuspected levels, when human values have been trodden underfoot as never before.
>
> How do we explain this paradox? We can say it is the inexorable paradox of atheistic humanism. It is the drama of people severed from an essential dimension of their being—the Absolute—and thus confronted with the worst possible diminution of their being. *Gaudium et spes* goes to the heart of the problem when it says: "Only in the mystery of the Incarnate Word does the mystery of the person take on light."[67]

In the face of horrors such as World War II, the Shoah, the Gulag, and totalitarian regimes, the pope saw that the key for genuine politics was to establish it on the firm foundation of an authentic humanism. For John Paul, the agenda was to explicate how a Christian humanism might shape a better politics. In such a humanism, human rights plays a large part because they specify the social conditions that make human dignity possible.

Furthermore, the Christian dimension of humanism means Christology will play a significant role in establishing what true humanity looks like. For John Paul, the important aspects of humanism, including the effort to defend and promote human rights, flow from Christology. For the pope, human rights have a theological basis.[68] Later in the same year as the Puebla speech, John Paul referred to human rights as a "humanistic criterion" for assessing all social systems.[69] Speaking before the United Nations he put the matter directly: "It

---

67. John Paul II, "Speech at the Third General Conference of the Latin American Episcopate" (January 28, 1979), I.9, quoting *Gaudium et spes*, no. 22. Available at http://www.vatican.va/holy_father/john_paul_ii/speeches/1979/january/documents/hf_jp-ii_spe_19790128_messico-puebla-episc-latam_en.html.

68. John Paul II, *Redemptor hominis* (Redeemer of Humankind, 1979), no. 17.

69. John Paul II, "Speech to the 34th General Assembly of the United Nations" (October 2, 1979), no. 17. Available at http://www.vatican.va/holy_father/john_paul_ii/speeches/1979/october/documents/hf_jp-ii_spe_19791002_general-assembly-onu_en.html.

is a question of the highest importance that in internal social life, as well as in international life, *all human beings* in every nation and country *should be able to enjoy effectively their full rights under any political regime or system.*"[70]

As the distinguished political scientist Samuel Huntington has observed, Roman Catholicism since Vatican II and particularly during the pontificate of John Paul II became one of the dominant forces for advancing democracy and human rights in the world.[71] The rationale for that was provided by developments such as the ones noted above. It was not only at the level of ideas, however, that things changed. There was also action that made Catholicism a strong presence in the movement for the promotion of human rights.

Church Activity on Behalf of Human Rights

Broadly, the action of the church on behalf of human rights may be divided into action in the realm of Vatican diplomacy and activity in support of popular movements at the national or subnational levels. At the level of Vatican diplomatic pursuits, the work is mainly done through IGOs like the United Nations, or in one-to-one engagement by members of the Holy See's diplomatic corps with government officials in various states.

Within the United Nations, diplomats from the Holy See usually participate in the preparatory consultations, debates, and negotiations that occur in the creation of documents on human rights, whether these are covenants or conventions that are legally binding on the ratifying states or declarations and recommendations that are without legal force.[72] Vatican diplomats also involve themselves in regional conferences and at the level of states, often negotiating behind the scenes on behalf of individuals or groups whose human rights are threatened.

Of course, it is the pope himself who is the most visible actor in the church's involvement in international politics. Huntington cites papal trips to numerous countries where the pope upheld the cause of human rights and energized forces working for justice: Mexico in 1979; Poland in 1979, 1983, 1987; Brazil in 1980; the Philippines in 1981; Argentina in 1982; Guatemala, Nicaragua, El Salvador, and Haiti in 1983; Korea in 1984; Chile in 1987; and Paraguay in 1988. As Huntington wryly observed, "The purpose of these visits, like that

---

70. Ibid., no. 9.

71. Huntington, "Religion and the Third Wave."

72. Fortunatus Nwachukwu, "The Work of Human Rights," in *The Holy See: A Face of Another Globalization*, ed. Bianca Nicolini (Geneva: Pax Romana. ICMICA/MIIC, 2007), 104-22 at 117.

of his many visits elsewhere, was always said to be pastoral. Their effects were almost invariably political."[73]

History provides ample evidence that, as ruler of the Papal States, the pope behaved like any other temporal sovereign, entering into political alliances, taking part in military activities, and engaging in international power politics. With the end of the Papal States that earlier phase of activity also came to a close. Eventually, and perhaps reluctantly at first, the papacy was able to adopt a new perspective. No longer is the Holy See an actor in the European balance of power. But now "its whole relationship in the international order is of a moral and humanitarian nature."[74] As the modern papacy has evolved it has become one of the most significant voices on behalf of human rights on the international stage.

Besides the human rights activity of the Holy See and its diplomatic service there has been an upsurge of activity by local churches on behalf of human rights. As to be expected, the action here is often in protest of a specific national government or in support of a popular movement seeking redress of human rights abuses. In Brazil during the 1960s and 1970s the bishops there stood up to the military and called for an end to that government's human rights abuses. Subsequently, many church leaders in Brazil have voiced support for popular movements in favor of land reform, poor assistance, housing development, and the rights of workers.

In Chile the Catholic Church made a dramatic break between the clergy and the government due to the harsh nature of the military regime in the 1970s. A Vicariate of Solidarity was created in 1976 to assist the families victimized by the government and its right-wing supporters. The church became the center of information for documenting the human rights violations of the government.

Cardinal Jaime Sin, the leader of the Catholic Church throughout the Philippines, demanded the end of martial law as well as that of the Marcos regime. Similar challenges to governments by church leaders happened in Argentina in 1981 and Guatemala in the mid-eighties. In almost every instance, the regimes that were criticized initiated attacks on Catholic clergy, activists, and organizations.[75] Perhaps the most famous case of a government's brutal response to church advocacy for human rights was the assassination of Archbishop Oscar Romero in El Salvador in 1980.

As a transnational organization with more than one billion members the Catholic Church has the potential for building networks of support that can

---

73. Huntington, "Religion and the Third Wave," 34.

74. John Quinn, "A Moral Voice Raised in the International Dialogue," *Origins* 13 (February 2, 1984): 571-73 at 571.

75. Huntington, "Religion and the Third Wave," 32-33.

promote human rights. Members of such networks can call on their own governments to act in putting pressure on an offending regime to cease human rights violations. In the United States this was evident in the activity of many Catholics opposed to the human rights violations during the Salvadoran civil war. The mobilization of church members has the promise of developing globalized church action in solidarity with the victims of human rights abuses.

The theme of human rights in Catholic teaching and practice has become a major illustration of how the Christian faith engages in the affairs of international life. Although no longer a temporal power in Europe, the Catholic Church has become a moral force in the global struggle for human rights.

WAR

There are few topics in the political life of humankind that the Christian tradition has confronted more regularly than the topic of war. Partly that is due to the persistence of war in human history, but it is also partly due to the insistence of human beings to think about war in moral terms. Even those political leaders who are most indifferent to moral judgments have couched their war decisions in the language of morality, if for no other reason than to sway others to support a war. Though the forms of war have changed throughout history, from its origins the Christian community has believed that warfare must be held up to moral scrutiny.

The Teaching of Jesus

For early Christians, Jesus of Nazareth was understood as the Prince of Peace about whom the prophet Isaiah spoke (9:6). Throughout history, the disciples of Jesus continually reflected on the Sermon on the Mount in Matthew's Gospel with its commandment to love one's enemies (5:44) and the beatitude "Blessed are the peacemakers, for they will be called children of God" (5:9). Without question, the first generations of Christians saw an inconsistency between the teaching of Jesus and the violent shedding of blood. And yet history amply documents that the Christian faithful have resorted to violence that was extensive and deadly.

Of course, it is not only in the area of violence that the later followers of Jesus failed to live by his teaching. So the gap between Christ's teaching and the practices of Christians is no shock to students of history. But are moral weakness and half-hearted discipleship the only or even main reason why Christians have taken up arms? The study of history also reveals the complexity of adequately grasping the meaning of Jesus' teaching when living in situations quite different than first-century Palestine.

The Gospels were not written to provide a "how-to manual" for the moral life. They were faith-inspired reflections by early followers of Jesus on the meaning of his life and what it means to be a disciple of the one whom these early followers called Messiah and Lord.

As was seen in chapter 3 in the analysis of Jesus' comment about paying the Roman tax, the statement "Render to Caesar the things that are Caesar's, and to God the things that are God's" (Mark 12:17) did not settle all questions. While not everything can be read into Jesus' teaching, there is a range of plausible interpretations. As reviewed in earlier chapters, history documents that *precisely what things* belong to Caesar and *what things* belong to God has been hotly contested. So, too, in the present case with the effort to understand the Sermon on the Mount, not every interpretation can be treated as plausible, but there are legitimate differences in understanding the text.

Regarding the implausibility of some interpretations, it is certainly doubtful that any specific command of the sermon should be taken literally as a universally applicable norm. Recall that just prior to the teaching about love of enemies Jesus recommends self-mutilation to avoid sinning and forbids all divorce and any swearing of oaths. None of these teachings were literally followed by the earliest disciples.

Concerning the legitimate range of interpretations, the biblical scholar Joachim Jeremias has nicely summarized four schools of thought regarding the Sermon on the Mount. The first sees the sermon as a perfectionist legal code that is to be followed. Avoiding the difficulties with literalism noted above, this approach sees the law as binding but limited in its applicability. That is, the sermon is interpreted as referring to inner attitudes not external behavior, or personal relationships but not public duties, or binding on certain classes, for example, the clergy but not others such as temporal rulers.

A second approach treats the sermon as the articulation of an impossible ideal that is designed to teach fallen humanity about our inability to live truly good lives. Starkly faced with our shortcomings, we are confronted by two options—either despair of our salvation or trust in God's mercy and forgiveness. The sermon teaches us that we cannot save ourselves.

The third interpretive school reads the Sermon on the Mount as reflective of how one is to live if one expects the imminent arrival of the end-time. It sees the sermon as proposing an "interim ethic," an ethic that lost much of its salience as the expectation of the end-time receded from the everyday consciousness of Christians.

A fourth school of thought, the one that Jeremias supports, is that the sermon provides a depiction of what life within the reign of God looks like. It is a description of how a truly converted community of God's people would live. The sermon presumes that those uncommitted to the way of Jesus could never live by the vision portrayed, but that those in the process of undergoing genuine conversion by divine grace can live their way into an anticipation of the fullness of God's reign. The sermon is a portrayal of authentic human life from the perspective of conversion.[76]

The sermon expresses what God's future intention is for a restored creation. The moral challenge for any generation of disciples is to live so there is some correspondence between their present and the future. Lisa Cahill nicely captures this approach to reading the Sermon on the Mount: "the Scriptures offer an impetus toward community formation, or rather a living source of re-experience and renewal of the impetus that was provided by the life, death and resurrection of Jesus. But they do not offer a blueprint for the practical shape of that community including its moral identity." The ongoing task of discipleship is not simply to repeat what the first Christians thought nor to mimic the first disciples. Rather, the ethics of discipleship must be worked out "in subsequent communities as it was in the earliest one, in interaction with concrete human experience and historically available sources of insight."[77]

What Does Love Require?

An example of the intellectual effort that was required to translate the New Testament teaching for later Christians is understanding how the commandment to love the neighbor changed as the social contexts for Christians developed. What does love of neighbor mean? That one ought not do any harm to another? That one ought to prevent harm or evil from befalling the neighbor whenever possible? That one ought to remove evil or harm inflicted on the neighbor? That one ought to promote the neighbor's good? While no particular Christian thinker in the early church may have phrased the question as posed, there was a growing appreciation for the complexity of what neighbor love might entail as Christianity spread within the Roman Empire.

If neighbor love is understood as causing the neighbor no harm, with bloodshed being an obvious harm, then it was unacceptable for Christians to shed blood. This meaning of the love commandment had priority at the outset. When considering what love requires when self-interest clashed with another's interests, the Christian community enjoined a spirit of service on its members so that self-interest gave way.

The problem became more difficult when believers tried to sort through what love required when the interests of two neighbors conflict. If X was attacking Y, what then? Here the second and third meanings of love, as preventing harm or removing evil, might justify the use of force to deter X,

---

76. Joachim Jeremias, *The Sermon on the Mount* (Philadelphia: Fortress Press, 1963).
77. Lisa Sowle Cahill, *Love Your Enemies* (Minneapolis: Fortress Press, 1994), 8.

especially if Y was an innocent victim. Since love might not be able to meet everyone's needs at the same time, protecting the innocent party would have priority. Implicit here is a sense of justice that allows various determinations of who is innocent and who is guilty. Viewed this way, the Christian soldier might violate the first meaning of love yet follow the second and third.

A further complication occurs when one neighbor's understanding of another neighbor's interests differs. Although it might be paternalistic, is there a duty to stop the neighbor from unjust violence and thereby avoid sin? Might the fourth meaning of neighbor love as promotion of the neighbor's good result in acting against a neighbor's will but in his or her true best interest?

By the fourth century, as Christians attained various roles of prominence within the empire, these dilemmas came to the fore. What accountability for evil exists if one can stop the harm of others but does not? Would failing to prevent or remove harm also be a failure of justice? Is there a difference between killing Y and letting Y be killed when one has the power to prevent Y's death?

Since moral agents can bear responsibility not only for what they do but also for what they omit doing, what do we make of public officials who have power to alter a harmful state of affairs but do not do so? Christians holding public office, wielding authority over others, are in a different situation than a marginalized group of Christians residing in a distant part of the empire. As the influence of the Christian community grew in the ancient world there was an appreciation for the substantial consequences of Christians' actions and inactions.

To understand the moral logic involved, consider the example of a drowning person in a river. An individual on the shoreline who cannot swim herself has a different responsibility than the person who is an excellent swimmer capable of saving the drowning individual without serious risk to herself. There is no duty for the nonswimmer to dive into the river, thereby creating a situation where two lives are put at risk. The obligation to act must be measured in accord with the ability to act. As centuries passed, Christians developed new capabilities of acting that had a marked influence on society. As a result, the church as an institution, and specific Christians as individuals, acquired new responsibilities that prior generations of disciples did not know.

Within the Christian community the conviction that neighbor love was the absolute imperative remained in the forefront, yet circumstances very different than Matthew's Gospel envisioned led believers to disagree over whether the love command logically required nonviolence as an absolute rule. While nonviolence might in many cases be a proper expression of the love of neighbor, there was no clear consensus that nonviolence was the only way to express the moral duty to love the neighbor.

Just War and Pacifism as Ethical Traditions

Within the life of the Christian community one finds different traditions regarding how to think about war. Though they represent the last of the traditions to emerge, the crusades were undeniably a part of Christianity's history, as were the ideas that supported them. The crusades were wars sanctioned for a holy purpose, but at the outset they were not seen as differing significantly from a just war ethic since the stated aim was the defense of innocent civilians, those pilgrims traveling to shrines in the Holy Land. Wars are waged for a variety of reasons, however, and eventually the crusades altered, adopting a rationale of support for "true religion" against infidels. That cause would reappear centuries later in the religious wars of Europe.[78]

Based on themes in the Old Testament that describe Yahweh as a warrior and the tales of the conquest in the books of Joshua and Judges, as well as select passages in the New Testament, the crusades morphed into the idea that combat against Islam was divinely sanctioned. Historical and social circumstances certainly influenced the shaping of this ethic. The mass conversion of the Franks and other northern people who were heirs of a warrior culture and who were not adequately evangelized or catechized in preparation for their entrance into the church was an important factor. The great and violent movements of people across the face of Europe placed weak social institutions under severe stress. Central authority had broken down in the feudal period. Islam was spreading as a presence not only in northern Africa but also on the Iberian Peninsula in the west and in the Turkish Empire to the east. There was a sense of fear, anxiety, and social dislocation in Europe that encouraged hostility toward Islam, which was judged a rising threat.

Both in age and influence, however, the more important treatments of war in Christian thought are the just war and pacifist traditions. Augustine articulated the emerging sensibility among Christians in the empire that taking up arms might be a duty, if there were proper cause. Using the analogy of police and criminals, Augustine viewed war as a punishment against wrongdoers and even as a requirement of neighbor love. The context, of course, was the place of the church in a political order that was, by Augustine's time, officially Christian. War and its accompanying evils were viewed harshly, but that did not mean such evils might not be justifiable in the face of even greater evils. Augustine and later adherents to his position were concerned about the

---

78. An excellent analysis of the nature of the crusades and their connection to the holy war idea can be found in Cahill, *Love Your Enemies*, 119–48.

church's responsibility to preserve order and defend the empire against forces that threatened social chaos.

Centuries after Augustine's defense of the moral legitimacy of some war, the early medieval canonists were the next great influence on thinking about the justice of war. These lawyers sought to develop criteria for determining the morality of war in the new situation of Christian princes taking up arms against one another. The breakdown of political order meant that there was no effective authority capable of mediating disputes or deterring violence by local nobles. The practices of the Truce of God, ruling out violence at certain times of the year (e.g., Christmastide or Lent), and the Peace of God, forbidding violence against certain persons (e.g., clergy or peasants), reflect a residue of uneasiness regarding war. The canonists' attempt to establish criteria based on justice for governing medieval warfare testifies to the ongoing hope of the Christian conscience to live morally in a complex and sinful world.

Thomas Aquinas systematized many of the teachings of the canonical literature in his treatment of war. Aquinas established three elements as crucial for a war to be morally acceptable: the existence of a just cause, the decision of a legitimate authority, and the maintenance of right intent. In accord with Augustine, Thomas held that war might be an obligation derived from the virtue of charity. Protection of the innocent from aggression was a requirement of the common good.

Subsequent Christian teaching had to deal with the dramatic changes brought on by the Protestant reform, the rise of nation-states and sovereign monarchs, the discovery of the Americas and indigenous people, the rise of colonialism, and in later times the existence of large conscripted armies, new weapons technology, and the economic devastation of war in urban, industrial regions. Catholics such as Francisco de Vitoria and Francisco Suarez, along with Protestants such as Hugo Grotius and Alberico Gentili, blended Christian morality with legal reasoning to develop the foundations for what we think of today as international law. Religiously inspired opposition to violence motivated much of their work to place moral restraints on war.

Understood properly, the just war tradition recognizes the horror of war and believes that a justifying argument for war must be presented since there is a presumption against war. Adherents of the just war tradition hold that in some cases the moral justification for armed force can be established, overriding the initial presumption against war. Throughout history the criteria for when, why, and how force may be used have been refined and extended.

Traditionally, the criteria are grouped under two headings; the *jus ad bellum* (addressing the why and when criteria for going to war) includes the first seven criteria, and the *jus in bello* (concerned with the how criteria for waging war) the final two criteria. Of late, there has been growing interest in the idea of determining criteria for ending war and reestablishing peace (*jus post bellum*), although this development has not yet established a consensus on the criteria.

One influential account of the criteria is that found in the U.S. Catholic bishops' pastoral letter of 1983.

- Just cause: War is permissible only for a sound moral reason such as the protection of innocent life or the defense of basic human rights. With the devastating force of modern weaponry, the harm of war has been increased to such an extent that a cause that may have justified war in an earlier age, when the harm was less, may not now be sufficient.
- Competent authority: War is not a private vendetta but a public act and must be declared by those who can legitimately speak and act on behalf of the state. In a democracy like the United States it is important that the nation's leaders follow the legally established processes for declaring and undertaking war.
- Comparative justice: The use of the modifier "comparative" is meant to signify that neither side in a conflict may be simply "just" in an unqualified way. Nor may the opposing side be characterized as purely evil or unjust. This criterion requires that on balance, the case must plausibly be made that one side has a clear "edge" in its claim that the values it defends outweigh the claim made by the opponent.
- Right intention: This criterion is closely linked to just cause. The actual intent of those waging war cannot be different than the cause that is publicly espoused; for example, war is declared to defend against an unjust aggressor while the real intent of the war is to seize territory or destroy the culture of the enemy.
- Last resort: Since war is always regrettable, all realistic alternatives must be utilized before going to war. This requires a willingness to take prudent risks and to explore options short of armed force to avoid the tragedy of war.
- Probability of success: This is not an expectation that we can predict the future but a reminder that if war is to be seen as a morally rational activity there must be a plausible expectation that the good(s) for which a war is fought are, in fact, obtainable. A reckless and foolhardy call to arms, even for the sake of a just cause, is ruled out by this criterion.
- Proportionality: When viewed under the *jus ad bellum* rubric this requires a judgment that the overall harm caused by war is proportionate to the good gained by armed conflict. Obviously as the devastation of war increases it becomes more difficult to satisfy this criterion.
- Proportionality: When seen under the heading of *jus in bello* this criterion means that the particular strategies, tactics, and individual actions employed in the conduct of war must be proportionate in terms of the

evil brought about in pursuit of the good. Even within a war that has satisfied the first seven criteria the means of fighting war can be unjust, for example, torturing prisoners of war as a way to gather military intelligence or using weapons that will cause long-term devastation of the environment.

- Discrimination: This final criterion proposes that some persons and places are not legitimate targets for attack. Deliberately attacking hospitals or shooting at civilians extends the range of war's damage beyond proper bounds. Even in war there are crimes, and denying to noncombatants immunity from direct attack is one of the clearest crimes.[79]

Although the just war tradition dominated Christianity, the pacifist tradition was never completely forsaken. The overwhelming spirit of the New Testament was understood as a message opposed to violence. Disciples in the earliest era of Christianity did not participate in the military or wage war. No persuasive evidence exists of Christians in the military until late in the second century.

Authors of the patristic era reflect an awareness that converts to the faith, including soldiers as well as others who might use armed violence, were not asked to give up their occupations. As noted earlier, shifts in the social roles of Christians also led to rethinking what love of neighbor might mean and whether violence could ever be justified. Still, writers such as Tertullian and Origen opposed Christians serving in the military. For these writers, the opposition to shedding blood was joined to a sense of Christian vocation so that, as in the case of Origen, a disciple should not be in the military even when there is an acknowledgment that some wars may be just. Whatever the actual practice of Christians, there are no arguments supporting Christians in the military to be found in writings prior to Constantine.

After Ambrose and Augustine, the pacifist witness of the church continued in the example of hermits, monks, and clerics who did not take up arms because of their personal understanding of Christian duties. This movement to a "vocational" pacifism permitted the great majority of Christians to wage war but prohibited small classes of disciples from serving in the military. It was part of a larger trend distinguishing between "higher" and "lower" states of life within the church.

Throughout the centuries, the nonparticipation in warfare by members of the clergy and religious orders reflected a residue of the idea that the violence of war was incompatible with gospel living. Francis of Assisi, in the beginning of the thirteenth century, called on the lay members of his movement to abstain from

---

79. U.S. Conference of Catholic Bishops, "The Challenge of Peace: God's Promise and Our Response" (May 3, 1983), 86-107. Available at http://old.usccb.org/sdwp/international/TheChallengeofPeace.pdf.

war and violence because of his belief that all Christians, not just an elite minority, were called to live the gospel ethic. The Franciscan example was not isolated because a variety of men and women in the medieval period saw opposition to war and the establishment of peace as a vital expression of their faith.[80]

Although Luther, Calvin, and other significant leaders of the reform did not adopt pacifism, their challenge to the idea of gospel perfectionism only for some and a less demanding way of life for the mass of Christians led to movements that placed nonviolence and pacifism at the center of a discipleship ethic. The reformers' emphasis on the biblical foundations for any true morality inspired movements, such as that of Menno Simons, who, along with other Anabaptists, formed churches, that continue into the present era to emphasize pacifism as a key dimension of Christian living.[81]

Catholic Theology and the Just War Tradition

Traditions encompass many possible theories. Just as there are many different understandings of Christ, or grace, or the church within the Christian tradition, so, too, there are many theories of just war within the just war tradition and many theories of pacifism within the pacifist tradition. Traditions are the genus and theories the species. To achieve clarity when discussing the just war or pacifist traditions, therefore, it is important to understand what unites the various theories into a tradition.

Essentially, the just war tradition makes three claims: (1) violence, though always regrettable, is not inherently or necessarily a moral wrong; (2) the harm caused by war's violence may be justified, at least in some cases, by an appeal to the goods protected or obtained by war; and (3) the use of armed force within war is a rule-governed activity because even war is subject to ethical assessment and governance. From the Christian perspective, standing behind these claims about violent force is a set of theologically informed judgments. These can be summarized under several headings.[82]

Eschatology
There is tension between our experience of the present and our hope for the establishment of the fullness of God's reign. Because the reign of God is not

---

80. For a brief overview of the variety of peace movements in the twelfth and thirteenth centuries, see Ronald Musto, *The Catholic Peace Tradition* (Maryknoll, NY: Orbis Books, 1986), 80-87.

81. The Mennonites, along with the Church of the Brethren and the Religious Society of Friends (Quakers), constitute what have traditionally been called the Peace Churches.

82. I have taken the headings, though not their exposition, from Charles Curran, "The New World Order and Military Force," *New Theology Review* 5 (1992): 5-18.

simply present but yet to be established, the harmony and peace longed for can be only partially experienced. There is a historical moment—one in which competition, conflict, and conquest occur—that places constraints on what can be achieved by those who long for the manifestation of God's reign on earth. The present moment tolerates a role for armed force in human affairs.

Violence ought not be simply identified with God's cause, however, because it increases human suffering and death. Because the establishment of God's reign is a firm hope, limits must be placed on the role of violence in human life. At times, violent force may appear to be a morally legitimate option, but it cannot be utilized as if the present situation is normative for Christian disciples. Believers should always find violence regrettable, even when necessary. It is necessary because of the limited possibilities available to those living in a situation that is not fully redeemed, and regrettable because the hope that spears will be transformed into plowshares is once more delayed.

Sin

That God's promised future is yet to be fully manifested is evident by the reality of sin in our midst. No theory of Christian ethics can ignore the sin dimension of our experience. Regardless of all attempts to overcome alienation, there remains enmity between people, and misunderstanding can overtake efforts at cooperation. Genuine communion among peoples is not easily or readily attained. Despite humanity's fervent hope and desire for peace the innocent are still attacked and still suffer at the hands of wrongdoers. The cries of these suffering innocents pose the challenge of what must be done to resist evildoers who prey on their victims.

Even those who countenance self-sacrifice and nonviolence when under personal attack are given pause when called on to decide what ought to be done when innocent third parties are involved. For many persons the obligations of neighbor love give rise to a sense that counterforce may be employed to protect those who are incapable of protecting themselves. Resistance to the sin of those people who employ violence wrongfully can lead to consideration of whether counterviolence may ever be employed rightly.

Ecclesiology

A third element in the theological background to the just war tradition is an ecclesiology that posits the church must accept some responsibility for the promotion and protection of temporal aspects of common good. The mission of the church is to serve as a sacrament of God's reign. It is not possible to signify the fullness of God's reign, however, if the church restricts its mission to some "religious" sector apart from the rest of human life.

It is improper to describe God's reign in a manner suggesting that the embodied, historical person is not saved but only a disembodied soul. The religious mission of the church extends to the realms of politics, economics, and culture. This is not because the church has a direct mission to these areas but because of its committed witness to the universality of God's grace and power.[83] No realm of creation is left untouched by the transformative grace of God, and this entails the entire range of those goods that constitute human betterment. The church must not be indifferent to those temporal goods listed in declarations of human rights.

Ethical Theory

Catholic moral theology has never set human life as the highest value of all. The honor accorded to martyrs who died for the sake of their faith shows that from the beginning of the church's life other values counted for more than the preservation of life. The Catholic moral tradition is a complex scheme of valuation that has resisted absolutizing any value other than the *summum bonum*, the highest good, of union with God.

In particular, the value of peace has never been accorded as an absolute value. This is certainly true when peace is understood in the minimalist sense of the absence of violence. Traditionally, Catholic teaching maintains that peace requires more than "merely the absence of war." For peace "is rightly and appropriately called 'an enterprise of justice.'"[84] When peace is understood properly, and not as the absence of violence, it is no contradiction to state that war can be fought in the name of peace. Rather, the outbreak of armed violence can be understood as an effort to establish a true peace in a situation where injustice prevails.

Even with the above theological background for a theory of the just war, Christians must remember that few things can skew the moral deliberations of a community more than ignoring the experience of those harmed by the decisions of the group. If the community of disciples continues to employ the just war tradition as a framework for assessing the legitimacy of war it must respect the experience of war's victims, their pain, suffering, and death. As an exercise of practical reason, the debate over just war must confront the harsh reality of war's effects.

Pacifism and the Catholic Tradition

Modern wars are different than in the past, and one of the dramatic differences is their effect on civilians. In World War I the percentage of casualties who were civilians was 5 percent. In World War II that percentage rose to 50 percent. In the Vietnam conflict the figure rose even higher to 80 percent. In more recent

---

83. *Gaudium et spes*, nos. 40–42; see chap. 9 for more extended commentary on the role of the church in secular life.

84. Ibid., no. 78 (quoting Isaiah 32:7).

conflicts of the past decades, 85 percent to 95 percent of war's victims were civilians.[85] No discussion of just war principles can ignore such dismal realities.[86]

Behind these statistics is the human face of the tragedy. Thousands of children have witnessed brutality against their parents, siblings, and neighbors. Millions of children have themselves been the victims of war. In some places a generation of youth has been traumatized by the experience of war in ways that shall only be discovered in the future. Also disturbing is the use of child soldiers, pressed to take up arms to fight in causes they cannot possibly understand and who then play the role of victimizer as well as victim. Untold numbers of women have been raped and beaten, as well as having lost husbands and children in war. Yet one more sad facet of modern warfare is the huge number of war refugees, a number that often does not include the internal displacement of persons forced to flee a combat area.

In the twentieth century, the experience of war and the devastation it causes presented a challenge to just war thinking and an impetus to those who opposed warfare. When the Catholic bishops met at Vatican II they called for "an evaluation of war with an entirely new attitude."[87] This new attitude did not mean outright condemnation of all war but the adoption of a different vantage point when assessing war. Starting with John XXIII and continuing through the papacies of Paul VI, John Paul II, and Benedict XVI, a teaching developed "that a presumption against war lies at the very center of Catholic thinking on war and peace."[88]

Whereas earlier theories of just war saw a presumption for justice, with war understood as a moral means to establish justice, the newer formulation of the church's teaching holds for a moral presumption against war. The "new attitude" called for at Vatican II sees war within the modern context of its destructive power and has led the church to voice much stronger opposition to resorting to war, while affirming a commitment to developing alternative ways of securing true peace.

The opposition to war grew in strength with the experience of twentieth-century wars. Some of those who have adopted the "new attitude" have challenged the idea that the moral presumption against war can ever be overcome,

---

85. Caritas Internationalis, *Working for Reconciliation: A Caritas Handbook* (Vatican City, 1999), 1. Available at: http://www.caritas.org/upload/wkg/wkgreconc.pdf.

86. Two recent works by social scientists have offered compelling evidence of the widespread suffering of civilians in warfare and formulated theories to understand the phenomenon and ways to mitigate it. See Daniel Rothbart and Karina Korostelina, *Why They Die* (Ann Arbor: University of Michigan Press, 2011); and John Tirman, *The Deaths of Others* (New York: Oxford University Press, 2011).

87. *Gaudium et spes*, no. 80.

88. Robert McElroy, "Why We Must Withdraw from Iraq," *America* 196, no. 15 (April 30, 2007): 10-14 at 11.

given the evils brought on by warfare. Early in the twentieth century the word "pacifism" was coined for the stance of "anti-warism."[89] The term pacifism can be a source of confusion since it is employed to denote a wide array of positions regarding the morality of armed force. In some circles pacifism is equated with nonviolence, a broader reality. In its original meaning of being antiwar, pacifism does not address violent acts by a domestic police force or violence in a situation of personal self-defense.[90]

Understood in one way it is inadequate that a person simply oppose war in order to be a pacifist. The objection to war must be on the grounds of moral principle, not simply pragmatic judgment nor because of inconvenience, cowardice, political opportunism, or distaste for bloodshed. Pacifism entails the view that war is to be opposed because of the immoral nature of armed conflict between states.

The most noteworthy aspect of Catholic teaching regarding pacifism is the development that has taken place in modern times. As recently as 1956, Pius XII stated that a Catholic could not cite conscientious disagreement with the legitimate leaders of a state as a reason to refuse participation in war. In this he echoed the views of his recent predecessors. In 1965, however, the bishops at Vatican II wrote, "We cannot fail to praise those who renounce the use of violence in the vindication of their rights and who resort to methods of defense which are otherwise available to weaker parties too, provided that this can be done without injury to the rights and duties of others or of the community itself."[91]

As with the just war tradition, the pacifist tradition also has many theories about why a person ought to oppose all war. Because Roman Catholic teaching approves of pacifism, it cannot be assumed that any or all theories of pacifism are thereby endorsed. The pacifism of Catholic teaching is of a particular sort.

In Part I of *Gaudium et spes* there is a profound concern expressed for the dignity of individual conscience both in the religious and the civic realms. The approval of pacifism later in the document fits with the Council's emphasis on the dignity of conscience.[92] With the rise of the limited constitutional state and the sad experience of abusive state power in fascism, Nazism, and communism, the bishops wanted to endorse the freedom of individual conscience before the state.

What the bishops affirmed was the right of the individual to refuse participation in war on the basis of personal conscience. At the same time, the

---

89. Jenny Teichman, *Pacifism and the Just War* (Oxford: Basil Blackwell, 1986), 1.

90. Ibid.

91. *Gaudium et spes*, no. 78.

92. The key passage for the treatment of conscience in *Gaudium et spes* is paragraph 16.

bishops maintained that states have a right to use armed force in national self-defense. Thus, the approval of pacifism was more in deference to the conscience of the person than a result of a conciliar preference for pacifism over just war as an ethical theory.

Pacifism within Catholic teaching must be placed in a context of concern for justice and human rights. A pacifist may not be indifferent to the "rights and duties of others or of the community itself." Thus, pacifism in this perspective cannot be equated with nonresistance. All Christians must defend the cause of justice, must protect human rights, must resist evil. Individuals may differ on the matter of how that is to be done, and the pacifist may seek methods other than war in order to resist evil and promote the good.

At Vatican II the bishops also declared, "It seems right that laws make humane provisions for the case of those who for reasons of conscience refuse to bear arms, provided that they accept some other form of service to the human community."[93] The conciliar text was addressed to the makers of public policy. The bishops proposed that laws be passed allowing for conscientious objection to military service but affirmed that the duty of the individual to serve the common good remains and ought to be fulfilled in another way.

Alternative service is a duty correlative with the right of the conscientious objector to dissent from the nation's decision to engage in war. The requirement of alternative service reveals that pacifism within Catholic teaching is not a "higher" or "purer" calling. Rather, it is a right of individual conscience that necessitates an expression of good faith on the part of the individual and a willingness to contribute to the nation's struggle against injustice in some way.[94] The presumption is that the nation is just in resisting the evil of aggression and that all citizens have an obligation to contribute to that effort even if not all are required to bear arms. Both pacifism and just war have the same goal, the preservation of a just social order, which is the foundation for true peace.

This understanding of pacifism in the Catholic tradition means that it is committed not only to the abolition of war but to the establishment of an authentic peace. Pacifism is not an expression of sectarian withdrawal by Christians who do not value the secular order, nor may pacifism be founded on a dismissal of the state's right to self-defense. In these matters, Catholic pacifism will differ with certain strands of Protestant ecclesiology or radical countercultural movements that support anarchical political theories.

---

93. Ibid., no. 79.

94. Rene Coste, "Commentary on Part II, Chapter V," in *Commentary on the Documents of Vatican II*, vol. 5, ed. Herbert Vorgrimler (New York: Herder & Herder, 1969), 354.

In sum, Catholic teaching on pacifism makes three claims: (1) pacifism is an option that individuals may choose based on sincere belief that war is incompatible with Christian discipleship; (2) pacifism requires a clear commitment to resist injustice and a desire to promote human rights and the common good; and (3) pacifism is based on the freedom of the person and the right of individual conscience. It is not a duty for all but a legitimate option for those who discern a moral calling to oppose war.

PEACE AND PEACEBUILDING

The Christian tradition does not always have the same understanding of a word as the popular usage. A good example of that is the word "peace." For most Americans, peace is what you have when the shooting stops. Peace is what exists when you do not have war. That understanding, however, is not what the Christian tradition means by peace. Peace is best understood not in a negative way, as the absence of war, but in a positive sense, as the creation and promotion of a particular vision of communal life. This positive sense draws on the writings of both Scripture and the patristic era.

In Hebrew the word for peace is *shalom*, and this term encompasses far more than the absence of violence. *Shalom* refers to a community experiencing a full and rich life. *Shalom* is a state of abundance wherein all the members of the community are able to enter into a shared life that is materially adequate, spiritually rich, and relationally satisfying. When people live together in fidelity to the covenant between God and God's people, and they know the blessings of God's generosity, then they are said to live in peace (*shalom*).

New Testament writings present peace as a dimension of the reign of God. Peace is God's gift to us through the ministry of Jesus who regularly wishes peace as a greeting to his disciples and urges them to use it in the same way as they go forth into the world (Luke 10:1-9). Peace is a gracious outcome when the followers of Jesus live in accord with the values and norms of the reign of God.

So, for the biblical authors, the experience of peace entails far more than putting down one's weapons; it requires building up a community that offers its members a richly rewarding taste of divine blessing and human well-being.

Early church writers such as St. Augustine carry forward the positive sense of peace. He employs the Latin word *pax*, or "peace," in one or another form over 2,500 times in his writings.[95] There are several aspects of Augustine's understanding of peace that merit notice.

---

95. Donald X. Burt, O.S.A., "Peace," in *Augustine through the Ages: An Encyclopedia*, ed. Allan Fitzgerald, O.S.A. (Grand Rapids, MI: Eerdmans, 1999), 629.

First, peace is multidimensional. There is the peace that can be called eschatological, related to the final end of humankind in enjoyment of life with God. This eternal peace is beyond the reach of temporal life and human achievement. The peace that is available to humanity in this life also has its origin and destiny in God. It has, however, been corrupted due to sin and as such retains a weakened connection to the first kind of peace. Yet it is real, and it is a blessing when attained in earthly existence.

This earthly peace, discussed in book XIX of *The City of God*, is what Augustine calls "civil peace."[96] It is a particular incarnation of the form of all peace, namely, *tranquillitas ordinis*. The "tranquility of order" is attained when there is a proper ordering of each part in relation to the whole. Thus, there is a peace of the individual, of the family, of the city, and of the world. When one achieves civil peace the citizens of the political community are in right relation with one another as well as with the subunits that make up the community and the higher units of which the community is a part. There is a right order existing between family, city, state, and, ultimately, God.

Temporal peace includes material and historical goods such as food, shelter, safety, and security. For Augustine, the aim of any war is peace, to restore a measure of right order within the human community when this has been disturbed. The goal of such peace is to permit human community to develop and flourish.

In the biblical and Augustinian texts we can see certain aspects of the Catholic view of peace that continue in the development of the tradition right to the present time.

- Peace is understood as a positive reality, entailing the establishment of justice and right order in and between societies.
- Peace is a universal human desire and is more fundamental than either war or violence. Humans are capable of peace and war is not inevitable, even if conflict is.
- There can be a false peace. The mere absence of violence is not peace since there may still be serious injustice in a society and an oppressive fear that cannot be equated with genuine peace.
- Because peace is not simply the absence of violence it is not self-contradictory to speak of fighting for peace. Peace may require the use of violent force in order to establish justice and resist aggression.
- War cannot create peace. At best, war can be employed as a means of removing obstacles to peace, but war cannot of itself create the tranquility of order that is true peace.

---

96. Augustine, *The City of God* (New York: Modern Library Classics, 2000), bk. XIX, chap. 13.

Contemporary Catholic Teaching on Peace

At Vatican II, in 1965, the bishops proclaimed that peace is the work of justice. They also declared, "Peace results from that harmony built into human society by its divine Founder, and actualized by persons as they thirst after ever greater justice."[97] One sees in their comments not only the communitarian perspective of justice found in the Bible but also the Augustinian theme of an order of tranquility that eventuates from harmonious relationships.

Two years later, Paul VI put it this way: "peace is something that is built up day after day, in the pursuit of an order intended by God, which implies a more perfect form of justice" among persons.[98] In other words, peace in the political realm was not simply a blessing from God but a task that was to be undertaken by human beings. Peace could be actualized as people of good will worked to create a more just social order.

It is within this framework that one can properly interpret Paul VI's famous statement that "Development Is the New Name for Peace."[99] During the decade of the 1960s, there were competing theories of development as well as a growing disenchantment with the word itself, as the residents of poor nations found that many initial hopes for development were dashed. Catholic social teaching began to place modifiers in front of the word "development" to distinguish the church's viewpoint from other perspectives deemed less adequate.

Paul often used the expression "integral development" to express the conviction that development cannot be reduced simply to economic advancement; other aspects of human existence—cultural, political, psychological, religious—had to be included in any satisfactory understanding of genuine development.[100] Especially important for Catholic social teaching was that any theory of development worthy of the name had to address the stubborn resistance of social structures that hindered the genuine advancement of people toward a better life. Justice was seen as the key virtue when discussing this need for social transformation.

Linking development and justice revealed the moral dimension of development. Economies might expand, but distribution of the benefits of such growth may be heavily skewed toward an elite. Authentic development must lead to a widely shared participation in the benefits of any economic and social progress. Justice demands the creation of a social system that promotes the

---

97. *Gaudium et spes*, no. 78.
98. *Progressio populorum*, no. 76.
99. Ibid. The phrase is the subtitle of Part II, section 4.
100. Ibid., no. 21.

common good and secures each person's right and ability both to contribute to, and benefit from, the common good.

This way of thinking in modern Catholic social teaching led to the idea that both justice and development were "placeholder" terms for political peace. There can be no *tranquillitas ordinis* without justice, and the particular shape of justice needed in our time is just development. Only by promoting the well-being of the millions trapped in crushing poverty throughout the world can there be a realistic hope for peace. Peace built on military or economic power may be a "peace of a sort," but it is not the Catholic understanding of political peace. For Catholic social teaching the surer path to peace in our world is just development.

Further, solidarity serves as the motivating energy that fosters a desire to work for truly just development by establishing proper national and international practices, policies, and institutions. Twenty years after Paul VI issued *Populorum progressio*, John Paul II wrote that solidarity is "the path to peace and at the same time to development." For the pope, solidarity, as noted earlier, is the virtue that allows us "to see the 'other'—whether a *person, people, or nation*—. . . as our 'neighbor,' a 'helper,' to be made a sharer, on a par with ourselves, in the banquet of life. . . ."[101] True peace will emerge from this work of solidarity in the pursuit of just development. "The goal of peace, so desired by everyone, will certainly be achieved through the putting into effect of social and international justice, but also through the practice of the virtues which favor togetherness, and which teach us to live in unity. . . ."[102]

To sum up the papal vision, peace is the outcome of a committed engagement (solidarity) to the project of social progress for individuals and societies (just development). Paul VI promoted this understanding by his linkage of development and justice as new terms for peace. John Paul II, while echoing Paul's viewpoint, emphasized solidarity as the crucial step in working for justice. Solidarity is the path to development, and peace is the end result of working for development that is just.

A New Emphasis

When one reflects on the multiple developments in Catholic thought on war and peace, it is easy to see why the Catholic tradition has become more and more interested in what is called peacebuilding. The just war tradition has focused on war avoidance or war limitation, and the pacifist tradition on opposition to war. Peacebuilding takes a different tack, and focuses attention on

---

101. *Sollicitudo rei socialis*, no. 39.
102. Ibid.

conditions for creating peace. It presumes, in agreement with the Catholic tradition, that peace is something positive, not simply the absence of violence. In its positive sense, strategies to establish peace and advance its maturation need to be devised and promoted.

Although Catholic social teaching does not focus on peacebuilding expressly, peacebuilding is implied whenever Catholic teaching talks about just development. The multiple levels of development demand that peacebuilding be understood broadly. Indeed, while some in the policy community identify several distinct tasks, the Catholic tradition stresses the way that the different tasks are related modes of working for peace and not separate stages hermetically sealed off from one another.

First, there is the realm of what can be called prevention, that is, identifying situations that might produce conflict and then through diplomacy removing the sources of violence before it erupts. A second concern entails peacemaking, efforts to resolve issues that have already led to conflict. Yet another task is peacekeeping, working to preserve fragile ceasefires or interim solutions in order to create space for implementing agreed-upon measures to achieve a lasting change in tense relations. And, finally, there is building peace by means of renewing institutions and infrastructure destroyed by war, encouraging actions of mutual benefit to opposing groups, and addressing the larger cause of conflict found in economic, social, and political injustice.

The "four Ps" of prevention, peacemaking, peacekeeping, and peacebuilding were given further clarification in a United Nations report issued in 1992. There one finds terms defined this way:

> Preventive diplomacy is action to prevent disputes from arising between parties, to prevent existing disputes from escalating into conflicts and to limit the spread of the latter when they occur.

> Peacemaking is action to bring hostile parties to agreement, essentially through such peaceful means as those foreseen in Chapter VI of the Charter of the United Nations.

> Peacekeeping is the deployment of a United Nations presence in the field, hitherto with the consent of all the parties concerned, normally involving United Nations military and/or police personnel and frequently civilians as well.[103]

> Peacebuilding, according to a separate paragraph in the report, is a "concept" that is "critically related" to the above terms; it is understood to address "post-conflict" issues including "action to identify and support structures

---

103. Boutros Boutros Ghali, *An Agenda for Peace* (New York: United Nations, 1992), no. 20.

which will tend to strengthen and solidify peace in order to avoid a relapse into conflict."[104]

Simply put, peacebuilding follows upon successful efforts at preventive diplomacy, peacemaking, and peacekeeping; it is aimed at halting recurrence of violence. This way of understanding peacebuilding, as a distinct and separate stage, is but one way that the term is often used.

Besides the UN-influenced usage, many workers in NGOs use another, more inclusive version of peacebuilding. This second understanding proposes that peacebuilding subsumes peacemaking and peacekeeping. "In this view, peacebuilding includes early warning and response efforts, violence prevention, advocacy work, civilian and military peacekeeping, military intervention, humanitarian assistance, ceasefire agreements, and the establishment of peace zones."[105] This broader sense is closer to how Catholic activists and theorists use the term. Peacebuilding embraces both short- and longer-term strategies aimed at transforming existing situations that either may lead to violent conflict or have already resulted in such conflict.

At the hierarchical level of the Catholic Church, the Holy See has tended to focus on preventive diplomacy. Various conferences of bishops as well as individual bishops have also offered to assist in mediating disputes and peacemaking. The work of the episcopacy of Guatemala is one example of a sustained effort at peacemaking during that country's civil war and subsequent civil unrest. Bishops Oscar Romero of El Salvador, Laurent Monsengwo of the Democratic Republic of Congo, Samuel Ruiz of Mexico, and Carlos Belo of East Timor are individual church leaders who have been widely hailed for their efforts at bringing peace and reconciliation to violent societies.

It is in the area of peacebuilding, however, where the wider church membership has been most visible and engaged. Many church-related organizations work at peacebuilding through advocacy, fundraising support, service projects, microlending, offering expertise and material resources. The largest of these organizations, Catholic Relief Services, has been involved all over the globe in a wide array of projects that help heal and rebuild societies ravaged by violent conflict.. These efforts are led by lay professionals and involve salaried and volunteer workers in dozens of countries who dispense funds provided by the U.S. government as well as money raised in local American congregations. The church's involvement in the work of peacebuilding goes far beyond preaching and teaching the message of peace to include "walking the walk" as well as "talking the talk."

---

104. Ibid., no. 21.

105. Michelle Maiese, "What It Means to Build a Lasting Peace," posted on Beyond Intractability.org (www.beyondintractability.org/essay/peacebuilding) in September 2003.

Clearly, a process of development has been under way in Catholic thinking about peace. Building on the ancient wisdom of the Scriptures and the patristic writers, there has been further reflection on the nature of justice as it leads to peace. Finally, the new emphasis on peacebuilding, which hearkens back to the traditional claim that peace is positive and not simply the absence of violence, gives additional evidence that Catholic teaching continues to evolve.

QUESTIONS FOR DISCUSSION/REFLECTION

1. What issues on the global agenda do you consider the most significant for the Christian community to address?
2. Can you provide a working definition of globalization? On balance do you consider globalization good or bad?
3. What "ethical coordinates" or guideposts do you think of as most important for the future development of globalization?
4. What is the "democratic deficit" in globalization? What can Christian churches do to remedy the problem?
5. How can subsidiarity be understood at the level of global governance?
6. What do we mean by human rights? Has the language of rights evolved over the centuries? In what ways?
7. How does Catholic social teaching understand human rights? How did Paul VI and John Paul II differ in their approaches to formulating the social teaching?
8. How does the teaching on human rights function as a political strategy for church activity?
9. What was the early church's attitude toward violence and war? How do you understand the teaching of the Sermon on the Mount? Why do you think the teaching evolved as it did in the first few centuries?
10. What is the just war tradition? What is the meaning of pacifism? How would you describe the strong points of both traditions?
11. What is meant by peace in the Christian tradition? What is meant by the contemporary term "peacebuilding"?

Conclusion

Empires rise and fall; monarchs come and go; popes and prophets appear on the scene and then disappear; politicians have a brief hold on power and then find how contingent is their place in the march of time. Through all of the centuries there are men and women, some known to us and more who are anonymous, who have done their best to live their faith in a morally serious way. One aspect of their effort is that they entered the political arena and made choices about how to build a good society.

There is no doubt that Christians have from the earliest days in the life of the church distinguished between the spiritual and the temporal realms of existence. History demonstrates that terrible abuses have occurred when the distinction between temporal and spiritual orders was ignored. Be it royal absolutists of the sixteenth and seventeenth centuries, papal absolutists of the medieval era, or totalitarian regimes of the twentieth century, those who collapse the distinction have taken both church and state down perilous paths. On the other hand, those who have turned the distinction into an impassable divide have fundamentally misunderstood Christianity's incarnational character. This latter error may also deny to political life the insights available from one of the great wisdom traditions within the human family.

If the vital distinction, but not unbreachable divide, between Christianity and political life must be preserved there is still the complex task of maintaining a proper balance within the relationship. This volume provides ample evidence that Christians throughout the ages have proposed multiple approaches in pursuit of getting the relationship right. From the perspective of history, the fairly recent experiment of the United States with its constitutional arrangement can be seen as a significant effort to fashion a normative framework for striking the proper balance. Of course, the framework has not settled the question, as numerous Supreme Court decisions testify; but it has provided a structure for the ongoing discussion.

History provides awful examples of the political order corrupted and the Christian faith debased by failed formulas for relating Christianity and temporal politics. Christians who have been less than sincere in their profession of faith or who were simply misguided about their religious beliefs and/or the political realities before them have made choices that will scandalize any reader of history. That is one of the lessons to be learned from the story of Christianity and the political order.

There have also been marvelous incidents where Christians have worked for justice, mercy, compassion, peace, and reconciliation in the political realm.

As in the past, so, too, in the present, despite much crassness and misunderstanding in relating the two spheres, there is much good being done by people of faith who use political power and employ political institutions to serve the common good at local, national, and global levels. That also is a lesson to be remembered from the story of Christianity and the political order.

With this book I have sought to blend historical narration and textual analysis along with theological and ethical reflection in order to study the relationship of Christianity and the political order. For example, several key biblical texts that have had great influence throughout the centuries were examined so that the foundations of the Christian tradition might be better understood.

Through an examination of select events, institutions, and persons this book presents a story of the development of the Christian tradition's engagement with the realm of politics. That story necessarily involved far more than the logical unfolding of ideas, for the important developments reflect the contingent nature of history in which unique and specific individuals, locales, institutions, and societies determine the course of events. Without any claim to comprehensiveness, this book focused on a few of the key actors and circumstances that profoundly shaped the evolution of Christianity's involvement with temporal politics and explained to some degree how we have arrived at the present state of affairs.

The third and final part of this book treats four topics that sketch the contemporary shape of perennial concerns in the relationship of Christianity and politics. Because the state is the most important institution in political life a chapter was devoted to discussing how the Christian tradition, particularly Catholic Christianity, viewed the state. Another chapter presented a theological rationale for why the church's interaction with political life is not to be treated as optional or of no religious significance. Rather, the case was made that the Christian community has a proper and vital role in the temporal order, including political life. Finally, two chapters offered an overview of topics in domestic U.S. politics and in international politics that have been a concern for Christians as political actors.

Of course, the vast expanse of issues that could be treated under the heading of Christianity and politics makes the process of writing a book such as this an exercise that forces an author to be aware of all that has not been included in these pages. What can be offered by explanation is the acknowledgment that the author's personal commitment to Catholic Christianity as well as professional experience of teaching for more than three decades has influenced the selection and treatment of material. Despite my limitations it is my hope that this presentation of *Christianity and the Political Order* offers readers a helpful perspective for understanding how Christians have thought about and interacted with the political order.

Select Bibliography

CHAPTER 1

Bellin, Eva. "Faith in Politics: New Trends in the Study of Religion and Politics." *World Politics* 60 (January 2008): 315-47.

Casanova, Jose. *Public Religions in the Modern World.* Chicago: University of Chicago Press, 1994.

Congregation for the Doctrine of the Faith. "Doctrinal Note on Some Questions Regarding the Participation of Catholics in Political Life." November 24, 2002.

Hehir, J. Bryan. "Why Religion? Why Now?" In *Rethinking Religion and World Affairs.* Edited by Timothy Shah, Alfred Stepan, and Monica Toft, 15-24. New York: Oxford University Press, 2012.

Vatican II. *Gaudium et spes* (Pastoral Constitution on the Church in the Modern World), 1965.

CHAPTER 2

Birch, Bruce. *Let Justice Roll Down: The Old Testament, Ethics, and Christian Life.* Louisville: Westminster/John Knox Press, 1991.

Heschel, Abraham Joshua. *The Prophets*, vol. 1. New York: Harper & Row, 1962.

Machinist, Peter. "Hosea and the Ambiguity of Kingship in Ancient Israel." In *Constituting the Community: Studies on the Polity of Ancient Israel in Honor of S. Dean McBride, Jr.* Edited by John Strong and Steven Tuell, 153-81. Winona Lake, IN: Eisenbrauns, 2005.

Roberts, J. J. M. "In Defense of the Monarchy: The Contribution of Israelite Kingship to Biblical Theology." In *The Bible and the Ancient Near East: Collected Essays*, 358-75. Winona Lake, IN: Eisenbrauns, 2002.

———. "The Davidic Origin of the Zion Tradition." In *The Bible and the Ancient Near East: Collected Essays*, 313-30. Winona Lake, IN: Eisenbrauns, 2002.

CHAPTER 3

Bruce, F. F. "Render to Caesar." In *Jesus and the Politics of His Day.* Edited by Ernst Bammel and C. F. D. Moule, 249-63. Cambridge: Cambridge University Press, 1984.

Bryan, Christopher. *Render to Caesar.* Oxford: Oxford University Press, 2005.

Matera, Frank. *New Testament Ethics: The Legacies of Jesus and Paul.* Louisville: Westminster John Knox Press, 1996.

Pilgrim, Walter. *Uneasy Neighbors.* Minneapolis: Fortress Press, 1999.

Schrage, Wolfgang. *The Ethics of the New Testament*. Philadelphia: Fortress Press, 1988.

Tolbert, Mary Ann. *Sowing the Gospel: Mark's World in Literary-Historical Perspective.* Minneapolis: Fortress Press, 1989.

CHAPTER 4

Augustine. *City of God*. Edited by David Knowles. Translated by Henry Bettenson. New York: Pelican Classics, 1972.

Chadwick, Henry. *The Early Church*. New York: Penguin Books, 1967.

Dyson, Robert. *St. Augustine of Hippo: The Christian Transformation of Political Philosophy*. New York: Continuum, 2005.

Meeks, Wayne. *The First Urban Christians*. New Haven: Yale University Press, 1984.

Oakley, Francis. *Kingship*. Malden, MA: Blackwell Publishing, 2006.

O'Donovan, Oliver, and Joan Lockwood O'Donovan, eds. *From Irenaeus to Grotius: A Sourcebook in Christian Political Thought*. Grand Rapids, MI: Eerdmans, 1999.

Stark, Rodney. *The Rise of Christianity*. Princeton, NJ: Princeton University Press, 1996.

CHAPTER 5

Canning, Joseph. *A History of Medieval Political Thought 300-1450*. London: Routledge, 1996.

Oakley, Francis. *Kingship*. Malden, MA: Blackwell Publishing, 2006.

O'Donovan, Oliver, and Joan Lockwood O'Donovan, eds. *From Irenaeus to Grotius: A Sourcebook in Christian Political Thought*. Grand Rapids, MI: Eerdmans, 1999.

Sabine, George. *A History of Political Theory*. 4th ed. Revised by Thomas Thorson. Hinsdale, IL: Dryden Press, 1973.

Tierney, Brian. *The Crisis of Church and State, 1050-1300*. Englewood Cliffs, NJ: Prentice-Hall, 1964.

CHAPTER 6

Calvin, John. *Institutes of the Christian Religion*. Edited by John McNeill. Philadelphia: Westminster Press, 1960.

McKim, Donald, ed. *The Cambridge Companion to Martin Luther*. Cambridge: Cambridge University Press, 2003.

————. *The Cambridge Companion to John Calvin*. Cambridge: Cambridge University Press, 2004.

Porter, J. M. "The Political Thought of Martin Luther." In *Luther: Selected Political Writings*. Edited by J. M. Porter, 1-21. Philadelphia: Fortress, 1974.

Shepherd, John. "The European Background of American Freedom." *Journal of Church and State* 50 (2008): 647-59.

Williams, George Hunston. "Introduction." In *Spiritual and Anabaptist Writers*. Edited by George Hunston Williams and Angel Mergal, 19-38. The Library of Christian Classics 25. Philadelphia: Westminster Press, 1957.

CHAPTER 7

Brown, Stewart, and Timothy Tackett, eds. *Enlightenment, Reawakening and Revolution 1660-1815.* The Cambridge History of Christianity 7. Cambridge: Cambridge University Press, 2006.

Burleigh, Michael. *Earthly Powers.* New York: HarperCollins, 2005.

Coffey, John, and Paul Lim, eds. *The Cambridge Companion to Puritanism.* Cambridge: Cambridge University Press, 2008.

O'Brien, David. *Public Catholicism.* New York: Macmillan, 1989.

Vidler, Alex. *The Church in an Age of Revolution.* The Penguin History of the Church 5. London: Penguin Books, 1990.

CHAPTER 8

Calvez, Jean-Yves, and Jacques Perrin. *The Church and Social Justice.* Chicago: Henry Regnery, 1961.

Camp, Richard. *The Papal Ideology of Social Reform.* Leiden: E. J. Brill, 1969.

Curran, Charles. "Just Taxation in the Roman Catholic Tradition." *Journal of Religious Ethics* 13, no. 1 (1985): 113-33.

Hollenbach, David. *The Common Good and Christian Ethics.* New York: Cambridge University Press, 2002.

Miller, David. *Political Philosophy: A Very Short Introduction.* Oxford: Oxford University Press, 2003.

Niebuhr, Reinhold. *The Children of Light and the Children of Darkness.* New York: Charles Scribner's Sons, 1944.

Rommen, Henri. *The State in Catholic Social Teaching.* St. Louis: Herder Book Company, 1945.

Vatican II. *Gaudium et spes* (Pastoral Constitution on the Church in the Modern World), 1965.

Wogaman, J. Philip. *Christian Perspectives on Politics.* Revised edition. Louisville: Westminster John Knox Press, 2000.

CHAPTER 9

Marty, Martin. *The Public Church.* New York: Crossroad, 1981.

McBrien, Richard. *The Church: The Evolution of Catholicism.* New York: HarperCollins, 2008.

Vatican II. *Lumen Gentium* (Dogmatic Constitution on the Church), 1965.

———. *Gaudium et spes* (Pastoral Constitution on the Church in the Modern World), 1965.

———. *Dignitatis humanae* (Decree on Religious Liberty), 1965.

CHAPTER 10

Cochran, Clark E., and David C. Cochran. *The Catholic Vote: A Guide for the Perplexed.* Maryknoll, NY: Orbis Books, 2008.

Congregation for the Doctrine of the Faith. "Doctrinal Note on Some Questions Regarding the Participation of Catholics in Political Life." November 24, 2002.

de Tocqueville, Alexis. *Democracy in America.* Edited and translated by Harvey Mansfield and Delba Winthrop. Chicago: University of Chicago Press, 2000.

Massaro, Thomas. "Catholic Bishops and Politicians: Concerns about Recent Developments." *Josephinum Journal of Theology* 12, no. 2 (2005): 268-87.

United States Conference of Catholic Bishops. *Forming Consciences for Faithful Citizenship.* Washington, DC: United States Conference of Catholic Bishops, 2011.

CHAPTER 11

Cahill, Lisa Sowle. *Love Your Enemies.* Minneapolis: Fortress Press, 1994.

———. "Globalization and the Common Good." In *Globalization and Catholic Social Thought.* Edited by John Coleman and William Ryan, 42-54. Maryknoll, NY: Orbis Books, 2005.

Coleman, John. "Making the Connections: Globalization and Catholic Social Thought." In *Globalization and Catholic Social Thought.* Edited by John Coleman and William Ryan, 9-27. Maryknoll, NY: Orbis Books, 2005.

Cooper, Richard, and Joseph Nye, Jr. "Ethics and Foreign Policy." In *Global Affairs.* Edited by Samuel Huntington and Joseph Nye, Jr., 23-41. Lanham, MD: University Press of America, 1985.

Groody, Daniel. *Globalization, Spirituality, and Justice.* Maryknoll, NY: Orbis Books, 2007.

Hollenbach, David. *Claims in Conflict: Retrieving and Renewing the Catholic Human Rights Tradition.* New York: Paulist Press, 1979.

———. *The Common Good and Christian Ethics.* New York: Cambridge University Press, 2002.

Huntington, Samuel. "Religion and the Third Wave." *National Interest* 24 (Summer 1991): 29-42.

Jeremias, Joachim. *The Sermon on the Mount.* Philadelphia: Fortress Press, 1963.

Rahner, Karl. "Towards a Fundamental Theological Interpretation of Vatican II." *Theological Studies* 40, no. 4 (1979): 716-27.

Index

abortion, 8, 9, 275, 284, 285, 286
  and Catholic politicians, 282
  and single-issue voting, 265, 266
  and U.S. bishops, 9
absolutist rule, 153, 154, 155
Act of Supremacy, 140, 141, 144, 167
Act of Uniformity, 167
actual sin, 248
African-American religious leaders, and
  civil rights struggle, 255
African Union, 13
Althusius, Johannes, 134
Ambrose of Milan, 65-68, 82, 97, 281
  conflict with Auxentius, 66, 67
  on relation of church and state, 65-68
American Revolution, and Christianity,
  166, 167
Anabaptists, 144, 145, 146, 147
  and pacifist tradition, 325
anarchy, in Aquinas, 103
Anglicanism, 140-44, 167, 168
anti–Vietnam War movement, 263
Apostolicam actuositatem (Decree on the
  Apostolate of the Laity), 236, 237
Aquinas, Thomas 112
  and forms of governance, 102-4
  and just war tradition, 322
  and need for the state, 203
  on papal and kingly power, 104
  political ideas of, 101-4
  on relation of law and morality, 277,
  278
  support for papacy, 104
  use of Aristotle, 101, 102
Aristotle, 101, 102, 109, 112, 113
  and politics, 3
Ark of the Covenant, 22
arms race, 285

Attila, 84
Augustine, 97, 101, 122, 136, 226
  on church and state, 68-78, 82
  defense of Christianity, 69-71
  and just war tradition, 321, 322
  on peace, 331, 332
  and political life, 71-75
Augustinianism, political, 77-78, 113
authority
  in Calvin, 129
  God as source of, 48, 50, 51, 52, 74,
  75, 83, 86, 87, 97, 119, 202
  legitimate, of rulers, 103
Auxentius (Arian bishop), 66, 67
Avignon papacy, 111-14

baptism
  and Anabaptists, 144, 145, 146, 147
  infant, 145, 147
Baptists, in New World, 178
beast, as symbol of Roman state, 53, 54
beliefs, imposition of Christian, on
  others, 258
Belo, Bishop Carlos, 336
Benedict XVI (pope), 209, 214, 247,
  251, 252, 267, 304, 328
Bible, authority of, 170
  in Luther, 122
Bill of Rights, 180
Birch, Bruce, 18, 24, 29
bishop-prince, 90, 91, 94
bishops
  appointment by secular authorities,
  99, 100
  Catholic, and political responsibility,
  271, 272
  Latin American, and engagement in
  politics, 235, 236

bishops (*continued*)
    nomination by kings, 87
    on religion and politics, 5, 6
    role in medieval period, 99, 100
    temporal wealth and power of, 100
bishops, U.S.
    and Catholic politicians, 281-88
    and engagement in politics, 235, 236
    and health care reform, 286
    on levels of moral teaching, 285, 286
Boadt, Lawrence, 21, 25
Bodin, Jean, 126
Boniface, St., 88
Boniface VIII (pope), 104, 105, 106, 107,
    111, 154
    dispute with Philip IV, 105, 106, 107,
    110
Book of Common Prayer, 141, 142
Bradford, William, 173
Bread for the World, 260
Bruce, F. F., 46
Brueggemann, Walter, 22
Bryan, Christopher, 54
Bucer, Theodore, 129
Bultmann, Rudolf, 37

Cahill, Lisa, 319
Calvin, John, 128-35, 170
    and pacifist tradition, 325
    and political authority, 149
    and social humanism, 26
Calvinism, 134, 135, 144, 170, 171
capitalism, global, 292, 293
cardinals, as electors of pope, 94
Casanova, Jose, 243, 292
Catherine of Aragon, 167
Catholic Action, 237, 287
Catholic Church
    in American public life, 255
    and promotion of human rights, 306,
    308-17
    and United Nations, 12
    See also Catholicism; Catholics, U.S.;
    church(es)
Catholic politicians
    personal and public positions of, 284

and U.S. bishops, 281-88
Catholic Relief Services, 13, 336
Catholic school system, 183, 184, 185
Catholic social teaching. *See* social
    teaching, Catholic
Catholic theology, and just war tradition,
    325-27
Catholic tradition, and pacifism, 327-31
Catholicism
    and absolutist rule, 154
    animus toward, in U.S., 183, 184
    and democracy, 217-23, 268
    as transnational, 291, 292
Catholics, U.S., pluralism among, 282,
    283
causality, chain of, and responsible
    voting, 272
Chadwick, Henry, 13, 65, 74
Charlemagne, coronation of, 89
Charles I, 168, 169
Charles II, 169
Charles V, 120
Christ
    as embodiment of true humanity,
    240, 314
    as king, and temporal monarchs, 98
    See also Jesus
Christian churches, and U.S. public life,
    7, 8, 9, 10
Christian faith, and Christian church,
    4
Christianity
    appeal of, in ancient world, 62, 63
    after conversion of Constantine, 63-
    64
    and international affairs, 10, 11, 12,
    13
    and justice in the state, 72, 87
    in New World, 171-76
    and U.S. domestic politics, 8, 9, 10
    and U.S. immigration, 182, 183
Christians
    early, and empire during patristic age,
    61-68
    early, and love of neighbor, 250
    early, and Roman Empire, 48-55

early, persecution of, 53
equality among, 148
moral duties toward state, 79
separation of, from Jewish
community, 53
Christiansen, Drew, 196
church(es)
and city of God, 70
as communion, 235-36
constitutional authority within, 110,
111
and dominion over all property, 108
as ecumenical, 238-39
and freedom from emperor, 66
global, and human rights language,
311, 312
global, pluralism of, 312, 313
as global institution, 310, 311
and God's reign in history, 70
and imposition of morality, 275, 284
mission to call to conversion, 248-50
mission to engage in politics, 230-52
mission to evangelize, 244-48
mission to oppose sin, 248-50
mission to proclaim reign of God,
240, 241, 245, 267, 291
mission to promote unity, 291
in New Testament, as model, 145,
146
as people of God, 236-37
and political conservatism, 1
and public realm, guidelines for, 289
relationship to temporal governance,
112, 113
as sacrament, 232-33
as servant, 233-35
and single-issue politics, 265-67
as transnational, 235
as universal society, 80
church activity, engagement in, 260
church and politics
changing attitudes, 1, 2
Vatican II on, 239-43
church and state
in Augustine, 71-75
Byzantine view of, 65

East and West views of, 79
harmony between, 65
under Napoleon, 162-65
separation of, 140, 149, 161, 164, 181,
185-88
and *Unam sanctam*, 107, 110
in U.S. context, 182, 183
Vatican II on, 242-43
church and state relations, New Testament perspective on, 55, 56, 57
church membership, and public skills,
260, 261
City of God, 68, 69, 72, 75, 76, 77, 78,
332
city of God
and Christian church, 70, 77
and Christian empire, 73, 77
as communion of saints, 70
and earthly city (Augustine), 70, 71,
75, 76
city council, authority of, in Calvin, 129
Civil Constitution of the Clergy, 157,
158, 161, 163, 219
civil courts, in New Testament, 49
civil government
accountability of, 52
as noble work for Christians, 132
purpose of, 51
See also government
civil law, modern Thomistic approach to,
279-81
civil religion, 160, 161
civil rights movement, 255, 258, 263
Clement V (pope), 111
clergy
and authority of the state, 113
interference in secular politics, 118
position on Civil Constitution of the
Clergy, 158, 159, 160, 161, 163
taxation of, 105, 106
Clergy Constitution. *See* Civil
Constitution of the Clergy
Clovis (Frankish king), 88, 164
Cluniac reform, 91, 92
Cluny, Benedictine monastery at, 91,
92

coercion, and conversion to Christianity, 74
Cold War, 11
colonialism, 151
common good, 55, 58, 72, 73, 87, 102, 103, 109, 113, 117, 200-13, 215, 216, 222, 225-27, 229, 238, 239, 264, 268, 272, 277, 279, 280, 288, 289, 294, 296, 301, 313, 310, 322, 326, 330, 331, 334, 339
    duty to contribute to, 210
    and globalization, 297-99
    and the state, 203-7
Communist Manifesto, 307
communitarian ethic, in Catholic social teaching, 198, 199
communitarian themes, in Catholic social teaching, 214
communitarian vision, and Catholic social teaching, 196
community, and personal faith, in Puritanism, 175, 176
Compendium of the Social Doctrine of the Church, 197, 204, 267, 281, 313
conciliarism, 110, 111
Concordat of 1801, 163, 164
Concordat of Worms (1122), 96, 100
Congregational Church, 176
Congress of Vienna, 165
conscience
    primacy of, 7, 286, 287, 329, 330
    and voting, 269-70
conscientious objection, 329, 330
consistories, 129, 130
Constantine, 84
    conversion of, 61, 63
Constitution, U.S., 179, 180, 181, 185-88
conversion, 248-50
    as central message of Jesus, 38
    social dimension of, 249, 250
converts, to early Christianity, 62
cooperation, principle of, and responsible voting, 271, 272
coronation of king, papal role in, 89, 92, 112

Cotton, John, 174
Counterreformation, 138, 139, 149
covenant, and Israelite religion, 17, 18
Cranmer, Thomas, 141
critical-constructive stance, on church-state relations, 55, 56
critical distancing, ethic of, 57
critical-resistance stance, on church-state relations, 56
critical-transformative stance, on church-state relations, 55, 56
Cromwell, Oliver, 168, 169, 170
cuius regio, eius religio, 126, 151, 201
Cuomo, Mario, 9

Damasus I (pope), 85
David (Israelite king), 18, 19, 20, 21, 22, 23
De ecclesiastica potestate (Giles of Rome), 108
De officiis (Ambrose of Milan), 66, 281
De potestate regia et papali (John of Paris), 109
de Tocqueville, Alexis, 254, 255, 256, 257, 259, 262
Declaration of the Rights of Man and of the Citizen, 202, 220
Defensor pacis (Marsilius of Padua), 112
Democracy in America (de Tocqueville), 254
democracy
    and Calvin, 132, 133
    Christian presumption for, 227, 228
    as the form of the state, 216-228
    and Protestantism, 223-28
    and the Romantic movement, 218, 219
    theological basis for, in Niebuhr, 225-27
denominationalism, 147
diaspora, Jewish, and approach to political authorities, 50
Dickens, Charles, 307
Diet of Worms, 120, 127

Dignitatis humanae (Decree on Religious Liberty), 239, 242, 243, 279, 310, 311

Discourses on the First Ten Books of Titus Livius (Machiavelli), 116

dissent, religious, in England, 167, 168, 171

Diuturnum (On the Origin of Civil Power), 201

divine-right kingship, 136-37, 139

"Doctrinal Note on Some Questions regarding the Participation of Catholics in Political Life," 287

Domitian, and persecution of Christians, 53

Donatist controversy, 73, 74, 77

dualism
of Ambrose of Milan, 66
of authority in medieval period, 114

Dyson, Robert, 63

Ecclesiastical Ordinances (Calvin), 129

ecclesiology, and just war tradition, 326, 327

economic order, and role of the state, 207

Edict of Nantes, 155

Edward VI (king), 141, 167

Edwards, Jonathan, and religious renewal, 177

egalitarianism, in Catholic social teaching, 295

election, 173, 174
Calvin's doctrine of, 131

Elizabeth I, 141, 142, 167, 168

Elizabethan settlement, 141, 142, 143, 144, 151, 167

emperor
and authority to govern in temporal matters, 67
as head of the church, 63, 64
as *pontifex maximus*, 63, 64
worship, 53
See also king(s); kingship; monarchy

empire, Christian, in Augustine, 73

Employment Division v. Smith, 186

end-time, nearness of, and Christian attitude to state, 51, 52

Engels, Friedrich, 307

England, national church of, 140-44

English Revolution, 168, 169

environmental issues, and common good, 206

equality
and justice, 209
political, 221, 222

eschatology, and just war tradition, 325, 326

establishment clause (First Amendment), 180, 181, 182, 185, 186, 187, 189, 192, 275

ethical coordinates, for globalization, 293-305

ethical theology, Catholic, and just war tradition, 327

Europe, fragmentation of, after Charlemagne, 90

Eusebian accommodation, 64, 65

Eusebius of Caesarea, 64-65, 82
on empire as part of God's plan, 64, 65

evangelical Protestantism, and public life, 255, 256

evangelical spirit, Protestant, in U.S., 182, 183

evangelization
and early Christianity, 61, 62, 63
as mission of the church, 244-48

faith, Christian, and the state, 80

Falk, Richard, 303

Farel, William, 129

fascism, 221, 268, 308, 329

feasibility, prism of, and law, 280, 281, 285

Federal Election Campaign Act, 263

Ferraro, Geraldine, 9

First Amendment (U.S. Constitution), 179, 180, 181, 185-88
and Supreme Court, 181, 186, 188, 189, 190

First Amendment (*continued*)
    tests for judging violation of, 189
    See also free-exercise clause;
    nonestablishment, of religion
*Forming Consciences for Faithful
    Citizenship* (U.S. Conference of
    Catholic Bishops), 267, 269, 270
Francis of Assisi, and pacifist tradition,
    324, 325
Frankish kings, 88
Frederick, Elector of Saxony, 120
free-exercise clause (First Amendment),
    180, 181, 185, 186, 188, 189
freedom
    in Luther, 123, 124, 128
    of religion. *See* religion, freedom of
French Catholicism, 155-66
    post-Revolution, 160-162
French church, as eldest daughter of the
    church, 164
French Revolution, 155-66
Fukuyama, Francis, 225

Gallicanism, 154, 157, 162, 163, 164,
    165, 166, 220
Gaudium et spes, 236, 237, 238, 239, 240,
    241, 243, 330
Gaustad, Edwin, 177
gay marriage, 275
Gelasius I (pope), 81, 83, 84, 86, 97,
    104
Genseric, 84
Gentili, Alberico, 322
Gerson, Jean, 111
Giles of Rome, 108, 109, 110, 112
global policy networks, 305
globalization, 291-305
    and Catholic social teaching, 293
    and the common good, 297-99
    ethical coordinates for, 293-305
    and solidarity, 295, 296, 297
Glorious Revolution, 169
God
    absolute rule of, in John Calvin, 130,
    131
    allegiance owed to, 44, 45, 46

    as source of all authority, 48, 74, 75,
    83, 86, 87, 97, 119, 202
    as Trinitarian, 197
governance, in Aquinas, 102-4
government
    as agent for religious society, 148, 149
    bad, 133, 134, 135
    definition of, 3
    nature and form, for Calvin, 131, 132,
    133, 134, 135
    positive role for, in Middle Ages, 87
    resistance to, in Calvin, 133, 134, 135
government authorities, duties of, 51
Great Awakening, 176-78
Greeley, Andrew, 195, 196
Gregory I (pope), 84, 85, 86, 87, 97, 136
Gregory VII (pope), 93-98, 104
Gregory XVI (pope), 165, 217
Groody, Daniel, 293
Grotius, Hugo, 303, 322
Gustafson, James, 233, 234

health care reform, 286
Henry III (king), 92
Henry IV (emperor), 93-98
Henry V (king), 104
Henry VIII, 140, 141, 155, 167
Henry, Patrick, and religious liberty, 178
Herodians, 43, 44, 46
Heschel, Abraham, 28
higher education, and subsidiarity, 212
Hitler, Adolf, 221
Hobbes, Thomas, 126
holiness, universal call to, 237, 261
Hollenbach, David, 297
Holy Roman Empire, 89, 92, 120, 151
Hooker, Richard, 142, 143, 144, 149
    on civil law, 143, 144
Hughes, Archbishop John, and school
    controversy, 184, 185
Hugo, Victor, 274
human beings
    as *imago Dei,* 198, 222, 225, 240
    as *zōon politikon,* 102
human development, 245, 246, 247, 248,
    294, 303, 304

human dignity, 197, 198, 294, 295
   mission of church to preserve, 240, 241, 265, 267, 294, 295
human law, and natural law, 103
human person, as political animal, 71, 72
human rights, 291
   and Catholic social teaching, 301, 306-17
   and common good, 309
   and globalization, 301, 306-17
   mission of church to protect, 240, 241, 265, 267
humanism, authentic, 294, 295, 314
humanity, as single global family, in Catholicism, 291
Huntington, Samuel, 306, 314
Hutchinson, Anne, 172, 174, 175, 176, 180, 185

iconoclasm, 85
Ignatius of Loyola, 138
imago Dei, humans as, 198, 222, 225, 240
immigration
   Catholic, 183, 184, 236
   U.S., 182, 183
Immortale Dei (On the Christian Constitution of States), 201
indifferentism, and freedom of religion, 218, 310
individualism, religious, 122
individuals, and duty to contribute to the common good, 210
indulgences, 118, 119, 120
inequality
   Israelite social, 32, 33
   and neoliberal capitalism, 293
Innocent III (pope), 104
Innocent IV (pope), 104
integral development, and human rights, 312, 313
International MonetaryFund, 305
International Religious Freedom Act of 1990, 12
intrinsic evil, and responsible voting, 271, 272, 273

Investiture Controversy, 93-101
Isidore of Seville, political thought of, 87
Islamic revolution (in Iran), 11
Israel, as client of Rome, 42-48
Israelite people, political organization of, 17-19
Ivo of Chartres, 99

James I, 168
James II, 169
Jansen, Cornelius, 156
Jansenism, 156
Jefferson, Thomas
   and nonestablishment of religion, 178, 179
   and "wall of separation," 188
Jeremias, Joachim, 318
Jerusalem, as capital of monarchy, 22
Jesuit Refugee Service, 13
Jesuits, opposition to absolute monarchs, 138-40
Jesus
   lordship of, in Calvin, 130, 131
   and love of neighbor, 250, 251
   as messiah, 38-40
   miracles of, 41
   parables of, 41, 42
   politics at time of, 42-48
   as Prince of Peace, 317
   and recognition of two realms, 46, 47
   and reign of God, 37, 38, 234, 245, 247
   on taxation, 318
   teaching on war and peace, 317, 318, 319
   See also Christ
John of Paris, 109, 110
John Paul II (pope), 4, 9, 206, 214, 293, 295, 300, 303, 306, 313, 314, 328, 334
John XXII (pope), 111
John XXIII (pope), 213, 238, 297, 301, 309, 328
jus ad bellum, 322
jus in bello, 322
jus post bellum, 322, 323

just wage, 300
just war, criteria for, 323, 324
just war tradition, 320-24, 325
justice
　　and Catholic social teaching, 299-301
　　and common good, 208
　　and deposition of kings, 99
　　and development, 333, 334
　　distributive, 204, 209, 210, 211
　　and globalization, 299-301
　　as goal of kingly rule, 87
　　and Israelite political order, 29-32, 35
　　and love of neighbor, 251, 267
　　and public policy, 258
　　and role of the state, 207-11
　　and the state, 72, 87; in Catholic
　　　　social teaching, 204
justification by faith, in Luther, 120, 121

Karlstadt, Andrew, 126
Kennedy, John F., 284
Kerry, John, 9
king(s)
　　and appointment of bishops, 93
　　authority over church affairs, 87, 88
　　deposition of, 98, 99, 109
　　divine right of, 111, 119, 136-37
　　by the grace of God, 86, 87
　　heretical, resistance to, 118, 119
　　(Israelite), political and religious role
　　　　of, 25, 26, 27, 35
kingdom of God. *See* reign of God
kingship
　　in Aquinas, 102, 103
　　biblical view of, 19-28, 35
　　in medieval period, 86-90
　　sacral nature of, 98, 99
　　supported by church, 90, 91
Knox, John, 133, 134, 135

language of human rights, 306, 307, 308
Laud, William, 168, 171, 172
law
　　in Aquinas, 103, 104, 142, 143
　　and morality, 275-81
　　in Richard Hooker, 143, 144

laws, public attitudes toward, 279, 280,
　　281
Laws of Ecclesiastical Polity (Hooker),
　　142, 144
laws of the free market, and natural law,
　　307
lay investiture. *See* Investiture Contro-
　　versy
laypersons, engagement of, in secular
　　life, 236, 237
Lemon v. Kurtzman, 189
Leo I (pope), 84, 86
Leo III (pope), 89, 205, 207, 208, 209,
　　210, 211, 212, 220
Leo IX (pope), 92, 93, 94
Leo XIII (pope), 197, 199, 201, 202, 255,
　　300, 312
liberals, and skepticism about religion in
　　politics, 1
liberalism
　　classical, and Catholic social teaching,
　　　　198, 203, 204, 206, 207
　　free market and utilitarian, 307, 308
liberation theology, 11
liberty, personal, 275, 276
libido domandi, 72
lobbying, by religious groups, 259, 260
local church, and political engagement,
　　235, 236
Louis XIV (king), 155
Louis XVI (king), 156
love ethic, in New Testament, 49
love of neighbor, 250-52, 267
　　and nonviolence, 320
　　and war, 319, 320
Lumen gentium (Dogmatic Constitution
　　on the Church), 232, 236, 238
Luther, Martin, 117-28
　　alliance with secular leaders, 127,
　　　　128
　　and indulgences, 119, 120
　　and pacifist tradition, 325
　　and peasant wars, 126, 127
　　and political authority, 149
　　political legacy of, 127, 128
　　on politics, 121-28

and public service, 261
and role of power in political life, 127

Machiavelli, Niccolò, 114, 116, 117, 126
Madison, James, and religious liberty,
    178, 179
Manegold of Lautenbach, and
    deposition of kings, 99
Mann, Horace, 184
market economies, and distributive
    justice, 209, 210
Marsilius of Padua, 112, 113, 114
Martel, Charles, 88
Marty, Martin, 238
Marx, Karl, 307
Mary (sister of Edward VI), 141, 167
Mary (wife of William), 169
Massachusetts Bay Colony, as Christian
    commonwealth, 171, 172, 173,
    174, 175, 183
Mater et magistra, 213
Mazarin, Cardinal Jules, 152, 153
McBrien, Richard, 234
McConnell, Michael, 190
mediation, Catholic principle of, 234,
    235
messiah
    as heavenly figure, 39
    Jesus as, 38-40
    as prophet or priest, 39
    royal, 38, 39
messianic secret, 39, 40
militancy, of New World Christians, 171
Minogue, Kenneth, 62, 82
monarchs, national, growth in power of,
    118
monarchy
    Calvin's view of, 132, 133, 134, 135
    constitutional limits to, 109
    right to rebel against, 137, 138
monarchy (Israelite), 19-28
    prophetic critique of, 27, 29, 30, 31,
    32
monasticism, destruction of, 158, 161
monasticism and clericalism, rejection
    of, 148

Monica (mother of Augustine), 68
Monsengwo, Laurent, 336
Mooney, Christopher, 180, 181
Moore, Jeremiah, 178
morality
    and law, 275-81
    and public policy, 282, 283, 284, 285,
    286, 287, 288
Morrill Act of 1890, 212
Münzer, Thomas, 126
Murray, John Courtney, 181
    on law and morality, 279
Mussolini, Benito, 221

Napoleon
    attitude toward papacy, 162, 163,
    164
    church and state under, 162-65
National Assembly, 156, 157, 158
national churches, 148, 149
national identity, 148
national kingdoms, autonomy of, 109
nationalism, and democracy, 219, 220
Native Americans, and Roger Williams,
    173
natural law
    and civil law, in Aquinas, 277, 278
    and governance, 103
    and laws of the free market, 307
    and the state, 109
natural rights, 306, 307, 308
Nazism, 221, 268
need, and justice, 209
neutrality, of government toward
    religion, 180, 181, 185-88
new internationalism, 12
New World, Christianity in, 171-76
Nicholas II (pope), 94
Nicholas of Cusa, 111
Niebuhr, Reinhold, 225, 226, 227
    on democracy, 223, 224
non-Catholics, in post-Revolutionary
    France, 164
nonestablishment, of religion, 178,
    179, 180, 181, 182. *See also* First
    Amendment

Nostra aetate (Declaration on the Relation of the Church to Non-Christian Religions), 238, 239

O'Connor, Cardinal John, 9
Oakley, Francis, 64, 104
Obama, Barack, 286
obedience
    to civil authorities, 133, 134, 135
    to ruler, in Luther, 125
    to the state, in Augustine, 74, 75
Octogesima adveniens, 301, 302
organization, political, 263, 264
Organization of American States, 13
Origen, and pacifist tradition, 324
original sin, 69, 73, 142, 226, 248
    in Augustine, 69
    consequences of, 69
    and the state, 72, 73

Pacem in terris, 238, 297, 301, 309, 310
pacifism
    and Catholic tradition, 327-31
    in context of justice and human rights, 330
pacificism, vocational, 324
pacificist tradition, 324-25
papacy
    authority over secular rulers, 139
    Babylonian Captivity of, 111
    as both spiritual and temporal ruler of Italy, 84
    call for new approach to global governance, 304, 305
    constitutional limits to, 109
    diminution of power of, 154
    emergence of, 84-86
    and Frankish kings, 84
    Jesuit support for supremacy of, 139
    as ultimate seat of all power, 108
    universal, and national monarchy, 104-10
    See also pope(s)
papal authority, challenged by Luther, 120, 128

papal elections, 94
Papal States, 88, 89, 106, 139, 149, 166, 219, 220, 316
Paris Commune, 307
participation
    and Catholic social teaching, 301, 302
    and globalization, 301-2
    in processes of democracy, 222
"Participation of Catholics in Public Life," 9
pastors and elders, authority of, in Calvin, 129
patriarchates, 85
Paul (apostle), on obedience to political rulers, 48-52, 119, 125
Paul (apostle) and John (author of Revelation), differing attitudes toward the state, 54, 55
Paul VI (pope), 221, 244, 294, 301, 312, 313, 328, 333, 334
Pax Christi, 13, 260
peace, 291
    in Christian tradition, 331, 332
    contemporary Catholic teaching on, 333-34
    and integral development, 333
    in New Testament, 331
    and reign of God, 331
Peace of Augsburg, 151, 153
Peace of Westphalia, 10, 152, 153, 154
peacebuilding
    and Catholic tradition, 334-37
    and just development, 335
peasant wars, 126, 127
Pepin (Frankish king), 88, 99
person, inner and outer, in Luther, 125
Pharisees, and politics, 43, 44
Philip IV (king), 105, 106, 107, 154
    dispute with Boniface VIII, 105, 106, 107, 110
Pilgrim, Walter, 46, 47, 55, 57
Pius VI (pope), 159, 162
Pius VII (pope), 163, 164
Pius IX (pope), 217, 220
Pius XI (pope), 211, 212, 213, 237

Pius XII (pope), 203, 206, 217, 268, 308, 309, 329

Plato, 52
and politics, 3

pluralism
in Catholic social teaching, 215, 216
religious, 180, 181, 185-88

Plymouth Colony, 172, 173

polis, 2, 7, 251

political authority
Augustine's negative view of, 73
as derived from God, 78

political order, as part of God's plan, 58

political parties, decline of, 263, 264

politicians
Catholic, autonomy of, in public life, 287
episcopal displeasure with, 9

politics
Augustine's transcendent and historical approach to, 75, 76
Christian promotion of, 148, 149
definition of, 2, 3
in Hebrew Scriptures, 28-34

pontifex maximus, emperor as, 63, 64

Pontifical Council for Justice and Peace, 197, 267, 313

poor, preferential option for, 205

pope(s)
appointed by king, 92, 94
deposition of, 109, 110
involvement in international politics, 315, 316
opposed to Civil Constitution of the Clergy, 159
and *plenitudo potestatis*, 104, 107, 108, 109
as political leaders, 116
and right to depose monarchs, 96, 97, 99
as ruler of Rome and environs, 84, 85
as temporal ruler, 88, 89
See also papacy

Populorum progressio, 294, 334

Porter, J. M., 126

pragmatism, and relation of law and morality, 276, 277

predestination, 131
and Augustine, 69, 77

priesthood, of all believers, 148
in Luther, 122, 125

The Prince (Machiavelli), 116, 117

principle, and preference, 284, 285

privatization, 6, 7

property
church's dominion over, 108
ownership and regulation of, 110

prophets
and accountability of civil government, 52
(Israelite), and kings, 27
and politics, 28-34

Protestantism
and democracy, 223-28
English, in sixteenth and seventeenth centuries, 167
in New England colonies, 255

Providence (settlement in New World), 173, 176

prudence, and responsible voting, 270

Pseudo-Dionysius, 108

public church, 238, 239

public morality, 206, 275, 279, 280

public office
as Christian service, 66
and Christians, 281

public officials, religious and professional roles of, 284, 285

public philosophy, Christian contribution to, 256-59

public policy, Christian contribution to, 257-59, 287

Public School Society, 183

public school system, 183, 184, 185

public skills, and church membership, 260, 261

public spirituality, 261, 262

public virtue, 259, 260, 261

Puritanism, American, 170, 171, 172, 173, 174, 175

Puritans, 142, 143, 144, 147, 168, 169, 170
and religious freedom, 175, 176

Quadragesimo anno, 211
Qumran community, and politics, 42

Radical Reformation, 145, 146, 147
Rahner, Karl, 311
Ratzinger, Cardinal Joseph, 9. *See also* Benedict XVI
realms, spiritual and temporal, 80, 81. *See also* two kingdoms; two powers
Reason, cult of, 160
rebellion
right of, 137, 138
against temporal sovereign, 165
"Render to Caesar," 44-47, 83, 318
Reformation, political legacy of, 147-49
reformers
Protestant, and engagement in civic life, 261
radical, 144-47
regimes, 305
regnum (temporal power), 83, 86-90
reign of God, 37-38, 40-42, 58, 247
as future reality, 40, 41, 58, 245, 246, 247, 252, 280
and image of mustard seed, 42
priority over political realm, 47, 58
and Sermon on the Mount, 318, 319
at work in history, 245, 246, 247, 252, 253, 280
Reign of Terror, 160
relationality, and Catholic social tradition, 196, 197
religion
in American public life, 254-62
definition of, 3, 4
freedom of, 153, 176, 177, 178, 179, 180, 181, 185-88, 242, 243, 310, 311. *See also* First Amendment
and international politics, 151-53
need for unity in, in patristic age, 80
in New England colonies, 255
and privatization, 7, 11

repentance, and reign of God, 41
Republic (Plato), 52
Rerum novarum, 205, 207, 211, 255, 312
resistance, ethic of, 56, 57
Restoration, 165, 166
Revelation, and Christian attitude toward the state, 52-55
revivals, 176, 177
Richelieu, Cardinal, 151, 152
Risorgimento, 219, 220
Roberts, J. J. M., 27
Roe v. Wade, 8
romanticism, and democracy, 218, 219
Rome
Augustine's assessment of, 75, 76
invasion by French troops, 162
medieval growth in importance of, 85, 86
sack of, 69
Romero, Archbishop Oscar, 316, 336
Rosenberger v. University of Virginia, 190, 191
Rousseau, Jean-Jacques, 220
Ruiz, Bishop Samuel, 336
rulers, Christian, Augustine's view of, 74, 75. *See also* kings; monarchy

Sabine, George, 79, 110, 135, 144
sacerdotium (spiritual power), 83, 84-86
Sadducees, and politics, 43, 44
salvation
in Calvin, 131
of sinners, 173
Samuel (Israelite judge, priest, prophet), 20, 21
Sant'Egidio community, 13
Saul (Israelite king), 20, 21
Schelkle, Karl, 57
Schrage, Wolfgang, 49
Second Great Awakening, 182
sectarian temptation, 233, 234
secular leaders, interference in church life, 118
secularization, 6, 7
self-interest, 74, 199, 204, 219, 224, 237, 259, 260, 264, 269, 289, 319

of Catholic Church, and democracy,
219, 220
Semon on the Mount, on peacemaking,
317, 318, 319
Simons, Menno, and pacifist tradition,
325
simony, 93, 94
sin
    intrapersonal and interpersonal,
    248
    and just war tradition, 326
    mission of church to oppose, 248-50
    reality of, 248
    social, 248-50
    transpersonal. *See* sin, social
Sin, Cardinal Jaime, 316
sinfulness, of human beings, in Luther,
    122, 123
single-issue politics, 262-67
    and decline of political parties, 263,
    264
single-issue voting, and the churches,
    265-67
slavery, 284
Smith, Adam, 307
Social Contract (Rousseau), 220
social distinctions (Israelite), 18, 33, 34
Social Gospel movement, 255
social humanism, 261
social imagination, Catholic, 195, 196,
    222, 223
social institutions, and love of neighbor,
    251, 252, 267
social teaching, Catholic, 195-201, 203,
    205-7, 209, 211, 212, 214, 216,
    221, 223, 229, 238, 293-97, 299-
    303, 309-13, 333-35, 337
    high and low tradition of, 195, 196,
    223
socialism
    and Catholic social teaching, 198
    critique of capitalism, 307, 308
sociality, and Catholic social tradition,
    197
socialization, and Catholic social
    teaching, 213

society
    as organic body, 222, 223
    and the state, 199
solidarity
    and Catholic social teaching, 199,
    200, 267, 295, 296, 297
    and peace, 333, 334
Solomon (Israelite king), 23, 24, 30
sovereignty
    cosmopolitan approach to, and
    Catholic social teaching, 310
    cosmopolitan school understanding
    of, 309, 310
    and individual rights, 309
    of the state, 201, 202, 203
spiritual power, as greater than temporal
    power, 108
St. Bartholomew's Day Massacre, 136
state
    in Catholic social teaching, 196-201
    and Christian faith, 80
    and common good, 113, 203-7
    definition of, 3
    inner moral necessity of, 200, 201
    and justice, 72, 77, 87
    limits to authority of, in Luther, 127
    and moral duties of Christians, 79
    as natural institution, 101
    and natural law, 109
    nature of, in Catholic social teaching,
    196-99
    as necessary institution, 78, 79
    as part of God's created order, 197,
    198
    as perfect society, 113
    purpose of, in Catholic social
    teaching, 203, 204
    purpose of, in Luther, 123, 124
    role in creating order, 73, 74
    in thought of Aquinas, 101, 102
Stephen III (pope), 88, 89
Suarez, Francisco, 139, 322
subordination, ethic of, 57
subsidiarity
    and Catholic social teaching, 302-5
    and globalization, 302-5

subsidiarity (*continued*)
    and higher education, 212
    and state intervention, 211-16
Supreme Court, and First Amendment,
    181, 186, 188, 189, 190

Talleyrand, Charles, 158, 159
taxation
    Ambrose of Milan on, 66, 67
    dispute between Boniface VIII and
        Philip IV on, 105, 106, 107, 110
    progressive, 210, 211
    See also "Render to Caesar"
taxes, payment of, 44, 45
temporal authority, autonomy from
    spiritual authority, 109, 110, 111,
    112
temporal ruler, in Luther, 125
Tertullian, and pacifist tradition, 324
Theodosius (emperor), 66
theology and politics, in Calvin,
    130-34
Thirty Years War, 151, 152, 201
Tierney, Brian, 84, 97, 100, 306
Tirimann, Vimal, 294
toleration, principle of, and law and
    morality, 278, 279
torture, 271, 272
Trent, Council of, 138
tribal social organization, and Israelite
    people, 17, 18, 19
Troeltsch, Ernst, 122
Truce of God, 322
two kingdoms
    in Calvin, 132
    in Luther, 124, 125, 127
two powers (realms), 82, 83-93
    Aquinas on, 104
    and *Unam sanctam*, 107
tyrannicide, 103, 104, 154
tyranny, 165, 224
    in Aquinas, 102, 103, 104

ultramontanism, 162
Unam sanctam, 107, 110

unemployment, 213
Unitatis redintegratio (Decree on
    Ecumenism), 238, 239
United Nations, and peacebuilding, 335,
    336
Universal Declaration of Human Rights,
    309

Valentinian II (emperor), 66, 67
Vatican
    and peacebuilding, 336
    and United Nations, 315
Vatican Council II
    on the church and politics, 239-43
    on church and state, 242-43
    and civil law, 279-81
    and human rights, 309, 310-11
    on peace and justice, 333
    on temporal involvement of the
        church, 231-39
Vidler, Alec, 161
Vindiciae, contra tyrannos (Vindication,
    against Tyrants), 134, 137, 138
Virginia statute, 178, 179
Vitoria, Francisco de, 322
voluntary associations, 260
vote
    failure to, as sin of omission, 268
voting
    and conscience, 269-70
    considerations in, 273, 274
    responsible, 267-74

war(s), 291, 317-37
    presumption against, in Catholic
        tradition, 328
    religious, 135-40, 151, 152, 153, 154
wealth
    of the church, seizure of, 158
    disparity of, in French Catholicism,
        155
The Wealth of Nations (Adam Smith),
    307
Western Schism (Papal Schism), 113
Westphalian synthesis, 152, 242

Whitefield, George, and religious renewal, 176, 177
Widmar v. Vincent, 190
William and Mary, 169
William of Occam, 112
William of Orange, 169
Williams, George Hunston, 145
Williams, Roger, 172, 173, 175, 176, 178, 180, 185, 187
   and Native Americans, 173

Winthrop, John, 171, 172, 173, 174, 183
Wogaman, Philip, 227, 228
World Bank, 305

Yahweh, as king of Israelites, 26, 27

Zachary I (pope), 88, 99
Zealots, and contemporary politics, 43, 44
Zwingli, Ulrich, 129